into the jaws of hell
pickett's charge at gettysburg

56th Virginia Infantry

2nd Edition

This Regimental history is dedicated to all men who served in Virginia Units during the War Between the States. Its purpose is to preserve, as a part of our heritage, the deeds and sacrifices of these gallant men. Your support of this meticulously researched project is greatly appreciated.

William A. Young, Jr.   Patricia C. Young

Copyright 2009, Authors William A. Young, Jr., Patricia C. Young, and Publisher James Keir Baughman.

All rights reserved. No part of this Second Edition may be reproduced or transmitted in any way, form, or by any means, electronic or otherwise, including photocopying, recording, or by any information or retrieval system, or posted on the Internet or World Wide Web without written permission of the authors and publisher. This edition has been dramatically changed from the original and new copyright applies.

Re-published 2009, 2nd Edition, by James Keir Baughman, Fort Walton Beach, Florida with permission of the authors and original publisher. Manufactured and printed in the United States.

www.baughmanliterary.com

ISBN # 978-0-9790443-7-3

Cover background art, the painting "Give Them Cold Steel, Boys," is the artist's depiction of Pickett's Charge at Gettysburg created by famed Civil War artist Don Troiani. An Artist and Publisher, Troiani's work may be found at Historical Art Prints. His web site address is www.historicalartprints.com

Original Copyright 1990 H. E. Howard, Inc.
First Edition manufactured and printed in the United States by H. E. Howard, Inc., Lynchburg, Virginia

TABLE OF CONTENTS

Fate Denied Them...

Dedication and Acknowledgements

Chapter 1... The Call To Arms

Chapter 2... The Colonel

Chapter 3... Camp Lee

Chapter 4... Conflicting Orders

Chapter 5... Fort Donelson

Chapter 6... Fort Drewry and Chaffin's Bluff

Chapter 7... Gaines Mill and Frazier's Farm

Chapter 8... 2nd Manassas, Boonsboro, Sharpsburg

Chapter 9... Fredericksburg to Suffolk

Chapter 10...Gettysburg and Pickett's Charge

Chapter 11...Cold Harbor to Appomattox

Chapter 12...Prisoners of War

Chapter 13... Introduction to the Roster

Chapter 14... Roster 56th Virginia Regiment, A thru E

Chapter 15...Roster 56th Virginia Regiment, F thru L

Chapter 16... Roster 56th Virginia Regiment, M thru R

Chapter 17... Roster 56th Virginia Regiment, S thru Y

Chapter 18...Photographs and maps

Bibliography

*"Fate denied them victory,
but crowned them
with glorious immortality."*

Lines from a Confederate monument.

DEDICATION

We dedicate this book to the men of the 56th Virginia with admiration and affection.

Before we began our research, they were just names. Now we know them personally, and they are our friends. We call the 56th Virginia "our regiment."

Someone once asked us, "Why do you refer to it as 'our regiment?' You make it sound like you served in it."

We replied, "We did."

Patsy and Bill Young

Acknowledgments:

There is an old Greek proverb that says, "We enjoy life through the help and society of others." We could not have written the story of the 56th Virginia infantry without the help and society of lots of other people. All of them fit into one or more of the following three categories: (1) descendants of the soldiers, (2) public servants, and (3) lovers of history. They not only made the men of the regiment live again, but they made our trip up and down the winding trail of the 56th Virginia fun, exciting, and rewarding.

We thank Harold E. Howard, our publisher, for having the vision and dedication to undertake the Regimental Histories Series. if it were not for his foresight, the stories of the Virginia regiments and their soldiers would be lost to posterity.

We are greatly indebted to the National Park Service. Bob Krick at the Fredericksburg and Spotsylvania National Military Park got us off to a good start; we left his office clutching his thick file of references and burning with his fire of enthusiasm. Jim Jobe at Fort Donelson National Battlefield Park opened all of his file cabinets on the Battle of Fort Donelson and made copies of everything that we wanted. Chris Calkins of the Petersburg National Battlefield Park offered suggestions and gave us information on the Howlett Line.

We felt like we had hit the mother lode the day we visited Lieutenant General Richard H. Groves, United States Army (Retired). General Groves is the great-grandson of Lieutenant John Thomas Chaffin of the 56th Virginia. The General had done exhaustive research on the history of the regiment during its first two years, and we walked away from his home with a large cardboard box filled with his typed manuscript and supporting documents.

Grady T. Turner of Dallas, Texas inspired us when he sent us a copy of a history that he wrote in 1931 of the 56th Virginia. His father, Lieutenant Stephen D. Turner, was a member of Company B, 56th Virginia.

Diane Jacob, archivist at the VMI library, provided us a stack of flies on the alumni of VMI who served in the 56th Virginia. The VMI files led us to Glen L. Alleman of Nevada. He wrote his master's history thesis on Colonel William Dabney Stuart and the 56th Virginia when he was a student at Brigham Young University. His thesis was a treasury of quotations from letters that Colonel Stuart wrote his wife Clinkey during the war - letters that are now lost.

Guy Swanson at the Museum of the Confederacy dazzled us when he opened a box marked "56th Virginia" in the storage vault and took out the red banner that the regiment carried beyond the stone wall in Pickett's Charge at Gettysburg. The staff of the Virginia Historical Museum was always attentive and helpful. We were thrilled to handle the original documents there. The letter that Colonel Stuart sent from camp at Chaffin's Bluff to the regimental surgeon in Richmond in March 1882 was still in its original envelope complete with Confederate postage stamp.

The staff in the archives of the Virginia State Library spent countless hours in the past two and one half years bringing books to our table and helping us locate information. When the library closed suddenly and unexpectedly a month after we started working on the book, Conely L. Edwards advised and helped us so that our research did not come to a complete halt.

Ray W. Gunn, Gerald W. Harlow, Scott W. Hutchinson, F. Lawrence McFall, and Carl F. Stein mailed us the cemetery lists that they have painstakingly compiled over the years. B. David Mann sent his file on VMI students who served with the 56th Virginia. Their information made the muster rolls far more complete and much more accurate. The clerks of the circuit courts of the eight counties that raised companies for the 56th Virginia beat the drum and told their constituents about our project.

Bill James of Bealton, Virginia, a Civil War buff and relic hunter, caught our enthusiasm for the project. We appreciate his frequent words of encouragement and his constant search for information on the soldiers of the 56th Virginia. Horace W. Daniels of Alberta, Virginia generously lent us the newspaper articles "Our Civil War Soldiers" by Dr. W. M. Pritchett. Mr. Daniel collected the articles over the 10 year period that they appeared as a weekly column in The Brunswick Times Gazette, and then he assembled them in a book. He also showed us the way down the road in Brunswick County to the home of Mrs. Caleb Short.

Mrs. Short gave us copies of letters that William B. Short, the tallest man in Company E, wrote to his wife Babie during the period 1863-1865. Richard L. Baird of Blackridge, Virginia gave us a photograph of his great- grandfather,

Charles W. Thomas of Company B, and copies of letters that Thomas wrote to his wife Mary during the period 1861-1865. Thomas told it like it was and nearly always ended a letter by asking Mary to send him "something to ate." Richard Baird was mindful of Thomas's complaint because he did not send us away hungry. We left his home laden with fresh fruits and vegetables from his garden.

    Just when we thought that we had finished our manuscript, Richard L. Armstrong told us that Colonel Robert J. Driver, Jr. had made an exciting find in the Bridgewater College Library. He found a manuscript of over 100 letters written by John Holt of Company I, 56th Virginia to his wife Ellen. The original letters belong to Holt's great-grandfather. They filled in many important gaps and provided new facts as well as fresh insights.

    The list of persons who should be thanked individually goes on and on. We wish that we could mention everyone by name, but it would take another book just to list the people who telephoned or sent us helpful material. We know who you are, and you know who you are. Please be content with the satisfaction of knowing that you have helped to preserve information that may have been lost, destroyed, or forgotten with the passage of time. Accept our sincere thanks for all of your interest, encouragement, and help. It has been a pleasure to know you and to work with you on this labor of love. The story of the 56th Virginia belongs to each and every one of you.

Patsy and Bill Young

CHAPTER 1

The Call To Arms

"...Men of the South, the hour has come."

In the summer of 1861, the sharp blast of the bugle, the shrill squeal of the fife, and the long roll of the drum called the sons of Virginia to arms. The hour had come for them to defend the Old Dominion against the Yankee invaders. Virginians saw the outbreak of war between North and South as a second American Revolution. They passionately believed that Virginia had played a key role in forming the union and that she had an absolute right to leave it whenever she chose.

The hot-blooded young men of Virginia considered themselves patriots who were duty bound to fight the northern tyrants for the honor of the Commonwealth and the new Confederacy of Southern states. James H. Mason was a typical Virginian of the era. When he was elected Captain of Company K, 56th Virginia infantry Regiment, he selected stationery that had the following quotation printed at the top:

> *Gather round your country's flag*
> *Men of the South the hour has come*
> *None may falter and none may lag,*
> *March to the sound of the fife and drum.*

Just to the right of the quotation, there was a printed drawing of the first Confederate flag bearing one white bar between two red bars. In the upper left hand corner, there were seven white stars in a circle on a blue field. The men who answered Virginia's first bugle call, who gathered around their new country's flag, and who tried to march in step to the fife and drum were all volunteers. They rushed to join new military companies in their home counties with their friends, neighbors, and relatives. They gave their companies intimidating names like "Spartans," "Guards," and "Defenders" that showed fierce determination, local color, and deep pride. The Ebenezer Grays of Brunswick County took their name from the old Methodist academy where they camped and drilled in the yard. They later became Company E of the 56th Virginia.

When the Confederacy mustered the volunteer companies into the army, it assigned them to regiments. It took ten companies to make one infantry regiment. The army discarded the fancy company names and identified the companies by letters of the alphabet. Each company in a given regiment received its letter according to the date when its officers were commissioned. The company whose officers were first became Company A; the company whose officers were commissioned second became Company B, and so on. The Confederacy gave each regiment a number, and the regiments became the backbone of the army. The Virginia regiments were destined to become a part of the legendary fighting force known as the Army of Northern Virginia.

The 10 military companies that were to become the 56th Virginia were organized between June and September 1861. As each company came into existence, the Confederacy ordered it to report to Camp Lee to be mustered into the service and wait for assignment to a regiment. Camp Lee was the base of instruction for Confederate raw recruits and was located at the Hermitage or New Fairgrounds in Richmond. The camp was not named for Robert E. Lee, but for his father, General Richard Henry or "Light Horse Harry" Lee. "Light Horse Harry" won fame when he served in the cavalry in George Washington's army during the American 'Revolution.

Nearly all of the companies that became the 56th Virginia arrived at Camp Lee a month or two before the regiment was officially formed. For example, the Mecklenburg Spartans enlisted at Tanner's Store in Mecklenburg County in June 1861. They drilled in the neighborhood for a few weeks before they marched to "the front" in Richmond. Miss Carrie Audelia Gee, a 16 year old local belle, presented them a beautiful, hand-sewn flag that the ladies of Mecklenburg had made for the company. When the Spartans became Company B of the 56th Virginia, they had to put the flag away because Confederate regulations allowed the men to carry only the regimental flag. The Charlotte Grays enlisted at Reese's Church in Charlotte County in July. They took a pleasant train ride to Richmond, marched from the depot to Capitol Square to be inspected by the Confederate inspector General, and paraded through the city to Camp Lee. They later became Company I of the 56th Virginia.

A total of 800 civilians traveled to Richmond by train, canal barge, and on foot to join the 56th Virginia. They were a motley group that came in all shapes, sizes, and uniforms. The last name of the tallest man in Company E was "Short." Many of them could shoot; nearly all detested spit and polish. Most of them were in their early twenties. Most worked on small farms, but there were also carpenters, millers, stonemasons, shoemakers, clerks, tanners, miners, wheelwrights, blacksmiths, laborers, and overseers. There was a sprinkling of plantation owners, merchants, accountants, doctors, lawyers, teachers, surveyors, and ministers. One was a watchmaker and another a bartender. One was a musician; one was a sailor; and one was Patrick Henry's grandson. A lot of them had never been away from home.

Jeffress of Company G owned a large manufacturing mill, while Major John McPhail raised silkworms at his ancestral home "Mulberry Hill." Major William Green owned two plantations - one in Virginia and one In Mississippi. Captain Thomas T. Boswell paid for the uniforms of every man in Company A out of his own pocket. His son, William Nelson Boswell, was only 11 years old in 1861, but he insisted on following his father into the field. He became a drummer boy in the regiment. President Jefferson Davis saw young William on the parade ground at Camp Lee and was so impressed with his military bearing that he presented a little sword to the boy.

The men got their first taste of army life at Camp Lee. On July 15 Private Charles W. Thomas, a farmer in Company B, wrote to his wife Mary to tell her that the food was "tolerably good" and that the men were having a fine time. Then he added, "There is great confusion here and guards on every side. We have to get a written pass from our Captain to get out of the lot ... there is so much crowding that we can't do anything." Nevertheless, Thomas managed to get his picture taken. He sent Mary a "likeness" of himself in uniform, complete with musket at his side, bayonet fixed to the muzzle, Bowie knife on his belt, and Colt Model 1860 Army revolver in his hand.

Private John L. Holt of Company I, a tobacco grower and country schoolmaster, wrote to his wife Ellen to say that he enjoyed camp life as much as he thought he would. He was quartered in a large, comfortable building in the center of the fairgrounds. The men sang and prayed together every night. Holt had to do guard duty, but he got time off to explore the city. He traveled all over town and even went down to the wharf to see the "strictly guarded" steamboats. Holt had his likeness taken too. He had it mounted under glass in a breastpin and sent it to Ellen. (Ellen wore the pin until the day she died in 1922.)

Both Privates Thomas and Holt were impressed by the number and variety of soldiers who went into the melting pot at the camp of instruction. Thomas wrote:

We have a great many Mexicans here. You can't understand nothing they say. . . We have a great many troops from New Orleans... We have troops here now I tell you... There are more people here who are soldiers than I ever saw at fifty times in my life.

Private Holt wrote Ellen:

... a large Louisiana Regiment has come in, all well-

armed and equipped, and made a great display marching through the fair grounds. They had one lady in their ranks who attracted great attention, and none of us could help saying, "Hurrah for Dixie!" ... but we are continually seeing something new.

On the night of July 21, the news of the Confederate victory at Manassas reached Camp Lee. Private Holt described the scene to Ellen:

Sunday, after we had all laid down about 9 o'clock at night news was received of the great victory we had gained at Manassas when a scene occurred the like of which I never witnessed before and I cannot describe it to you: drums began to beat and men to shout and soon nearly all the soldiers in the Fair Ground had assembled together and commenced marching round through the camp with flags waving, drums beating and men shouting, which continued until after 12 o'clock. Several short but stirring speeches were delivered in the meanwhile. I never witnessed such a Sunday night before.

Four days later Private Thomas wrote Mary to report the rumors of the battle that were buzzing about the camp:

They had a tremendous fight at Manassas Gap last Saturday and Sunday. We lost 25 thousand men and killed 45 thousand Yankees. We took 12 hundred prisoners and we have 950 of them in Richmond in the old tobacco factory under guard. We expect 500 more prisoners to come in tonight. We have to send men there every two days to stand guard.

Private Holt was one of the men ordered to Rocketts, an industrial and dock area of Richmond about five miles from the fairgrounds, to guard the Yankee prisoners and bring them water. Holt described the captured Federals:

The most of them are very good looking fellows and say they are sick and tired of the war... There are about 40 or 50 officers among them and one member of Congress. Some of the officers are fine looking men, but they may have very black hearts. The most of them say they have been deceived. They say they had no doubt when the attack was made on Manassas but that it would be but a small job to come through and come on to Richmond, but they were sadly disappointed. Many of them say their time is out and if they can get home again they are done with the war.

There was talk in camp that the war would soon be over. Private Holt hoped so, but he said to Ellen, "Who is not willing to give up all, even their lives if necessary, that our posterity may be freed from tyranny and oppression? I feel, for one, that I am."

On the evening of July 31, President Jefferson Davis, Governor Letcher, Robert Toombs, the Confederate Secretary of State, and Senator R. M. T. Hunter came to the fairgrounds with the Richmond brass band and a smart-looking military escort. A crowd of thousands of soldiers and civilians gathered around the President as he walked to the Texas encampment. Private Holt said that Davis presented a flag to a Texas regiment and then made a thrilling speech to the solid mass of human beings. Most people in the crowd could not get close enough to hear the President, but Holt was one of the lucky ones. Holt reported: he was one of the favored few who got close enough to hear him distinctly. I have seen him several times before, but that was the first time I had the pleasure of hearing him speak. He spoke with much feeling and in a loud, distinct voice and, although there were so many around him, all kept as silent as the grave during its delivery. He seems to have the entire confidence and esteem of all the soldiers who flock around him and follow him whenever he comes till he leaves the Fair Grounds.

According to Holt, by the end of August there was less noise and bustle at the fairgrounds. Most of the recruits had been assigned to regiments. They left the camp and headed for the battle areas; the soldiers who stayed behind were nearly all Virginians. The men who were to become the 56th Virginia still needed one more company before they could become a regiment. They were getting bored. They could see "heavy breastworks" going up in a ring around the city, but they still had not drawn their muskets. Holt wrote Ellen, "We are still in Richmond with no . . . prospect of leaving." The recruits still in camp had to wait in suspense and hope for the army in the field to win a decisive battle without them. The wait was doubly hard because no one knew what was really happening outside the camp. On September 10 Holt wrote Ellen:

The movements of the army are kept entirely secret. We are expecting daily to hear of a big fight somewhere about Washington City, as I understand the advanced lines of our army are close enough to that place to count the panes of glass in the windows of the Capitol.

While the men listened to rumors and waited to get into a regiment so they could see action, Private Peyton Lawson and his brother, Tom Lawson, of Company I returned to the fairgrounds from furlough with a big box of fresh chickens and a barrel of assorted vegetables. Private Holt said that for the next few days, the men made batches of Brunswick stew ". . up right and. .. pitched into them with a good will."

During the first week of September, Captain Dabney Harrison marched his newly-formed Harrison's Guards from Hanover County to the fairgrounds.

CHAPTER TWO

The Colonel

> ". . . a gentleman and a soldier, as
> Lear was a king - every inch."

When the 56th Virginia was formed, Governor Letcher was at a loss to select a colonel for it because its men came from so many different counties. The governor decided to let the junior officers name the colonel of their choice. They elected William D. Stuart almost unanimously.

William Dabney Stuart was born in Staunton, Virginia on September 30, 1830, and was christened there in St. Paul's Episcopal Church. He was the oldest son of Thomas Jefferson Stuart, a member of the Virginia legislature. William's father was named "Thomas Jefferson" because William's grandfather, Judge Archibald Stuart, had been a friend of "the sage of Monticello." Judge Archibald Stuart was the brother of Judge Alexander Stuart who was the grandfather of General Jeb Stuart. Thus, William D. Stuart and Jeb Stuart were second cousins.

William Stuart completed his early education at Staunton Academy. The headmaster of the school wrote a letter of recommendation for him when he applied for admission to Virginia Military Institute. The headmaster praised Stuart's good conduct, studious habits, and high moral character. Stuart won a scholarship to VMI and entered the military college as a state cadet in 1847. He was graduated in 1850 first in his class in artillery and infantry tactics and third in his class overall. In his senior year, he was the First Captain (commanding officer) of the corps of cadets and a member of le Societe' de Militaire.

Shortly after graduation, Stuart became assistant

professor of math and assistant instructor of tactics at VMI. When Major Thomas J. Jackson, the future "Stonewall," joined the VMI faculty in 1851, he lived on the post near Stuart. Jackson and Stuart saw each other every day and soon became close friends. They remained friends and corresponded with one another for the rest of their lives.

In 1853, Stuart left VMI to become the headmaster of a classical school in Georgetown, Virginia near Washington, D.C. While Stuart was in Georgetown, he received a letter from one of his old VMI classmates who gave him some good advice about teaching that he could use when he commanded the 56th Virginia:

> *School teaching like everything else, has its reverses, its calms, and its storms. We can find no profession that is made up entirely of sunshine. We must expect the life of man to harmonize with all nature, having its passing clouds and refreshing sunshine in equal turns... and industry, wherever it is found - is in the course of time rewarded.*

When war broke out in April 1861, Stuart was the headmaster of a classical school in Richmond and the captain of a militia company called the Richmond City Guard. He promptly offered his sword to Virginia and was appointed executive officer of the 3rd Virginia infantry Regiment with the rank of Lieutenant Colonel. Stonewall Jackson offered him a place on his staff as quartermaster, but Stuart graciously declined because he preferred the duties of a line officer.

Stuart commanded the 3rd Virginia as acting colonel in the Battle of Big Bethel on the Peninsula and helped to rout a Yankee force under General Ebenezer W. Pierce. Colonel D. H. Hill, Stuart's commanding officer, commended Stuart in his official report of the battle for handling the 3rd Virginia under fire in "the most heroic manner." General J. B. "Prince John" Magruder, the Confederate commander on the Peninsula, wrote to the Adjutant General to request that Stuart be promoted to full colonel. Magruder described Stuart as "... a man of knowledge of his profession and firmness." General George W. Randolph, the Confederate Secretary of War, called Stuart "an educated soldier... and a gentleman," and A.S. Rives, the acting Chief of the Bureau of Engineers, said that he heard Stuart "... uniformly spoken of as a gallant, efficient, and accomplished officer." Stuart impressed a fellow officer, Captain Briscoe Baldwin, so much that Baldwin wrote a letter of commendation to the War Department and said, "I declare him [Stuart] to be a gentleman and a soldier, as Lear was a king - every inch."

Stuart was a man of strong personality, stern discipline, and firm leadership. Private Holt said, "...Col. Stuart is invincible when he sets his head to anything. There is no getting around him." Stuart did not drink and would not tolerate laziness. He was an honorable, respectable, capable, and courageous leader. He also had a commanding appearance because he was over six feet tail. His military career looked bright. He longed to become a brigadier general, but it was not to be his destiny

CHAPTER THREE

Camp Lee

"The Sons of Virginia, Volunteers of the 56th Virginia Regiment will never do discredit to the sacred cause in which they have enlisted."

On September 7, 1861, William D. Stuart was promoted to full colonel and ordered to take command of the newly formed 56th Virginia. On September 23, the War Department issued Special Order No. 285 that mustered the regiment into Confederate service. The ten companies of the 56th came from eight counties scattered throughout the state, and the regiment was initially organized and staffed as follows:

Colonel - William Dabney Stuart
Lieutenant Colonel - Philip Peyton Slaughter
Major - William Edwin Green
Adjutant - Lieutenant Edward Branch Goode
Surgeon - Dr. Marlon Howard
Commissary - Captain Robert Richards
Asst' Quartermaster - Hilliard W. Carter
Company A - Mecklenburg Guards, Mecklenburg County - Captain Thomas Taylor Boswell
Company B - Mecklenburg Spartans, Mecklenburg County Captain George W. Davis
Company C - Louisa Holliday Guards, Louisa County - Captain Timoleon Smith,
Company D - Buckingham Yancey Guards, Buckingham County - Captain Camm Patteson
Company E - Ebenezer Grays, Brunswick County – Captain Thomas James Taylor

Company F - Louisa Nelson Grays, Louisa and Nelson Counties - Captain John Richardson

Company G - Charlotte Defenders, Charlotte County - Captain Thomas Daniel Jeffress

Company H - White Hall Guards, Albemarle County – Captain John Augustus Michie

Company I - Charlotte Grays, Charlotte County - Captain William Edwin Green

Company K - Harrison's Guards, Hanover County - Captain Dabney Carr Harrison.

Colonel Stuart was already at Camp Lee training recruits when he got his promotion and orders to command the 56th Virginia. He wasted no time in putting the regiment through five one hour drill sessions a day starting at 6 a.m. The men soon complained that they had no spare time because all they did was drill, drill, drill. Stuart knew all too well that it took long hours of hard work to teach the hayfeet-strawfeet how to do a manual of arms with their newly-issued, heavy, clumsy, smoothbore .69 caliber muskets converted from flintlock to percussion. (Some of the recruits did not know their left foot from their right, so the drill sergeant tied a wisp of hay to each recruit's left foot and a small bunch of straw to his right. Instead of marching the recruit to the words "left, right," the sergeant moved him with the commands, "hayfoot, strawfoot." The recruit soon got the idea; the men called all new recruits "hayfeet, strawfeet.") The recruits also had to learn how to load and fire on command and how to maneuver as a unit on the battlefield. The men were pleased to be armed at last. Private Holt said, "if we will only be men and use them [the muskets] as brave men fighting for their native land is all that is necessary."

The men did not realize at first that their living together in a large group under poor sanitary conditions exposed them to all sorts of illnesses. Sickness and disease raced through the ranks. Men came down with colds, diarrhea, jaundice, and worse. Private Holt wrote to Ellen, "... there is a great talk here of typhoid fever." Private Thomas reported to Mary that and some of the men in the "horse pittle" died from illness contracted in camp long before they ever met the first bluecoat on the battlefield.

A soldier named Steel of Company I broke out with the measles on the train before he even got to camp. An epidemic of measles soon swept through the 56th Virginia. Nearly every man in the regiment broke out with red spots, and some of them died. Private Peyton T. Scoggin of Company E died of measles on September 2. Captain Thomas Taylor, his company commander, had the unpleasant duty of writing a consoling letter to the boy's father. Captain Taylor said about all that he could say to justify the boy's death when he wrote, "Although not on the field of battle, yet he (Scoggin) has died in the defense of his country."

It was not long before the men began to shed their gaudy militia uniforms that differed so much from company to company and to substitute a simple, practical, single-breasted, gray Jacket and trousers in their place. Captain Timoleon Smith requisitioned 68 flannel shirts and 68 pairs of pants from the C.S. Quartermaster for Company C. Some of the men wrote home to their wives and asked them to make uniforms according to their directions. Thomas sent Mary these instructions:

The buttons, you must put them on in one row straight down before and four behind. 2 on each sleeve (1) one on each shoulder to fasten the straps. Like our other suit, the wrist band is open and the buttons on the wrist is to fasten the cuff with. Straight breast, trim the coat with black tape.

Private Holt also asked his wife to make his uniform. He told Ellen to get the wool from "Pa" and to mix the wool about 1/4 black to 1/4 white to make it the proper color, "a tolerably dark gray." Holt went on to say, "I had much rather have a good home made suit if I can get it than a suit that would cost me $15.00 here."

The men were beginning to feel like old soldiers, and they started to exercise the old soldier's right to grumble. Private Thomas wrote to Mary that he had no fault to find of Captain Davis, but "... our eatings are very scanty as we don't get but about half enough to eat and that is very rough ... we can't draw any shoes without paying $4.00 ... some days they say we must leave in a few days, then it is contradicted." Private Holt wrote Ellen, "We get plenty to eat but it needs woman's hands to cook it to make it good. You would laugh to see us cooking." The usually cheerful Holt complained, "I shan't be surprised if we are sent off at any moment, or if we were to stay here all the winter ... it seems like they can't do without the 56th here, we have been here so long ... we are tired of staying here doing nothing."

During the month of October, the 56th Virginia received orders to be ready to march at a moment's notice. The orders had an urgent tone this time and sounded like the real thing. The men did not know where they were going, but they believed it was Manassas, Yorktown, or West Virginia. No marching orders came; they remained stuck at the fairgrounds. The only excitement they had came one Friday when a sudden gust of wind ripped through the camp and blew down many of the tents. It tore the large preaching tent all to pieces.

There was more excitement on October 22 when a company of 80 men from Mobile, Alabama had a falling out with their officers and refused to serve under them. General John H. Winder, the head of the military police in Richmond, ordered the 56th Virginia to take the mutineers into custody. One instant the regiment was sitting down to eat dinner in the pouring down rain, and the next it was marching to headquarters to draw cartridges for its muskets. The regiment marched to the camp of the troublemakers and formed a line of battle around them. No one was sure what to do if the Alabamians resisted arrest, but, fortunately, they gave up cheerfully and easily.

A week later the 56th heard that the army was going to send one of the companies of the regiment on a special detail to escort some Yankee prisoners from Richmond to Columbia, South Carolina. Private Holt said that everybody wanted to ride the train to "the Sunny South" at government expense. Captain Camm Patteson of Company D wasted no time in asking Colonel Stuart for the assignment, but Stuart was a drillmaster and said that he would award the South Carolina trip to the company that looked the best on the parade ground. The next evening, Stuart held a regimental drill competition. According to Holt, Company D made a bad showing. Stuart gave the prize to Company I because it was "... the finest looking and the best drilled company in the regiment."

The happy men of Company I cooked two days' rations, and the next morning they marched down to Rocketts, picked up the bluecoat prisoners, and boarded the train for South Carolina. When the train pulled into the depot at Columbia two days later, a military band, two cadet companies, two regular infantry companies, and a crowd of thousands of civilians were on hand to greet the arrivals. Company I marched the prisoners about a half mile to the jail while the band played "Dixie." All along the way, people looked out of second story windows, stood on top of fences, and climbed trees to catch a glimpse of the Yankees.

The South Carolinians relieved Company I of the prisoners at the Jail. Then the band, cadets, and soldiers escorted the entire company to two of the main hotels of the city and treated every man to a hot meal. Private Holt reported that Company I spent the next two nights In the hotels "... four to a room with two good beds in each room." Holt said that the men almost forgot they were soldiers and that the city with its houses, yards, and gardens was so pretty that it looked "...something like enchantment, not reality." Holt wrote Ellen, "I don't think Columbia can be beaten anywhere for pretty women. There is hardly a single man in our company but says he is going back to Columbia when the war is over."

Just before Company I boarded the train to return to Richmond, the ladies of Columbia presented the men a large box of "segars," some fine chewing tobacco, and a box of palmetto rosettes to be worn on their hats as an ornament of uniform. Company I gave three cheers for the ladies of the Palmetto State, waved their hats, and cheered lustily. The ladies answered with three cheers for Virginia. Private Holt said, "We then got on the cars and left and we all felt almost as if we were parting with brothers and sisters, fathers and mothers, they treated us with so much kindness."

Just after Company I reached Richmond at the end of its South Carolina adventure, Captain Thomas S. Henry began to hemorrhage from the lungs. The doctors told him that he could not possibly survive the winter in the army, so he resigned his commission. The men elected John T. Palmer to be captain in his place.

Slowly, but surely, the 56th Virginia took shape, and by November the men received orders once again to be ready at a minute's warning. They had heard those orders many times before and nothing happened, but they got ready anyway. Although the regiment bore the number "56," the men already identified directly with Colonel Stuart Colonel Stuart. They were getting used to him, and in their minds, they belonged to "Stuart's regiment."

The regiment received its first official battle flag on November 15. It was a hand sewn, blue flag of the Commonwealth of Virginia that bore the state seal. The seal showed an ancient, Greek woman warrior standing in triumph over the body of tyranny. The two figures were surrounded by a circular wreath that bore in white letters the state motto "Sic Semper Tyrannis" (Thus Always To Tyrants) and the word "Virginia". Colonel S. Bassett French presented the banner to the regiment on behalf of the governor at a special ceremony at Camp Lee. The festivities included a review of the entire regiment and the trooping of the colors. It was a grand occasion because the wives of some of the officers and men were present. Colonel Stuart made a short speech to the men while they stood at parade rest in the ranks in front of him. Stuart said:

Soldiers of the 56th Regiment of Virginia, the flag which now graces your line is presented through the Executive of Virginia by the people in convention assembled. It is emblematic of the honor and virtue of our Mother State. Hitherto unsullied, it will be your part to see that this honor remains unblemished in your hands. The commanding officer feels highly gratified to assure the Governor and through him the Convention and people of Virginia that he commands true Virginians whose every pulse beats more strongly and whose steps grow more firm as they march to battle against tyranny and oppression under the banner and motto of Virginia. Soldiers, you have discharged the duties of your profession thus far well. It only remains for you in the more trying days of the future to bear your part as faithfully as you have heretofore done.

There was a dance after the ceremony. Later that evening Colonel Stuart sent a note to Colonel George W. Mumford of the War Department to thank him officially for the flag. Stuart wrote:

Sir, I have the honor to receive at the hands of Col. S. Bassett French the flag of Virginia intended for the Regiment I have the honor to command, also the accompanying letter of presentation from you.

As the Commanding Officer of the Regiment and its organ upon this occasion I need not assure you that I have received it with pride and satisfaction. Regarding it as the emblem of the honor and purity of our Mother State, hitherto unsullied in Council or War it shall be carefully guarded that it receive no defilement at the hands of the Regiment to which you have confided.

I think I can with all safety assure you that the sons of

Virginia, Volunteers of the 56th Va. Reg't, will ever be found at their post of duty and that they will never do discredit to the sacred cause in which they have enlisted. The Daughters of Virginia whose fair hands have wrought this beautiful emblem of Virginia's honor, will never have cause to blush for shame at the conduct of their brothers.

Six days later the 56th Virginia received definite orders to proceed without delay to join the small force of Brigadier General Humphrey Marshall defending the region of southwest Virginia and eastern Kentucky. Private Holt reported that there was a sudden stir and bustle in camp. The 600 men of the 56th who were fit for duty became "as busy as bees." They drew 20,000 rounds of buck and ball cartridges and percussion caps from the quartermaster at headquarters, filled their cartridge boxes, and started their fully loaded supply wagons on the road. They were all in high spirits as they marched to the railroad station, boarded the train, and headed west. According to Private Thomas, they were "...going to start to the salt mines to protect them from the Yankees."

CHAPTER FOUR

Conflicting Orders

"I am in the worst quandary I ever was in my life."

Private Thomas said that the 56th Virginia rode a slow train "over, under and through" the mountains to the town of Abingdon on the Virginia-Tennessee border. The men got a good, long look at some beautiful scenery because the feeble, little engine could hardly make it up the mountain sides. The regiment arrived in Abingdon late on the night of November 27, 1861.

The men spent the next few weeks in an old college building on a hill overlooking the town. Then they moved to a camping spot at the foot of a small mountain about one and a half miles south of town and pitched their tents beside a creek with a mill nearby. They called their campsite "Camp Robertson" after the man who owned the land. Private Holt wrote Ellen, "...we have excellent tents with good flyers to them and our bed ticks well filled with leaves and plenty of covering so that I think we could keep quite comfortable in almost any weather."

On December 1st a courier rode into camp with a letter for Colonel Stuart from General Marshall. The letter directed the regiment to move through Pound Gap and report to Marshall in the town of Prestonburg, Kentucky "...as soon as possible after the reception of this order, unless you should receive other directions from Maj. Genl. George B. Crittenden at Knoxville." Stuart was puzzled by Marshall's conditional order, but when 48 hours passed and he did not receive a contrary order from Crittenden, he decided to head for Pound Gap to join Marshall.

Private Holt's wife Ellen was distressed to hear that the regiment was going to Kentucky, but Holt consoled her:

> We ought to be willing to go anywhere to meet the invaders of our soil, who would crush and bind us to the earth and take from us all that is worth living for, and I would fight as freely to free Kentucky from the galling yoke under which she is groaning as for my own native Virginia...so let us console ourselves with the thought that we are in a just and holy cause, a cause for which our children's children will rise up and call us blessed for delivering our beloved South from such a tyrant's grasp as Abraham Lincoln.

Holt enclosed the words of "A Southern Song" in his letter to Ellen. He said that he wanted her "to particularly notice the last verse"

> Now when the war is over
> And we go home to see
> Our wives and little children
> Old Abe must let us be.

The move to join General Marshall was easier said than done because Pound Gap was 50 miles away, and the regiment had no horses or wagons to carry its heavy equipment over the rough mountain roads. Wagons were supposed to be on the way from Richmond, but a telegram arrived from Captain W. Gibboney, an assistant quartermaster in the War Department, stating:

> Some of the waggoners I hired and started left their teams on the road. I am compelled to go to Abingdon by private conveyance and will purchase some wagons and teams by the way and hire other waggoners.

The wagons crawled into Abingdon one at a time, and Captain Gibboney was able to buy a few more wagons and hire new drivers on the road. After several days, the regiment had enough wagons to carry its basic supplies, heavy baggage, and essential equipment, although it would have to leave some things behind. The wagons were piled high, and the regiment was about to begin the march to Pound Gap when an order dated December 5 arrived for Colonel Stuart. It was from General Crittenden in Knoxville and said, "You will move with your Regiment as soon as transportation can be furnished you to Nashville, Tennessee."

Colonel Stuart assumed that Crittenden's direct order overrode Marshall's conditional order. The regiment needed a train - not wagons to get to Nashville. Since Stuart could not use the wagons to carry out Crittenden's directive, he immediately ordered all of the wagons unloaded. He reloaded them with ordnance supplies and other stores that belonged to General Marshall and started them on the road through Pound Gap to Marshall's army in Kentucky. Stuart sent the regimental quartermaster to Lynchburg to arrange for a train to carry the regiment to Nashville. The men of the 56th pitched their tents in the mud and laid down inside them to wait for the train. According to Stuart, the weather was "very warm," but the ground was "very damp."

By December 10th the quartermaster had secured the train for Nashville. The men cooked seven days' rations, struck their tents, packed their baggage, and carried everything to the depot. Just as it was getting dark on the night of the 10th, the 56th finished loading all of its equipment on the railroad cars.

Some of the companies were preparing to board the train when another telegram came over the wires. The train should have left the station before the telegram arrived, but one of the steam pipes of the engine burst, and the train was late departing. The telegram was addressed to Colonel Stuart and said, "General A. S. (Albert) Sidney Johnston, the commander of all Confederate forces in the

West] orders that your regiment remain with Gen'l Marshall."

As Stuart read the telegram by lantern light, he must have felt like pulling his hair out by the roots, but he dutifully ordered the companies to unload the regiment's equipment from the train. The men of the 56th probably stood on the platform moaning, muttering, and cursing under their breaths as they watched the train chuff slowly away. Then they pitched their tents in the mud again.

It would be three more weeks before the regiment got its final marching orders, so the men found ways to pass the time. Private Holt and a large group of his companions explored an underground cave. Its entrance was about 50 yards beneath Abingdon. The men took several candles with them, but it was so dark inside the cavern that they could hardly see. They squeezed from one underground chamber to another and found a well and a large stream of clear water. Holt said, "it was a very curious sight."

The men had to spend a part of every day at drill, and they were becoming skilled in the manual of arms and the school of the soldier. Private Holt reported:

Our regiment has received a great deal of praise since we came to Abingdon. I saw a piece in the Abingdon Virginian last week complimenting us very highly. It said ours was the best drilled regiment they had seen, and they thought it second best to none except, perhaps, the Virginia First.

On Christmas morning the officers treated the entire regiment to a fine eggnog. There was enough for every man to have a good cupful. Private Holt drank a cup, but he was of the opinion that "... in camp life, as well as everywhere, . . . the most temperate are generally the most healthy, and by far the most peaceful soldiers."

Two of the men went home for Christmas without leave. Private Holt wanted to spend Christmas with his family too, but he wrote Ellen, "...bad as I want to see you all, if I can't go honorably, I don't want to go at all." He added that the two men ". . .will have to pay very dearly for their enjoyment, besides the disgrace of desertion, as I fully expect they will be Court Martialed and may have a very severe punishment inflicted on them.

On December 29 Captain Camm Patteson's Company D left camp to take a few additional cannons and ordnance wagons through Pound Gap to General Marshall. The men got to put their knapsacks and muskets in the wagons, but they had to wade through mud knee deep most of the way. Private Holt reported that when they rejoined the regiment, they gave a dreadful description of their trip and said that the other companies "...made a good miss not to go there."

On New Years Day, 1862, Private Holt went into the town of Abingdon to buy "some little presents" for his family. He sent a comb to Ellen, a watch to his little son Manly, and a string of beads to his infant daughter Viola. He said that the gifts were the best he could do, and he called them "love's offering." That night Holt returned to town to see a concert that was put on to raise money for the benefit of the sick soldiers of the regiment. Several of the officers of the 56th were in the cast. They acted and sang on stage with some of the faculty and young ladies of Martha Washington College. According to Holt, it was "...a very rich and entertaining scene." He sent Ellen a copy of the program.

While the men of the regiment were finding ways to enjoy the Christmas holidays, Colonel Stuart and the executive officer of the regiment, Lieutenant Colonel Slaughter, were trying to get the snarl of conflicting orders untangled. The two colonels realized that they and the regiment were impaled on the horns of a dilemma. They were caught squarely in the middle of a tug of war between General Marshall in Kentucky and General Crittenden in Tennessee. There were not enough troops to go around, and both of the generals wanted the 56th Virginia. On December 10 Stuart telegraphed the War Department in Richmond to ask whose orders he should obey. His answer came the next day by telegram from Adjutant General Samuel Cooper, "Proceed with your Regiment to Pound Gap and report to Gen'l Marshall. The Quartermasters Dept. is ordered to furnish transportation."

General Cooper's order was clear enough, but the Richmond quartermaster could not provide transportation because there was none. The regiment had to have wagons, drivers, and horses to get its supplies over the almost impassable mountain roads through Pound Gap to Kentucky, but all of the wagons, drivers, and horses were long gone. Some of them were loaded with ordnance and well on their way to General Marshall, while others were empty and already on the return trip to Richmond.

At this point, Colonel Stuart's health broke down. His poor physical condition was probably due to his continual sleeping on the wet, muddy ground combined with his constant worry about moving the regiment. He wrote home that he had been "quite unwell with jaundice" for some time. The regimental surgeon refused to be responsible if Stuart made the trip to Pound Gap and Kentucky. Stuart turned over the command of the regiment to Colonel Slaughter and went back to his home in Richmond where he was confined to his room with a severe attack of rheumatism.

Colonel Philip Peyton Slaughter was an 1857 graduate of VMI (Virginia Military Institute) and a fine officer. According to Stuart, there could be found in the service "...no officer more active, intelligent, and competent to the discharge of the duties of his position..." than Slaughter. Slaughter did his best. He cancelled all furloughs until after Christmas, and he and the men scoured the countryside surrounding Abingdon for the next two weeks to find transportation. They needed twenty wagons (two per company) and eighty horses (four per wagon). They were able to scrounge eight or nine wagons, but not a single horse. Slaughter did not want to seize wagons or horses from the local people because it would be "particularly harsh" on them and could destroy the economy of the region. Unfortunately, General Marshall was not sympathetic. By December 21, he was getting impatient. He sent a special order to the 56th which stated, "Colonel Stuart is directed to move his Regiment from Abingdon immediately with such transportation as can be procured." Marshall followed up with a letter to Colonel Stuart the next day in which he told Stuart "...to move your regiment without delay."

Obviously General Marshall did not know that Stuart was ill in Richmond and that Slaughter was in command of the regiment. He also did not know that lack of transportation was only one of the regiment's problems. Major Green was absent. He had gone on furlough to visit his plantation in Mississippi and became sick before he could return. Slaughter was the only field grade officer of the regiment left on duty. The health of the men had gotten steadily worse since Stuart left. Dr. Marlon Howard, the regimental surgeon, wrote to Stuart on December 27 to advise that 40 of the men were sick in the hospital, that the number of sick in camp and in private homes was hardly to be believed, and that "... if 250 men rank and file are able to march now more than I expect." However, the doctor hastened to assure Stuart that "... we 'what can go' are going - and no mistake."

Colonel Slaughter fully intended to move the remaining fragment of the regiment through the freezing mountain pass at Pound Gap at the earliest moment possible, but it was utterly impossible to move without wagons and horses. Slaughter wrote to Stuart to say that "entre nous" he was afraid that the regiment's reputation had suffered because of the "...embarrassing circumstances by which we are surrounded." Slaughter confided that he heard ugly rumors from Richmond that the regiment declined transportation for its supplies to Kentucky on account of the ". . .onerous march across the mountains."

Slaughter wanted Stuart to represent the men of the 56th Virginia "in our true colors" to the War Department and suggested that a Court of Inquiry be held because it "... would be beneficial to us; and at all events it could not injure us." Slaughter concluded his letter with a plea, "Can you do anything for us? I am in the worst quandary I ever was in my life."

There would be no Court of Inquiry. On Christmas Eve another telegram arrived from the War Department. It was addressed to "Lt. Col. Slaughter or commanding officer of the 56th Reg Va Vols." It directed the regiment to report for duty to General Marshall "immediately." On December 27, Slaughter wrote to General Marshall to explain the regiment's multiple problems of sickness, lack of transportation, and conflicting orders. He assured Marshall that he would do his utmost to move at the earliest hour possible. That same day the plot thickened; a third general claimed the regiment. Brigadier General John B. Floyd passed through Abingdon on his way to join his command In Bowling Green, Kentucky. Floyd discovered the 56th Virginia ". . .awaiting transportation, which is slow and difficult to procure."

Floyd telegraphed Adjutant General Cooper in Richmond and asked to have the 56th transferred to his brigade. Floyd told the War Department that General Marshall could not supply the troops he already had and that the region he was defending was of no military value anyway. When Marshall learned of the contents of Floyd's telegram, he flew into a rage. His anger was too hasty because Richmond promptly denied Floyd's request. General Cooper sent a staff officer, Colonel Dees, from Richmond to Abingdon to inspect the regiment and to hasten it to join General Marshall. On December 30 Marshall wrote a stinging letter to General Cooper:

I regret that Colonel Stuart has not moved from Abingdon yet. I learn that both officers and soldiers of that regiment are very averse to this service, and I suggest that in such mood they will be of very little service. I have no inclination to command men who pick soft places, and I would prefer regiments that are willing to sacrifice comfort to the cause they serve. It is not with me the best sign to know that a regiment loiters on the wayside when its absence endangers the safety and efficiency of a whole command. I am willing, so far as I am concerned, to exchange Colonel Stuart's regiment for any other the Department may think proper to send me.

On January 3, 1862, General Marshall complained in

desperation to General Albert Sidney Johnston, the Confederate commander in the West, about the 56th Virginia. He wrote Johnston:

Colonel Stuart's regiment is still in Abingdon - himself sick in Richmond - the regiment having only about 200 fit for duty and these trifling with the question of transportation. I have sent the most positive orders for them to move with such transportation as they can get, but to march at once, and they have received like order direct from the Department of War, to march with what they have, if it is but ten.

General Marshall did not know it, but the day before he wrote to General Johnston, the War Department resolved the issue of the destination of the 56th Virginia once and for all. For some reason, now unknown, the Secretary of War sent Special Order No. 1 to the regiment. The order plainly stated:

Colonel Stuart's 56th Regiment Virginia Volunteers is detached from General Humphrey Marshall's Command and will immediately proceed to Bowling Green, Kentucky and report to General A. S. Johnston for duty with General Floyd's Brigade.

It was relatively easy to get a train to Bowling Green, Kentucky. The moment Colonel Slaughter received the special order, he told the 56th to break camp and prepare to move out. He was determined to head for Kentucky before the War Department changed its mind again. The regiment had to leave behind 30 men who were sick in the hospital, including Dr. Howard, the regimental surgeon. Every able-bodied man was glad to get up out of the rain and mud of Abingdon and out from under the thumb of General Marshall. Slaughter summed up the mood of the regiment when he wrote Stuart on January 4 and said, ". . .our great objective is to get away, as fast as possible, from the road to Pound Gap."

Somehow, someway, General Floyd got his way after all. Maybe Floyd, a crafty old politician, pulled some strings behind the scenes. Maybe the War Department decided to stop the tug of war between Generals Marshall and Crittenden by assigning the 56th to neither. Needless to say, General Marshall was furious when he learned that the 56th would never be joining his command. On February 15 (the very day that the 56th was charging and breaking through the Union lines at Fort Donelson, Tennessee) Marshall wrote again to General Cooper and fired his parting shot:

I have no hope of preserving any Virginia regiment in this difficult and unwelcome service after the success of the 56th Regiment in getting away from it. I do think, however, when the frontier of Virginia herself is the line of contest, her sons had as well take the snows of her mountains as any other troops. ..

In spite of what General Marshall thought, the 56th Virginia tried hard to comply with his orders as well as the conflicting orders that it received from General Crittenden and the War Department. The regiment did not deserve the tarnished reputation that Marshall did so much to create. However, it is to Marshall's credit that six weeks later when he learned the true facts of the regiment's unsuccessful struggle to join him, he wrote a gentlemanly letter to Colonel Stuart in an effort to forgive and forget. He said:

Your vindicating note has been successful, I imagine, in proving that you did not delay marching last winter intentionally ..I am ready . . . to look forward and not backward, and hope our acquaintance may be as agreeable in its continuance as it was awkward in its beginning.

In any event, it was a great relief to the men of the 56th Virginia to receive clear, final marching orders at last. The paper war with the Confederate high command had severely damaged their spirits. They looked forward to their trip to Kentucky with enthusiasm. They were eager to meet the enemy because they hoped to regain their high morale and lost prestige on the battlefield.

CHAPTER 5
Fort Donelson

"Those who experienced it will never forget it."

On January 4 six companies of the 56th Virginia boarded the train for Bowling Green, Kentucky. The other companies did not leave Abingdon until two days later because there were not enough cars to carry the whole regiment at one time. Private Holt's Company I rode on the second train. Holt reported that some Union sympathizers burned the railroad bridge across the Holston River. Holt said, "We had to get off the cars and march and wagon our baggage about a mile and a half round by another bridge." The Union men were such a constant threat that the train ran only in the daytime. The 56th slept in the cars at night.

There were other problems too. Holt said that the train passed through mountainous country. "There were some very heavy upgrades and we came to one so tight that the engine couldn't pull us ... but... they got three engines hitched to the train, one behind and two before, and after much squealing and puffing and blowing they got us up."

By January 10th the 56th Virginia was in Bowling Green. It was now part of General Floyd's Brigade of the Central Army of Kentucky. The regiment set up camp on a rocky hill about three miles northwest of town. it joined a tent city of regiments from Tennessee, Kentucky, Texas, and Mississippi. The camp was so big and spread out that the tents of the 56th Virginia were 400 yards from the tents of the nearest other regiment. No one else was in sight. it was a beautiful camping spot with plenty of wood and pure limestone water as clear as crystal.

The men heard plenty of rumors in their new camp about the Yankees. Sometimes they heard that the bluecoats were advancing on them, and other times they heard that there would never be a fight at Bowling Green. While they waited, the regiments took turns sending details of 100 men per day to work on fortifications around the camp. The infantrymen at Bowling Green did not have to go out on picket because the cavalry patrolled the whole area and kept a constant lookout for the enemy.

Private Holt was happy with camp life at Bowling Green. He wrote Ellen on January 18:

We have got very well fixed here and are almost as comfortable as if we were in a house. We have built us a good rock chimney to our tent and made us a good floor of fence rails covered over with cornstalks. Our bedticks are filled with wheat chaff, and you would not suppose that anyone could be as comfortably situated in a tent. In fact, it Is almost as good winter quarters as we could expect anywhere. Nearly every tent in the regiment has a chimney, and this answers a fine purpose. It is raining very hard today, but we have a good fire and can sit around it and keep as comfortable as if we were in a house. We are getting better rations here, too, than we have had; that is, we have a greater variety. We draw flour, meat (some pork and some beef), sugar, coffee, Irish potatoes and molasses, besides candies and soap in abundance.

On the same day that Private Holt wrote his cheerful letter home to describe the food and housing, Captain Dabney Harrison, the commander of Company K, wrote to his father to tell about his living conditions. Harrison's letter was not as enthusiastic as Holt's, but its overall tone was still cheerful:

My tent is on a hi-side, and has a flue instead of a chimney. it rained hard all last night, has rained all of today, and is raining yet. The water has risen in my tent, the fire has been drowned out, the floor is nearly all mud, and I have been writing all the morning in a chair stuck deep in this mud. My bed is kept out of it by some fence rails, and my larder is a basket on the ground at the bed's head, containing a piece of pork and a bag of flour ... but I am 'contented.' I sleep soundly, work hard, eat heartily, and am fattening.

A day or two later Harrison wrote to his father again, " I have just finished a large stone chimney to my tent, and shall have it floored with poles tomorrow; then I shall be in great state."

Private Holt and Captain Harrison were content with life in camp at Bowling Green, but Private Thomas was not. Thomas was homesick. He wrote Mary that he was "... nearly one thousand miles from you all... the people are all gone from about here for they were Union men... we don't get enough to eat up here for it ain't to be had." To make matters worse, although there was strict military discipline in the tent city, somebody stole three pairs of socks from Thomas's knapsack while he was on guard duty.

On January 25 the regiment broke camp at Bowling Green and took the train to Russellville, the Confederate capital of Kentucky. It was the longest train of cars that Private Holt ever saw. It carried two full regiments, the 56th Virginia and another regiment of Floyd's Brigade, plus all of their baggage. The train arrived In Russellville at sunset on the 25th.

As soon as the men of the 56th took their gear off the train, they pitched their tents about 300 yards from the edge of town. The area was such a bad camping spot that General Floyd soon moved the regiment into the woods on the side of a hill about a mile and a half west of town where food, water, and firewood were plentiful. There was little for the men to do except to drive mule teams that pulled wagons with feed and to take turns on the guard detail to enforce martial law in town. Private Holt wrote Ellen, " I don't know when we will leave here or where we will go from here. There is some talk of fortifying this place, but I don't know how true it is, as it is by accident if we hear the truth often here."

Some of the men came down with the mumps at Bowling Green and had to be left behind in the hospital when the regiment moved to Russellville. Other men got sick with other illnesses at Russellville and had to go to the hospital. It was hard to stay well when the weather was so bad. it rained heavily or snowed lightly almost every day during the whole month of January. Colonel Slaughter himself was on the sick list as were the regimental adjutant, commissary, and quartermaster. The men longed for home. Private Holt reported that his older brother Meredith ". . has always been of a rambling disposition but ... he says that if he can get safely back to Old Virginia, he will be satisfied to remain there the rest of his days, for he has seen as much of the world as he wants to see." Private Thomas, the farmer, said simply, "Old Virginny land is the land for me."

Even though there was little for the regiment to do, there was always drill. One Sunday evening, Brigadier General Simon B. Buckner drilled the entire brigade. The men of the 56th Virginia got to see him up close, and they liked what they saw. Buckner was a West Pointer who knew what he was doing. He made such a good impression on the regiment that Captain Thomas Jeffress of Company G said, "He looked every inch a typical military man and leader."

The men of the 56th thought that they had settled into sleepy, long term winter quarters at Russellville where they could stay out of the cold until spring. They were sadly mistaken, for events were about to happen so soon and so fast that they would remember them vividly as long as they lived. President Lincoln was tired of Union failures in the East and stalemates in the West. He wanted action. One of his generals, an unknown named Ulysses Grant, was determined to give it to him.

Forts Henry and Donelson were the keys to the Confederacy in the West. They were 11 miles apart and controlled a narrow peninsula between the Tennessee and Cumberland Rivers. On February 6, 1862, Grant unleashed a powerful army and an ironclad navy against little Fort Henry on the Tennessee River. The heavy guns of the Union ships pounded the tiny fort and its token garrison into submission at point blank range before the Union army even got into attack position. Only Fort Donelson on the Cumberland River remained to challenge the Federals. If it fell, the gateway to the western Confederacy would be wide open.

General Albert Sidney Johnston, the supreme Confederate commander in the West, was in a desperate situation. He had expected a Union invasion for months and had kept the Yankees from coming mainly by bluff, but time had run out. Johnston was short of troops. He could not fight the two armies of Ulysses Grant and Don Carlos Buell on two fronts, so Johnston sent the brigades of Generals John B. Floyd, Gideon S. Pillow, Simon B. Buckner, and Bushrod R. Johnson to Fort Donelson to hold Grant's army at bay. If these brigades could protect his flank, Johnston could withdraw the rest of his army from Bowling Green, Kentucky and fall back to Nashville, Tennessee. Under Johnston's plan, as soon as the Confederates at Donelson completed their mission, they were to abandon the fort and join Johnston in Nashville.

The earthworks of Fort Donelson stood on the top of a hill in Tennessee about 100 yards above the Cumberland River. Log cabins filled the center of the fort; a moat twelve feet wide and six feet deep surrounded the entire post. The front of the earthworks bristled with heavy guns. Twelve pieces of seacoast artillery loomed from emplacements dug into the side of the bluff that overlooked the river. Walls of sandbags protected every gun position. The whole area outside the fort was hilly, rugged, and covered with a thick growth of scrub black-jack and oak trees.

The Confederate engineers cut all of the surrounding trees down and cleared away brush to provide open fields of fire from the fort in all directions like spokes of a wheel. They left the fallen trees on the ground, sawed off the tips of the branches, and sharpened the blunt ends with axes to form a protective abatis ring around the fort. They dug a line of shallow rifle pits in the yellow clay on the outer perimeter and strengthened them with logs. The reinforced trenches extended around the entire works in an arc on the land side.

The little village of Dover lay one mile south of the inner fort, but within the outer defense line of rifle pits. Dover was important to the overall defense because it housed a hospital and supply depot. it also had a wharf at the river's edge where steamboats could land and deliver troops and heavy equipment. At 4 p.m. on February 8, 1882, the 350 men of the 56th Virginia jumped off the boat at Dover Landing. They made camp near the wharf beside the 51st Virginia.

Most of the soldiers inside Fort Donelson came from Tennessee, but there were also units from Alabama, Kentucky, Mississippi, Texas and Virginia. There were only 4 infantry regiments from Virginia at the fort - the 36th, 50th, 51st and 56th Virginias. A small number of Virginia artillerymen were there too. The Virginians were the only Easterners who fought in the battle on either side.

General Floyd restructured his brigade for duty at Donelson. He called it a "division" and divided it into two "brigades." Floyd assigned the 51st and 56th Virginias to the First Brigade under the command of Colonel Gabriel G. Wharton, the commander of the 51st. Thus, the 56th Virginia became a part of Wharton's Brigade, Floyd's Division, Central Army of Kentucky. Colonel Stuart, Colonel Slaughter, and Major Green were all absent sick, so Captain George W. Davis of Company B assumed command of the 56th and led it through the coming battle.

On Wednesday, February 12, Wharton's Brigade took its place in the center of the line of rifle pits on the outer perimeter of the fort. The 56th Virginia spent the next few days digging new rifle pits and deepening the old ones. in the meantime Grant marched his army from Fort Henry straight to Donelson. By noon on the 12th, the defenders of Donelson found themselves encircled along a four mile front by a ring of iron and steel. There was frequent skirmishing along the line, and Union snipers constantly harassed the Confederates from the outer edges of the arc. The snipers were Birge's Sharpshooters, 66th Illinois infantry, but they called themselves the "Squirrel Tails."

Union Lieutenant Colonel John M. Birge of Missouri commanded the "Squirrel Tails." His expert marksmen carried the American deer and target rifle, complete with powder horn and bearskin bullet pouch. They wore gray uniforms and gray felt hats shaped like a sugar loaf. Each hat was trimmed with three squirrel tails dyed black and tied on top in a knot. The regimental first sergeant turned the "Squirrel Tails" loose at dawn every day a few hundred yards from the Confederate outer trenches with the single command, "Find your holes, boys."

The riflemen scattered and took cover Indian style behind logs, stumps, rocks, bushes, and trees. Sometimes they climbed into the treetops, and sometimes they 'stayed close to the ground and crawled into shallow holes. They were not only crack shots, but they were trained to load their weapons while lying down so that they did not have to expose themselves as targets. While the men of the 56th Virginia wielded shovels, picks, bayonets, and tin cups in the ditches, the rifle balls of the "Squirrel Tails" whistled past their heads.

Late Wednesday afternoon Union field artillery began to lob shells into the Confederate rifle pits, while Union infantry inched forward to feel out the defenses. On Wednesday night the Confederates captured a Union captain who commanded a company in an Indiana regiment. They brought the prisoner under guard to the camp of the 56th Virginia. He sat by the campfire with Captain Jeffress. Jeffress asked him, "Who commands your army?" The Federal replied, "General U.S. Grant." Nobody in the 56th had ever heard of Grant. "What do the initials 'U.S.' stand for?" Jeffress asked. "Unconditional Surrender," the Federal answered, "and you will know him well enough before Saturday night." Years later, Jeffress wrote, "His predictions were verified, much to our astonishment."

On Thursday the 13th, General Floyd himself stepped off the boat at Dover Landing with the rest of his Virginians. Floyd immediately took command of Fort Donelson. Floyd was not sure what plan of action to follow, but Grant solved the problem for him by immediately attacking the Confederate right and center with infantry and the entire front with artillery. At times the opposing riflemen blasted each other blindly at a range of only 40 yards. Somehow the Confederates were able to hold their ground and drive the Yankees off.

Late that afternoon the spring-like weather snapped suddenly without warning. Rain fell in torrents, then turned to sleet, and then became snow. The temperature dropped to 20 degrees below freezing. The wind knifed in from the north and cut the soldiers to the bone. The men on both sides had no overcoats. The Union troops had been fooled by the unusually warm weather and had thrown their overcoats away on the hike from Fort Henry. The Confederates never had overcoats, but they were great improvisers. They covered themselves with horse blankets, bed quilts, tablecloths, pieces of carpet, and even piano covers.

The officers on both sides would not let the men build fires because the opposing lines were so close together. After the sun went down, the men's clothing began to freeze to their skin. Icicles started to form and hang down from their caps. Several soldiers froze to death during the night. The next morning the men crept from their holes to behold a winter wonderland. The trees were sheathed in ice, and the ground was covered with a three inch blanket of snow. Years later, Captain Jeffress of the 56th Virginia still remembered. He wrote:

That week at Donelson was one of exposure, peril, exhausting trials, and almost unbroken sleeplessness. The weather was very cold, February 12-16. Rain fell in torrents, and driving snow and sleet followed. Those who experienced it will never forget it.

On the morning of February 14, General Floyd held a council of war with his fellow generals at the Dover Inn, a two story frame building in the village. The generals decided to mass their troops on the left under General Pillow and hurl them against the Union right. It was late in the afternoon before the men got into attack position. By that time a Union flotilla of four ironclads and two wooden gunboats under the command of Flag-Officer Andrew H. Foote had steamed right up to the fort. The ships began to fight a heavy gun duel with the river batteries at point blank range just as they had done at Fort Henry.

General Pillow felt it was too late in the day to accomplish anything. After putting the men through much tiresome marching and counter marching, he ordered the 56th Virginia and the other assault regiments back into the trenches while the water battle still raged. The Yankee gunners on the ironclads overshot the inner fort. Many of their shells exploded in the outer rifle pits, but no one in the 56th Virginia was hurt. The men of the 56th loudly cheered the gunners in the fort as they severely damaged all four ironclads and sent them drifting downstream helpless and out of action.

General Floyd had now accomplished the first half of his mission. He had kept Grant's army away from Johnston during the retreat from Bowling Green so that the bulk of the Confederate army could concentrate safely at Nashville. All that remained was for Floyd to break out of the trap at the fort and join Johnston for the defense of Tennessee. There were several roads that led from the fort to Nashville. Grant's army was stretched across all of them. If the Confederates pushed the Federals back from just one of the roads, they could open an escape route to Nashville.

Floyd held another council of war with his fellow generals on Friday night. They decided again to try their bold breakout plan. They agreed to mass their troops under General Pillow on the extreme Confederate left and strike a sudden, hammer blow on the far Union right. Their goal was to push the Yankees back and open the Forge Road to Nashville and freedom.

Confederate officers labored all though the night to

move their regiments into attack position. It was pitch black dark, and it started snowing again. The men suffered, but at least the cruel weather gave them an advantage over the bluecoats. The howling wind and softly falling snowflakes masked the sounds of tramping feet, murmuring voices, and creaking cannon wheels. The Confederates were able to find a little bit of warmth and comfort just by moving about. The unsuspecting Yankees could only burrow down deeper into the frozen ground and hope that the morning sun would hurry up and rise.

Shortly before 4 a.m. on Saturday, the 56th Virginia was standing in the outer trenches awaiting the order to move to the assault line. Captain Dabney Carr Harrison called the men of his Company K to attention. The 31 year old Harrison was a brave soldier and an outstanding human being. He was a descendant of two signers of the Declaration of independence, Thomas Jefferson and Benjamin Harrison. Benjamin Harrison was also the father of William Henry Harrison, President of the United States.

Captain Harrison was a Presbyterian minister who held degrees from three universities. He was a lawyer, theologian, and former chaplain of the University of Virginia. When his brother, Lieutenant Peyton Randolph Harrison, was killed at First Manassas, Dabney Carr pledged to take his brother's place. He raised a company of infantry from Hanover County where he was preaching, called the unit "Harrison's Guards," and marched it to Camp Lee in Richmond in 1861. It became Company K of the 56th Virginia.

There was a certain glow about Captain Harrison because he was the epitome of the Christian soldier. He led by example; he never said "go on," but always "come on." According to Captain Jeffress, Harrison's good character "... permeated the entire regiment." He really cared about the men. When the 56th Virginia was in Abingdon, Harrison wrote to Colonel Stuart in Richmond to ask Stuart to find a chaplain for the regiment. Harrison urged:

Do try to get us a Chaplain, we are famishing for one. . .

The soul of a soldier, even in the poorest earthly point of view, is far more important than his body. And if you ever get a word with a Congressman, do beg him to raise the Chaplain's pay and rank at least to a Captain's. We could better spare any officer in a regiment, I say it with deference, than the Chaplain. Strike off the Majors, or Third Lieutenants, if economy be the object. We could possibly spare them; but never the Chaplain. If a judicious man, he would cure as many sick men as the surgeon.

Harrison was frail, but he rolled up his sleeves and swung a pick alongside the men of Company K to deepen the rifle pits. He got sick Friday afternoon and spent Friday night in the hospital in Dover, but the moment he heard of the plan to attack at dawn, he left his bed. He rejoined the regiment in the trenches in the wee hours before sunrise on Saturday morning. The sun had not come up when Harrison asked his men to bow their heads in prayer while he recited the 27th Psalm by heart. Men from other companies of the regiment crowded around the Captain. Many of them took off their hats and solemnly repeated the words after him:

The Lord is my light and my salvation. Whom shall I fear? The Lord is the strength of my life. Of whom shall I be afraid?... Though an host should encamp against me, I will not fear. Though war should rise against me, in this I will be confident.

Soon after the prayer ended, the 56th Virginia climbed out of the trenches and took its place in the line of attack. The four Virginia regiments were on the left of the battle line and stood, left to right - 56th Virginia, 51st Virginia, 50th Virginia, and 36th Virginia. A hush came over the ranks as the four generals and their aides rode across the front of the line. The senior officers passed close to the colors of the 56th Virginia. The regiment was not carrying a red Confederate banner, but the blue flag of the Commonwealth that it received at Camp Lee in Richmond.

General Floyd came first. He kept his eyes straight ahead and passed on by. Generals Buckner and Johnson came next. They simply touched their right hands to their caps in salute to the flag. General Pillow came last. When he reached a point opposite the flag of the 56th Virginia, he reined in his horse and faced the regiment. He pointed to the blue banner and said in a firm, clear voice, "I trust to old Virginia my safety and my honor." According to Captain Jeffress, the effect of his words on the men of the 56th ". . .was electrical and Inspired the Virginians with renewed hopes and courage."

At 5 a.m., two hours before sunrise, the Confederates struck the Federal right with all their might. Captain Dabney Harrison drew his sword and gave the order, "Follow me," to Company K. The men of the 56th Virginia screamed the high keen of the rebel yell for the first time in battle and surged forward. They stumbled clumsily in the soft snow, slipped up gullies, slid down ravines, and slapped the ice-laden tree branches out of their faces as they drove in the Yankee pickets. They only had to go about 200 yards before they plunged headlong into the camp of the Illinois troops of Richard J. Oglesby's Brigade, General John A. McClernand's division.

The attack was a complete surprise. The bluecoat buglers were Just beginning to sit up in bed and starting to rub the sleep from their eyes when the Confederates, howling like demons, ran into them. The Yankees did not panic and run, however. They jumped to their feet, grabbed their muskets from the stacks, and fired cartridges as fast as they could bite, pour, ram, cap, and pull the trigger.

The ground was so rugged and criss-crossed with chasms, gullies, and rises that all organization broke down on both sides. It was every man for himself. A wild melee of clubbing muskets and thrusting bayonets see-sawed back and forth through the snow-capped underbrush. Private Holt said, ". . . the balls rattled around us sometimes almost like hail."

Three rifle bails tore through the hat of Captain Harrison. A fourth cut the skin across his temple. A fifth ripped through his right lung. He pitched forward into the snow while the men of Company K swarmed, twisted, and lunged around him. Eighteen year old James H. Jeffress, a private in Company G, charged ahead of the whole regiment. He died instantly when a rifle bail struck him between the eyes.

The bluecoats stubbornly contested every inch of ground, but they began to fall back steadily. They regrouped on the next ridge, stood, and fought again. They continually fell back, regrouped, stood, and fought. The path of the battle was plainly marked in the snow by the litter of canteens, cartridge boxes, knapsacks, blankets, broken bodies, and bright red bloodstains. The Confederates captured General Grant's head-quarter's tent, 5000 small arms, and 7 cannons. By noon, they had pushed the Union right wing (five brigades) back about two miles. McClernand's division was bent back at a right angle to the rest of the Union line. The Forge Road was swept clean of Yankees; the gateway to Nashville was wide open. The entire garrison of Fort Donelson was safe.

The fighting sputtered and died down. The soldiers on both sides asked the same question, "What happens now?" While they were waiting for the answer, General Pillow and General Buckner got into an argument. Bucker, the West Pointer, wanted to hold the road open with his troops while Pillow marched the rest of the army to Nashville immediately. Pillow disagreed. He was wounded twice in the Mexican War and considered himself an accomplished soldier. He insisted that the Confederates had won a great victory. He thought that they had plenty of time to return to their trenches, pick up their gear, rest overnight at the fort, and then march to Nashville the next morning.

At that moment General Floyd rode up to Buckner and Pillow. Floyd was a poor choice for fort commander because he had little military experience and no military aptitude. He had been Secretary of War under President Buchanan and was under Federal Indictment for malfeasance in office. He was really just a politician in uniform. Even Ulysses Grant said of him, "He is no soldier."

Buckner appealed to Floyd, and Floyd agreed with him. Then Pillow, an old politician, argued with Floyd, and Floyd changed his mind. Floyd ordered the entire Confederate attack force to retrace its steps, give up all the ground it had paid for in blood, and return to the trenches. When Captain Davis, the acting colonel of the 56th Virginia, heard the order, he could not believe his ears. He thought that there must have been a mistake, so he sent a courier to General Floyd for confirmation. Floyd promptly confirmed the order, and the 56th joined the other regiments in trudging back to the outer ditches that arced around the fort.

While the Confederates were withdrawing, Ulysses Grant arrived on the field. With the stump of a cigar clenched between his teeth, he took command of his reeling army in person. The first thing that he did was to order a savage counterattack on the Confederate right. He reasoned correctly that if the Confederates struck with such force on their left, they must be weak on their right. Within a few hours, the original Federal line was restored. The gate to the Confederate escape route over the Forge Road to Nashville was slammed shut. The 56th Virginia suffered 8 killed, 37 wounded, and 115 missing - for nothing.

That night General Floyd held his last council of war. He met with Generals Buckner and Pillow at the Dover inn. After some debate, they all agreed that their situation was hopeless; they had to surrender the fort. Before the battle Floyd had pledged to fight until "liberty or death"; he chose liberty. He was afraid of what the Federals would do to him if he fell into their hands. He decided to escape from the fort and to take as many of his Virginians with him as he could. He turned the command over to General Pillow who immediately tossed it like a hot potato to General Buckner. Buckner accepted the responsibility as a good soldier. He agreed to surrender the fort, the garrison, and himself to Grant the next morning.

Back in the trenches the men of the 56th Virginia were in good spirits. They were not aware of what was going on at the Dover inn. Their army had just whipped the Yankees on water and on land, and they were ready to fight them and whip them again in the morning. They were content as they ate their supper and went to sleep. Early the next morning the men of the 56th were sick, angered, and disgusted to hear that the fort was to be surrendered. Some of them protested when they heard the order to march to the wharf at Dover Landing and board the steamboat General Anderson that had arrived during the night. Orders were orders and had to be obeyed.

When the 56th Virginia got to the landing, the soldiers learned that the steamboat had already carried McCausland's Brigade (36th Virginia and 50th Virginia) across the river to the Kentucky side. it was rapidly filling up with the 51st Virginia, so the 56th scrambled to get aboard too. General Floyd stood beside the rail on the lower deck of the steamboat with his sword drawn. "Come on, my brave Virginia boys," he encouraged. Before all of the 56th could climb on board, the boat suddenly started to pull away from the dock and to back out into the river. Floyd had run out of time; he was also afraid that the boat would swamp. He ordered the Captain of the General Anderson to get up a full head of steam. The boat sailed up the river to Nashville while part of the 56th Virginia and all of the other regiments that were left behind stood on the riverbank and howled.

Floyd had ordered the 20th Mississippi Regiment to guard the steamboat so that the Virginians could get aboard first. The men of the 56th Virginia felt that Floyd had dishonored them by leaving the faithful Mississippians behind. Captain Davis protested loudly to Colonel Wharton and Wharton agreed with him, but there was nothing they could do at the moment to help the abandoned Mississippians.

Later that morning General Buckner surrendered the 12,000 men who were still inside Fort Donelson. He had no choice but to accept Grant's harsh terms of "unconditional surrender." About 80 men of the 56th Virginia were caught in the trap; 6 of them were young lieutenants. The enlisted men soon found themselves in the Federal prisoner of war stockade at Camp Morton in Indianapolis, Indiana, while the officers were sent either to Camp Chase in Columbus, Ohio or to Johnson's Island in Lake Erie near Sandusky, Ohio.

On the afternoon of the surrender, Captain Dabney Harrison, the ideal soldier of the 56th Virginia, died. He fell in the breakout charge and had been in a deep sleep ever since he was wounded. Suddenly he awoke with a start. He sat up in bed and called to his men, "Company K, you have no Captain now, but never give up! Never surrender!" Then he closed his eyes forever. Since he was a true Christian soldier, it was fitting that he was born on a Sunday and died on a Sunday.

The General Anderson landed at Nashville on February 17th. The people of Nashville were in a panic and on the verge of rioting because they heard that the Confederate army intended to abandon the city and its citizens to the oncoming bluecoats. For the next few days the 56th Virginia and its three companion regiments guarded and shipped Confederate government stores. They got most of the supplies away safely before they were ordered to start their long journey back to the Old Dominion. Their first stop on the way home was Murfreesboro. The morning report of the 56th Virginia for February 24 stated that the regiment was encamped "near Murfreesboro" and that 184 officers and men were present for duty. in less than two months, the regiment had lost two-thirds of its men, most of its equipment, including tents and cooking utensils, and all of its baggage.

At least the regiment could find a little comfort in Colonel Wharton's official report of his brigade's performance at Donelson. Wharton mentioned the 56th Virginia specifically: "Captain George W. Davis gallantly led the 56th Regiment ... all the officers and men of both regiments (51st and 56th) behaved with commendable coolness and bravery."

The 56th Virginia marched with the other Virginia regiments from Murfreesboro to Chattanooga where they all camped at the foot of Lookout Mountain. At that point morale reached an all time low. The men called the campsite "Camp Bitter" to show how they felt about the Donelson campaign. General Floyd issued an unusual order allowing the men a 60 day furlough, but then he suspended the order because he expected to meet the enemy momentarily. Floyd's order only made things worse. The troops knew that their generals had mishandled them; they felt that Donelson was a disgrace. On March 17 the 56th Virginia quietly boarded the train for Knoxville.

While the regiment was on its slow, torturous route back to Virginia, Colonel Stuart recovered from his fever enough to get out of bed. He even managed to recruit some new men for the regiment. On March 8 Stuart left Richmond with his recruits and headed for Knoxville to meet the regiment. His wife, whose nickname was "Clinkey," felt that he was not well enough to go and that he was acting rashly, but she could not hold him back any longer. He had to see his men. He had heard the grim news of the failure of Fort Donelson, but he was not fully prepared for what he saw when the soldiers of the 56th Virginia got off of the train in Knoxville. Only 88 officers and men fit for duty stood on the platform. Stuart wrote to Clinkey, "Never has my soul been so grieved as when I looked upon those grieving faces of my men."

The next day the War Department relieved General Floyd of command and put Colonel George Meaney in charge of the division. Meaney was responsible for all the Confederate forces at Knoxville. He was so impressed with Colonel Stuart that the next morning he turned what was left of Floyd's division over to Stuart. Stuart found himself in temporary command of the 36th, 50th, 51st and 56th Virginia infantry regiments plus some Virginia artillery units and a few quartermasters. His job was to regroup and reorganize them.

Stuart received a flurry of orders to march, then not to march, then to prepare to march, then to march, and then not to march. Fortunately the red tape was unsnarled after a few days. The War Department told Stuart to take his little division on foot through the Cumberland Gap to Morristown, Tennessee and then to board the train for Abingdon, Virginia. Before the men began the long hike, the chief quartermaster had a surprise for them. He had been hoarding rations for a special occasion, and the time had come. As if by magic, he produced bacon, flour, real coffee, and other almost forgotten delicacies. The hungry soldiers lost no time in building cooking fires. Colonel Stuart remembered that for a whole day "... the camp haze was rich with the smell of corn bread and chicory coffee." It was surely one of the most pleasant days in the life of the 56th Virginia since it left Richmond.

The regiment spent the last part of March and most of April in the rain and mud at its old campground in Abingdon. The headquarters's huts were still there, and the town still had plenty of liquor, saloons, vice dens, and camp followers. Colonel Stuart did his best to keep the men away from corruption, but it was an impossible task. Stuart was disgusted by any soldier's drunkenness and troubled that even some of the youngest soldiers contracted venereal disease.

Stuart's days in Abingdon were filled with administrative duties. His work load increased because he sent many of the junior officers to their home counties to find new recruits to refill the ranks of the regiment. He had to put pen to paper every day for a variety of reasons. He wrote letters to release an under-aged boy from the army, to approve specifications for a court martial, to console a mother who lost a son at Fort Donelson, and to explain to a wife that he did not know what had happened to her husband who was listed as "missing."

Some of the men who were sick or wounded at Fort Donelson rejoined the regiment in Abingdon; Private Holt was one of them. He walked out of the trap at Donelson and managed to get about 100 miles from the fort before he became too "sick and feeble" and collapsed from cold and fatigue. He then traveled by train with other sick and wounded men to Atlanta, Georgia. He stayed in the Empire Hospital, a former tavern on White Hall Street, about six weeks. At first he was too sick to write and lived on milk, mush, and chicken soup. When he felt strong enough to hold a pen, his handwriting was shaky and misshapen. He reported to Ellen that the ladies of Atlanta visited the hospital every day with something good for the men to eat and that he ". . never was amongst kinder and more hospitable people." When Holt rejoined the regiment in Abingdon, he felt much better, but he still had not regained his full strength. He said with conviction, "I feel quite glad that we have got into Old Virginia again and I hope we will stay here now till our time is out."

On March 24 Dr. R. M. Evans, the assistant surgeon of the regiment, gave physicals to all of the men. He reported to Colonel Stuart that they were suffering from diarrhea, fatigue, exposure, and coughs. According to Evans, the whole regiment was in a broken condition. The doctor recommended that the men be allowed to go home to recover their strength and health. Stuart sent Evans's report to Richmond and asked for the furloughs, but General Robert E. Lee himself denied the request because the army could not spare the men at that time.

The mental state of the men of the 56th Virginia was as bad as their physical health. Private Holt said, "The fall of Fort Donelson has caused a great gloom to be cast over our cause." The war was no lark for the men of the 56th. Except for the first giddy day or two when they enlisted at their community stores and churches, it had never been a lark. The men could live with General Lee's decision that there would be no furloughs. They could accept the fact that war was dirt, mud, rain, sleet, ice, snow, cold, exhaustion, blood, and death. They could pull their minds and bodies together and keep on fighting, but they had to have self-respect. They needed a genuine victory on the battlefield in order to feel like real soldiers. They would soon get another chance to prove themselves.

CHAPTER SIX
Fort Drewry and Chaffin's Bluff

"The Yankees gave us a salute as we arrived.. .."

By April 26, 1862, the 56th Virginia was camped on Fulton Hill about three miles down the river from Rocketts in the east end of the city of Richmond. The company commanders kept busy filling out requisition forms "for the comfort of the men" to replace the equipment that the regiment had lost at Fort Donelson. The ranks were filling up fast with new hayfeet-strawfeet recruits who had to be taught the school of the soldier. Every now and then a man who was listed as "missing since Fort Donelson" would show up in camp unexpectedly. He had escaped through the Union lines and walked all the way over the mountains to come back to the regiment.

The Confederate army reorganized in the spring of 1862, and each officer had to stand for reelection. The 56th Virginia held its election of officers at Fulton Hill on May 3 and 5. Colonel Stuart notified Brigadier General John H. Winder, the commander of the Department of Henrico, of the results of the election and verified that the voting was conducted fairly. Colonel Stuart, Lieutenant Colonel Slaughter, and Major Green were all reelected as the field grade officers of the regiment. Most of the junior officers were reelected also. However, a few of the privates became officers, and a few of the officers found themselves out of a job. Private John W. Thomas was elected First Lieutenant of Company B. Thomas T. Boswell was not reelected captain of Company A, and First Lieutenant John B. McPhail became company commander in his place. Boswell resigned, transferred to the reserves, and rose to the rank of colonel by the end of the war.

On the day of the election of officers, Private Holt wrote Ellen to say that under the new Confederate Conscription Act all men between the ages of 18 and 35 would be held in the army until the end of the war. Holt was almost 33 years old, but he accepted his fate with his usual cheerfulness and resolve. He looked forward to the $50 bounty and the furlough that came with reenlistment. He said to Ellen: "I think that every Southern heart should now respond to the language of our great Patrick Henry in the days of '76 and say, 'Give me liberty or give me death!' If money were all we were fighting for, I would not serve in the army for $100,000 a year so you may know it is no pleasure for me to be in the army, but I feel that we are fighting for all that is worth living for, and this braces me up to bear the hardships of camp life, the greatest of which is my separation from you and my dear little babes."

Holt also wrote to Ellen, "There can be no possible doubt that there will be a big battle or battles fought around this place (Richmond) in a very short time. The enemy's gunboats are said to be moving up the James River and are within 12 or 15 miles of this place." Holt was right. While the 56th Virginia was recruiting and refitting at Camp Fulton, Union General George B. McClellan began his "On to Richmond" campaign. He landed what he called "the finest army on the planet" (the Army of the Potomac) at Fort Monroe and advanced up the Virginia Peninsula between the York and James Rivers to seize the Confederate capital.

The Federals captured the Norfolk Navy Yard on May 10. The next day, the Confederates blew up the C.S.S. Virginia (formerly the U.S.S. Merrimac, a wooden ship cut down close to the water line and covered with thick plates of railroad iron), so she would not fall into Union hands. As long as the Virginia was afloat, she guarded the mouth of the James River at Hampton Rhoads and held the Union navy at bay. The moment she exploded, the James River was defenseless; the river was wide open almost all the way to Richmond. Under General McClellan's plan, the Union navy would steam up the James River and bombard Richmond from the water while the army attacked the city on the land.

There was only one thing of any consequence that stood between the Union gunboats and Richmond - Fort Drewry. The fort was a small square of earthworks located in Chesterfield County about seven miles below Richmond on a bluff overlooking a sharp bend in the James River. The garrison consisted of the Southside Heavy Artillery and a small detachment of Confederate marines under the command of Captain Eben Farrand, C. S. Navy. A farmer, Augustus H. Drewry, owned the land on which the fort was built. Drewry was a captain in the Southside Heavy Artillery, so when he took his battle station in the fort, he was literally defending his home and fireside. The Confederates called the earthworks Drewry's Bluff or Fort Drewry; the Yankees called the post Fort Darling. All of a sudden, events thrust the little fort on the south side of the river into the national spotlight.

The 56th Virginia received sudden orders to go to the defense of the fort. The regiment hurriedly broke camp at Fulton Hill and marched overland through the rain and mud towards Drewry's Bluff. The men set up a new camp at Chaffin's Farm on Chaffin's Bluff across the river from the fort and about a half a mile downstream. The regiment carried extra firepower - a battery of light field artillery and a rifled 30 pound gun. Colonel Stuart must have been glad that he finished first in his class in artillery and infantry tactics at VMI as he set the men to work positioning the cannons and digging a line of rifle pits on the high bluffs along the north bank of the river. On May 10 Stuart sent word to Captain Farrand at the fort that the 56th Virginia's advance pickets downstream had just sighted "...enemy transports (fourteen) at City Point with troops."

On May 11 the Confederate high command ordered the former officers and crew of the Ironclad Virginia to report to Fort Drewry as fast as they could get there. They traveled all night by train and arrived at the fort on the 12th. There was not a minute to spare because only three of the fort's seven heavy guns were in position. For the next three days the newly arrived sailors, the regular garrison, and some of the men of the 56th Virginia on special detail dragged the remaining four guns into place. It poured down rain the whole time, but the laborers did not stop pushing, pulling, lifting, digging, and sandbagging. They also sank old, wooden, paddlewheel steamboats filled with stones and scrap iron into the muddy river below the fort. They drove wooden pilings deep into the soft river bottom among the hulks and dumped every big rock, tree stump, and loose object they could find into the water beside them. Then they wrapped the whole mass with lengths of iron chains. The result was a barrier of obstacles that forced any ship coming up the river toward the fort to swing wide around the barrier and come into the narrow channel. At that point the middle of the channel was the dead center of the field of fire from the guns of the fort.

The fort was thrown together almost overnight, but it was a perfect place for a heavy gun battery. It stood on a sheer bluff that dropped straight down 90 feet to the water's edge. The three guns on the front parapet were giant Rodmans (Columbiads). Their barrels were newly cast at nearby Bellona Arsenal and weighed 8,800 pounds apiece. Each gun was mounted on a round Barbette carriage so that it could swivel on wheels to the left or right with ease. Each could fire a shell that was eight inches in diameter and weighed sixty-four pounds for a distance of two and a half miles. All of the fort's guns could deliver a plunging fire on any target below.

The Confederates on both sides of the river stood by their guns and braced themselves for the attack. It was not long in coming. On the morning of May 15, Commander John Rodgers, U. S. Navy, led five Union warships (Monitor, Galena, Aroostook, Port Royal, and Naugatuck) up the James River toward Richmond. The ships easily brushed past one or two shore batteries along the way. They did not stop until they reached the sunken barrier about a mile below Fort Drewry.

As the Yankee flotilla approached the fort, Colonel Stuart crossed the river from the south bank to the north. Stuart had spent the night of the 14th in the fort. Late in the evening, he received an order from General Lee telling him to cross the river as soon as possible and to take charge of the 56th Virginia men who were standing by the artillery pieces and lying in the rifle pits along the north bank. Stuart deployed six companies of the regiment and several light cannons in line of battle across the Richmond Road below Chaffin's Bluff in case the gunboats landed troops on shore. The gunboats did put some infantry ashore, but the bluecoats got right back on board. The boats steamed past the regiment and opened fire on the men on shore. Later that day, Stuart wrote to his wife, "The Yankees gave us a salute as we arrived but without any harm." The men of the 56th raced through the woods ahead of the ships. They took their positions in the rifle and cannon pits beside the other four companies and waited for the gunboats to arrive.

The Confederates called the Union ship Monitor "a cheesebox on a raft" because that is what she looked like. The Monitor was already a famous fighting ironclad because of her recent historic duel with the Virginia in the harbor at Hampton Rhoads, but her two big Dahlgren guns would not elevate enough to hit the fort. The Aroostook, Port Royal, and Naugatuck were wooden ships, so the ironclad Galena had to take the lead in the fight. According to Commander Rodgers, the Galena bravely "...steamed up to within seven or eight hundred yards of the Bluff, let go her starboard anchor, ran out the chains, put her head inshore, backed astern, let go her steam-anchor from the starboard quarter, hove ahead, and made ready for action before firing a gun."

All five Union ships opened fire on the fort at the same time; the guns of the fort immediately returned the fire. The Confederate cannoneers took careful aim because they were short on ammunition for the big guns. However, the marines inside the fort and the men of the 56th Virginia in the rifle pits on the north bank of the river were not short of rifle ammunition. They kept up a constant musket fire. Some of the men of the 56th were armed with fine British Enfield rifles and picked off a number of Yankees on deck. The Yankee sailors and marines had to take refuge below deck and stay out of the fight. Even then the bluejackets were not out of danger because the Confederate sharpshooters sent a steady stream of minie balls pinging through the open gunports on the sides of the ships.

Select men from Company K of the 56th Virginia fired the rifled 30 pound gun as fast as they could sponge down the barrel, reload, and jerk the lanyard. There were five huge targets floating on the water directly below them which made it hard for them to miss. The rifled gun on the river bank and the giant cannons in the fort had great penetrating power. At such close range, they easily damaged the two ironclads and tore the wooden hulls of the other three ships to splinters. After three hours and twenty minutes, the Union flotilla stopped firing. The Galena was hit 28 times and holed in 14 places; 7 of her crew were dead and another 20 were wounded. All five gunboats turned and headed downstream away from the fort at top speed. The rebel yell rang out from both sides of the river. The 56th Virginia had won its first battle; the stigma of Fort Donelson was starting to wear off. For the first time, the men began to feel like real soldiers.

The Union navy did not make a serious effort to pass the guns of Fort Drewry again until April 1865. By that time, the Confederates had evacuated Richmond and abandoned the fort. Of course, on May 15, 1862, the authorities in the Confederate capital expected another attack at any moment. Private Holt said, "We are looking every day for the gunboats to come again." The 56th Virginia received orders to construct additional earthworks for an artillery battery along the north river bank and a second barrier of sunken boats at Warwick Bar downstream near Chaffin's Bluff. The Confederate high command ordered the regiment to mount the rifled 30 pound gun at the center of the new defense line until it could be replaced by something heavier.

It was dirty, backbreaking work, and the rain continued to pour, but the morale of the regiment was way up. The men had seen how dirt could stop bullets and cannon balls. They worked all night. They leaned into their shovels and swung their picks, axes, and tin cups with a will. Two weeks later there were nine heavy gun emplacements on Chaffin's Bluff. Private Holt considered Chaffin's Bluff so well fortified that he called it "Fort Chaffin."

At 1 p.m. on May 25 Colonel Stuart sent a letter to Dr. William P. Palmer, the new regimental surgeon, at Meade and Baker's Drug Store on the corner of Main and 16th Streets in Richmond. Stuart wrote:

What has broken loose this morning in the direction of Hanover? All the guns in creation must have been congregated and fired there this morning. There has been one incessant roar since sunrise. The gun boats were reported on last night as advancing up the river, but some of our sharpshooters lower down the river gave them one or two volleys, whereupon the boats shelled the bluffs, then retired. Everything quiet, the rain descending in torrents.

The next day Stuart developed a bad chill, fever, and dysentery. In a few more days, his health broke down completely again. Stuart turned the 56th Virginia over to Colonel Slaughter for the second time and went to join his family at Edgemont House, a farm just outside of Richmond. The farm was only a few miles from the battle area. Slaughter sent dispatches to Stuart nearly every day for the next two weeks telling him the general whereabouts of the regiment and what action was expected.

By May 22 the men of the regiment were making themselves at home all over the widow Chaffin's farm. Private Holt wrote Ellen:

"*We have sent all our tents back to Richmond and are staying in the houses of a widow lady, Mrs. Chaffin, who has moved off. Some of our boys are in the dwelling house, some in the kitchen, some in the Negro houses, some in the stables, and some in the strawstack - anywhere we can get a shelter. We have plenty of straw to lie on and plenty of rails to burn to cook with. Fence rails fare very badly where soldiers go along.*"

The regiment ran out of meat for a few days at Chaffin's, and the men had to live on bread alone. The officers impressed some fat sheep in the neighborhood, paid $15 apiece for them, and ordered the men to slaughter and cook them. Private Holt ate roast sheep for breakfast and said that "... it was as good mutton, I believe, as I ever ate."

On May 31 the Confederate army, under the command of General Joseph E. Johnston, fell upon two corps of General McClellan's Army of the Potomac at Seven Pines near Richmond. While the battle raged through the woods, the 56th Virginia guarded the river defenses at Chaffin's Bluff. The men could hear the sounds of severe fighting 13 miles away. Private Holt reported that they could hear ". . .heavy firing. . . and cannonading very distinctly ... all day." The next morning, the regiment learned that General Johnston was wounded and that Robert E. Lee was the new commander of the Army of Northern Virginia.

On June 9 the regiment was suddenly caught squarely in the middle of another tug of war between two generals. Major General D. H. Hill needed replacements. He wanted the 56th to Join his division on the firing line in the woods and swamps around Richmond. Brigadier General Henry A. Wise, a former governor of Virginia, was responsible for defending Fort Drewry, Chaffin's Bluff, and the James River. Wise wanted the 56th to stay right where it was. Couriers galloped back and forth between Hill and Wise with dispatches. Each general claimed the 56th Virginia and asked the other when the regimental commander was going to report to him for orders.

When Colonel Stuart heard what was going on, he wrote to General Wise to request that the 56th be transferred to General Hill. Stuart had fond memories of Hill from the Battle of Big Bethel. Stuart knew that Hill was a fighter; he was sure that the regiment would see action under Hill. General Lee settled the matter on June 17 when he wrote to both Hill and Wise. Lee said firmly:

"The Fifty-Sixth and Sixth Virginia Regiments were

ordered to Chaffin's Bluff as a supporting force when the position was first occupied. They have now been ordered to their respective brigades, as it is considered advisable to keep brigades united, if practicable."

The 56th Virginia was now part of General George E. Pickett's Brigade, James H. Longstreet's division. The other regiments in the brigade were the 8th, 18th, 19th, and 28th Virginias. The 56th had found its niche at last; it would stay there until the end of the war. It was about to see the elephant (meet the bluecoats on the battlefield) for the first time as part of the first team. On June 26 Colonel Slaughter sent a dispatch rider to Edgemont House to tell Colonel Stuart that the regiment was going into battle at any moment.

CHAPTER 7

Gaines's Mill And Frazier's Farm

"Colonel Slaughter, with Corporal Guill, the color bearer, rushed ahead, shouting to us, 'Charge them !'"

The instant that Colonel Stuart tore open Colonel Slaughter's latest dispatch and started to read, he got out of bed. He buttoned up his double-breasted, gray frock coat trimmed in sky blue with the three gold stars on the collar and buckled on his VMI presentation sword. He was still sick with fever, but he was not going to miss the regiment's next battle. His wife Clinkey begged him to stay home until he got well, but it was no use. Late in the evening of June 26, Stuart swung into the saddle and rode in the direction from which the last sounds of gunfire had come.

As Stuart rode along Nine Mile Road, he passed what seemed to be an endless line of wagons carrying the badly wounded and the dying into Richmond. He also met the walking wounded, and he asked them all the same question, "Where is the 56th Virginia?" He did not find the regiment's camp until after midnight. It was beside the tents of the 18th Virginia about a half mile from Fulton in full view of Richmond.

Colonel Slaughter sat with Stuart by the fire and told him about the events of the past week. A few days before, the regiment was drilling with the regiments of General Samuel Garland's Brigade when a courier rode up to General Garland. The horseman told Garland to get the men ready because McClellan's whole army was about to attack. Garland rode down the line and asked Colonel Slaughter if the men of the 56th Virginia were ready for action. Slaughter replied that they were, but it was a false alarm. On the evening of June 20, the Yankees raised an observation balloon twice in plain view of the regiment.

Colonel Slaughter then explained the current situation to Stuart. The Union army was divided. Most of it was on the south side of the Chickahominy River, but General Fitz John Porter's Fifth Corps was dug in on the high ground on the north side of the river to protect the Union right flank. The Confederate army attacked Porter at Ellerson's Mill on the afternoon of June 26. In order to get to the Federals, the Confederates had to charge across Beaver Dam Creek, a stream that was waist deep and bordered by swamps. The gray and butternut soldiers charged again and again, but the Yankees beat them back every time with terrible slaughter. The 56th Virginia was kept in reserve all day and did not see any action.

While Stuart and Slaughter were talking beside the campfire, General Porter abandoned his strong, defensive position at Ellerson's Mill. Under the cover of darkness, he moved the entire Fifth Corps about six miles down the north bank of the Chickahominy to Gaines's Mill. He formed a new line of battle in the woods on another piece of high ground called Turkey Hill. The hill sloped down to Powhite Creek and rose to a height about 50 feet above the water.

Turkey Hill was a good position to defend. General Porter's men dug three rows of trenches. The first row was in a washout or ravine five feet wide and four feet deep that ran parallel to the narrow, sluggish creek at the bottom of the hill. The second row was about half way up the side of the hill and 100 yards behind the first row. The third row followed the crest of the hill and was about 100 yards behind the second row. The Yankees chopped down trees and sharpened the protruding branches with axes to form an abatis. They erected log barriers along the fronts of the trenches and filled them with fence rails and knapsacks.

General Porter posted batteries of artillery in rows along the crest of the hill so that they could fire over the heads of the infantry in the trenches below. Porter made his headquarters in the Watt House, a white frame building located on top of the hill a few hundred yards behind the artillery positions. Porter's mission was to hold the right flank at all costs until General McClellan could change his base from the York River to the James River.

The Confederates attacked the Yankees at Gaines's Mill on the afternoon of June 27. General A. P. Hill struck the center of the Union position while Stonewall Jackson hit the left and "Old Pete" Longstreet the right. Pickett's Brigade, which included the 56th Virginia, did not reach the field until about 4 p.m. The brigade moved toward the sound of heavy firing and formed a line of battle in the woods on the Confederate right to support Longstreet's division. Every man carried 80 rounds of ammunition in his cartridge box. The 56th Virginia was directly in front of the Yankees on Turkey Hill on the other side of Powhite Creek.

The regiment lined up with the 8th Virginia on its right and the Texans of Brigadier General John B. Hood on its left. The 56th advanced over a ridge and passed through an apple orchard while Captain James Dearing's battery of the Lynchburg Artillery fired from the rear. Dearing's gunners lobbed shells over the heads of the men of the 56th and dropped them on Turkey Hill. The cannon fire made the bluecoats keep their heads down. According to Lieutenant W. F. Clarke of Company I, the 56th was ordered ". . .to move by the right flank in double quick." The regiment obeyed instantly. It crossed a narrow, deep-gullied stream and reformed its line in an open field on the edge of Powhite Creek.

The regiment was only 30 or 40 yards from the enemy's first row of trenches as it dressed its line under fire. Men fell like leaves from the trees in an autumn wind. Had it not been for the smoke, casualties would have been even heavier. The woods on Turkey Hill across the creek were so thick with black powder smoke from the blasting muskets and booming cannons that neither side could see the other. The air was full of flying lead and iron. One of the Confederates recalled later, "The roar of musketry was so terrific that it was impossible to hear anything else."

The men of the 56th Virginia instinctively threw themselves to the ground. They fired one or two volleys straight across the creek, but it was obvious to everyone that they could not stay out in the open long. The sun was setting as Colonel Slaughter and Corporal William T. Guill of Company I, the regimental color bearer, stood up and rushed ahead of the regiment. Slaughter waved his sword and shouted, "Charge them!" The men of the 56th must have had trouble hearing Slaughter's command over the battle noise, but they understood exactly what he wanted them to do. They jumped to their feet and fixed bayonets.

The wild cry of the rebel yell burst from every throat in the regiment. Some men jumped over Powhlte Creek; others splashed straight across it. When the Yankees in the first line of breastworks heard the yelling and saw what was coming through the smoke, they panicked and fled. A blue mass of jumbled humanity swarmed up Turkey Hill and carried the defenders of the second and third lines of trenches with it. The 56th Virginia was right behind the bluecoats and poured musket fire directly into them. It was almost impossible to miss such a big, struggling target at such close range.

The men of the 56th leaped into the ravine, climbed out on the other side, and kept going. They scrambled up and over the second and third rows of Union breastworks. They were so close on the heels of the Yankees that the Union artillery on the crest of the hill could not fire but once. In the next instant, the Confederates were among the guns. They planted the flag of the 56th Virginia on top of a captured Union cannon. Somebody gave the order to halt, but most of the men did not hear it. They kept running ahead and chased the Union infantry past the Watt House. General Porter saw the disaster coming just in time to bolt from the house and avoid capture.

The charging Confederates ran for another 500 yards and stopped. They were scattered, disorganized, and out of breath. At that moment, a squadron of the 5th U.S. Cavalry charged them in an effort to recapture the artillery pieces. The

Confederate foot soldiers coolly took careful aim and blew the charging horsemen out of their saddles. The ground was covered with the bodies of dead cavalrymen and horses. The Union infantry continued to flee towards the swamps of the Chickahominy. That night, General Porter hustled all of his remaining troops across the river.

The 56th Virginia was not able to regroup until after dark. While the roll was being called, a large group of Yankees carrying their muskets at trail arms rushed down Turkey Hill. The bluecoats were trying to escape. The 56th cut them off, took them all prisoner, and turned them over to General Pryor's Brigade for safekeeping. Pryor's men were fresh and had just arrived on the field. The 56th marched back over the same ground where it had charged and bivouacked for the night in the woods. It had been in one of the hardest fights it would ever experience.

When the men of the 56th Virginia sat down around their campfires that night to swap stories, they made a few discoveries. As the regiment was charging up Turkey Hill, Lieutenant Clarke saw neat lines of knapsacks sitting on the ground with the letters "P. R. C." stenciled on them. The 56th had fought against and overrun the Pennsylvania Reserve Corps. Captain Jeffress of Company G "behaved with marked bravery," and Colonel John B. Strange of the 19th Virginia would say so in his official report of the battle. The Confederates captured 14 cannons, including a battery of Parrott guns, and nearly a whole regiment of infantry. The 56th Virginia paid for the victory in blood. The regiment suffered seven killed and sixty-five wounded; nine of the wounded were officers.

A soldier named Trice from the 13th Virginia went into the charge with the 56th Virginia. He was one of five brothers from Louisa County who served in the Confederate army. In 1861 they all joined the Louisa Blues, a unit that became a company of the 13th Virginia. One brother, Corporal Addison L Trice, was discharged because of bad health. He promptly joined the 56th Virginia. He was wounded in the breakout charge of the 56th at Fort Donelson. He did not let his wound stop him, but used his musket as a crutch and kept going forward at the head of the regiment until he was hit by a dozen rifle balls. One of them pierced his heart.

The second and third brothers were killed at the same instant at Gaines's Mill and fell side by side. The fourth brother was badly wounded at Gaines's Mill. The fifth brother captured several prisoners on the skirmish line at Gaines's Mill. He was sent to the rear with his captives, but he turned them over to someone else and hurried back to the front line. In the confusion of the battle, the fifth brother could not find his own regiment, the 13th Virginia. When he saw the 56th Virginia about to charge, he asked permission to take the place of his brother who was killed at Fort Donelson. He charged with the 56th and was wounded five times. He refused to leave the field and fell to the ground unconscious. After the charge, someone remembered seeing the badly wounded fourth brother taking care of the fifth brother whose wounds were even worse. Later, the fourth brother prepared the bodies of his two dead brothers to send home to the widowed mother Trice.

Colonel Slaughter was also a casualty of the charge of the 56th Virginia at Gaines's Mill. Slaughter had been First Captain of the corps of cadets at VMI and was a man of personal charm, unusual ability, and much promise. He was a classical scholar who taught Romance languages at VMI before the war. He read Latin and spoke French, Spanish, and Italian. He carried a book of popular quotations in his saddlebag and jotted sayings that he wanted to remember in the margins with a pencil. One of his favorite quotes came from Shakespeare's Julius Caesar, "Cowards die many times before their deaths; the valiant never taste of death but once." Slaughter must have recited the two lines from Julius Caesar to himself just before he drew his sword and shouted, "Charge them!" During the wild scramble up Turkey Hill, a Union shrapnel shell smashed into Slaughter's hip and caused his field glasses to be driven into his groin.

Slaughter's wound was so severe that he was never

able to return to the battlefield. He kept his commission for the next two years in hopes that he would recover. He drove out in a buggy to visit the regiment in the field whenever he could. He wanted to return to duty, but his wound forced him to resign from field service in 1864. He retired as a full Colonel and served to the end of the war as a staff officer with Colonel Robert Quid and General James Kemper. On the day of his retirement, someone presented him an exquisite pair of ivory field glasses made by Ringard Opticien in Paris. The glasses were beautifully engraved in flowing script: "Col. P. P. Slaughter, 1864, 56th Reg. Va., Infty, A. N. Va." The gift probably came from his wife, his fellow officers, or perhaps the entire regiment.

By Sunday morning June 29, the whole Union army was in full retreat. The bluecoats were trying to reach their gunboats on the James River. General McClellan planned to load his men and equipment on troop transports at Harrison's Landing and sail back to Washington. Union infantry and wagon trains choked both the Long Bridge and Quaker Roads that led to the river. When General Lee discovered McClellan's plan, he decided to hit the bluecoats with everything he had. Lee ordered Longstreet and Hill to attack the Union left flank while Benjamin Huger struck the right flank. Jackson was to cross the White Oak Swamp and smash into the Union rear. Longstreet decided to intercept the Federals at Frazier's Farm near the Charles City crossroads.

The 56th Virginia marched 14 miles on the 29th with Longstreet's division and camped for the night at the intersection of the Darbytown and New Market Roads about three miles southwest of Frazier's Farm. The men were exhausted after the fight at Gaines's Mill, but there was little straggling on the march. One day of rest was all it took to restore their strength. While the 56th was in camp for the night, Colonel Stuart received orders for the regiment to attack the next day as part of the whole division.

Early the next morning, June 30, Longstreet marched his division to Frazier's Farm. Union General George A. McCall, a good soldier, was already at the farm with 10,000 bluecoat infantry of the Pennsylvania Reserve Corps. It was the same corps that had fought against the 56th Virginia at Gaines's Mill three days before. Once again the Yankees held the high ground, and the Confederates had to charge across the low ground. The 56th formed its line of battle in the woods in front of the Federal position. The ground where the regiment began its attack was cut up by ravines, cluttered with heavy timber, and covered in tangled undergrowth, so for the moment the Yankee bullets did no harm.

Longstreet was supposed to wait to attack until he heard the firing of Huger's guns. The 56th Virginia waited for the signal all morning and almost all afternoon, but it did not come. Late in the afternoon, Longstreet decided that he could not wait any longer; he ordered the whole division forward. Pickett's Brigade struggled through a deep marsh that was almost impassable. As soon as the brigade reached solid ground, it started to reform its line. At that moment, Union infantry, hidden in the woods to the right, poured a terrific, unexpected rifle fire into the brigade. At the same time, Union artillery blasted a shower of grape shot into the Confederates from across an open field in front. Pickett's men were thrown into disorder and confusion, and the brigade started to fall back.

Captain W. Stuart Symington of Pickett's staff was on horseback. Symington galloped to the front of the 56th Virginia. He seized the regimental flag from the color bearer, held it aloft, and called loudly to the brigade to rally. His horse was shot through the neck; men dropped all around him. Somehow his voice carried over the storm of shot and shell, and the men saw the flag of the 56th Virginia waving through the smoke. The brigade stiffened and rallied. As the brigade started to move towards the enemy again, Huger's North Carolina division arrived on the field and came to its support with a yell.

A tall, whiskered North Carolinian charged past Captain Jeffress of the 56th Virginia. The tarheel kept his musket pointed towards the Yankees and said, "They got you boys, but get out of the way and we will give them hell." The Virginians and North Carolinians charged together and broke the Union line. They captured several batteries of artillery, but the Yankee cannoneers and infantrymen pulled back slowly and stubbornly. The bluecoats kept up a constant cannon fire to cover their withdrawal; their shells did not stop falling until 9 p.m. By that time, the entire battlefield belonged to the Confederates, and General McCall was a prisoner of war.

The Union army fell back to Malvern Hill where Lee attacked it again the next day. Once again the Yankees held a good defensive position, and they threw the Confederates back with frightful losses. Longstreet's division was held in reserve, so the 56th Virginia did not see action. After Malvem Hill, McClellan managed to get his men and equipment aboard the transport ships on the James River. The Union army was so large that the rescue operation took several weeks. The bluecoats stayed within the protection of their gunboats at all times. The finest army on the planet had failed to take Richmond. Private Holt wrote Ellen:

"Old McClellan says it was not a defeat but merely a retreat to a better position. But he may say what he pleases; he can't deceive the world as much as that. He thought he had Richmond almost in his clutches, but he found out he was slightly mistaken. .. .he may try to get round and cut us off and try to starve us out. But I don't believe they can do that. . . , for they will have to leave the water too far, and that is all we want them to do, for we don't ask them any odds off the water. But we can't do much with them under cover of their gunboats, unless they were close to some of our heavy batteries. If we could get them up to Fort Drewry I think we could give them a lively time on land and water."

The 56th Virginia suffered two killed, twenty-two wounded, and two missing at the Battle of Frazier's Farm. Private Lee Smith of Company K was one of the missing.

The regiment could not find him on the field, so it assumed that he was a prisoner. The regiment had fought well. Colonel John B. Strange, the acting commander of the brigade in the absence of the wounded Pickett, stated in his official report that "Lieut. J. W. Jones, Company B, and Private Rozall Lockett, Company G, Fifty-sixth Regiment Virginia Volunteers... deserve special mention for courage and daring."

The men of the 56th Virginia must have grinned at one another as they stood on the field at Frazier's Farm and wiped the blood and black powder grime from their hands and faces. They had been in a terrible battle, but the official reports had praised them. They had removed the stain of Fort Donelson. Colonel Stuart wrote to Clinkey that the men of the regiment felt that ". . . they had redressed the misfortunes of their western campaign." The 56th Virginia could now take its rightful place as a crack light infantry regiment in the Army of Northern Virginia.

CHAPTER 8

Second Manassas, Boonsboro, and Sharpsburg

"Our little regiment fought with conspicuous gallantry."

For the next few weeks the 56th Virginia camped in several places on the outskirts of Richmond. One of its campsites was in the woods beside the Darbytown Road. While the regiment was in its Darbytown camp, Private Holt's father sent him a box of soap. Holt said that he shared the luxury with the other men in his company because they did not draw enough soap to wash their hands, "much less" their clothes. The 56th was in a lull before its next storm. it was during this lull that Colonel Stuart received a letter from Stonewall Jackson. Stuart had written his old VMI friend on June 20 to ask If Jackson could find a place for him in his command.

Stuart told Jackson how the War Department had mishandled the 56th Virginia by giving it conflicting orders before finally deciding to send it to Fort Donelson. Stuart then gave Jackson an account of the tug of war between Generals Hill and Wise for control of the regiment after the Battle of Fort Drewry. The reputation of the regiment had been tarnished unfairly. Finally, Stuart explained that if he could return to the drier climate of the Shenandoah Valley, he might be able to recover from the fever that had plagued him since the beginning of the war. Jackson's letter in reply was dated July 9 and read:

Colonel, Your letter of the 20th June is at hand. No recommendations are necessary for you. When my command will return to the valley I am unable to say; but whether it remains here (Richmond) or goes there, I would always be gratified to have you with me. Should the Secretary of War direct you to report to me, you would for the present be assigned to duty as inspector Gen'l; as my inspector Gen'l is absent wounded. There are regiments here without colonels; but I do not see that you could legally be assigned to command any one of them, though I would if practicable have you in command of a regiment.

When Stuart received Jackson's letter, he went straight to the Secretary of War in Richmond to ask for a transfer to Jackson's command. The War Department denied Stuart's request on the ground that he could serve the cause better by remaining with the 56th Virginia. While Stuart was in Richmond applying for his transfer, he learned that Humphrey Marshall's quartermaster was spreading the rumor that the previous winter Stuart had refused transportation to move the 56th from Abingdon to join Marshall's command. Stuart was incensed. He handed copies of all the conflicting orders, letters, and telegrams to the Secretary of War and demanded a board of inquiry if there was "the slightest doubt" as to the propriety of his actions. The War Department notified Stuart by letter that it was satisfied with his conduct. The matter was officially dropped, but it may have cost Stuart a place in Stonewall Jackson's command.

Stuart did not complain about his bad luck. He did his utmost to administer, train, and strengthen the 56th Virginia for the battles that lay ahead. On July 29 the regiment had a turn of luck — it got its first chaplain. Colonel Stuart and the regiment needed him. Private Holt was delighted and wrote Ellen:

We now have a chaplain to our regiment, the first we have had since we have been a regiment. He is a Methodist preacher and his name is Waggoner (Rev. James R.). He preaches for us twice on the Sabbath, in the morning and at night, and every Wednesday night. He holds prayer meetings every other night and distributes tracts and religious newspapers to us. He is a fine preacher, and I hope his service among us may be blessed with good consequences. If any people need religious instruction it certainly is soldiers.

By August 11 the 56th was back in its old campsite on Fulton Hill. While the regiment was in camp in Richmond, Major General John Pope took command of a new Union army. Pope called it "The Army of Virginia." Pope had fought the Confederates in the West with some success. He bragged to his new troops that he was used to seeing "the backs" of his enemies. He supposedly went on to announce that his "headquarters would be in the saddle." His second bombast was too much for the Confederates. When they heard what he said, one of them replied, "We can lick anybody who doesn't know his headquarters from his hindquarters." Private Holt said, " I hope we will be able to give Old Pope's army a complete rout."

About the middle of August, General Pope led his Army of Virginia south across the Rappahannock River and headed towards Richmond. Lee sent Stonewall Jackson north to challenge him. Pope did not know that he was in trouble until Stonewall's men captured the main Union supply depot at Manassas Junction. The hungry Confederates gorged themselves on such rare delicacies as canned lobster, pickled oysters, and Rhine wine that were intended for Federal officers. The ragged, butternut soldiers put on new pairs of shoes and hung extra pairs around their necks. They tucked thick socks and blue wool overcoats into their knapsacks and blanket rolls to save for the next winter. They set fire to all the supplies they could not carry; millions of dollars worth of Federal stores and equipment went up in smoke. The odor of burned bacon drifted through the countryside for miles.

General Pope rushed all of his troops to Manassas. Pope planned to bag Jackson's small force before Lee could send the rest of his army to support Jackson. The 56th Virginia and the rest of Longstreet's division were coming from Richmond as fast as they could, but Jackson had to hold Pope at bay long enough for help to arrive. Jackson moved his men out of Manassas Junction and ordered them to dig in along the embankment of the Manassas Railroad line near the Warrenton Turnpike. The railroad was supposed to connect Gainesville with Alexandria, but it was still under construction. There were many cuts and fills behind the embankment. It was a good place to stand and fight.

Colonel Eppa Hunton of the 8th Virginia was acting commander of Pickett's Brigade as it raced north with

Longstreet's division first by train and then on foot to rescue Stonewall Jackson's men. General Pickett had not recovered from the wound he suffered at Gaines's Mill, and Hunton was senior colonel of the brigade. The brigade spent the night of August 29 in Thoroughfare Gap on the main route through the mountains. Early the next morning, the brigade joined the division in marching along the Warrenton Turnpike towards Manassas.

Hunton's men reached Gainesville about noon. They could hear the sound of firing coming from the direction of the Manassas Railroad line up ahead. Pope was attacking Jackson with wave after wave of bluecoat infantry. Jackson's situation was desperate. Stonewall's soldiers were holding on by their fingernails. They had run out of ammunition and were swinging their muskets like clubs. Some of them were picking up chunks of rock in the railroad cuts and throwing them at the Federals.

General Longstreet arrived on the field at a gallop with his whole division trotting right behind him. Longstreet took in the situation at a glance and ordered the entire division to charge. Longstreet's men struck Pope's army in the center and flank at the same time. Pickett's Brigade was on the right; Hood's Brigade was on the left. The Yankees immediately gave way to the charge of Pickett's Brigade, but they did not give ground to Hood's men. The Yankees directly in front of Hood were the 5th and 10th New York Zouaves, elite units whose men wore red fezzes with tassles, short blue jackets trimmed with red piping, and bright red baggy pants tucked into white canvas leggings. The Zouaves sang their own song on the march. Part of it went.

> *We belong to the Zoo, Zoo, Zoos.*
> *Don't you think we oughter?*
> *We're coming down from Washingtown*
> *To fight for Abraham's daughter.*

The Zouaves were not just natty dressers and lusty singers; they were also fierce fighters. They were determined to maintain their reputation - they were not going to pull back.

Fate handed Colonel Hunton a golden opportunity to rout the Zouaves. Hunton discovered a ravine that ran downhill from the Chinn House; a tiny creek flowed through the middle of the hollow. The ravine was deep enough so that once the men started into it they would be hidden from view and protected from the bullets of the Zouaves. A plan of action sprang into Hunton's mind; Hunton decided to take the whole brigade up the ravine in a column. The five regiments could then wheel to the left, change front, and charge right over the edge of the ravine into the flank of the unsuspecting Zouaves.

Hunton gave the order in a loud voice so that all of the regimental commanders could hear it. To be sure that there would be no mistake, Hunton sent a messenger to each regiment to explain the order. Hunton took his place beside Colonel Stuart at the head of the lead regiment, the 56th Virginia, and started up the ravine. When Hunton and Stuart climbed up the ravine far enough for the whole brigade to have room to change front and charge, they turned around. They were startled to see that only the 56th Virginia had followed them. Hunton learned later that Colonel R. C. Allen of the 28th Virginia refused to obey the order because it was not in writing. The 28th was to the immediate left of the 56th in line of battle and should have been right behind the 56th. Since the 28th did not follow the 56th up the ravine, the other regiments could not follow either.

Hunton was bitterly disappointed at the missed opportunity to catch the Zouaves by surprise, but, luckily, General James H. Kemper's Brigade rushed forward and helped Hood's brigade overrun the Zouaves. The field was so littered with the bodies of dead and wounded Zouaves that, at a distance, it looked like the ground was strewn with red, white, and blue flowers.

The 56th Virginia joined the rest of Pickett's Brigade in driving the Yankee infantry and artillery from the hill beside the Chinn House. One Confederate said that the bluecoats ran "pell mell" from the field. The Confederates captured one cannon, several regimental flags, and a large number of prisoners. The fighting kept on until 10 p.m., when the firing spluttered out. Pope's army escaped across Bull Run Creek before sunrise the next morning. President Lincoln relieved General Pope from command and sent him back to the West to fight Indians.

The 56th Virginia suffered one killed and twelve wounded at Second Manassas. Colonel Stuart wrote to his wife Clinkey and told her that he ". . .grieved over the loss of his men." Stuart did not mention the regiment's lost opportunity to rout the Zouaves.

Two days after Second Manassas President Lincoln disbanded the Union Army of Virginia and added it to the Army of the Potomac under the command of General McClellan. Lincoln was not happy with "little Mac," but McClellan, "the little Napoleon," was so popular with the troops that Lincoln decided to give him one more chance. McClellan withdrew the Army of the Potomac from Virginia and moved it into the outer defenses of Washington, D.C. As soon as the Union army went on the defensive, Robert E. Lee decided that it was time to gamble. Lee made plans to invade the North with his Army of Northern Virginia.

On the night of September 2, the 56th Virginia received orders to march north the next day with Longstreet's division. All men who did not have shoes were excused from the march, so many soldiers in the 56th did not go. The Confederate daily ration on the march consisted of a small piece of unsalted beef and an ear or two of green corn. The poor diet made a large number of the men so sick with diarrhea that they could not keep pace. In addition, the long, hard hike north caused other men to straggle and stop by the wayside. At least the men of the 56th got to leave their knapsacks behind in the wagons so they could travel lightly.

By the time Longstreet's division splashed across the Potomac River at White's Ford on September 6 and set foot on the soil of Maryland, the 56th Virginia could count only 80 muskets. The regiment was not even as large as a full strength company.

The Confederates were low in number, but high in spirit. Private Holt wrote Ellen, "I reckon we have marched 200 miles, taking all the crooks and turns we have taken. We sometimes marched by day and night, but it seems to agree with us pretty well." As the soldiers waded across the river with their muskets and powder held high above their heads, one of the bands struck up "Maryland, My Maryland." Suddenly, the bass drummer stepped into a deep, underwater hole. The men hooted and hollered as the big drum bobbed away downstream.

Colonel Stuart rode his horse at the head of the column of the 56th Virginia. Since Major Green was absent and Colonel Slaughter was badly wounded, Captain John B. McPhail of Company A served as acting Major and second in command. Even McPhail was unable to march into Maryland with the regiment. He was delayed for a day or two, but he walked alone 125 miles across what he called "desolate countryside" to catch up with the 56th. There was nothing on the roadside for money to buy, so he hurried to join the regiment at its camp near Frederick.

The 56th spent the next few days in bivouac at Frederick taking a much needed rest. The men stood for hours in front of well-stocked shop windows and gawked at things they had not seen for months. A few lucky men in Company C had "shinplasters" — Yankee greenback paper money. Colonel Stuart said that they bought themselves new hats that made them "...the envy of the whole command."

General Lee decided to gamble again, and he divided his army into three parts. He sent Jackson to capture Harper's Ferry and Longstreet to Hagerstown to drive out Federal cavalry that was reported there. A. P. Hill was to hold Turner's Gap at South Mountain near the village of Boonsboro in order to shield Jackson and Longstreet against any Union movement from Washington. The 56th Virginia arrived in Hagerstown with Longstreet's division on the 11th. There was no Federal cavalry there, so the 56th had another day or two to rest and window shop. Colonel Stuart bought himself a hat that he needed badly. He also bought some cloth for his wife to make herself a new dress.

On September 13 while the 56th Virginia was still in Hagerstown, McClellan's army arrived in Frederick. The Yankees pitched their tents on the same spot where the Confederates camped just a few days before. Private B. W. Mitchell of the 27th Indiana Volunteers saw a pack of three cigars lying on the ground. Mitchell was interested only in the cigars, but he glanced at the paper they were wrapped in before he lit one. The paper outlined Lee's entire plan for the Maryland campaign in detail. Mitchell gave the paper to his sergeant, and within a few hours, the lost order was in McClellan's hands.

Now that McClellan knew Lee's intentions, he moved with unusual speed. McClellan marched his army to South Mountain and threw both Joe Hooker's First Corps and Jesse Reno's Ninth Corps at Hill's little division. Hill rushed a courier to Lee for help. Lee, in turn, sent a rider to Longstreet in Hagerstown with an order to go to Hill's aid as quickly as possible. Early Sunday morning, September 14, the 56th Virginia moved out of Hagerstown with Longstreet's division on a murderous forced march. The division hiked 18 hot, dusty, and fatiguing miles and reached Boonsboro about 4 p.m. When the division arrived, a terrific fight was already in progress. Hill was battling for his life and trying to hold the mountain pass. There was no time to waste.

The 56th Virginia formed a line of battle in an open field. A Union artillery battery on the heights to the right immediately opened fire on the exposed right flank of the regiment. A piece of shell grazed Captain McPhail on his right hip. it cut the flesh slightly and made ". . quite a severe bruise as large as your two hands," but McPhail did not leave his post. He continued to relay Colonel Stuart's orders to the regiment, encouraged the men, and assisted Stuart in every way that he could.

The 56th was ordered to support General James L. Kemper's Brigade. Colonel Stuart took the regiment into a line in a corn field between Kemper's Brigade on the right and the 17th Virginia on the left. Kemper's Brigade was already hotly engaged with the bluecoats. The Yankees did not appear in front of the 56th Virginia or the 17th Virginia right away, so both regiments held their fire for the moment. For the next 15 minutes Kemper's Brigade bore the brunt of the fighting.

Colonel Stuart studied the bluecoats closely through the smoke with his field glasses. He could tell from the angle of the Union battle flags and the direction of their rifle flashes that they were concentrating on Kemper's Brigade. If Kemper's men gave way, the right flank of the 56th Virginia would be in real danger. Stuart ordered the right flank of the regiment to swing back and prepare to meet the enemy from the right.

Darkness fell, and the firing on the right died down. Colonel Stuart realized that Kemper's Brigade had pulled back, so he sent a messenger to tell Colonel "Old Puss" Corse of the 17th Virginia to drop back about 15 or 20 steps and take cover behind a fence. (Colonel Corse was short and stocky; he wore high boots that came up over his knees. The men of Pickett's Brigade called him "Old Puss in the Boots" or "Old Puss" for short.)

The 56th and the 17th fell back to the fence quickly and in good order. The two regiments reformed their defense line behind the fence and continued the fight side by side even though they were vastly outnumbered. Colonel Stuart reported that they kept up a brisk, right oblique fire on the enemy for an hour or more. The 56th Virginia was under "a severe fire of musketry" from its right flank and front, but it stayed in place and kept on firing.

The 56th fought until long after dark. The men ran completely out of ammunition, but they ransacked the cartridge boxes of the dead and wounded whose bodies littered the ground around them and fired every cartridge they could find. Colonel Stuart sent Lieutenant Ira A. Miller to the rear to tell General Richard B. Garnett, the acting brigade commander, that the regiment had to have ammunition or re-enforcements right away. Lieutenant Miller soon met Captain Fry, General Kemper's adjutant. Fry told Miller that Garnett's Brigade had been ordered from the field some time before and that the 56th and 17th Virginias should abandon their forward position.

By that time the two regiments did not have a single bullet left between them. Luckily, the Yankees stopped firing and left the 56th and the 17th in possession of their part of the battlefield. It was almost 9 p.m. The 56th tried to carry off its wounded, but the field was so dark that the ambulance corps was not able to find all of them. Forty men of the 56th lay killed or wounded; five were missing. The regiment had lost over half of its men.

Captain McPhail wrote home to say that the enemy's numbers were "overwhelming" and that the regiment fought against odds of "at least 10 to 1." At times, both flanks of the regiment were "entirely exposed." McPhail said that although most of the Confederate soldiers were exhausted and did not fight with their accustomed valor, "Our little regiment fought with conspicuous gallantry. "McPhall added that Colonel Stuart "greatly distinguished himself." Stuart, in turn, stated in his official report of the battle that he was "...indebted to Captain McPhail for gallant services on this occasion, who, although severely bruised by a shell, remained on the ground, encouraging the men, until the engagement ceased." Stuart also officially reported that "Sergeant Tucker of Company K and Sergeant Newton of Company E are deserving of honorable mention for their bravery."

As far as Captain McPhail knew, the 56th Virginia and the 17th Virginia were the only regiments at Boonsboro that held their ground. However, Longstreet's and Hill's divisions did their job. They kept McClellan's army in check at South Mountain long enough for Lee to pull his scattered forces together and concentrate them at a town nearby called

Sharpsburg.

Late on the night of September 14, the 56th Virginia began the march to Sharpsburg. The regiment recovered its five missing men, but it had to leave its wounded in the hands of the enemy. Early the next morning, the 40 able-bodied survivors of the regiment reached what Colonel Stuart called "a commanding position" on one of the hills that surrounded the town. The hill was just east of Sharpsburg and sloped down to Antietam Creek. The high ground overlooked the whole area in front of the town and covered the approaches to the town over the Boonsboro Turnpike. The men of the 56th were just getting settled when they saw huge dust clouds appear in front of them; the Yankees were coming after them in hot pursuit. Soon the opposite hills crawled with bluecoats as McClellan moved his men into position. Colonel Stuart watched the approaching Federals through his field glasses. To him the long, massive column of Yankees looked like ". ..a great blue snake wending its way towards us."

The Yankees opened fire with part of their artillery, but it was only a half-hearted attempt and amounted to nothing. The next day, both sides blazed away at one another with all of their cannons until nightfall. Captain McPhail called the duel "...one of the grandest artillery battles ... that ever came off." The cannons made a lot of noise and cloaked the battlefield in a haze of black powder smoke, but they did little harm to anyone.

That night Colonel Stuart became violently ill. His whole body was wracked with pain; his temperature was extremely high. His fellow officers wrapped him in blankets and gave him what attention and comfort they could, but he was not fit to command any longer. Stuart turned the regiment over to Captain McPhail. The first thing McPhail did was to put Stuart into an ambulance and to send him back to Virginia in the company of Dr. Evans, the assistant regimental surgeon.

Captain McPhail reported that the next morning, September 15 ". . . the great fight came off." McClellan's infantry advanced and attacked. The badly outnumbered

Confederates had their backs to the wall, and they fought for survival. The 56th Virginia was ordered to protect several batteries of the Washington Artillery, an elite unit from New Orleans. The regiment stayed with the Louisiana cannoneers most of the day. The Yankee artillery poured a continuous enfilade fire of solid shot, shell, and spherical case on the regiment and the gunners, but it was not well directed and did not cause much injury. In the afternoon, the bluecoat skirmishers moved toward the cannons of the Washington Artillery and tried to pick off the gunners.

The men of the 56th Virginia were ordered to deploy like skirmishers and drive the bluecoats off. According to Captain McPhail, the regiment was soon "hotly engaged." The 56th endured "...heavy musketry and terrific artillery fire. . . for something less than an hour." The 56th held its ground until other regiments could come to support it. The skirmishers of the 56th then rallied on the left of the brigade and fought "with unflinching courage." Captain McPhail stated in his official battle report that Lieutenant Frank W. Nelson, commanding Company A, Lieutenant John W. Jones, commanding Company B, and Lieutenant Matthew Brown, commanding Company D, were conspicuous for their "gallantry" and "courage" under fire.

At one point the fighting became so fierce and the odds against them so great that the officers of the 56th Virginia felt that only a miracle could save the whole Confederate army from total destruction. The miracle happened. A. P. Hill's division made a forced march from Harper's Ferry, rushed to the field out of breath, and without stopping smashed straight into the Union right flank. Hill was wearing his famous red battle shirt as he led his light infantry in a fierce charge that swept away everything in its path. Three days later, Captain McPhail summarized the battle in a letter home:

"I could not describe it. We may have lost more in other battles, but the destruction of the field and the other circumstances made this one of the grandest on record. The

battle was fought with varying fortunes. Sometimes the enemy drove us, and sometimes we drove him. Night closed upon the scene, leaving us everywhere in possession of our position. The enemy had made an attempt to dislodge us but failed. Some counted it a drawn battle; some a victory. The enemy's numbers were overwhelming. Our army straggled until it was reduced by half; otherwise I think we would have won a most signal victory. Our little brigade supported by the Washington Artillery fought with distinguished gallantry. The Major General commanding paid it a glowing compliment at the close of the battle. Colonel Stuart was taken very ill the day before and I had the honor to command the regiment in this great battle. I was very proud of its conduct.

On September 18 Lee's army stayed in position on the hills outside Sharpsburg all day. Lee expected McClellan to attack again, but he did not. Instead, the bluecoats sent over a flag of truce and asked for time to bury their dead. Captain McPhail was afraid that if he walked any more, his bruised hip would become inflamed, so he asked and received General Garnett's permission to go to the rear. That night the Army of Northern Virginia crossed the Potomac and headed for home. McClellan let the Confederates go in peace; he did not pursue them. The Confederate army had plenty of fight left in it, but Lee had gambled on his invasion plan and lost.

The 56th Virginia carried only 40 men into the fight at Sharpsburg; 8 of them were wounded. The regiment could count only 32 sound muskets when it waded back across the Potomac and stepped ashore on the Virgina side. A captain commanded the regiment; lieutenants commanded the companies. Captain McPhail reported that the regiment was reduced "to a handful."

CHAPTER 9
Fredericksburg To Suffolk

"...pride in victory, but not joy."

For the next two months of 1862, the Army of Northern Virginia camped in the upper Shenandoah Valley in the hills around Culpeper. The 56th Virginia's campsite was near Winchester. Lee used the time to rebuild his army. He prescribed lots of rest, food, refitting, and discipline; his prescription was remarkably successful.

As the rest period began, Private Holt was war weary and wanted to go home. He dipped his pen into watered down ink and wrote to Ellen on poor quality paper:

"There is a pretty general belief that the war won't last much longer, but that it will close before the winter is out. I hope and trust that it may be so. Nothing could afford me more relief now than to hear that peace was made and all of us had received marching orders to go home. Generally, when we receive marching orders, there are some who set up a shout and halloo, but if we could get marching orders to go home, I feel like I could halloo some myself."

As the 56th Virginia began the fall season, its ranks were woefully thin. On October 8, there were only eight men fit for duty in Company G. Two days later, Lieutenant Talley resigned his commission as an officer of Company K. Talley wrote, "My Company, always below the minimum number, is now reduced to a number that renders my office a sinecure. It now consists only of 7 men with me." There were many reasons why the ranks were empty. Bullets, disease, absence without leave, and desertion had all taken their toll.

Some able-bodied men were lost to special service. They became full-time shoemakers, harness makers, tanners, woodchoppers, teamsters, ambulance attendants, and foundry workers. Private G. H. Wright of Company K was detailed to tend to the wounded at the Masonic Hall in Richmond. Sergeant G. W. Reevly of Company G signed a contract with the State of Virginia to alter the Hall's breechloader rifle and was transferred to the C. S. Arsenal in Richmond. Private Burnet Trainer of Company C was ordered to build gunboats on the James River. Captain Thomas D. Jeffress of Company G was assigned to be temporary commandant of Libby Prison in Richmond. After three weeks at the prison, Jeffress was appointed provost marshal of Lynchburg. Jeffress found the duties of provost marshal to be "easier and higher than Capt. of Infantry," and he never returned to the 56th Virginia. The special service details were necessary, but in every case they resulted in one less rifle or revolver on the firing line.

Colonel Stuart did his best to fill up the ranks of the 56th Virginia in every possible way. Stuart gave some of the junior Lieutenants leave and sent them back to their home counties to bring in absentees. The young officers met with varying degrees of success in rounding up the strays. The typical Confederate soldier was a rugged individualist and an independent thinker. He saw nothing wrong with "running the block" to go home for a visit when there was a slump in the fighting. He fully intended to return to his regiment when the action began again. He was not a deserter. He was just absent without leave, and if his lieutenant could find him, the officer was usually able to bring him back to the front.

On the other hand, some of the soldiers were deserters - plain and simple. They went "over the wall" the first chance they got, and they never intended to come back. The most conspicuous group of deserters in the 56th Virginia was the Shiflett clan. Ten Shifletts enlisted in Company H in Albemarle County in 1861; nine of them deserted at the same time. On November 26, 1861, one John Hunter sent a telegram to the Confederate Secretary of War to report:

Seven (7) soldiers whose surname is Shiflett belonging to Capt. Michie's company from Albemarle attached to Col. Stuart's command lately ordered to South Western Virginia were discovered in Louisa County yesterday. Three (3) of the number were captured and lodged in jail; the others escaped. They admit they are deserters.

There was only one member of the Shiflett clan who left the regiment in an honorable way. Wesley Shiflett died on March 6, 1862, of wounds that he suffered at Fort Donelson. The Shifletts must have believed that a family that deserted together stayed together!

Colonel Stuart sent the rest of his junior officers back to their home counties to recruit new blood for the regiment. The trouble was that there were precious few men left to recruit, and all of the other regiments were after them too. Most of the men who stepped forward to volunteer were either too young or too old; the recruiters were forced to rob both the cradle and the grave. Colonel Stuart was particularly worried about the very young. In a letter to Colonel Slaughter he said, "...in my mind there is some doubt about these fuzzy faced youths and their ability to become soldiers, but we must take what we can get."

By October 1, 1862, the men of the 56th Virginia who were captured at Fort Donelson had been exchanged. They had been prisoners of war for more than six months. They were so unused to the harsh climate up North that about 30 of them died in prison; the rest of them were sick. Most of the survivors returned to the regiment, but first they had to go to the hospital for several months before they were fit for duty. Private Thomas was confined at Camp Morton, Indiana and exchanged at Vicksburg, Mississippi in September, 1862. On September 15 Thomas wrote Mary from Jackson Town, Mississippi:

"I am happy to inform you that I have got out of the cut throats' land once more. We were on our way to Vicksburg 19 days and on the boat for 17 days. We were exchanged at Vicksburg last Thursday. We took the cars for this place Friday evening and we arrived here that evening. We had a dreadful trip on the boats, eating old crackers and they had bugs and worms in them. There were old things we could not eat at all. They gave us raw meat and we had to eat it raw or boil it on a pit coal fire which made it taste dreadful. It is useless for me to

try to explain how we have been treated since the 16th day of last February."

There was only one way left to fill up the ranks of the regiment - conscription. The 56th Virginia began as an all-volunteer unit, but it had to resort to the draft to supply the men it needed so badly. Company A applied to Adjutant General Samuel A. Cooper for 25 conscripts to bring the company to standard strength. The Lieutenant commanding the company stated in his application, "My company only numbers 31, total present and absent, having never received any conscripts since its entry into service."

The conscription system was only a partial success. Some of the conscripts deserted the first time they got the chance, but others adapted to army life and made good soldiers. Private William B. Short was a conscript who became a good soldier in the 56th Virginia. Short was conscripted into Company E from his farm in Brunswick County on February 9, 1863. Short's nickname was "Sambo"; his wife's nickname was "Babie." Sambo wrote a series of letters to Babie after he joined the 56th Virginia. His letters clearly revealed what the first few weeks in the life of a conscript were like.

In order to report for duty, Sambo walked from his farm to the train station at Belfield (now Emporia), Virginia. He was wet and cold. He laid down on a wooden bench until four o'clock the next morning when the train arrived. He rode the train to Petersburg and stepped off the car about sunrise. A Confederate officer took Sambo and some other conscripts ". . .down to a room down in town that was worse than any hog pen you ever saw." The conscripts stayed in the room one day and two nights before they boarded the train for Richmond. They got to Richmond after dark, marched five miles to Camp Lee through mud that oozed up over their shoes, and stayed in another room with about 300 other men. At least 50 of the other men were sick.

The next day the brand new soldiers marched five miles out of the city under an armed guard of twelve soldiers. They reached the camp of the 56th Virginia after dark and were "put in" the regiment. Sambo was not used to so much walking. His feet were sore, and he "came very near giving out." For the next few days, he slept outside in the open without a tent and got wet. Then he was quartered in a ten pin bowling alley. He complained to Babie, "The soldiers roll balls from daybreak until 10 o'clock at night. it disturbs me mightily."

For the next few weeks the regiment toiled and trudged through the mud all day. Sambo reported to Babie that Oscar Short, another soldier in the regiment, got sick one night, became delirious, and went out of his head. The doctors did not think that there was anything wrong with him. Sambo said, "They stripped him naked and threw basin after basin of water on him... The surgeons don't show a man any respect at all." Oscar Short died soon after of typhoid fever.

Sambo also reported that the men were issued hard tack without grease or salt, corn bread without sifting, about one half as much beef and other meat as they could eat, plenty of sugar, and no coffee. He grumbled that they had nothing but green pine to burn and that he had not changed his drawers yet. He added that he had never tried to get a discharge because it was no use. Sambo said, "They won't discharge a man as long as he can put one foot before the other." Sambo was in an army that needed every man.

On October 11, 1862, one of the army's best men, Stonewall Jackson, was promoted to Lieutenant General. Jackson wrote Colonel Stuart to offer to make him one of his brigade commanders. Stuart was grateful for the offer. He very much wanted to be with his old VMI friend, and he longed to wear the gold star and wreath of a brigadier general. However, he was still sick with the fever that seized him at Sharpsburg. Since War Department policy stated that a general officer could not be appointed unless he could take the field immediately, Stuart was not able to get his star or to join Jackson. Stuart had lost his last chance to tie his destiny to that of the great Stonewall.

On October 26 General Richard B. Garnett sent a letter

to Colonel Stuart. Garnett and Stuart became friends during the Maryland campaign when Gamett served as acting brigade commander. Garnett wrote:

"*I have received your report of the battle of 'South Mountain' and with it your very kind note. I can truly assure you I was much gratified with the expressions of regard and esteem you therein expressed towards me. My brief association with you was among the most pleasant I have formed during the war, and I sincerely trust it may be resumed at no distance and time, and under such auspices that we may be able to cultivate a still closer intimacy. With many prayers for your safety and happiness, I remain truly your friend...*"

Gamett and Stuart did not know it, but their destiny was to be linked together. Their safety and happiness was to be short-lived. The day was not far off when they would both meet the same fate because of the same charge on the same battlefield.

By November 1 Stuart's fever was gone. He rejoined the 56th Virginia in camp near Winchester. One of the first things he did was to take a long, hard look at the regiment. There was good news and bad news. The good news was that the junior officers had returned and brought some recruits and conscripts with them; the ranks were filling up again. The bad news was that the men looked like ragamuffins. Their muskets and bayonets were clean and bright, but they wore whatever they could requisition, beg from home, or strip from the bodies of their dead friends and foes on the battlefield. No two were dressed alike. The lucky ones wore yellow butternut suits and misshaped, wide brimmed hats. Most of them were barefooted. Winter weather was fast approaching; they would soon have to wrap their feet in old clothes to ward off the frost.

Although the men grinned and said they were "tolerably comfortable," they would never be able to march without shoes in the snow or across frozen ground. Stuart was angered by the plight of his men. He wrote to his uncle, Alexander H. H. Stuart, a Confederate congressman, to ask him to use his influence to get the basic necessities to the soldiers in the field. Stuart said, "I have heard from several that there are many who are living in luxury, especially in the deep South. Do they not believe in our cause?"

At least Stuart was able to get a short, round jacket for himself and two pairs of pants for his servant Jacob from the C.S. quartermaster. Jacob was Stuart's right hand man; he went into the field with Stuart and assisted him in countless ways. The previous winter when Stuart's health forced him to leave the regiment in Abingdon and go home to Richmond to recover, Stuart left Jacob behind to look out for Colonel Slaughter. Slaughter soon wrote Stuart to praise Jacob:

Jacob, during our troubles, has been invaluable to me; Indeed, while attending to my innumerable duties I think I would have starved but for his providing hand, and it is almost certain I would have lost everything I have but for his care.

Stuart fully appreciated Jacob as a "valuable and reliable servant" and frequently mentioned Jacob's love and affection for him in his letters to his wife. Jacob was an ardent Confederate; he hated the bluecoats. Stuart reported to Clinkey in one of his letters that, "Jacob said that he was 'gwine' to shoulder a musket and get him one 'ob' those damn Yankees who were causing his folks so much trouble."

Stuart had a servant in the field on whom he could depend, but Abraham Lincoln was still looking for a dependable general to command his army. On November 5, 1862, Lincoln relieved McClellan of command. Lincoln was tired of McClellan's timidity, cautiousness, and constant demands for more men and equipment. In desperation, Lincoln named Major General Ambrose E. Burnside to take over the Army of the Potomac. Burnside did not think that he was the right man for the job; his troops did not think so either.

Burnside was keenly aware that Lincoln wanted prompt action; he decided to give it to him. On November 15 Burnside ordered the Army of the Potomac to break camp near Warrenton and head south. Three days later, Confederate scouts reported to Lee that thousands of bluecoats were moving towards Fredericksburg. Lee ordered Longstreet's corps to make a forced march to Fredericksburg to stop Burnside.

The 56th Virginia marched from Winchester to Fredericksburg with Pickett's division. The regiment arrived on the hills behind the town about 3 p.m. on the 21st and dug in on the top of Telegraph Hill, the highest point on the field. Telegraph Hill was later called "Lee's Hill" because General Lee set up his headquarters and observation post there. The hill to its immediate left was called "Marye's Heights." It was the place where the bluecoats would attack in strength. All of the hills were natural places to defend because they were high, steep, and rugged. The Confederates piled up earthworks to make them even stronger.

After an absence of two months, Private Holt rejoined the ranks of the 56th Virginia in the trenches on Telegraph Hill. Holt had been so weak and sick after the Maryland campaign that the regimental surgeon had declared him unfit for duty. The doctor had sent Holt in an ambulance with other sick and wounded men to the hospital in Winchester. The hospital was set up in an old Presbyterian church. While Holt was recuperating, he served as a clerk for the hospital staff. He stayed quite busy most of the time writing reports, requisitions, passes, and transfers. He returned to active duty just as soon as the doctors pronounced him fit, but he wrote Ellen, "I never was so tired of anything in my life as I am of a soldier's life."

For the next three weeks the two armies confronted each other from opposite sides of the Rappahannock River. The 56th Virginia camped in the woods behind the trenches. The ground was covered with new fallen snow; the weather was cruelly cold. The men of the regiment spent most of their time just trying to stay warm. They cut and burned all of the trees nearby and hoped to move camp closer to another supply of firewood. Private Thomas was convinced that there was no likelihood of a fight because "...they are on one side of the river and we the other and they aren't going to come over to us nor will we go to them."

Private Thomas was wrong. On the morning of

December 13, the plain at the foot of Telegraph Hill, Marye's Heights, and the other Confederate high ground was completely hidden by a thick, gray fog. The waiting Confederates could hear the unmistakable sounds of infantry on the move. The slapping of canteens, the rattling of mess kits, the creaking of leather, and the murmuring of the voices of officers came up through the mist. The bluecoats had crossed the river in force and were going to try to take the heights. From the earthworks high on top of Telegraph Hill, Colonel Stuart trained his field glasses on the fog below. He described what happened next in a letter to Clinkey:

The morning was bitterly cold and when the sun shone through the mist, it seemed to vanish like magic. The whole Northern Army stood arrayed before us in all its glory, ready to shatter itself against our fortifications.

The bluecoats attacked Jackson's corps on the Confederate right. The Yankees advanced with grim determination. According to Colonel Stuart, they came with ". . .not much shouting, just a general forward movement." The 56th Virginia was on the alert to charge down Telegraph Hill and strike the Union flank if the bluecoats pierced the line below. The men of the 56th were itching to get into the fight, but they were not needed. Jackson's men held their ground against repeated attacks while Pickett's Brigade stayed in reserve.

The Yankees then charged Marye's Heights to the left and below the trenches of the 56th Virginia. There was a sunken road in front of Marye's Heights with a stone wall in front of it. The 56th was ordered to move out of its earthworks and take a new position high above and far behind the wall. The regiment was to support the defenders below in case the Yankees broke through. The South Carolinians of General Joseph B. Kershaw's Brigade and the Georgians of General Thomas R. R. Cobb's Brigade stood behind the wall four ranks deep. They did not need the help of the 56th Virginia or anyone else. The first rank fired, stepped back to reload, and made room for the second rank to step forward and fire. The second rank then stepped back and made room for the third rank which fired and yielded its place to the fourth rank. The Confederate scheme forced the Yankees to walk into steady sheets of rifle fire. Colonel Stuart saw the bluecoats charge the wall six times "with valor becoming any army," but they were hurled back six times.

By nightfall all the Yankees had to show for their courage were piles of dead bodies dressed in blue overcoats in the snow. The men of the 56th Virginia watched the panorama-turned-slaughter from their vantage point on the hill while a few artillery shells roared harmlessly over their heads. Since they did not fire a single shot, they saw the battle from a different perspective. When the fight was over, Colonel Stuart said, "We were all so relieved when the sun set and the useless slaughter was ceased. Never have I seen men die so bravely or so needlessly." Stuart wrote Clinkey that the 56th Virginia took "...pride in victory, but not joy." Three days later Private Thomas gave Mary his account of the battle:

"Saturday we had a hard fight on our right and left but we cleaned the Yankees out on both sides ... I was right where I could see them fight . . . but our regiment did not fire a gun. They sent in a flag of truce yesterday to bury their dead and this morning we expected to have it again but they took a wise plan on last night and moved their troops back across the river, so I don't know where our next battle will be. I am just off the battle field. I went on just to see and a sight it was. The Yankees were lying on the ground thick enough, besides what was buried."

A few days after the battle, the 56th Virginia moved its camp into the woods on the left of Telegraph Road. On the morning of December 19, the regiment was ordered to get under arms in quick time because the Yankees were going to cross the river again, but it was another false alarm. The bluecoats thought that the Confederates had left the Fredericksburg area, but when they discovered their mistake they gave up their plan to advance. Private Holt said, "We are well fortified here and have a very commanding position and have no fears that they can pass us here, even though they may have a much larger force than we have."

During the week before Christmas, a considerable number of men throughout the army left their posts and went home without leave. About 25-30 men were missing from the ranks of the 56th Virginia. The army sent out squads of cavalry to arrest all of the absentees and bring them back. Private Holt wrote Ellen:

It will be very apt to go very hard with them, deserting, as they did, in the face of the enemy.... I wish to go home very much indeed, but not in that way. Colonel Stuart says that no effort shall be liking (lacking) on his part for those who have faithfully stuck to their duty, to go home this winter if there is any chance.

Holt wrote Ellen again on Christmas Eve and said sadly:

"Today is Christmas eve. Tomorrow is Christmas again, and here we are around our campfires once more instead of being at home enjoying ourselves with those we love best, as we were want, in days gone by, to spend the Merry Christmas Holy Days."

On January 6, 1863, Private Holt's uncle, John Wood, visited the camp of the regiment. He brought Holt some heavy, warm clothes from home, including a wool overcoat. Everything fitted Holt exactly. When Holt reached into the overcoat pocket, he found some sweet, juicy apples inside. Holt thanked Ellen and said, "They were quite a rich treat." All Holt could find to send to his family as New Year's gifts in return were two bone rings and $10 cash.

A week or two later the 56th drew picket duty for three days on the banks of the Rappahannock River near Fredericksburg. The regiment did not have any wagons, so the men could bring only small picket tents with them. They stretched the little tents up with blankets and oil cloths and built huge log fires. According to Private Holt, they were "tolerably comfortable" in spite of the snow that poured down in torrents. The ground was so rain soaked that the snow would not stick to it. Some of the men stood at the water's edge and talked to the Yankee pickets on the opposite side of the river. They carved little wooden boats and pushed them across the river to trade Southern newspapers and tobacco for Northern newspapers and coffee.

After its disaster at Fredericksburg, the Union army withdrew to its base camp at Falmouth and prepared to go back to Washington. Even the weather was hostile to the bluecoats; heavy rain turned the roads into quagmires. Men, animals, and equipment got stuck in the soft, boggy ground and sank almost out of sight. The men called the retreat "the mud march." One Yankee joker stared at the ground, scratched his head, and said in a puzzled voice, " I know there's a mule in there someplace. I can see the tops of his ears sticking out."

General Burnside was humiliated by the stinging defeat; Lincoln started looking for another general. On January 25, 1863, Lincoln removed Burnside from command of the Army of the Potomac and replaced him with General "Fighting Joe" Hooker.

The 56th Virginia spent the next six weeks at Camp Hollydays near Guinea Station about seven miles below Fredericksburg. The men had light duty. They still had to drill, stand guard, tidy up camp, wash their clothes, and clean their rifles, but they could spend the rest of the time improving their living quarters. They used dirt, rocks, branches, logs, barrel staves, and whatever else they could scrounge to enlarge and improve their tents in every way imaginable. They even added stone chimneys, fireplaces, and other comforts not usually found in the field. Their canvas and what-not houses were so big and so well furnished that the men called them "mansions." Private Thomas wrote Mary and said, "Our boys are all quite well. ...we are very comfortably situated."

It snowed again on February 5, and this time the snow stuck. The men of the 56th Virginia passed the morning away sitting by the fires in their snug houses and looking through the cracks of the tent flaps at the falling snow with pleasure. That afternoon, Garnett's Brigade got into a snowball fight with Kemper's Brigade. it looked a lot like a real battle with officers on horseback and color bearers with flags flying. Sometimes one regiment would charge another; first one side would fall back and then the other. The "battle" ended when Kemper's Brigade charged, but Garnett's men routed it and drove Kemper's troops back through their camp. Private Holt thought that it was "great sport."

On the day of the snowball fight, Private Holt wrote Ellen to report on the food in the winter camp. He said:

"We don't draw as much as we can eat, but we make out very well most of the time by buying a little cornmeal once in a while and now and then a beef's kidney . . . we hardly ever eat beef kidney at home but we consider them great delicacies here. Nothing we can get here is like anything sent from home, and there are many things we would hardly touch at home but think them great treats here."

Colonel Stuart often visited Stonewall Jackson's headquarters while the 56th Virginia was in winter camp at Hollydays. Stuart and the general spent many afternoons together sitting in front of the fire and talking about the old days at VMI. Sometimes Stuart brought a few of the officers of the regiment along for a visit. Most of them found Jackson to be "forbidding and cold," but Stuart thought he was ". . .the warmest, kindest person I have known."

Jeb Stuart's headquarters were also nearby, and Colonel Stuart had a standing invitation from his famous cousin to drop by any time. There was always something going on. It might be a play or even a minstrel show, but regardless of the activity, there was sure to be music and laughter. Wherever Jeb went, a banjo, fiddle, and pair of bones were not far behind. Colonel Stuart thought his cousin was "a little too flamboyant," but he had to admit that Jeb was "always good company."

The Confederate army's winter camp provided much needed rest and relaxation for the troops, but it caused a serious problem. After the army spent six weeks in the same place, there was a critical shortage of food and fuel. Sanitary conditions got worse with each passing day, and there was always a chance that an epidemic like measles or smallpox would break out. To remedy the situation, General Lee decided to move part of the army. On February 18 Lee ordered Garnett's Brigade to go to Washington, North Carolina to report to General D. H. Hill and to forage for food. Garnett was now the permanent commander of the brigade, Pickett was head of the division, and Longstreet was the Corps Cornmander.

Colonel Stuart told General Garnett that he was worried that the men were going on such a long march when they were so ill clad. Most of the men in the brigade still did not have shoes. Stuart pointed out that they were wrapping their feet in torn blankets and overcoats. Corporal George W. Smith of Company C had shoes, but he said that they were "... worn out and bursted open." According to Smith, even when the Confederate quartermaster had new shoes to issue, they were of "but little account."

A good many of the men had no hats, and at least one of them did not have a whole pair of trousers. Private Thomas had only one pair of "... very nasty ... old pants." The seat was worn completely through, and his rear end was "out." Orders were orders; the brigade marched south. Sambo Short wrote Babie that as the brigade passed through Petersburg, "The ladies cheered us and waved their handkerchiefs and flags mightily." Hopefully, Private Thomas marched in the middle of the column!

The 56th Virginia also passed through Greenville and Tarboro, North Carolina on the way to Washington. The country was low, flat, and covered with pine trees. Sambo Short reported that Tarboro was "a very pretty town," but he complained that "...the water we have to drink is as black as tar and tastes like it." Private Holt and three of his companions in Company I had the good fortune to spend the night In the home of a rich old gentleman somewhere between Tarboro and Washington. After the men ate a sumptuous supper, the ladies of the house came into the parlor, played the piano, and sang.

By March 30 the regiment had set up camp near the town of Washington. Private Thomas reported that the Yankees held the town, but the Confederates had cannon "planted all around it" within a range of only a few hundred yards. The 56th Virginia joined General Hill's command in laying siege to Washington. The regiment had to stand picket duty every third day. Thomas wrote, "We have the place surrounded and it is thort that we will bum bar it." A week later, Thomas said, "...we are shelling the town some every day. I reccon they entend to shell the place or to perrish them out." Private Holt said, "I believe the intention of the generals is to hold the Yankees in and starve them out." General Hill ordered the pickets to keep cattle, hogs, and other livestock from passing through the lines. A citizen sneaked out of town one night and reported that the Yankees were living on crackers and horse meat.

Sambo Short's Company E was held in reserve to support one of the artillery batteries that ringed the town. Sambo wrote Babie to say that his company was standing guard behind some houses when ". . .a cannon ball struck within 20 steps of us. Several balls popped over our heads." Private Thomas laughed his "belly full" at one of the men in his Company B who was scared every time a cannon fired. Private Holt wrote Ellen:

"They send a good many shells over us... Our men would shell the town to pieces, I expect, if it were not for the women and children. The Yankees won't let them come out."

The Confederates besieged the town of Washington from March 30 to April 16. It was an uncomfortable time for the men of the 56th Virginia because they had no personal belongings. The army sent their knapsacks and baggage to Greenville when the regiment left Virginia, but the packs did not get to Greenville until after the 56th left Greenville and moved to Washington. The regiment's tents did not arrive on time either. Since the men were in "tar country," they had to burn swamp cypress and pitch pine logs in their camp and cooking fires. They were soon covered from head to toe with black pitch. They slogged through the mud, slept in the rain, shivered in the cold, and wore no clean clothes for weeks. Sambo Short told Babie, " I caught a pouncing Confederate off my flannel shirt the other day." Private Holt reported to Ellen that the daily ration per man was cornmeal and bacon. He said with tongue-in-cheek, "Bread without sifting and a quarter pound of meat a day! Who wouldn't be a soldier?"

The Yankees stubbornly held on to Washington. The siege did not force the bluecoats to surrender, but it did keep them bottled up inside the town while the brigade scavenged the surrounding countryside for food. Private Holt was probably right when he said, "We failed to take Washington, and some seem to think they had no idea of taking it, but merely pretended to try to take it to deceive the enemy in order to carry on our foraging purposes." The 56th Virginia was able to pile a number of wagons high with tons of bacon and corn and to start them on the road back to the main army in Virginia. Private Thomas wrote Mary, ". . .they made a sweep stake of corn and meat down there."

On the night of April 16, the Yankees ran two transport ships filled with food up the Pamlico River past the Confederate shore batteries and unloaded them at the dock in Washington. The Confederates had to abandon their plan to starve out the garrison. The very next day, the 56th Virginia received orders to leave North Carolina and to report to General Longstreet in Suffolk, Virginia.

Colonel Stuart was delighted. He wrote to Clinkey, "it

will be such a relief to move North and once again be united with the rest of the Division." Private Holt wrote to Ellen to share a laugh with her at the expense of the tarheels:

> *You would be amused to see the merriment the boys have at the ignorance of some of the North Carolina people of the low country. Some of them seemed to be ignorant of the war going on, and said, when asked something about it, that they believed they had heard something about a war going on somewhere. They believed it was a way out in Virginny, or somewhere out that way. One old lady, on seeing the brigade pass, was mightily disturbed to know where all them men would get their suppers.*

General Gamett, the brigade commander, did not get along well with General Hill during the siege of Washington. Colonel Stuart admired Hill when they fought side by side at Big Bethel in 1861, but Hill was no longer the same man. He was moody and irritable. Stuart thought that Hill had lost his nerve and was no longer able to seize the initiative. To make matters worse, General Pickett neglected the Washington siege operation to see his sweetheart. Stuart wrote Clinkey to complain that Pickett "...was continually riding off to pay court to his young love, leaving the division details to his staff." For a while the men of the 56th Virginia were afraid that they would be permanently attached to General Hill's command. They wanted to be back with the old division in Virginia. Private Thomas said that he would rather be with the rest of Pickett's division "than any other troops."

The 56th Virginia marched back to Tarboro and then took the train to Franklin, Virginia. The men rode over 100 miles while sitting on the hard, wooden slats of the railroad cars. Sambo Short reported that the weather was cold and disagreeable. The regiment got off the train at Franklin about 9 p.m. The next morning the men "took the tramp" all day. They marched about 25 miles to Suffolk through rain, mud, and creeks and made camp beside the Blackwater River. Sambo did not get dry until the following day.

The 56th Virginia joined Longstreet's corps in the siege of Suffolk. The country surrounding Suffolk was low, flat, and swampy. One end of the Confederate line extended to the Dismal Swamp, but the regiment found a dry hill with good water nearby to set up camp.

The 56th did little fighting at Suffolk, although the regiment came close to clashing with the bluecoats several times. Private Thomas reported that every day the men could hear the Yankee snare drums beating often and the sound of heavy cannonading. Thomas said that on April 24 the regiment marched two miles in double quick time to meet the advancing Yankees, but it was another of many false alarms. Two nights later there was heavy firing on the picket line that lasted a half hour or more. Later the Confederate and Union pickets reached an "understanding" that neither side would fire unless the other advanced.

The 56th drew picket duty in the swamp on the night of April 29. The men had to stand in water all night long. They could not sleep because there was no place to sit or lie down. To add to their misery, it rained all night, and they ran out of chewing tobacco. Two days later, Private Holt wrote Ellen:

> *"There is a continual cannonading going on pretty much every day, as at Washington. I have heard cannon so much since I left home that I have become so accustomed to it that I don't think any more of it, I reckon, than you would of a spinning wheel running in the house."*

The 56th Virginia was ordered to dig in, erect fortifications, and be ready in case the bluecoats attacked. Sambo Short wrote Bable, "I expect to have to cut trees and build breastworks where the water is knee deep. I can assure you that the life of a soldier is very tough."

The Confederates had no more success in trying to capture the city of Suffolk by siege than they had in trying to take the town of Washington. The men of the 56th Virginia must have smiled with relief when the brigade got new orders to hurry to Petersburg to repel a Federal cavalry raid. On the morning of May 3, the regiment began to break camp and prepare to march to Rice's Turnout in Chesterfield County. At breakfast time, the men discovered that there was no food. The regimental quartermaster was supposed to have drawn two days' rations the day before, but by mistake he drew only one day's food. The cook wagons had already gone ahead and were miles up the road. The regiment marched all day and all night without a morsel and did not get anything to eat until noon of the second day. Private Thomas wrote Mary, "...we had a very mad set of fellows." Private Holt told Ellen that when the men finally caught up with the cook wagon, "You had better believe me we made the bread fly."

While the 56th Virginia was in camp at Rice's Turnout, it got news of the Battle of Chancellorsville. The regiment missed the battle because of its detached duty in North Carolina and Suffolk. Chancellorsville was the brainchild of Generals Lee and Jackson, and it was a stunning Confederate victory. Although it was Jackson's most brilliant achievement, it cost him his life. Colonel Stuart was deeply upset that Jackson was dead and that the 56th Virginia did not serve with him during the battle.

On May 9 the regiment went to Richmond to march in Jackson's funeral procession as part of the honor guard. The men carried their muskets reversed and marched in front of and behind the carriage. Four gray horses pulled the hearse through a crowd of thousands who lined the streets to say farewell to the man everyone knew as "Stonewall." According to Private Thomas, the ceremony was "a great to do." Sambo Short said of Jackson, "He is a great loss to the S. Confederacy, and his death has caused much sadness. I fear it will cause the Yanks to fight us much harder." Private Holt added that the funeral "...was a grand and imposing sight as well as deeply solemn and was nothing more than the respect due from this nation to the departed hero whose deeds of valor will live and be handed down from generation to generation as long as there is a spark of Southern liberty to breathe it." Private Thomas said simply, "He is dead, poor fellow. We could of spared 4,000 privates better, but their lives would have been as sweet as his."

The South lost Stonewall Jackson at Chancellorsville, and the North lost "Fighting Joe" Hooker after Chancellorsville. President Lincoln removed Hooker from command of the Army of the Potomac and replaced him with Major General George G. Meade. Meade was not a handsome man like Hooker. The bluecoat rank and file said that Meade looked like "a God damned, de goggle-eyed snapping turtle," but he was a fighter. General Lee was one of the most handsome men in both armies, and in battle he was a fighter and a gambler.

The Army of Northern Virginia was at its peak in the spring of 1863, but it was a paradox. On the one hand, the soldiers looked like scarecrows in their calico shirts, patched brown trousers, worn leather belts, and bare feet. Their uncut hair stuck out in shocks through holes in their misshaped, slouched hats. On the other hand, they were lean, tan, and in good physical condition. Their esprit de corps was sky high, and they marched with a spring in their step. They thought they were invincible; Lee thought so too. Private Robert B. Dameron of Company D, 56th Virginia said that Lee's men "...would go anywhere and had the courage of the Spartans."

Lee decided to gamble and invade the North again; this time he planned to take the army into Pennsylvania. The men began to prepare for the long tramp by lightening their knapsacks and sending their valuables home. Corporal George Smith, a watchmaker and musician in Company C, sent his sister Clara a pipe that he whittled from a brier root while the regiment was in North Carolina. Sambo Short wrote to Babie on May 15 to tell her that the regiment was under marching orders and expected to go north. He made a prophetic statement in his letter. He said, "The greatest fight that has ever taken place on the American continent is expected soon."

Chapter 10

Gettysburg and Pickett's Charge

"Men, you see that wall there? It's full of Yankees. I want you to help take it."

NOTE: Since 1990, Bill Young has traveled to 18 states and to London to present a first person impression of First Lieutenant George W. Finley who commanded Company K of the 56th Virginia Infantry Regiment in Pickett's Charge. Finley was captured at Gettysburg, spent two years in six Federal prisons, and became a Presbyterian minister after the war.

In 1904, Finley wrote a detailed account of the charge for "The Buffalo Evening News," a newspaper in Buffalo, New York. Young is 100 years younger than Finley, so when he tells the story he goes back in time 100 years. For example, in 2008 Young is the same age that Finley was in 1908. Young dresses as Finley actually looked in 1908 and speaks in the first person in the year 1908 as Finley looks back 45 years to his part in Pickett's Charge. The story is all true. Lt. Finley actually existed, and much of the story is in his own words or the words of his comrades.

Here is Lt. Finley's account as Young tells it:

Let us pray. May the words of our mouths and the meditations of our hearts be always acceptable in thy sight, O Lord, our strength and our redeemer. Please forgive what we have been, amend what we are, and direct what we shall be. Amen.

My name is George W. Finley. The W stands for Williamson. I am 68 years old. I stand before you today in the year 1908 – 1908! How time flies! I am wearing the black frock coat of a minister of the gospel, because for many years now I have been the minister of the Tinkling Springs Presbyterian Church in Augusta County, Virginia just outside of Fishersville. But 45 years ago, in the summer of '63, I stood on the battlefield of Gettysburg, and I wore the gray frock coat of a 24 year old First Lieutenant commanding Company K, 56th Virginia Volunteer Infantry Regiment, Garnett's Brigade,

Pickett's Division, Longstreet's Corps, Army of Northern Virginia – that magnificent army of legend that wrote its name in large, bold letters across the pages of history.

Every time I tell this story, the memories come rushing back to me across the years. I see the faces of my old comrades; I hear their voices again; and I often break down and weep. So if I shed tears today, you will understand why.

I am married to Margaret Elizabeth Booker of Charlotte County, Virginia. Her father is a professor of theology at the Union Theological Seminary at Hampden-Sydney, Virginia. Margaret and I have 14 children – seven boys and seven girls, and I am proud to tell you that we have taught our children to recite some of the basics by heart. And what are the basics, you might ask.

Well, they're such things as "The Westminster Shorter Catechism" that begins with a question, "What is the chief aim of man?" Answer: "Man's chief aim is to glorify God and to enjoy him forever." And they know the words of the 27th Psalm that Lt. Dabney Carr Harrison said for the men as they stood in the snow-covered trenches just before the breakout charge at Fort Donelson: "The Lord is my light and my salvation. Whom shall I fear? The Lord is the strength of my life. Of whom shall I be afraid? Though a host should encamp against me, I will not fear. Though war should rise against me, in this will I be confident."

They know the words of General Lee's last order – his farewell address delivered to the Army of Northern Virginia on the eve of the surrender at Appomattox Court House: "After four years of arduous service, marked by unsurpassed courage and fortitude, the Army of Northern Virginia has been compelled to yield to overwhelming numbers and resources. I need not tell the brave survivors of so many hard fought battles who have remained steadfast to the last, that I have consented to this result from no distrust of them, but feeling that valor and devotion…Well, you know how it goes. I get carried away with it sometimes.

And finally, Margaret and I have taught our children the words of the 56th Virginia's favorite marching song. Now if you could make one statement about the Confederate soldier without fear of contradiction from anyone, it would be that he was always hungry. We had a saying in our army that "misery and peanuts were plentiful." Only we didn't call it the "peanut" then. We called it a "goober" or a "goober pea," and the song went like this:

"Sitting by the roadside on a summer's day
Chatting with my messmates, passing time away.
Lying in the shadows underneath the trees.
Goodness, how delicious! Eating goober peas.

When a horseman passes, the soldiers have a rule.
They shout out at their loudest,
"Hey mister, here's your mule!"
But another pleasure, enchantinger than these
is wearing out your grinders eating goober peas.

Just before the battle, the general hears a row.
He says, "The Yanks are coming!
I hear their rifles now!"
He turns around in wonder,
and what do you think he sees?
The 56th Virginia eating goober peas.

(He sings the last verse and the chorus.)

I think my song has ended, it's lasted long enough.
The subject's interesting,
but the rhymes are mighty rough.
I wish this war was over
when free from rags and fleas,
We'll kiss our wives and sweethearts,
and gobble goober peas.

CHORUS: Peas, peas, peas, peas, eating goober peas.
Goodness, how delicious!
Eating goober peas.

All right. I freely admit it. It sounds better when the whole regiment sings it!
Our story begins on the night of July 1, 1863. The men of Pickett's Division were camped in and around Chambersburg, Pennsylvania when the order came down to cook three days' rations. Every man in the division knew what

that meant – a fight! So we cooked the three day's rations and promptly sat down and ate them up all at one time just like we always did. But that was not as foolish as it sounds, because in less than three days Pickett's men were going to march into the valley of the shadow of death and straight into the mouths of the Union guns.

    The bugler woke us up at 2:00 o'clock on the morning of July 2. We marched along the Chambersburg Turnpike that day and passed through Cashtown. We must have gone about 25 miles. At sunset we turned off the road to the left and bivouacked in the woods beside a place called Marsh Creek. As best as we could tell, we were near a little town called Gettysburg. Longstreet's fight was still going on in the woods off to the right, and we could distinctly hear the rattle of musketry and the crash of cannon that told of stern work on both sides, but the men were so worn down by the long day's march that they fell asleep as soon as their heads touched the ground.

    I couldn't sleep. I sat down on a log. I picked up a stick and poked the campfire into life. Then I reached inside my old gray, frockcoat – into my inner coat pocket just over my heart – and I took out this little New Testament. (He takes the Testament out of his pocket and holds it up.) Now I wasn't a minister then, but I always carried this little Testament in my inner pocket over my heart. I carried it for three reasons. First, because my wife gave it to me. Second, because nothing will give you greater spiritual comfort than a New Testament. And Third, because absolutely nothing will stop a minie ball better than a New Testament! With luck, that rifle ball will enter at the first chapter of Matthew and stop somewhere short of the last chapter of Revelation.

    I opened this little book at random, and my eye fell on a passage of scripture I had never read before. It was Paul's second letter to Timothy, Chapter 1, Verse 12. I read these words for the first time in my life: "I know whom I have believed and am persuaded that He is able to keep that which I have committed unto Him against that day." Against that day! And that day was surely going to come for the regiment and for me with the dawn.

    But you know, after reading that little passage of scripture, an inner peace came over me, and somehow I knew that everything would be all right. So I put my head down on the ground and fell fast asleep. And the bugler was kinder to us on the morning of the third. He didn't get us up until 3:00

o'clock. We marched along a dusty, farm road that morning about six or seven miles. It wasn't hot, because the sun wasn't up yet, but all of those thousands of marching feet stirred up such a terrible dust cloud that the men at the rear of the column could scarcely breathe.

Before dawn we turned off the road to the right and went into a little wheat field that was beside a patch of woods. The woods belonged to a local farmer named Henry Spangler. We stacked arms in that wheat field, and we rested. And the entire morning was allowed to while away. It was a relatively safe place to be on that battlefield. Oh, an occasional artillery shell passed overhead. Every now and then a minie ball sang among the tree tops, but few or none of us was hurt. About 11:00 o'clock, General Lee himself and his adjutant, Colonel Walter Taylor, walked out of the woods near us. The General opened up a map and spread it out on a tree stump, and soon the staff officers began to gather around him. Those men were holding a council of war – in full view of our regiment. We could see them plainly, but we couldn't hear a word they were saying.

After about a quarter of an hour, the General folded up his map, and he and Colonel Taylor walked into the woods off to our left and disappeared. The staff officers disbursed to the four points of the compass, leaving us standing there with our mouths wide open. We didn't know it then, but General Lee had made a decision that was going to make Pickett's Division immortal. For the past two days, the Army of Northern Virginia and the Army of the Potomac had stood toe to toe like two old prize fighters and had slugged it out.

The first day had gone to the South. The second day was about even, and this was the morning of the third day. So with food running low and ammunition running low, General Lee - who was always outnumbered and outgunned on the battlefield and had to be a gambler – whose very name might have been "audacity" – decided to risk it all on one last throw of the dice. He had tried the Union right, and he hadn't broken it. He had tried the Union left, and he hadn't broken it, so he reasoned that the only place left to strike was the Union center. His plan was to hurl Pickett's entire division, with the 56th Virginia as part of the spearhead, right down the middle – straight into the center of the Union line – and if we could punch through, it just might mean victory.

About that time, the boys spotted some green apple trees on the edge of Spangler's woods, and you know the old saying, "Boys will be boys." Before you could say "Jack Robinson," some of the boys shinnied up the apple trees and shook those apples down. The boys began to stuff themselves with green apples. They gorged themselves on green apples. Now I know what you're thinking – they got sick. Well, they didn't get sick. It would have served them right if they had. It might even have saved their lives.

But what do boys do when they've eaten their fill of apples? They throw the cores at each other - that's what they do. As if the Yankees weren't enough, we were fighting our own civil war on the back side of Spangler's woods with apple cores flying in all directions. When our colonel realized what was going on, he lost his temper. Our colonel was William Dabney Stuart of Staunton, Virginia. He was 33 years old and six feet two inches tall. He was a graduate of the Virginia Military Institute where he had been first Captain of the Corps of Cadets and a member of the Societe de Militaire. He was a cousin of Jeb Stuart and a personal friend of Stonewall Jackson.

Colonel Stuart was a gentleman and a soldier, as Lear was a king – every inch. And he reminded me of my mother, because once that man set his mind to something there was no getting around him. And when he told you to jump, you didn't ask "how high?" You just jumped as high as you could and hoped to heaven it was high enough! So when he said, "You boys stop throwing those apples," not another apple was thrown. Then he said, "Men, I want you to take your arms off the stacks and pass through this patch of woods. It's not very wide. When you come out on the other side, you're going to find yourselves on the reverse slope of a ridge. It's called Seminary Ridge, and it runs across the front of the woods. I want you to stoop down low, lie face down in the tall grass on the back side of the ridge, and await further orders. And keep the colors cased so the Yankees won't see you.

Now that order made sense to us. The Yankees were a lot of things, but stupid was not one of them. They knew that by regulation a Confederate regiment was allowed to carry only one battle flag. One flag – one regiment, so all they had to do was put a man with sharp eyes up a tree on the other side of the field and count the battle flags to know the strength coming against them. Hence, Colonel Stuart's order was to keep the colors cased and stoop down low so the Yankees won't see you.

We did as we were told, and as soon as the men of my Company K settled down on their stomachs in the grass on the reverse slope of the ridge, I lifted my head and looked around. There was the crest of the ridge just a few feet above us. On the top of the ridge as far as the eye could see to the right and as far as the eye could see to the left, there was a long row of cannons. There must have been 150 of them. I didn't know our army had that many guns. They were all under the command of Colonel E.P. Alexander of Georgia who was better known as "Porter."

Where my men went face down in the tall grass, we were directly below and behind the eighteen gun artillery battalion of Major James Dearing of Lynchburg. We were so close to his guns that I had to order the men to break to the rear to give the gunners at the limber chest room to handle the ammunition. The artillery caisson with its horses and drivers was right behind Company K.

I could see Major Dearing plainly. He was leaning against the wheel of one of his guns. He had his gold watch in his hand, and he had the lid up. And he was just studying that watch as though time meant something to him. Well, it didn't mean anything to us, because we had wasted the whole morning. But he kept studying that watch, and the sun's rays began to beat down vertically on us. Don't ask me how hot it was, but it was hot enough to scorch a feather, I can tell you that. Those sun rays felt like steel lances tipped in fire.

Every canteen in the regiment was empty, and every throat was parched and dry, but the orders were "Nobody moves. Nobody goes to the spring in the rear for water." At that moment it dawned on me that a great, strange stillness had come down over everyone and everything. The awful silence of that vast battlefield was profound. And then, all of a sudden, about 1:00 o'clock the ball opened. It was like the final day of judgment when the great scroll of life in the heavens is rolled shut with an overpowering clap of thunder!

There was a streak of orange flame way off to the right down near the peach orchard followed by a thick cloud of sulfurous, black powder smoke and a thick slap in the summer air. It was a single shot from a signal gun of the Washington Artillery of New Orleans. A few seconds later, on the far left end of the line there was a second streak of orange flame and a second cloud of smoke and a second slap in the summer air – a second shot from a signal gun of the Washington Artillery.

There was a pause, as though the earth itself were drawing its breath - aaaaaaaaaahhhhhhhhhh, and then with a great crash and crescendo, like the sound of the trumpets of a mighty organ being played with all of the stops pulled out, every gun on the Confederate line on Seminary Ride opened fire! General Hunt's Federal artillery about a mile away promptly returned the fire, and for the next two hours the greatest artillery duel that I have ever heard or witnessed took place. Our gunners stood to their pieces and fired peal after peal in salvos. The guns bucked and roared like caged lions, and we could feel the very ground tremble beneath our chests. The air was filled with murderous iron. The incoming storm of shot and shell killed or wounded many a man lying face down in the tall grass, and the moans and screams of the wounded and dying mingled with the sounds of the tempest, but the orders were "Nobody moves," and all we could do was lie there and sweat, swelter, suffer, grit our teeth, and take it. And that firing went on and on and on and on for two solid hours. I don't see how any man or beast could possibly have survived, but most of them did.

And then, about 3:00 o'clock, the firing stopped as suddenly as it had begun. The black powder smoke began to drift away from the muzzles of the guns, and it was like a curtain going up on the last act of a drama. I caught a movement out of the corner of my right eye and everybody else did too, because we all looked down that way. And there was a lone rider on horseback walking his horse across our front from right to left. Somebody called out, "Who is that out there?" The answer came back, "Its Ole Pete" – referring to General James Longstreet, the Corps commander from South Carolina.

"What's Ole Pete doing out there?" "He's inspecting the line." And sure enough, that's what he was doing. He acted like he was on a Sunday picnic. He was in full view of the enemy sharpshooters, and the rifle balls whistled past his head. Every now and then an incoming artillery shell plowed up the ground so close to him that he had to check his frightened animal more than once, but he paid it no mind. And some of the men lying face down in the tall grass began to remonstrate with the General for recklessly exposing his person so. They began to call to him in terms more emphatic than they were elegant. They yelled things like "Go to the rear…We'll fight without you leading us…You'll get your old fool head knocked off!" But he paid them no mind. He walked that horse calmly and leisurely across our entire front and disappeared safely into the woods off to our left.

A few seconds later, General Pickett, the Division commander, rode out of the same woods, dismounted, and gave the order "Up, men and to your posts! Remember today that you are from Old Virginia!" The men began to stand up all down the line, and oh, what a relief that was! We had lain under the hot sun under fire so long that we scarcely appreciated the danger. Anything was better than lying under that hot sun and cannon fire any longer. And when all of those thousands of men stood up – with the grunting and the groaning and the creaking of the leather and the slapping of the wooden canteens, we frightened a wild jack rabbit that was in a bush a few yards out in the front and center of our line. That old bunny rabbit was terrified. I can still see him today in my mind's eye. He was a light tan and had a white, fluffy, cotton tail like a lady's powder puff. He bolted and zig-zagged for the rear as fast as he could go.

A soldier in the 18th Virginia yelled, "That's right, run you little ole rabbit! If I was a little ole rabbit, I'd run too!"

The drummers began to beat the long roll, and the color bearer in each regiment uncased his colors and shook them out. The battle flags blossomed like red and blue flowers all down the Confederate line.

Forty two regiments of infantry – forty two battle flags like red and blue flowers. The red flower? That's the battle flag of the Army of Northern Virginia. Four feet by four feet square. A red field bordered in white, and on that red field a blue cross of Saint Andrew. And on the cross 13 white stars – one for each of the seceded Southern states and one each for the Confederate governments in Missouri and Kentucky.

And painted on our battle flag in white letters and numbers: "56th Va. Inf." The flag was the very soul of the regiment. Our color bearer was Alexander Lafayette Price Williams, better known as "Corporal Sandy." He shook out the very soul of the 56th and took his place with the color guard in the front and center of our line.

And the blue flower? That's the flag of the Mother of Presidents, the Old Dominion, the Commonwealth of Virginia. A blue field, and on that blue field a circle of leaves of the Virginia Creeper. And inside that circle a woman warrior who represents virtue. She is dressed in Greek light armor. She wears a helmet, a curass, and greaves. She holds a long spear in her left hand and a short sword in her right and has her foot planted across the throat of a fallen male foe who lies on his back with his crown at his side.

And beneath the seal the Latin motto of Virginia: "Sic Semper Tyrannis" which we always told the Yankees meant "Get your foot off my neck!" but you know means "Thus always to tyrants."

We had lain down in our usual order of battle, so when we stood up we were ready to move forward. My brigade, Richard Garnett's, was on the left. There are five regiments in a brigade. Left to right: 56th Virginia – Colonel William Dabney Stuart, 28th Virginia – Colonel Robert Allen, 19th Virginia – Colonel Henry Gant, 18th Virginia – Lieutenant Colonel Henry Carrington, and 8th Virginia – Colonel Eppa Hunton. And to our right, James Kemper's brigade, five more regiments of Virginians: the 1st Virginia, the 3rd Virginia, the 7th Virginia, the 11th Virginia, and the 24th Virginia.

And centered between the two brigades and a short distance behind them, Lewis Armistead's brigade – five more regiments of Virginians: The 9th Virginia, the 14th Virginia, the 38th Virginia, the 53rd Virginia, and the 57th Virginia. And to our left, 27 more regiments of Southerners under the command of Generals Pettigrew and Trimble.

The old Virginia 1st in Kemper's brigade was founded in 1754. Its first Colonel was George Washington, and its second was Patrick Henry. There was a young man in the color guard of the 53rd Virginia in Armistead's brigade that day who was the son of a president of the United States. And in my own regiment, the 56th Virginia, there was a 19 year old private named Stanhope Henry carrying a musket. He was the grandson of Patrick Henry. The first Captain of my Company K was a descendant of two presidents of the United States and two signers of the Declaration of Independence.

General Armistead walked over to the color bearer of the 53rd Virginia. The man's name was Sergeant Leander Blackburn. The General took the folds of the 53rd's battle flag tenderly in his hand, and he looked Sergeant Blackburn squarely in the eye. "Sergeant," he said, "Are you going to plant this flag on the enemy's works today?" Sergeant Blackburn replied, "Sir, I'm going to try, and if mortal men can do it, it will be done." Sergeant Blackburn would be one of the first men to go down in the charge, and it would take nine more color bearers in succession from the 53rd Virginia to plant the flag on the enemy's works that day, but mortal men could do it, and it was done.

General Garnett limped over to General Armistead, took him to one side, and whispered, "Lewis, I have seen the field, and it is a desperate thing to attempt."

General Armistead replied: "Yes, Dick, it is, but the issue is with the Almighty, and we must leave it in His hands."

General Garnett limped over because he had been kicked by a spirited horse a few days before the battle, and he could scarcely walk. General Lee had ordered that all officers were to go into the charge dismounted so as not to be ready targets for the Union sharpshooters, but because General Garnett could scarcely walk he got special permission to ride. He was mounted on his favorite bay thoroughbred "Red Eye" 18 hands high. He rode ole "Red Eye" right up to the front and center of the line and took his place beside Corporal Sandy and the color guard of the 56th Virginia.

Our Colonel Stuart and General Garnett were friends. Colonel Stuart walked over to the General, looked up, and said: "General, please don't make this charge. You're hurt. You're sick. Your place is in the rear. Watch us from the rear."

General Garnett smiled and said, "Dabney, I will make this charge today if I have to be carried." And then he added sadly, "Dabney, I fear that you and I are both near death today, and I do hope that you will be spared."

Neither one of them was going to be.

And then Colonel Stuart gave an order that he had never given before. There are 10 companies in a regiment, and he appointed one man by name in each company to be file closer.

He said, "If any man lags behind in this charge, the file closer is to shoot him."

Then he appointed one man by name in each company to be alternate file closer, and he said, "If any man lags behind in this charge and the file closer fails to shoot him, the alternate file closer will shoot the file closer."

But he needn't have worried. I tell you truly, there was no pulling the wool over the eyes of the men. They knew what was expected of them, and they would have made the charge that day had there not been a single officer on the field – but one.

The Commanding General was sitting on his favorite mount "Traveler" in the shade of a little wood off to the left with that grand, gray head uncovered watching as we formed up.

Both horse and rider were iron gray. The General's face

reminded me of the image on an ancient Roman coin, and his countenance was as tranquil as the morning sun. Being in his army was like being in his family. His tent was always open to every man regardless of rank or station. He always did the best he could for us, and in return we worshipped the ground that he walked on.

His name was Robert E. Lee, but to every man in our army he was simply "Marse Robert." We would have followed him anywhere...even into the jaws of hell itself..., and on the third day at Gettysburg..., that is exactly what we did.

The First Sergeants gave the final orders: "Advance slowly with arms at will. No cheering, no firing, no breaking from common to quick step, dress on the center, Fix bayonets. Forward..., March!"

We started up the reverse slope of Seminary Ridge, passed between Major Dearing's gunners, some of whom were wearing the little kepi caps trimmed in red to show that they were artillerymen. They lifted their caps to us as if to say, "We have done our job. It's the infantry's turn." We doffed our old, wide brimmed slouch hats, returned salute for salute, and clapped our hats back on our heads. We crested the ridge and saw for the first time the field that lay before us.

The best way I know to describe it for you is to say that it was a green field of gently undulating wheat about a mile long and three quarters of a mile wide.

It was completely open.

There was no cover of any kind.

It was like a shallow basin with high ground at each end – Seminary Ridge at our end and Cemetery Ridge at the Union end.

About three quarters of the way out you could see the Emmittsburg Road in the distance crossing the field. There was a fence that ran alongside the road, and behind that fence we could see the Union skirmish line waiting for us. The bluecoats were so thickly planted that they looked like a regular line of battle and so far away that they appeared almost toy like.

I was struck by the appearance of that Union infantry. Every man dressed like every other. Every man wearing a dark blue kepi cap with the trefoil badge of the Union Second Corps in the top, a dark blue shell jacket with a single row of brass buttons, sky blue trousers, and heavy brogan shoes. Each man clutching a shiny, new Springfield rifle-musket. You could see the sunlight gleaming on the barrels. The bluecoats represented all of the wealth and power and might of the Federal government.

And then I took a look at our boys.

No two dressed alike. Some of them bare footed. Many of them wearing butternut trousers.

Butternut? That's captured Federal sky blue trousers boiled in walnut juice, and they varied in shade from a light tan to a dark brown - depending on how long they had been boiled in the walnut juice.

And calico shirts with wide suspenders and brown, gray, or black wide-brimmed, slouch hats pinned up on the wide or rolled up in the front.

Confederate infantry did not wear kepi caps like Yankees. In the first place, it just wasn't dignified, and in the second place nothing is going to keep the rain and the sun off the back of your head better than a wide-brimmed, slouch hat.

To be honest with you, our boys looked like a pack of dirty, lean, gray, brown, hungry wolves. But they were ready, willing, and able to lay down their lives for their countries, and their countries were Alabama, Arkansas, Florida, Georgia, Kentucky, Louisiana, Maryland, Mississippi, Missouri, North Carolina, South Carolina, Tennessee, Texas, and Virginia.

And on the other side of the Emmittsburg Road the ground rose up gently to other high ground called Cemetery Ridge.

There was a long stone wall or fence that ran along the top of the ridge. It varied in height from about three to four feet. In the center of the line the wall made a sharp, right angle turn at a place later to be known as "the angle." There was a grove of umbrella shaped trees inside the angle on the Union side of the wall.

Colonel Stuart pointed towards the trees at the center of the wall and said in a loud voice, "Men, you see that wall there? It's full of Yankees. I want you to help take it."

The place where he was pointing was indeed full of Yankees. The angle was defended by Battery A, 4th United States field artillery – six three inch rifled guns under the command of First Lieutenant Alonzo H. Cushing, a West Point graduate and regular army soldier from Wisconsin. Cushing's men were stuffing the mouths of their cannons with double loads of canister shot. Canister is iron balls packed in sawdust inside tin cans.

Canister turns a cannon into a giant shotgun on wheels. Canister is so devastating against infantry at close range that the soldiers on both sides called it "canned hellfire."

Artillery is always supported by infantry, and Cushing's guns and gunners were protected by the men of the Philadelphia Brigade – the only brigade in either army to be named for a city – and ironically, the "City of Brotherly Love."

There were four regiments in the Philadelphia Brigade: the 69th, 71st, 72nd, and 106th Pennsylvanias. The 69th was to the left of the guns. The 71st was to the right. The 72nd was over the hill in reserve, and only a part of the 106th was on the field... and it was attached to the 72nd.

The 71st and 72nd Pennsylvanias had begun the war as Zouave regiments - Baxter's and Birney's Fire Zouaves. They had worn turbans and fezzes, dark blue shell jackets trimmed with red scroll work, bright red, baggy trousers, and white canvass leggings. They had their own marching song, and it went like this:

Oh, we belong to the zoo zoo zoos.
Don't you think we oughter?
We're coming down
from Washingtown
To fight for Abraham's daughter!

The 69th Pennsylvania had a Stars and Stripes flag, but it was proudest of its own special regimental flag of green silk. There were three things on the green field: a round tower, a sunburst, and a wolf dog to show that the regiment was solidly Irish.

About the time Colonel Stuart was telling us to take the wall, Colonel Dennis O'Kane of the 69th Pennsylvania was giving his men the old Bunker Hill command: "Don't fire 'till you see the whites of their eyes!"

And he was talking about us!

We started into the wheat at our end of the field.

In spite of Colonel O'Kane's orders, flames flashed from the mouths of kicking muskets and bucking cannons all across the Union front.

Men began to go down, even at that extreme range, but it was regular time, dress the line, a deadly dress parade.

We had taken but a few steps when something hot and heavy struck the gallant Colonel Stuart on his left side, and he sank to his knees. He must have been struck by a shell fragment or a skirmisher's rifle ball.

He didn't want to fall down, and he couldn't stand up, so he stood there doubled over, half down and half up, supporting himself on his V.M.I. sword.

Two men stopped to help him, but he waved them on. Colonel Stuart was the only officer of the regiment above the rank of Captain on the field, so Command of the Regiment immediately passed to the senior Captain, James C. Wyant of Company H. It was Captain Wyant's first battle as an acting regimental commander.

It was also going to be his last.

We came to a tree stump in that wheat field, and an officer coolly commanded "Pass obstacle."

Half of the regiment broke to the right, and half broke to the left. We re-dressed the line and continued on.

Corporal Sandy could feel the little tugs as the minie balls tore through our battle flag. The enemy fire grew hotter and faster. The bullets buzzed about our ears like angry hornets. The air was so full of flying lead that you could raise your hand above your head and catch a bullet.

Thank God the Yankees were shooting high like they always did! Had they fired properly, not a single Confederate would have reached the wall. The men began to pull their hats down low over their eyes and to lean forward as men do in walking against a hailstorm, but their discipline was perfect. Their pace never slackened. They marched with quiet determination as if they were on dress parade.

We came to a worm fence in the wheat field – a worm fence like we have in Virginia. Split rails piled alternately on one another at right angles. We half climbed the fence, half tore it down, and continued on.

We could hear the zip, zip, zip of the minie balls that missed, and when a minie ball struck a man's body you could hear his bones crash like broken glass.

A minie ball is not round, you know. It's conical shaped – bullet shaped. It's pointed on the front end and has two or three rings around the back end. It spins in flight. It is .58 caliber, and it has terrific knockdown power. If it strikes you in the tip of your little finger, it will bowl you over like you've been struck by the giant sledgehammer of Thor.

Men were falling from the ranks as a cart spills meal on the road, but it was regular time, dress the line, a fatal parade. And when we came to the center of the wheat field there was a swale there, a slight depression in the ground. We paused, stopped, and straightened up our line. A gasp went through the Union ranks on the other side of the field.

"What are the Johnnies doing out there?' The answer came back, "They're dressing the line!" Their first reaction was astonishment. Their second reaction was admiration.

And their third reaction was anger that we should be so contemptuous of their fire as to dress our line in full view of them. They began to pour lead into us as fast as they could bite, pour, ram, cap, cock, and pull the trigger – about four times a minute.

When we passed the center of the field, the Union artillery on Little Round Top off to our right began to open fire on us. Shells poured down upon us, and as they descended they shrieked and screeched and hissed like frightened birds.

The first shell landed in Company A. It knocked six men down and scattered them about like so many rag dolls – four killed, two wounded.

The second shell landed in Company D. It knocked five men down and scattered them about – three killed, two wounded.

The third shell struck on the extreme right of Company H – largest company in the regiment – 37 men. All 37 men were swept away by a single shell. Some of the men scrambled to their feet and resumed their place in line, while others would never get up again.

And through it all...through the roaring of the guns and the choking smoke and the searing flame where the very earth beneath our feet seemed to be on fire, we could hear the firm, clear voice of General Garnett,

"Steady men. Steady. Save your strength for the end."

By this time men were falling like stalks of grain before the grim reaper, but there was never a pause in that slow and steady movement. The gray and butternut ranks kept coming and coming and moving and closing and rolling on as a moving sea closes over the flaws and rips of the tide.

As we approached the fence at the Emmittsburg Road, the Union skirmishers pulled back, ran up the hill, jumped down behind the stone wall, and rejoined their comrades.

When we got to the fence at the Emmittsburg Road, we discovered to our horror that what we thought was going to be another worm fence was instead post and rail. That Pennsylvania Dutch farmer had dug post holes alongside the road, sunk upright posts in the holes, cut slots into the tops of the posts, and fitted them with slatted boards!

We had to climb the fence to get to the enemy! Men were falling all around us, and cannons and muskets were raining death upon us. The 56th was being torn to pieces, but the men never faltered or wavered. They kept coming on in strict formation. On and up the slope to the stone wall the Regiment steadily swept, without a sound or a shot, save as the men would clamber to return the fire that was being poured into them.

When we reached a point about 100 yards from the stone wall, a junior officer couldn't stand it any longer, and he gave the order we had all been waiting for: "Take good aim, aim low, fire!" We fired one time, and then he said, "Now let's holler!"

"Eeeeeeeeeeeeeeeeeeyaaaaaaaaaaaaaaaaaaaaaa!"

The rebel yell rent the air for the first time that day. We screamed like fiends and demons from hell, and it was awe inspiring, and the earth fairly trembled.

Some of the Yankees tucked their tails between their legs and ran for the rear like sheep. A Union cannoneer ran to the rear with a rammer on his shoulder.

Somebody in our ranks called, "Stop, you Yankee devils!" Some of them never could stand up to the rebel yell, but I'll give the devil his due. I never saw more gallant conduct from any men on any field at any time than that displayed by Cushing's gunners who stood manfully to their pieces as we approached that wall.

And when we reached a point about 50 yards from the wall, there were only two gunners left able to function in Cushing's battery. They both dropped down on their stomachs and watched us come through a crack in the wall. Each man had his hand on a lanyard, and each lanyard was attached to a three inch rifled-gun triple shotted with canister. When we were about 50 yards out, one gunner called to the other, "Let 'em have it!" They jerked the lanyards simultaneously, and the two cannons rocked back from the wall with a splitting report. They fired their last shots full into our faces and so close to me that I distinctly felt the flame of the explosion against my left cheek.

Their last shots cut a bloody swath in our ranks to my immediate left about 50 feet wide. Captain Wyant, our acting commander, was shot in the face and writhed in pain as he fell in front of the wall. No one in the path of that swath could possibly have lived, but I was on the outer edge of it and was untouched. And then we were at the wall.

Some of the Yankees put up their hands and shouted, "Don't shoot! We surrender! Where do we go? What do we do?' We told them to go to the rear, but you're supposed to escort prisoners to the rear, so I suppose they all got away.

For the next few minutes, there were no bluecoats in front of our regiment. We stood at the wall on our side and fired obliquely at the Yankees on the left. I picked up a musket that would not fire, cleared it, and used it on the Federals. I made every shot count. If we had been reinforced, we could have held the rock fence with ease, but no help came.

I looked back and saw General Garnett ride up to the wall. At that moment, the 72nd Pennsylvania came over the hill on the other side of the wall. They leveled their muskets as one, pulled the triggers, and fired a terrible volley straight into us. Now I told you that the Yankees tended to shoot high, and because General Garnett was on horseback he took a minie ball right between the eyes and toppled off his horse stone dead. I watched as ole "Red Eye" galloped alone through the battle smoke back to our lines.

We exchanged one or two volleys with the 72nd Pennsylvania, and then they pulled back and went over the hill from whence they had come.

Just as the 72nd withdrew, General Armistead arrived at the head of the remnants of his brigade. He had begun the charge with his hat on the tip of his sword, but by the time he reached the wall the hat had worked its way down the blade and was over his hand. The General leaped onto the stone wall right at the colors of the 56th Virginia. In fact, he bumped Lieutenant Henry Clay Michie of Company H on his right elbow.

The General stood on the wall for a moment with his hat in his hand with his sword sticking through and held aloft.

"Give them cold steel, boys!" he cried.

He jumped down from the wall, ran over to one of Cushing's guns, put his hand on the barrel, and was shot down and fell beneath the wheels. The men began to follow the General over the wall – that is, those of us who were still able to walk.

I estimate that 12,500 men began the charge. Now there couldn't have been more than several hundred of us left, but every man who was able followed the General over the wall.

I hesitated, and then I remembered the words that I had read from the little pocket Testament beside the campfire the night before - Paul's second letter to Timothy,

Chapter 1, Verse 12. Those words went through my head right there at the wall. "I know whom I have believed and am persuaded that He is able to keep that which I have committed unto Him against that day."

Against that day!

And this was surely that day! So I too jumped the wall, and I landed in the worst fight I have ever been in my life!

Both sides came ever closer to one another. We were so close that we were literally shooting into each other's faces. The muzzle flashes of the muskets were scorching the shirts off of our chests. In some places there wasn't room to load and fire, so the men threw down their muskets and fought fist to fist, rock to rock, tooth to tooth.

Every man fought on his own hook. Private James Norris of Company H had just fired his musket when a Pennsylvanian charged him from behind with fixed bayonet. Captain Michie saw the Yank coming and shouted, "Jimmy, look out!" Jimmy also had a fixed bayonet. He whirled around and caught the Yank in the stomach with his cold steel.

Private Audubon Smith of Company K stood inside the bloody angle and mechanically loaded and fired, loaded and fired, loaded and fired his musket until a minie ball struck him in the shoulder and spun him to the ground.

A soldier in the 72nd Pennsylvania saw Audubon go down. The Union soldier bent down under the line of fire and ran to Audubon's side. The Yank gave Audubon a drink of water from his canteen, slung Audubon over his back in a fireman's carry, and lugged Audubon to a field hospital. He saved Audubon's life.

Corporal Sandy, our color bearer, stood inside the wall within 15 paces of the Union line. He waved our flag defiantly right in the faces of the Yankees until he was bowled over by a bullet in his thigh. A bluecoat from the 71st Pennsylvania ran over to him and pried the flag from his fingers.

We were in full view of the Federal officers, and they could see that we were but few in number and well nigh exhausted by what we had already accomplished.

They had reserves in countless thousands, and they threw every man they had at us. We soon found ourselves fighting not only the Philadelphia Brigade, but fresh regiments from New York, Ohio, Massachusetts, Pennsylvania, and Vermont.

Captain Frank Nelson of Company A tried to take his handful of men to the rear to avoid capture, but they fell like leaves from the tree in an autumn wind. The minie balls came at us from all directions.

We were surrounded on three sides, and I could see that our situation was hopeless. So to avoid the further useless waste of blood, I..., a lowly First Lieutenant..., the highest ranking officer left standing at my end of the line..., I gave the order to the men around me...

"Cease fire! Lay down your arms and surrender!"

And soon, the sharp, quick "Huzza!...;Huzza!...Huzza!" of the Federals told of our defeat and their triumph. They didn't even cheer like we did!

Oh, I wish I could find the words to describe for you the bitter anguish that welled up in our hearts at that moment.

To have fought so hard, to have come so far, to have endured so much, to have given everything for our beloved Virginia, and to have failed only because it was impossible to succeed, it was almost more than we could bear!

I was led away from the wall a prisoner of war, and I spent the next two years in six Federal prisons..., but that is another story.

CHAPTER 11

Cold Harbor to Appomattox

"...a confused struggle of firing, thrusting, cutting."

The 56th Virginia spent the last part of July, all of August, and the first week in September 1863 in Orange County, Virginia.

Private Thomas wrote Mary on July 27 to say that the regiment stopped at Culpeper Court House "to recruit up a little." Thomas told her that the men and horses were exhausted. The regiment had not drawn any pay in three months, and Thomas had no idea when he would get paid. Thomas had lost his knapsack containing all of his clothes except the shirt on his back and his torn, ragged pants when he was in Pennsylvania.

On September 8 the regiment marched with Hunton's Brigade to Chaffin's Farm about eight miles below Richmond on the north bank of the James River. The men of the 56th Virginia knew Chaffin's and liked it. They had camped there the year before when they helped drive back the Yankee fleet at the Battle of Drewry's Bluff. After they had left Chaffin's, General Henry A. Wise's Brigade had moved in and built permanent quarters. It was like a little outpost town. There were sturdy log houses with built-in bunks, stone fireplaces, and even a few brick hearths; there were streets, vegetable gardens, a small herd of cows, and a few chickens. Wise's Brigade reluctantly moved out; Hunton's Brigade eagerly moved in.

For the next nine months Chaffin's Farm was home away from home for the 56th Virginia. The men were able to put the horrors of the battlefield out of their minds most of the time and to devote their days to the three "R's" — rest, recuperation, and reorganization. They sang and danced to the strum of the banjo and the hum of the violin. They converted lead minie balls into fishing sinkers and caught bream and catfish in the river for supper. They used their pocket knives to slice bullets into cubes and gouged holes in the fiat sides to turn the cubes into dice. They whittled chess sets out of pine knots and soup bones. They formed debating societies and reading clubs. They boxed, wrestled, high jumped, and ran foot races. They built a bomb proof chapel out of logs and kept the chaplain busy at revival meetings. One of their favorite pastimes was to "run the blockade" into Richmond.

While the 56th Virginia was at Chaffin's, the Yankees made two cavalry raids on Richmond. Hunton's Brigade left its camp at Chaffin's both times and marched to meet the enemy. The Confederate cavalry drove off the invaders easily the first time, but the second raid was more serious than the first. Union General Philip Sheridan attacked at the head of a strong force of horsemen. The 56th Virginia formed a line of battle along the Brooke Turnpike to stop them. The regiment was about to charge when it was ordered back to Chaffin's again — the Yankees had turned around and gone.

While the regiment was resting at Chaffin's, Major William Edwin Green, a lawyer from Charlotte County, was promoted to colonel and took command of the regiment. Green would lead the 56th to the end of the war. Captain Timoleon Smith became Lieutenant Colonel and the second in command; Captain John McPhail moved up to Major. At about the same time that the regiment was getting its final senior leaders, Abraham Lincoln finally found his general. The men of the 56th already knew the general because they had fought against him at Fort Donelson, their very first battle. His name was Ulysses S. Grant.

In March 1864 Lincoln named Grant commander of all the Union armies. Two months later Grant took charge of the Army of the Potomac In person. His main goal was not to capture Richmond, but to destroy the Army of Northern Virginia. He decided to wage a war of attrition. He planned to attack Lee's army and to keep on attacking relentlessly until it was worn down and out. He led his bluecoat host across the Rapidan River and into the Wilderness of Virginia.

Lee raced north with most of the Army of Northern Virginia and headed into the woods to meet Grant's army head on. For the next month the two armies slugged each other without mercy in a series of violent, vicious encounters in the tangled brush and undergrowth of the Wilderness. Men died by the tens of thousands. The fortunate casualties were killed instantly by flying lead and iron. The unfortunate were mangled, strewn on the ground, and burned beyond recognition by the fires that sprang up and ravaged the woods after each fight.

Grant's standard tactic was to strike hard all along the front and then to sidle crab-like off to the right or left in an effort to go around the Confederate army. Time and time again, Lee pulled his men back and formed a new line of battle to stop the bluecoats, but Grant's army edged closer and closer to Richmond. The last week in May, Grant executed one of his crab-like sidles and headed for a little village In Hanover County called Cold Harbor. Cold Harbor was a crossroads outside Richmond. The invading Yankees wondered why the village was called Cold Harbor when there was no harbor or large body of water nearby, and there was no ship within miles of the place. The men of the 56th Virginia who came from Hanover County knew that in earlier days the village had a fine grape arbor. The local farmers called it "Cool Arbor." Over the years, the name "Cool Arbor" became corrupted into "Cold Harbor."

Lee did not hesitate. He rushed the Army of Northern Virginia to Cold Harbor to block Grant. Lee was vastly outnumbered; he needed every soldier he could find. He ordered Hunton's little brigade to march to Hanover Court House to join the main army on the road to Cold Harbor. The 56th Virginia reached the court house on May 23; by the night of June 2, the regiment was at Cold Harbor on the far right of the Confederate defense line. The men spent the whole night scooping up the soft dirt with their spoons, tin cups, mess pans, and bayonets and piling it up high in front of them. General Thomas L. Clingman's North Carolina brigade was in the trenches to the right of the 56th. There was a swamp on the left of the 56th, and it was swarming with Union sharpshooters.

General Grant arrived on the field on the same night as the 56th Virginia. Grant was frustrated and impatient; he demanded action. His army outnumbered the Confederates two to one, but it was stymied. Grant rashly ordered his bluecoats to put their heads down and bull their way through the Confederate defenses. As soon as the sun rose the next morning, Grant's infantry attacked all along the front.

The family of Private Edward W. Kelley of Company K, 56th Virginia owned a farm on the battlefield of Cold Harbor. Kelley's sister stood in the doorway of the house and watched the Yankees charge with fixed bayonets across her front yard. At the same time that the bluecoats charged over the Kelley farm, the Union sharpshooters in the swamp on the Confederate left opened fire and began to pick off the men of the 56th Virginia in the trenches. The Virginians and Carolinians could not stand the constant sniping, so they climbed out of their earthworks to fight.

Clingman's Brigade formed a skirmish line and attacked the sharpshooters on the right flank while Hunton's Brigade struck them in front with everything it had. The two Confederate brigades drove the Union marksmen out of the swamp, and by 8 am. the entire Battle of Cold Harbor was over. Grant's men paid dearly in blood for his rashness; the battle was a blood bath for the Federals. The Yankees lost 7,000 men to the Confederates' 1,500. Grant's army turned Private Kelley's house into a temporary field hospital. Federal surgeons amputated so many arms and legs inside the house that the blood ran out the front door and down the porch steps. The Yankees ripped all of the family's sheets, pillow cases, quilts, and bolsters into strips for bandages. They tore down the barn to get wood for coffins and buried hundreds of soldiers in the Kelley's front yard.

In spite of his appalling losses, Grant would not quit. He stuck to his plan because slowly, but surely, he was winning his war of attrition. He stubbornly kept right on attacking and pursuing the Army of Northern Virginia. Instead of withdrawing and allowing the Confederates to catch their breath, he ordered his army to make a crab-like sidle to the left, cross the James River, and head for Petersburg. While the Army of the Potomac was on the move, a second Union force called the Army of the James stepped off the boats at City Point below Richmond and marched straight towards Petersburg. The second Yankee army was under the command of General Benjamin F. "Beast" Butler.

Petersburg was 25 miles south of Richmond. It was an important rail center with four railroad lines that supplied the Army of Northern Virginia. It was also the key to Richmond. If Petersburg fell, the Confederates would have to abandon Richmond. General P. G. T. "Old Bory" Beauregard, a Creole from Louisiana who won fame at First Manassas, was in command of the defenses in the Petersburg area. In May 1864 Beauregard constructed an elaborate line of trenches on the south side of the James River. Beauregard's men called the trench system the "Howlett Line" because it began at the 21 room mansion of Dr. John Howlett on a bluff overlooking the river a mile or two below Fort Drewry. The line extended in a southerly direction all the way to Dunn's Hill on the Appomattox River near Petersburg.

Beauregard's situation was desperate as "Beast" Butler and his bluecoats drew close to Petersburg. "Old Bory" and his scratch force had to hold "the beast" at bay until help arrived. Their only chance was to bluff. Beauregard pulled all of his troops out of the Howlett Line, abandoned the trenches, and concentrated his men in front of the city. The Confederates made as much noise as they could to deceive the Yankees. Beauregard's men played fifes and drums as loudly as they could, shouted commands until they were hoarse, and fired muskets and cannons into the air. They clashed briefly with the Federals, but held the line. "Old Bory's" ruse was a surprising success.

The trick worked because Butler was cautious, timid, and confused. His army could have walked right into Petersburg with little bloodshed, but instead it stopped short of its goal and waited for Grant and the main army to arrive. Butler did manage to take possession of the Howlett Line, and he threatened to prevent Lee from coming to Beauregard's rescue. Lee ordered Pickett's division to try to save Fort Drewry at the north end of the line.

At daybreak on the morning of June 16, the 56th Virginia left Chaffin's Farm with Pickett's division on what was to be the fastest march the regiment ever made. The Confederates were in such a hurry that they did not march on the roads as usual. Instead, they went cross-country. They hiked on a bee line through woods and fields, crossed the James on a pontoon bridge, climbed the steep bluff, and found that Fort Drewry was safe. In the afternoon they hurried about two miles down the Richmond-Petersburg Turnpike. When they reached a point near Chester Station, they discovered General Butler's bluecoats in the trenches of the Howlett Line.

Pickett's division quickly formed a line of battle and advanced toward the center of the Union position. As soon as the Virginians in the main body caught up to their skirmishers out in front, they charged the Yankees on the run. The Confederates yelled like demons, jumped into the trenches, and fired as fast as they could load. it was too much for Butter's men. A soldier in the 18th Virginia said, "They couldn't stand the yell, and bullets proved too much for them. They broke and ran like sheep." The Yankees did not stop running until they reached the James River. In a few minutes the Confederates recaptured the entire Howlett Line with little loss of life. General Lee was delighted. The Richmond Examiner printed a tongue-in-cheek account of the exploit and said, "General Lee has given orders for long-tail coats to be issued Pickett's men to hold them back while charging."

Beast Butler's Army of the James was pressed into the peninsula of Bermuda Hundred between the James and York Rivers as tightly as though it were corked in a bottle, and Pickett's division was the cork. Butler's army was no longer of any use to Grant; it could not even slow down Lee's effort to reach Beauregard. The "beast" was caged.

Somehow Lee's Army of Northern Virginia got to Petersburg ahead of Grant's Army of the Potomac. By the night of June 18, Lee was inside Petersburg kneeling in prayer at St. Paul's Episcopal Church, and the Army of Northern Virginia was manning the trenches that surrounded the city. The longest siege of any American city in history was about to begin.

The 56th Virginia spent almost every day of the next nine months on guard duty in the trenches of the Howlett Line. The regiment was at the northern end of the line within sight of the Howlett House. Private Thomas A. Patteson of Company D drew an elaborate map that showed the regiment's camp and its surroundings in detail. The camp was just to the east of the road to Chester. The men slept in tents pitched in two neat rows in an open field well behind the trench line. When Patteson was at his post in the trenches, he could see the tall masts of the wooden ships and the low silhouettes of the ironclad ships of both the Union and Confederate navies at anchor near Dutch Bend in the James River. He also had a bird's eye view of Union mortar batteries, cannon emplacements, picket lines, and a signal tower across the river.

The regiment's duty was to hold its part of the Howlett Line on the south side of the James at all costs. On July 1 Private Thomas wrote to Mary to describe life in the trenches:

"We are seeing a very hard time out here lying in fortifications and on picket every other day and night and on guard at our fortifications one hour and three quarters every night when off picket. Some of the company on fortifications

up all night... I don't like picket duty very much. We have a very hot time sometimes firing at each other. We have pits to get in to keep off the balls. I give them 20 rounds one night not long since ... I have been in a very hot skirmish. The pickets have stopped firing at each other but I don't like to trust them. They might crack a fellow."

Thomas went on to say, "Our boys are very sickly. A great many born to the horse pittle ...When I got to the Company the Regiment numbered 400 and now they ain't but 270, officers and all." On August 7 Thomas wrote, ". . .my bowels got out of fix and I weakened down so fast that I went to the hospitle to stay a while untell I could straighten up some."

Thomas did not stay in the hospital long, and it was partly because he got "old rusty herrings" every morning for breakfast. Thomas almost always mentioned food in his letters. In his letter home dated July 24 he said, "Our fare are enough to make out with if we could ate it but it is the very fattest of old bacon and about two good slices per day and two small corn doggers per day."

Thomas reported that frying chickens cost eight to ten dollars apiece. He directed Mary, "You must ... send me one or two baked chickens for I never wanted to ate a chicken so bad in my life."

The regiment's morale began to sag for a number of reasons. The men were sick, the food was bad, and life in the trenches was boring most of the time. The men had not drawn any pay for six months, and even if they had, there was no place for them to spend it. There was a standing order that no one could leave the line except to go to the spring.

Private Thomas said, 'We don't get no news only by papers and they are generally filled up with lies." The men could hear the sounds of fighting that came from Petersburg.

Except for an occasional picket fight, however, they saw little action for months on end. Their guard duty was heavier than ever. On September 19 Thomas was depressed because he had not received a letter from Mary for a while. He complained to her, "I am confined and bound like a highway robber in custody and treated like a pointer dog.... Nobody cares for me now.... I am dwindling away and I fear I will soon be gorn. I never entend to go to another Horse Pittle again."

On September 25 the Yankees on the north side of the river opened fire on the Howlett Line with 100 cannons to celebrate their cavalry's victory over General Jubal A. "Old Jube" Early's little force in the Shenandoah Valley.

The Yankees shelled the trenches for an hour. Cannon balls and shells landed all around the 56th Virginia, but no one in the regiment was hurt. During the cannonade Private Thomas was on picket duty in a rifle pit in front of the trenches. The artillery fire cut saplings in two within ten feet of Thomas as he hugged the ground. The next day the regiment feasted on some poor, but welcomed beef. The fresh meat came from cattle that General Wade Hampton's cavalry captured from the Yankees in what was called "the beefsteak raid."

During the last week of September, bluecoat infantry attacked the Confederates in the trenches that surrounded Chaffin's Farm on the north side of the James River. Although the defenders of the Howlett Line on the south side of the river could not hear the gunfire, they knew that a battle was in progress because they could see a thick cloud of black smoke hanging over Chaffin's. Lee ordered General Pickett to send a brigade to help the embattled butternut soldiers at Chaffin's. Pickett hastily organized a provisional brigade and assigned the 24th, 32nd, 53rd, and 56th Virginia regiments to it. Pickett named Colonel Edgar Montague, the commander of the 32nd Virginia, to lead the provisional force. The four regiments of the makeshift brigade were each from a different regular brigade and had never worked together before.

Colonel Montague was a no-nonsense, hard-hitting, tough fighter. He led the new brigade across the James River just above Drewry's Bluff and rushed it into action headlong. The bluecoats had broken through the Confederate defenses at one point, but Montague's men quickly plugged the hole and drove the Yankees back. The 56th Virginia lost three men killed and seven wounded. After the battle, the 56th re-crossed the river and resumed its place in the Howlett Line.

The Regiment brought some bluecoat prisoners back with it. The men forced the Yankees to work on the fortifications alongside a gang of Virginia State Penitentiary prisoners who were already wielding picks and shovels under guard. Private Julius C. Mosley of Company B was in a feisty mood. He told the Yankee captives that if one of them so much as crooked a finger at him, he would "send him up the spout."

After the brief fight at Chaffin's Farm, life in the trenches returned to the usual, dull routine for the 56th Virginia. In October Private Thomas wrote Mary:

"Our Regiment are on this side of the James River again, lying back in the rear resting. They are held as reserve. They don't have nothing to do, but they may have to ketch it. They caught fire and blazes when they went on the north side of the James but have not been in no engagements since."

By January 1865 desertions were increasing in the Army of Northern Virginia. One Saturday night three men of Company G of the 56th Virginia deserted their vidette post near the rifle pits on the picket line in front of the trenches. Privates Elder, Watson, and Webb took off their shoes, laid down their rifles, cartridge boxes, and canteens, tiptoed across no man's land, climbed into the Union trenches, and gave themselves up. The next morning, Private Thomas and several other men in the regiment followed the tracks of the deserters. They were still on the trail when a Yankee picket saw them and decided to have a little fun at their expense. The Yankee hallooed to them gleefully and asked them where Private Elder was - as if he did not know. Private Thomas yelled back a reply that is unprintable. Suffice it to say, Thomas told the Yankee picket where Elder was, and the bluecoat did not ask any more questions.

On January 11, 1865, Private Thomas wrote Mary his last letter that still exists. In his final report on life in the trenches, he said:

"We have had a very hard spell and yesterday it rained

all day and last night was my time to stand picket down on the river whare the mud and water was over shoe deep, so I gave a conscript $5 to take my place. I had rather paid $25 If I had of had it than to of gorn.... Times is very quiet now. They are shifting the troops about mighty lately. I don't know what it is for unless they are making preparations for a spring siege. Our boys are tolerable healthy. Some few cases of the itch. I have never got it yet but a good many of my Company have had it and are got it now."

Thomas ended his last letter on his usual theme — hunger. He complained, "What they give us to ate is nothing but half enough."

On February 2 word came to the men of the 56th Virginia in the trenches on the Howlett Line that Captain Charles W. Read of the Confederate navy needed volunteers for a secret mission. Read was stationed at nearby Fort Drewry. He was known as the "John Paul Jones of the Confederacy." He was a graduate of Annapolis and had served aboard the famous Confederate ram Arkansas. Seventeen year old Private Freeman W. Jones and his buddy, Private Francis R. Fraser, both of Company E of the 56th decided to volunteer for the mission. They hiked to Drewry's Bluff, reported to Read, and spent a quiet night at the fort.

The next morning after breakfast, Privates Jones and Fraser fell in line with about 120 other men. Most of them were sailors; 13 of them were Marines. Read issued every man a short, heavy, navy cutlass and a single-shot, flintlock pistol. A few minutes later four wagons drove up. According to Private Jones, they were "coupled at great length" and each carried a long boat with two or more heavy poles on each side. A torpedo was fastened to the end of every pole.

Captain Reid explained that he planned to take the expedition around Grant's entire army to a place called Burwell's Bay. Under cover of night, the men would board and capture one of the many Federal transport ships lying at anchor. They would then steam up the James River and take by surprise the first gunboat they met. Armed with the gunboat and their torpedoes, they could easily sink the entire Yankee fleet. Captain Read assured everyone that both General Lee and President Davis knew about the plan and approved it. Private Jones was shocked by the seafaring nature of the mission. He was a foot soldier in the army and had a horror of water over three feet deep, but it was too late to turn back. He and Fraser decided to go along with the plan and to make the best of a bad bargain.

The little band left Drewry's Bluff on the morning of February 3. The weather was bad, and it was hard to move the wagons in the mud, but the men made good progress nevertheless. At noon on the 7th, they were many miles behind the Union lines. As they stopped to get some forage for the horses, a courier galloped up to them. The messenger's horse had run so hard that he reeled from side to side like a drunken man. The exhausted rider handed Captain Read a dispatch from General Lee. The message said that after the expedition left Drewry's Bluff, a Confederate naval officer deserted to the enemy and told the Yankees the whole plan. For the next two days, the band hid in a swamp while Captain Read and a guide scouted ahead.

When Read returned, he reported that the Yankees were waiting to ambush the group with a large force of infantry, artillery, and cavalry. Had it not been for the messenger's timely arrival, the entire expedition would have been wiped out. Privates Jones and Fraser returned to the ranks of the 56th Virginia on the night of February 13. They were tired, hungry, and cold, but at least they were on dry land. Now they knew why the old veterans of the regiment did not volunteer for anything, and it is highly unlikely that they ever volunteered for any more secret missions.

While Privates Jones and Fraser of the 56th Virginia were trying their hands at marine warfare, General Grant was tightening his noose around Petersburg. Grant kept extending his line westward along a 35 mile front until it reached a creek called Hatcher's Run. Lee was forced to extend his line to counter Grant. The Confederate line was stretched so thin that it was ready to break everywhere. During the last few days of March, Grant ordered Sheridan's cavalry, Andrew A. Humphrey's Second Corps of infantry, and Gouverneur K. Warren's Fifth Corps of infantry to sidle around the Confederate right and seize the village of Five Forks. Five Forks was critical because it was dangerously close to Lee's railroad line. If the Yankees took the village, they could block Lee's withdrawal from Petersburg.

On March 29 Lee pulled Pickett's division out of the Howlett Line in the pouring rain and rushed it to Five Forks with orders to hold the village no matter what happened. The White Oak Road ran eastward from Five Forks to Hatcher's Run. On the night of March 30, the men of the 56th Virginia and the other regiments of Hunton's Brigade found themselves in deep breastworks in the woods along the White Oak Road. They were hungry, muddy, and soaked to the skin. Their orders were to sleep with their muskets in their hands.

The next morning Hunton's troops climbed out of the breastworks. They deployed in the woods beside the White Oak Road near Hatcher's Run with Martin L Stansel's Alabama brigade and Samuel McGowan's South Carolina brigade. General Lee himself was there in the woods with them. "Marse Robert" was mounted on his favorite horse Traveller and watched as they got into position. The three small brigades had just formed a line of battle when the bluecoat infantry of Romeyn B. Ayres's Second Division, Warren's Fifth Corps advanced on them and started to drive in the skirmishers in front of them. Samuel W. Crawford's Third Division was right behind Ayres.

A young lieutenant in Hunton's Brigade could not restrain himself. He drew his sword, waved it in the air, and yelled, "Follow me, boys." The Confederates were spoiling for a fight. They hollered the rebel yell and went at the Yankees on the run.

When they got close to the Union line, they opened fire. They kept running and struck the 5th, 140th, and 146th New

York regiments of Ayres's division on the left flank. The New Yorkers broke, turned, and ran back into Crawford's line behind them. Crawford's men could not hold their formation with their companions in Ayres's division fleeing headlong through their ranks, so they broke and ran for the rear too.

There was no order, it was every man for himself. The Confederates yelled like devils and kept coming. They struck a third Union battle line in the woods. The third line was also part of Crawford's division; it gave way, turned, and fled.

As the Confederates pursued the fleeing bluecoats, a minie ball struck General Hunton's adjutant, Captain E. C. Fitzhugh, in the forehead and knocked him to the ground. Colonel Green of the 56th Virginia glanced at Fitzhugh as he went down and said, "Poor Fitz. Forward, boys."

The butternut soldiers left Captain Fitzhugh behind and pushed on, but a few minutes later they were happily surprised when Fitzhugh caught up with them. The captain had only been stunned by the bullet. He was able to pick himself up and continue the charge.

By this time the Confederates had three separate Union lines of battle on the run. They chased them more than a mile to the bank of a creek called Gravelly Run. The butternut troops burst out of the woods and charged right up to the edge of the creek. They were flushed with success, but they were widely scattered and out of breath. Union General Charles Griffin's First Division was waiting for them on the opposite side of the creek.

General Joshua L Chamberlain, a fine soldier, commanded the First Brigade of Griffin's division. Chamberlain had skillfully massed his infantry and unlimbered two batteries of artillery opposite the very spot where the Confederates came out of the woods. Every Union cannon and musket that could be brought to bear suddenly erupted in flame.

The exhausted Confederates recoiled from the storm of lead and iron that burst upon them. Before the butternuts could reform their lines, the 198th Pennsylvania Regiment and the 185th New York Regiment of Chamberlain's Brigade splashed across Gravelly Run with the regiments of Edgar M.

Gregory and Joshua J. Barlett's Brigades close behind. The routed men of Crawford's and Ayres's divisions regrouped and rallied behind Griffin's division.

The Confederates fell back slowly at first, but they were so outnumbered and hard pressed that they began to run back over the same ground they had Just charged across. When the soldiers of Hunton's Brigade reached some shallow rifle pits that Ayres's bluecoats had hastily thrown up earlier in the day, they decided to stand and fight.

The men of the 56th Virginia did not have time to do any digging. They were still panting for breath as they tore paper from cartridges with their teeth and rammed rifle balls down the muzzles of their muskets.

The rifle pits were at the edge of a patch of woods. There was an open field in front of them with more woods on both sides.

General Chamberlain's first line of bluecoats soon reached the open field. Chamberlain took in the situation at a glance and made a snap decision. He asked Gregory's Brigade to move through the woods on the right side of the field and to fire on Hunton's men from the flank while his own brigade made a frontal dash straight across the field.

Gregory's men reached their objective quickly and opened fire; Chamberlain's bluecoats cheered and started forward. Hunton ordered his Virginians to hold their fire. When the Yankees got close, Hunton's men pulled their triggers. Hunton described what happened next:

"The Federal line wavered under the fire very decidedly, and a portion of it broke and ran. The balance of the line reformed under our fire, advanced, and drove us back. I thought it was one of the most gallant things I had seen... if we had not retired in haste all of us would have been captured."

The 56th Virginia did not fall back with the rest of the brigade, but stood its ground. The bluecoats kept coming with their officers leading out in front and their flags flying. They jumped into the rifle pits and fought hand to hand against the men of the 56th Virginia. There was a wild melee of clubbed muskets, clanging metal, and grappling men. According to Major E. M. Woodward of the 198th Pennsylvania, it was "...a confused struggle of firing, thrusting, cutting." The 56th Virginia was surrounded and cut off.

Private Augustus Zelber of Company D, 198th Pennsylvania seized the flag of the 56th Virginia. He handed it to General Chamberlain himself while men from both armies still struck each other with wood, steel, and fists and wrestled around them. Chamberlain handed the flag right back; he told Zelber to keep it and take the credit he deserved.

The bluecoats captured nearly the entire 56th Virginia Regiment — about 135 officers and men. The other regiments of Hunton's Brigade escaped and made their way back safely to their starting point, the deep trenches on the White Oak Road near Hatcher's Run where General Lee waited for them.

Only a handful of men in the 56th got away; the regiment almost ceased to exist as a unit. At 3:40 p.m. General Warren sent a dispatch to General Alexander S. Webb:

"We have driven the enemy, I think, into his breast-works. The prisoners report General Lee here to-day, and also that their breast-works are filled with troops. We have prisoners from a portion of Pickett's and Johnson's Divisions. General Chamberlain's brigade acted with much gallantry in this advance, capturing nearly the entire Fifty-sixth Virginia Regiment with its flag."

The next day the Yankees captured Five Forks. On the night of April 2, General Lee had no choice but to pull the Army of Northern Virginia out of the trenches at Petersburg and to start on a zig-zag course westward in an effort to save his men.

The Confederate army must have felt like a mortally wounded fox with a pack of fresh and healthy, but hungry, Union hounds snarling and snapping at his hind legs every step of the way.

The few men in the 56th Virginia who escaped capture at Hatcher's Run joined other regiments whenever and wherever they could and fought to the end. One or two men of the 56th were killed, wounded, or captured at every encounter between Hatcher's Run and Appomattox. They became casualties or prisoners at Sutherland Station, Amelia Court House, Harper's Farm, Rice's Station, Sayler's Creek, Burkeville, and High Bridge.

On the morning of April 12, 1865, when Lee's army stacked arms for the last time on the rain-soaked ground of Appomattox Court House, there were only 32 officers and men of the 56th Virginia left.

One Captain, two Lieutenants, one first sergeant, one quartermaster sergeant, one commissary sergeant, and twenty-five privates surrendered and accepted paroles.

Alexander L. P. Williams, the gallant color bearer who was shot in the thigh at Gettysburg in Pickett's charge, was one of the Lieutenants. He was promoted after Gettysburg and was present for duty at Appomattox in spite of his terrible wound. Captain John W. Jones of Company G, a junior officer, commanded the regiment.

The bluecoats stood at attention at order arms in ranks beside the lane and watched the gaunt and ragged scarecrows of Lee's army march proudly and tearfully past.

A bugle sounded, and a Union General ordered the Federals to shift from order arms to carry arms in a salute to their former enemies. The general was Joshua L. Chamberlain, the same man whose brigade had captured the 56th Virginia and its flag at Hatcher's Run 12 days before.

A month later, Major John McPhail of the 56th Virginia was still a prisoner of war. He was captured at Hatcher's Run and wrote to his aunt from prison while he was waiting for his parole. He spoke for every man in the 56th Virginia when he said"

"I have a heart for any fate that can possibly befall me... I am at the end of my tether."

Chapter 12

Prisoners of War

"It is enough to kill the old
and make the young old."

NOTE: Since 1990, author Bill Young has presented a sequel to his first person impression in costume of First Lieutenant George W. Finley and his account of Pickett's Charge at Gettysburg.

The sequel is called "Prisoners of War" and follows Finley from his capture at the stone wall on Cemetery Ridge at Gettysburg to his confinement in six Federal prisons and to his entry into the Presbyterian ministry after the War.

In 1901, Finley wrote an account of prison life for the magazine of the Union Theological Seminary of Virginia, and the sequel is based on the account plus the accounts of several of Finley's fellow prisoners. The story is true, and much of it is in Finley's own words, the words of his comrades, and some educated guesses by Young.

When Young puts on his black, beaver top hat, white shirt, black and gray striped tie, black vest, black and gray striped trousers, black frock coat, black high top shoes, and gray gloves, winds up his gold pocket watch with the initials G.W.F., and picks up his black walking stick with the pewter head of John Bull on the top, he becomes Finley.

The first time Young portrayed Finley, his teenage son took one look at him, shook his head, and said sadly, "Dad, one of these days you're going to become Finley and never come back."

Young replied: "Son, the inscription on Finley's gravestone says: 'George W. Finley, D.D., Pastor of Tinkling Spring Church from February, 1892 to April, 1908. Devoted husband and father, faithful minister, gallant Confederate soldier. This monument is erected as a tribute of love and admiration by his family, congregation, friends, and comrades.' I could do a lot worse than become the Rev. Finley and never come back." Here is Lt. Finley's story of prison life as Young tells it:

Let us pray: Lord, I asked you for strength that I might achieve. I was made weak that I might learn humbly to obey. I asked for health that I might do greater things. I was given infirmity that I might do better things. I asked for riches that I might be happy. I was given poverty that I might be wise. I asked for power that I might have the praise of men. I was given weakness that I might feel the need of God. I asked for all things that I might enjoy life. I was given life that I might enjoy all things. I got nothing that I asked for, but everything I had hoped for. Almost despite myself, my unspoken prayers were answered. I am, among all men, most richly blessed. Amen.

My name is George W. Finley. I am a Confederate veteran who served as a First Lieutenant in the 56th Virginia Infantry Regiment of the Army of Northern Virginia. The last time we were together, I told you that my wife Margaret and I have taught our 14 children to recite some of the basics by heart. One of the basics was the 56th Virginia's favorite marching song called "Goober Peas." As the boys of the regiment in rags of butternut and gray loped down the road like a pack of wolves, the song fairly rolled off their tongues. The boys weren't much to look at, but they had a spring in their step and their fighting spirit was a mile high.

The boys of the regiment sang a lot of songs during the war. Some of them were light-hearted, and some were melancholy. One of the light-hearted ones went like this:

> *A farmer came to camp one day with milk and eggs to sell,*
> *Upon a mule that oft would stray to where no one could tell.*
> *The farmer, tired of his tramp, for hours was made a fool,*
> *For everyone he met would holler, "Hey mister! Here's your mule!"*
> *Come on, come on, come on old man, and don't be made a fool,*
> *By everyone you meet in camp With "Hey mister! Here's your mule!"*

The boys loved to laugh. Whenever they saw a man wearing a big hat, they would shout, "Hey Mister! Come on out from under that hat! We know you're in there! We can see your legs sticking out!"

But a steady diet of rain, cold, mud, home sickness, exhaustion, disease, bleeding, fighting, and dying were a serious business, so the boys sang sad songs too. One of them went like this:

> *Why am I so weak and weary, fever on my heated breath?*
> *All around to me seems darkness. Tell me, comrades, is this death?*
> *Ah, how well I know your answer. To my fate I meekly bow,*
> *If you'll only tell me truly, who will care for Mother now*
> *Soon with angels I'll be marching with bright laurels on my brow,*
> *If you'll only tell me truly, who will care for Mother now?*

The story I am going to tell you is not a pretty one, but it does have a happy ending. It begins on the afternoon of July 3, 1863 on the battle field of Gettysburg. I was but one of the thousands of men of Pickett's Division who on that fateful day marched into the valley of the shadow of death, into the mouths of the Union guns on Cemetery Ridge, and straight into the jaws of Hell itself. I was among the handful of men still standing at the end of the charge who jumped the stone wall on the ridge and fought hand to hand with the Yankees.

There were countless thousands of bluecoats. They surrounded and overwhelmed us. Our situation was hopeless, so the few of us who were left laid down our arms and surrendered. The Yankees wasted no time in leading us off the field. They marched us directly to Fort McHenry in Maryland where they herded us into holding pens like cattle.

We stayed in the holding pens for a few weeks, and then the Yankees crammed us into train cars and took us to the Union prison at Johnson's Island in Sandusky Bay, Ohio.

The Ohio Home Guards watched the prisoners. Now those of you who are old soldiers know that when soldiers meet the enemy on the battlefield, they develop a grudging respect for him and treat him accordingly. For instance, just before the Battle of Fredericksburg, the Confederate pickets were on one side of the Rappahannock River, and the Union pickets were on the other. When they thought the officers weren't looking, the men on both sides carved little boats of bark, fitted them with paper sails, and pushed them across the river to the other side. Each Confederate boat contained a Southern newspaper and a twist of tobacco. Each Union boat was filled with a Northern newspaper and a pinch of real coffee.

Of course, the pickets couldn't resist bantering back and forth. One day a Union soldier called across the river to his Confederate counterpart and said: "Hey Reb! You look mighty dirty and ragged over there! Is that all the clothes your army gives you?" The Confederate shot back: "We don't get dressed up when we're about to butcher hogs!" And believe me, a lot of butchering went on once the battle started.

I'm told that during the siege of Petersburg the opposing trench lines came ever closer to one another. They were so near to each other in some places that the soldiers on each side could call across to the other side. Sometimes before the Yanks opened fired they would yell: "Down, Reb!" Our boys always returned the favor and would shout: "Down, Yank!" before they returned the fire. That way no one got hurt.

Every few days that winter the men would declare an informal truce. A Confederate and a Union soldier would climb out of their trenches, walk into the no man's land in between, chop down the same tree, cut the trunk into logs, split the logs, and divide the firewood into two equal piles. The man in the trenches would hold their fire until both men reached the safety of their lines with their wood.

But the Ohio Home Guards had never gone into battle. They had never "seen the elephant" as we called a fight, so they gave us unusually rough treatment. I was on Johnson's Island for nine months, and I was happy when the Yankees moved me to Point Lookout, Maryland.

Point Lookout was a tent city with a population of about 23,000 prisoners. It didn't take me long to realize that the Yankee guards at Point Lookout were worse than the guards at Johnson's Island. I had gone out of the frying pan and into the fire! The Point Lookout bluecoats constantly cursed us, insulted us, and fired their muskets into us without the slightest provocation. We were helpless. We got no relief until we sent word to the camp commander that we could not stand such treatment any longer. If it did not stop, we were going to break out, attack our guards with our bare hands, and kill or be killed.

After that, things got a bit better, but I was glad when after a few months the Yankees moved me again. This time they sent me to Fort Delaware, and once again it was a step down. Fort Delaware was the dirtiest, filthiest, and most unhealthy prison I have ever seen, and I've been in six. The captain of the guard at the fort was cruel and arrogant. He gave us a steady diet of bad water and scant rations, carelessly prepared, and issued at constant risk of being shot by some rash sentinel. The Yankees made life very trying for us captives.

It was at Fort Delaware that I discovered the secret to survival in prison. The key to survival lies within you. You must reach way down deep inside of yourself and find the strength, the courage, and the determination to go on. You must be like the British bulldog. When a British bulldog bites you in the pants leg, he clamps his teeth shut so hard that he won't let go. You can hit him with a stick and knock him unconscious, but he will still hang on to your trousers with his teeth. I made up my mind that I was going to be like the British bulldog and hang on by my teeth.

Every day I said to myself the little poem that the Cavalier poet, Richard Lovelace, wrote to his sweetheart Althea from prison:

> *Stone walls do not a prison make nor iron bars a cage.*
> *Minds innocent and quiet take that for an hermitage.*
> *If I have freedom in my love and in my soul am free,*
> *Angels alone that soar above enjoy such liberty.*

In late August, 1864 the Yankees moved me again. This time they loaded 600 Confederate officers, including me, onto an ancient, side-wheeler steamboat called "The Crescent City" and took us to the prison on Morris Island in Charleston Harbor, South Carolina.

I remember that slow and torturous trip in every terrible detail. The passage was horrible. My bunk, a single one, was way below deck. It was just under the propeller shaft and against the engine room of the steamer. I could not sit up in it nor lie down without squeezing myself under the revolving iron shaft, and the boiler on the other side of the wall was so hot that I could not bear my hand upon the metal partition. There in almost pitch black darkness, without any clothing, and drenched in my own perspiration, I had to remain for several days and nights. Our daily food ration was a few crackers with a bit of salt beef or bacon and the water that was condensed from the ocean as we steamed along.

In early September, the Yankees prodded us ashore at the point of the bayonet and pushed us into a wooden stockade that rose from the sandy beach on the island. Nearly all of the prisoners carried gray, wool blankets that they had captured on the battlefield. The blankets were stamped "U.S." in large, black block letters.

As each man passed through the gate and into the stockade, a Yankee guard wrenched his blanket from him. The guard said, "These blankets are the property of the United States. You rebels have been fighting against the United States. You have no right to them." As soon as all prisoners were inside, the guard threw the blankets into a big pile and set fire to them.

We lived in tents pitched on the sand within the stockade. The enclosure was directly in front of and between two Union heavy gun batteries called Battery Gregg and Battery Wagner.

All day long and all night long the guns fired their shells towards Fort Sumpter, Sullivan's Island, the City of Charleston, and other points around Charleston Harbor.

The Confederate guns on the other side of the harbor always returned the fire, so we were kept under the constant fire of our own guns. Luckily for us, the Confederate gunners had the range, and they fired their guns so that the shells arced over our heads and dropped on the Yankees behind us.

I was not a minister then, but the men came to me in prison and said, "George, every day in prison is like every other, and we don't want that. We want to have Sunday morning worship services and Wednesday night prayer meetings, and we want you to be our pastor."

I protested and said, "But I'm not a minister." They replied, "You're all we've got," so what could I say but "yes?" I had no choice.

I had no religious training whatsoever, but I turned to God in prison to help me get through each day. I became the de facto chaplain to my fellow prisoners and even conducted countless funeral services before I was released.

I soon promised the Lord that if I survived the war I would become an ordained Presbyterian minister and serve Him for the rest of my days. And it has come to pass. Truly

doth the Lord move in mysterious ways, His wonders to perform.
    I will never forget the first Sunday morning that a group of us held a worship service. We were sitting in a big semi-circle on the sand in front of the tents. We had just finished reciting the 23rd Psalm together. Please say it with me now:

The Lord is my shepherd, I shall not want.
He maketh me to lie down in green pastures.
He leadeth me beside the still waters.
He restoreth my soul.
He leadeth me in the paths of righteousness
for his name's sake.
Yea, though I walk through the valley of the shadow of death,
I will fear no evil, for Thou art with me.
Thy rod and thy staff they comfort me.
Thou preparest a table before me in the presence of mine enemies.
Thou anoinest my head with oil. My cup runneth over.
Surely goodness and mercy shall follow me all the days of
  my life,
And I will dwell in the house of the Lord forever.

    No sooner had we said the final word "forever," when there was a flash of bright light on the other side of the harbor followed by a billowing cloud of black powder smoke and a loud BOOM! A Confederate mortar had fired a giant shell in our direction. It darted into the heavens like a tiny, black speck, and when it reached its zenith it turned and rolled and descended upon us. I stared at it in horror, because I realized that it was going to fall short. It was going to land squarely in our midst, and there was no place to run, no place to go, no place to hide.
    They say that your whole life flashes before you at a time like that. Mine did. I saw the white frame house in Clarksville where I grew up with the big oak tree in the yard and the rope swing with the board seat. I saw my Mother's

sweet smile and heard my Father's stern voice. I saw the little, red school house with my desk in the third row and my slate on top of it with my sums done on it in white chalk. I saw the scowl on the face of the bank manager when I reported for work the first day. I saw my bride Margaret coming down the aisle of the church in her long, white wedding dress. I held my first born baby girl in my arms and heard her first cry.

I took my eyes off the incoming shell, but I could still hear it scream as it came down. The piercing sound grew louder and louder. I closed my eyes and said a quick, little prayer, "Here am I, Lord. Take me."

There was a loud THUMP as the shell struck the ground nearby, and I could feel the earth shake. I kept my eyes tightly shut as I waited for the explosion. I waited…and I waited…and I waited…"

I opened one eye. Then I opened the other eye. There was the mortar shell buried nose down in the sand not 15 feet away. My comrades and I were half buried in the sand. No one said a word. No one moved. The shell did not explode. It must have had a defective fuse. It was a miracle! Thank God for Confederate ordinance! I know that you will believe me when I tell you that we continued our worship service that morning with renewed enthusiasm.

The daily food ration at Morris Island was four small crackers and a cup of bean soup. The Union colonel in charge of the stockade boasted that he gave his prisoners an ample ration of fresh meat every day because the soup had plenty of worms in it. It was hard to make four crackers last for three meals when the stomach craved more than four crackers for one meal. We had to find a way to get our minds off of our stomachs and off of the incoming and outgoing artillery shells that crisscrossed over the stockade at all hours of the day and night.

Many of my fellow prisoners had some kind of expert knowledge that they were willing to share with their comrades, so somebody hit upon the idea of teaching school. What a joy the classes were! My favorites were the medical school, the law school, and the Bible school. In the medical school we learned the care and treatment of gunshot wounds and how to make a tourniquet out of a pair of suspenders. We found out that the Yankee doctors had sutures made from the finest silk. Since our doctors had no silk, they made do by boiling the long hairs from a horse's tail. The result was a suture that was as soft and pliable as silk but produced a lower infection rate than silk. Boiling the hairs in water cleansed and purified them in some way.

In the law school we studied the difference between an action at law and a suit in equity. We learned the fundamental maxims of equity like "He who comes into equity must come with clean hands" and "He who seeks equity must do equity." We learned the two Latin phrases that are the foundation of the law of agency: " Qui facit per alium, facit per se – What a man does through another, he does himself" and "Respondeat superior – The master shall answer." We studied the Rule against Perpetuities that limits the time in which title to real property must vest, although I must confess that I never really understood it.

We all loved to tell and hear the old, familiar Bible stories like Moses in the bulrushes, Daniel in the lions' den, Joshua and the Battle of Jericho, David and Goliath, and Sampson and Delilah.

One of the men told us the story of the boy Samuel who went to live in the temple and study under Eli, the old chief priest. One night after everyone had gone to bed, Samuel heard a voice call to him "Samuel. Samuel." Samuel thought it was Eli calling, so he went down to Eli's room and said, "Here am I." Eli was irritated and said, "I did not call thee. Go back to bed." Samuel went back to his room, but no sooner had he lain down when he heard the voice again, "Samuel. Samuel." Samuel was certain it was Eli, so he went down to Eli's room again and said, "Here am I."

Old Eli was even more irritated this time, and he said impatiently, "Go back to bed. I did not call thee." Samuel went back to his room, but the voice called to him a third time." It sounded like Eli. Surely it was Eli. The little boy went to Eli's room a third time and said, "Here am I." Eli was angry now, and he started to scold the child, and then it dawned on him that Samuel was hearing the voice of God. Eli said to the boy, "The next time thou hearest the voice, say 'Speak Lord, for thy servant heareth.'"

Another man told the story of King Belshazzar of Babylon who was sitting at the head of the table during the great banquet the night before the city fell. The king was dressed in his finest robes of purple and gold, eating from gold plates, and drinking from jeweled goblets when a hand appeared and wrote these words on the wall: "Mene mene tekel upharsin." None of the king's astrologers or wise men could tell him what the words meant, but the captive Jewish boy Daniel could. Daniel said to the king, "The words mean, Thou hast been weighed in the balance, and thou hast been found wanting."

A third man reminded us of how Ruth showed so much love and loyalty when she said to her mother-in-law Naomi, "Whither thou goest, I will go, and whither thou lodgest, I will lodge, and thy people shall be my people, and thy God, my God."

I got to teach school myself. Before the war I studied English literature at Washington College which has since become Washington and Lee University. I taught the men "Gray's Elegy in a Country Churchyard" that begins with these lines:

"The curfew tolls the knell of parting day, the lowing herd winds slowly o'er the lea. The plowman homeward plods his weary way and leaves the world to darkness and to me."

I told them how the immortal bard, William Shakespeare, described his homeland, "This royal throne of kings, this sceptered isle, this sacred plot, this earth, this realm, this England, this precious stone set in a silver sea."

I taught them these lines by William Wordsworth: "The world is too much with us, late and soon. Getting and spending we lay waste our powers. Little we see in nature that is ours. For a cap and bells our lives we pay. Bubbles we buy with a whole life's taking. Tis heaven alone that is given away. Tis only God may be had for the asking."

My greatest challenge was to teach my comrades how to recite the prologue to Geoffrey Chaucer's Canterbury Tales" in Middle English. It begins like this:

"Whan that Aprille with his shoures soote, the droghte of March hath perced to the roote..." but I stopped it short with these words: "Bifil that in that seson on a day, in Southwerk at the Tabard as I lay, redy to wenden on my pilgrymage to Caunterbury with full devour corage, at nyght was come into that hostelrye wel nyne and twenty in a compaignye of sondry folk, by aventure yfalle in felaweshipe and pilgrimes were they alle, that toward Caunterbury wolden ryde."

Can you imagine what it was like trying to teach 600 Confederate officers to recite Chaucer's Canterbury Tales in Middle English? They were convinced that I had gone over to the enemy and that it was another Yankee plot! But at least it took our minds off of our stomachs and the artillery shells that screamed overhead day and night.

We tried to tunnel out of the stockade twice, but both escape attempts failed. The first tunnel was about half finished when a sudden storm came up like storms do on the Carolina coast. It flooded the tunnel and caused it to cave in. We promptly started another tunnel, but a traitor in our midst betrayed us to the Federals. On November 19, 1864 the Yankees moved me again. This time they sent half of us by ship to the prison at Hilton Head, South Carolina. From that day on, those of us who were held under the fire of our own guns on Morris Island have been known as "The Immortal 600." I must say that I would like to be remembered for almost anything else.

We were at sea for what seemed like an eternity before the ship finally anchored at Hilton Head. Our Yankee guards kept us below deck in the hold of the ship for another day while sharks circled our floating prison. Then our captors escorted us ashore at bayonet point. In this camp, we lived in frame buildings about 90 feet long and 30 feet wide. There were 100 men to a building. There were no windows. Our light came from gas jet lamps fixed to the walls that burned continuously. Our bunks were made of pine poles. There was one blanket for every four men. Our guards were so cruel that we thought we were living over a powder keg that was liable to explode at any moment.

The daily food ration was five ounces of corn meal and a half pint of brackish water. The meal came from barrels that bore stencil marks showing that the crumbly corn was kiln dried in upstate New York in 1861. It was issued to us in the winter of '64-'65. It was so moldy, rotten, and swarming with vermin that if you set your daily handful down on the table, it would get up and crawl away.

Every now and then the Yankees gave us some pickles to eat, but they only sharpened the appetites that the corn meal could not satisfy, and it seemed to us that the main purpose of the pickles was to eat away the wooden staves of the barrels that were our only source of fuel. You can't live on five ounces of corn meal a day and a few pickles every now and then, so we supplemented our diet by catching wharf rats, searing them over the flames of the gas lamps, and devouring them. After all the rats were gone, we started on the cats.

We ate 32 cats that winter, and we know the exact number because Lieutenant Francis C. Barnes of Company C of my regiment made a mark with a sharp stone on the side of his bunk every time we ate a cat. I remember the last cat well. He was a great, big, old, gray bobbed-tailed fellow. Cats are intuitive creatures, and this cat suspected that if we got our hands on him, he was going into the cooking pot. Try to picture 100 grown men creeping around the building for hours and coaxing in a soft, low, deep voice, "Here kitty, kitty, kitty." We finally caught him, and he went straight into the pot. He tasted so good, I can taste him yet.

The winter of '64-65 was unusually cold. We had scant clothing, little covering, and no fires. Water froze in our bunks.

It was impossible to sleep on the hard planks of our berths. No one who heard it can ever forget the doleful sound of the tramp, tramp, tramp of the men who walked around the table in the center of the room all night long to keep from freezing to death.

And no one who saw it can fail to remember how strong, grown men dropped down on their hands and knees like dogs and crawled over the dirty floor trying to find a single crumb that might have fallen from the table. Soon sickness grew worse and multiplied. Great, black splotches appeared over the body and limbs, and men failed rapidly and died.

Oh, I wish I knew how many hundreds of times I stood over a fresh mound of earth in the prison yard and said, "In my father's house are many mansions. If it were not so, I would have told you. I go to prepare a place for you."

I always closed every funeral service with a little poem that I learned at my mother's knee:

"A little bird am I, shut from the fields of air, and in my cage I sit and sing to him who placed me there. And though my wing is closely bound, my heart's at liberty. My prison walls cannot control the flight, the freedom, of my soul."

The captain of the guard at Hilton Head had a beautiful, well-fed, sleek, fat setter puppy named "Ponto" who came into the prison yard every morning to romp with the prisoners. At first, we dared not entertain any thought of eating Ponto, but with each passing day Ponto began to look better and better.

Captain Tom Perkins, 4th Tennessee Cavalry, was in our building. Perkins was quite a character. He was an escape artist and had broken out of prison three or four times. He once got off of a prison ship by stealing a saw from the ship's carpenter, cutting a hole in the stern of the ship, squeezing through the hole, and swimming to shore. The only trouble was, every time he got away, the Yankees caught him and brought him back.

One night Perkins couldn't stand the thought of Ponto any longer. He said, "Boys, tomorrow morning I'm going to catch Ponto, kill Ponto, cook Ponto, and serve 'Ponto stew' to all of us. Everybody's going to get a piece – share and share alike." We stayed awake all night thinking about how good Ponto was going to taste. The next morning, sure enough, Ponto bounded into the prison yard as usual. Now I told you that cats are intuitive creatures. Well, dogs are intuitive creatures too, because Ponto took one look into Perkins' eyes, and he saw something there that he had never seen before. Ponto turned tail, bolted through the gate, and we haven't seen him since.

The Yankees always separated the enlisted men from the officers in prison. There was a private in Company C of the 56th Virginia whose name was Freeman Jones. He joined the Confederate Army in early 1865 when he was scarcely 17 years old. The Yankees captured him at Hatcher's Run and sent him to the prison at Point Lookout, Maryland. Jones was captured on a Friday, and on Sunday morning two days later the iron gates of the prison slammed shut behind him. His heart ached as he thought about his family going to church at that moment at home in Brunswick County without him.

The first thing that Jones heard in prison was the latest "dispatch" of the prison grape vine. The second thing he learned was to take it with a grain of salt. Jones heard rumors every day. Somebody would say, "The latest dispatch is that 2,000 prisoners will be taken out and shot tomorrow morning." An hour or two later, somebody else would say, "No, that's not right. The very latest dispatch is that we will all be paroled tomorrow morning at 9:00 o'clock and released to go home." None of it was true.

Every time the prisoners saw Major Brady, the camp commander, they asked him when they were going to be released. He always gave them the same answer – "Next week." One day a prisoner said to him, "Major, how come every time we ask you when we're going home you always say next week? It never comes true." The Major replied sadly, "I have to tell you fellows a few lies just to keep you alive."

The drinking water at Point Lookout was simply horrid. There were five wells inside the prison compound, but only the water in two of the wells was drinkable. The water in the other three was impregnated with a copperas solution. It always had a brownish, greenish, film on the surface that was so thick you could take a stick and write your name in it. It did have a sweet taste, however, and the prisoners learned to bring it to a boil, add pieces of burned bread that they stole from the back of the cook house, and enjoy what they called a delicious "bread crust" coffee.

There were only two meals a day at Point Lookout – breakfast and dinner. Dinner was the main meal and was always served at noon. Dinner was always the same – a cup of so-called bean soup. Some of the men called it "so-called bean soup" because it almost never had any beans in it, but you seldom failed to find one or more well cooked flies in it. The rest of the men called it just plain "fly soup." There was no supper.

One day at noon Jones was in a group of 300 men who marched to the cook house for dinner. The burly Yankee cook was standing in the yard behind a kettle of so-called bean soup. The kettle was hanging from a tripod over a small fire. The cook was stirring the kettle with a sawed off oar. The men formed a long line and presented their tin cups to the cook one at a time to be filled. When it came Jones' turn, the Yankee cook took one look at him and said, "You don't fool me, Johnny Reb. You're trying to flank a cup of bean soup." "Flank a cup of soup" was prison slang for going through the food line twice.

Jones was innocent. He had not tried to flank a cup of soup. He looked the cook squarely in the eye and said, "Sir, you accuse me of stealing your bean soup. It is not true."

The cook put down his oar, came around the kettle, thrust his face down into Jones' face and said, "It is true, Johnny. And I gotcha. I gotcha."

There was an agonizing silence. Three hundred men started at Jones and the cook. It looked like a Mexican standoff. At that moment, a grizzled old soldier from North Carolina walked up and stood beside Jones. "Stand your hand, Jones," the old soldier said. "I am here. I will back you. Throw the cup of soup in his damned face!" Jones didn't think that was such a good idea. The cook said again, "I gotcha, Johnny Reb. I gotcha." Then the old Tar Heel said to the cook, "Yeah, you got him, and a hellova git you got!"

The Carolinian went on, "You have got hold of the wrong man, my friend. You had better let him alone! Right boys?" YEEEEEEEEEEAAAAAAAAAAH! Three hundred men screamed the rebel yell. They beat their cups on the sides of trees, stomped their feet, and chanted in unison, "Turn him loose! Turn him loose! Turn him loose!"

The Yankee cook must have believed like Shakespeare's Falstaff that "the better part of valor is discretion," because he hurried back to his kettle and filled the cup of the next man in line. Jones walked away from the cook house and heaved a sigh of relief. He would not have to wear a sign with the word "THIEF" painted on it in large, red letters around his neck for 10 days after all.

A few days later, a rumor of the prison grape vine finally turned into truth. Major Brady rode through the prison compound on horseback and announced, "All boys under 18 years of age report to the front gate to be sent home." Jones was instantly sick. He had just turned 18. To make matters worse, he was over six feet tall and had grown a long, full beard. He ran to his tent, shaved as closely as he possibly could, ran down to the front gate, and stood in the line with a slump so he wouldn't look so tall. Then his conscience got the best of him. Jones was a Southerner, and a true Southerner is a man of honor. The enemy can take almost everything away from you, but he cannot take away your honor.

Jones got out of line, walked over to Major Brady, looked up at him, and said, "Major, I have just turned 18, and I sure would be glad to go home with the boys."

Now I'll give the devil his due. Major Brady took pity on Jones and said, "Get back in line, Jones, and go home." Years later, Jones said, "I bade adieu to Point Lookout, and I only hope I may never have to look out from that point again."

Major John McPhail of the 56th Virginia was captured at Hatcher's Run on March 31, 1865. He was first a prisoner in the Old Capitol Prison in Washington, D.C. and then at Johnson's Island. He did not gain his freedom until July 25, 1865, about three and a half months after the surrender at Appomattox. He did not leave behind an account of his days as a prisoner of war, but he expressed the essence of his life in captivity when he wrote to his aunt from prison on Johnson's Island and said,

"It is enough to kill the old and make the young old." Then, with a touch of pride and defiance and perhaps to

reassure her, he added, "...but you must not expect to see me very lean or my hair gray." And then he added, "I have a heart for any fate that can possibly befall me. I am at the end of my tether."

Many of the soldiers of the 56th did not survive prison. Private Charles Thomas, the volunteer who begged his wife Mary to send him "something to "ate" almost every time he wrote a letter home, was captured at Farmville on April 6, 1865. He died of pneumonia at Point Lookout. Private Sambo Short, the conscript who spent one of his first nights in the Confederate Army trying to get some sleep in a bowling alley, was captured at Gettysburg. The Yankees took Sambo to Fort Delaware. He got so sick he couldn't stand up, so the Yankees moved him to a hospital in Chester, Pennsylvania. Sambo wrote his last letter to his wife "Babie" on August 18, 1863 from the hospital. He began by saying that the doctors and nurses were kind and attentive. He ended with these words, "If we never meet on this earth again, I hope we may meet in heaven." He died three weeks later.

Private John Holt, the country schoolmaster and volunteer soldier, wrote more than 100 letters to his wife Ellen while he was in the army. He never lost his enthusiasm for the Southern cause, and he laid down his life for it. He was but one of the many, many men of the 56th Virginia who fell in Pickett's charge at Gettysburg and were never seen or heard from again. He never lost his faith in God no matter what happened. Back in 1861, when he was still a raw recruit at the fairgrounds in Richmond, he expressed the wish of every true Christian soldier for the past 200 years:

"I hope and pray that these times will not last long, but that the time will soon come when the implements of war will be changed to implements of husbandry (swords will be beaten into ploughshares) and all of us can return to our peaceful and happy homes and be with those we love, to enjoy their smiles through the remainder of life's short journey, and when life's journey is ended, to die in the arms of the dear Redeemer, and be wafted to the shores of everlasting blessedness where there will be no more parting, no more sorrow, no more crying, but all will be peace and joy, world without end."

I was still in prison when General Lee surrendered at Appomattox Court House. The Yankees immediately put relentless pressure on us prisoners to take the oath of allegiance to the United States. All of the officers from Virginia promised one another that we would not take the oath. We called the act of swearing allegiance "swallowing the yellow dog." Every hour on the hour the Yankees told us, "If you rebels don't take the oath, you will rot and die in prison." We still refused. Then one day we got word that General Lee himself wanted us to take the oath, and if Marse Robert said it was the thing to do, it was the thing to do. So we swallowed our pride and the yellow dog, and the Yankees set us free.

When the iron gates of my prison swung open on May 14, 1865, and I was free for the first time in nearly two years, I found myself broken in health, broken in body, broken in fortune – but not broken in spirit. I was almost blind. I had to walk home. It was 111 miles, and it took me 17 days to get there. As I walked, I thought to myself, amid the gathering gloom of the closing days of our beloved Confederacy, with much suffering of mind and body, those of us in prison had to wait until the end came. And God sent us back to our wasted land and stricken people to take up the work for which he had been preparing us. Truly does he bring the blind by a way that they knew not.

When I got home, my wife Margaret - bless her heart - had saved the last chicken for me. Scrawniest ole chicken you every saw in your life, and it tasted so good I can taste it yet!

And do you know that within one day of my eating that chicken my eyesight was miraculously restored? I never knew a chicken had such curative powers!

I promptly enrolled in the Union Theological Seminary at Hampden-Sydney, Virginia, and two years later I became an ordained Presbyterian minister. I have served the Lord as best I can ever since that day. Truly doth the Lord move in mysterious ways, His wonders to perform.

Hundreds of years ago, an English poet said:

"Gather ye rosebuds while ye may, old time is still a-flying, and this same flower that smiles today, tomorrow will be dying. And at my back I always hear time's winged chariot hurrying near."

I have reached the age in life when I realize all too well that one of these days like...Marse Robert...I'm going to have to strike the tent and...like Old Jack... I'm going to have to cross over the river and rest in the shade of the trees.

But that will be a happy day for me, because I know in my heart – I can feel it to the depths of my soul – that when I cross that river I'm going to find lying in the shadows underneath those trees my old comrades in the 56th Virginia, and those rascals will probably be eating goober peas.

My favorite Yankee is General Joshua Chamberlain of Maine. When he was Colonel of the 20th Maine Infantry Regiment, he was shot through both hips during the siege of Petersburg and left on the field to die. When General Grant heard what had happened, he said, "Let's promote Chamberlain to Brigadier so he can die a General for the sake of his family." Chamberlain got up, walked off the field, and became Governor of Maine and president of Bowdoin College!

And then...when the ragged, rawboned remnants of the Army of Northern Virginia marched down the sunken road at Appomattox Court House to surrender, they had to pass through two lines of Union infantry standing on both sides of the road with their rifle-muskets at the ready.

It was General Joshua Chamberlain who commanded the Federal troops that day. And as the head of the Confederate column approached Chamberlain, he turned to his men and gave the order, "Shoulder arms!" – the parade ground salute.

General John B. Gordon of Georgia was at the head of the Confederate column on horseback. The instant Gordon heard Chamberlain's order, horse and rider wheeled around as one. Gordon rose up in the stirrups, drew his saber, dropped the tip to his boot toe, turned to his men, and gave the order, "Carry arms!" – the marching salute.

It was salute for salute, honor for honor, and those starving, suffering, scarecrows in butternut and gray marched to the end of the sunken road, stacked arms for the last time, furled their shot torn red battle flags, and stood silently in the ranks until they were dismissed.

Then they melted away into the woods and sobbed their broken hearts out. Listen to how General Chamberlain described his former enemies that day:

"Before us in proud humiliation stood the embodiment of manhood, men whom neither toils and sufferings nor the fact of death nor disaster nor hopelessness could bend from their resolve – standing before us now – thin, worn, and famished, but erect, and with eyes looking level into ours, waking memories that bound us together as no other bond."

A new nation was born that day – a nation so strong, so powerful, and so bound together that the words of one of the Southern generals still hold true today: "Give me Confederate infantry - and Union artillery - and I will conquer the world!"

And now, may the God of battle and the Lord of peace, raise you up on eagle's wings, bear you on the breath of dawn, make you shine like the sun, and hold you in the palm of his hand – both now and forever more.

I bid you farewell.

Chapter 13

Introduction to the Roster

The names of the 1,598 soldiers who served in the 56th Virginia infantry Regiment were obtained from the Complied Service Records, pension applications, county lists, company records, tombstone markers, UDC files, and family records.

All names that were not found in the Compiled Service Records are followed by PWL (Post War List).

Because of illegible handwriting, deterioration of documents, and the fact that some lists were compiled 50 or more years after the War Between the States, some soldiers may be listed twice and/or with alternate spellings. Such listing seems preferable to omitting anyone who might have served the Confederate cause. Hopefully, the readers of this book and future researchers will be able to shed some light on the correct names.

Each soldier's military service record is given first and in chronological order. If no rank is given, the soldier entered and left the service as a private. If only one rank is given, that Is the highest rank the soldier obtained. If two ranks are given, the first is the one the soldier had when he entered service, and the second is the rank with which he left.

Roll calls for the 56th Virginia are very incomplete. When a soldier is listed as "present" on all rolls that means that he was present for roll call during the periods of July through October 1861, July through December 1863, July 1, 1864, and May through August 1864.

Clothing receipt and power of attorney information is only given if the event was the last entry in the soldier's Compiled Service Record. Men who are shown as AWOL were often actually away sick or had gone home for a short time, and they had no intention of deserting.

The biographical information found on each soldier

follows his military record. The facts found in pension applications are grouped together to distinguish the soldiers "official" record from his "unofficial" one. The pension amounts that were granted were paid annually. No corrections in ages have been made. The inconsistencies are due to poor records, lack of true facts, or pure forgetfulness.

The location of all hospitals and cemeteries given is Richmond, Virginia unless otherwise stated. All towns, cities, and counties are located in Virginia unless another state is named.

The following dates have been omitted from the roster for the sake of brevity:

August 24, 1862 — men sent from Camp Morton to Vicksburg, Mississippi for exchange
June 27, 1862 Battle of Gaines's Mill
June 30, 1862 Battle of Frazier's Farm
August 30, 1862 Battle of Second Manassas
September 14, 1862 Battle of Boonsboro
September 15, 1862 Battle of Sharpsburg
December 13, 1862 Battle of Fredericksburg
July 1-3, 1863 Battle of Gettysburg
June 3, 1864 Battle of Cold Harbor
March 31, 1865 Battle of Hatcher's Run
April 9, 1865 Lee's surrender at Appomattox
September 27, 1931 Soldiers buried in Green Lawn Cemetery were reinterred as unknowns in lot 285, Section 32 Crown Hill Cemetery, Indianapolis, Indiana.

Many of the soldiers of the 56th Virginia were prisoners of war in one or more of the following locations:

Camp Chase, Columbus, Ohio; Camp Morton, Indianapolis, Indiana; David's Island, Pelham, New York; Elmira, New York Ft. Delaware, Delaware City, Delaware; Ft. McHenry,

Baltimore, Maryland; Hilton Head, South Carolina; Johnson's Island, Sandusky, Ohio; Newport News, Virginia; Old Capitol Prison, Washington, D.C.; Pt. Lookout, St. Mary's County, Maryland.

The following abbreviations are used in the roster:

Adj. – Adjutant
Asst. – Assistant
Arty. Artillery
AWL - Absent With Leave
AWOL - Absent Without Leave
b. – Born
Batt. - Battalion
c..- Circa, About
Capt. – Captain
Cav. - Cavalry
Cem. - Cemetery
Col. - Colonel
Co. - Company or County
Com. - Commandant
Comdg. - Commanding
Cpl. - Corporal
CSR - Compiled Service Records
d. - died
Enl. - enlisted
Enr. - enrolled
Gen. - General
Hosp. - hospital
Inf. - infantry
KIA - killed in action

Lt. - Lieutenant
m. - married
MWIA - mortally wounded in action
Maj. - Major
n.d.g. - no date given
POW - Prisoner of War
pwl - Post War List
Pvt. - Private
Q. M. - Quartermaster - Regimental
Rt. - Route
Sgt. - Sergeant
UCV - United Confederate Veteran
UVA - University of Virginia
VMI - Virginia Military institute
Wd. - wound
Wded. – wounded
WIA - wounded in action

Chapter 14

Roster - 56th Virginia Infantry Regiment, A thru E

ABERNATHY, EDWARD (EDMUND) R. enl. 4/18/63 age 19 in Nablett's Heavy Artillery (later called Coleman's) - discharged 9/3/63 due to severe cough; conscripted later in war and assigned Co. E, 56th Va.; admitted Chimborazo 2/25/65 with bronchitis - returned to duty 4/4/65; POW Farmville 4/6/65 - took oath and released from Pt. Lookout 6/22/65; brown hair. hazel eyes, light complexion. 5'101/2"; b. about 1844 to Benjamin and Ann E. Pritchett Abernathy; brother of Percival Smith and William Mormon Abernathy; farmer before and after war in Brunswick; m. Lucy Frances Delbridge 12/13/65 - 6 children; member Bethel Methodist Church: died 1879 - bur. Oakwood Cem. Lawrenceville, Brunswick Co.

ABERNATHY, JOHN E. enl. 6/10/61 Co. E in Brunswick, Pvt/Cpl., POW Ft. Donelson - sent from Camp Morton to Vicksburg for exchange; admitted Richmond hosp. 11/25/62 - returned to duty 11/29/62; WIA and POW Gettysburg - escaped from battlefield by crawling but captured 7/7/63 Greencastle, Penn. - admitted Satterlee USA Hosp. 7/12/63 with bullet wd. in loft groin -transferred USA Hosp., Chester, Penn. 7/14/63 - on roll of paroled and exchanged prisoners at Camp Lee 8/31/63, admitted Richmond hosp. 4/1/64 with pneumonia; present 5/8/64; POW Farmville 4/6/65 - took oath and released from Pt. Lookout 6/22/65; light complexion, grey eyes, brown heir, 5'8"; b. Brunswick 3/28/37 to Buckner and Nancy Lewis Abernathy; Edward R Abernethy's uncle. Grandfather Ruel Lewis was last surviving Revolutionary War veteran in Brunswick; farmer before and after war', m. Catherine R. Lewis 4/6/59 - no children; 12/19/66 married Harriet B. Lewis - age 21, (sister of deceased wife) - 5 children; member Bethel Methodist Church; applied for pension 6/8/1909 *age* 73 living Alberta, Brunswick, Co. - $24 approved; probably died c. 1910 - bur. family plot on his farm.

ABERNATHY, MARCELLUS T. (L.,) enl. 9/1/64 Co. E in Brunswick 5/10/62 exempted by Brunswick Co. authorities from service because of "cachexie' (generally poor health): last received clothes 10/13/64: farmer before and after war; m. Nancy R. Delbridge 12/21/70 *(her* sister married Edward R. Abernathy) - 1880 census - 3 children.

ABERNATHY, PERCIPHER (PERCIVAL) SMITH: enl. 2/16//64 Co. E at Chaffin's Farm; admitted Richmond hosp. 3/12/64 with catarrh - returned to duty 3/18/64; present 4/1/64; admitted Richmond hosp. 6/8/64 with acute diarrhea - returned to duty 6/23/64; last received clothes 12/28/64; b. about

1845 - Edward R and William Mormon's brother, nicknamed "Sing"; m. Rosa R. B. Elmore *1/16/67* - 7 children; member Bethel Methodist Church; attended Lawrenceville reunion of CV 1908; received Cross of Honor at unveiling of Confederate Monument Lawrenceville 6/19/1911; d. 1916 Walthall's Store - bur. on John E Abernathy's farm, Alberta.

ABERNATHY, WILLIAM MORMON enl. 7/10/61 Co. E in Brunswick; sick furlough with measles 8/31/61; POW Ft. Donelson - sent from Camp Morton to Vicksburg for exchange; admitted Richmond hosp. 11/25/62 - returned to duty 11/29/62; reenl. 6/10/63; present on all rolls 1/4/64; roll dated 8/31/64 listed as deserted since last muster - also listed on sick furlough with measles; last received clothes 12/3/64; b. Brunswick 1/24/39 - Edward R. and Percipher Smith Abernathy's brother, farmer: m, Martha A. Daniel *12/7/59* - 8 children; member Bethel Methodist Church; applied for pension 5/5/1906 age 66 living Lawrenceville, Brunswick Co, - disabled by pneumonia due to exposure during war - said left service when war over - $15 approved; attended Lawrenceville reunion of CV 1906; d. 2/22/1918 Brunswick

ABRAHAMS, (ABRAHAM) SAMUEL F. enl. 7/8/61 Co. D. in Buckingham; wagon master on rolls of 7/63, 9/1263,1/64, and 6/64. WIA Cold Harbor - right arm amputated at shoulder joint on battlefield - 60 day furlough from Chimborazo 6/4/64; 8/12/64 retirement approved - unfit for duties of soldier - Medical Board recommended he be farmer; 1864 living Hardwicksville; on Farmville hosp. register 2/21/65; applied for pension 4/91888 age 48 living Buckingham - $30 approved; notary public in 1902.

ABRAHAMS, (ABRAHAM) *WILLIAM* B. enl. 7/8/61 Co. D in Buckingham; present 9/10/61; reenl. 8/11/62.

ACORS, THOMAS; enl. 7/26/61 Co, F. In Louisa; present on all rolls 9/61 – 6/64; deserted after mustered for pay 6/64; present 7/8/64; last received clothes 12/28/64; paroled Staunton 5/1/65 age 21; dark complexion and hair, grey eyes, 5'10".

ACORS, *WILLIAM* HENRY: enl. 7/25/61 Co. F in Louisa; reenl. 3/20/64; present 4/1/64 and 6/64; sick Chimborazo 11/21/64 with internal fever - furloughed for 60 days 12/14/64; paroled Staunton 5/1/65 age 19; dark complexion, brown hair, hazel eyes, 5'8".

ACRE, (ACHREE) EDWARD H. (P. H. on some lists) enl. 8/6/61 Co. K at Mechanicsville; AWOL from 8/31/61 on roll dated 9/2/61; present 9/10/61; POW Ft Donelson; d. of pneumonia c. 4/6/62 Indianapolis, Ind; bur. Green Lawn Cem. - reinterred Crown Hill Cem.

ADAMS, I. (J.) L: Co.G - from Charlotte; received clothes *12/28/64;* Surrendered by Lee at Appomattox.

ADAMS, JOHN: enl. 8/6/61 Co. K in Mechanicsville, age 27, Pvt/Sgt; present on all rolls; POW Ft. Donelson - sent from Camp Morton to Vicksburg for exchange; promoted to 5th Sgt. 8/18/64; admitted to

Chimborazo 10/31/64 with fever - returned to duty 2/13/65; paroled 4/21/65; b. Hanover Co.; farmer; florid complexion, dark brown hair, 6'1".

ADAMS, *WILLIAM* T.: enl. 2/3/64 Co. K at Chaffin's Farm; admitted Chimborazo 6/17/64 with rubeola - returned to duty 7/11/64 - readmitted 8/26/64 - furloughed to Hanover Co. 9/2/64.

ADCOCK, EZEKIEL A. (H.): enl. 7/8/61 Co. D in Buckingham; present 7/8/61 – 10/61; d. from camp fever in Atlanta, Ga.; death clam filed by father James H. Adcock 6/16/62; 1850 census - age 8 - brother of Reuben T. Adcock

ADCOCK, HENRY: PWL.; Co. D.

ADCOCK, JOHN H.: enl. 7/10/61 Co, A. in Mecklenburg; 9/2/61 sick with measles; present on all rolls; surrendered by Lee at Appomattox.

ADCOCK, REUBEN T.: enl *7/8/61* Co. D in Buckingham; in Medical College of Va 8/13/61 - 8/24/61; present 9/1/61; reenl. 8/11/62 present 9/10/63; listed as unfit for duty for 30 days due to chronic dysentery and debility 12/9/63; AWOL 4/64 – 8/64; took oath 4/28/65; b. 1843; d, 1901 age 58 at 816 Venable Street, Richmond - bur. 10/16/1901 Oakwood Cem. - Soldier's Section, row 16, grave 51; wife Susan received pension of $68 1920's - when she died oldest daughter received half the pension.

ADCOCK, WALTER H.: enl. 7/8/61 Co. D in Buckingham; present 7/8/61 – 10/31/61; reenl. 8/11/62 at Fulton Hill; absent-sick on all rolls 9/63 – 8/64; b. 10/1839 In Va.; 1900 census showed living Slate River District of Buckingham Co. with wife Willie A. age 49 and mother-in-law Sarah A. Cobbs age 82, m. 12 years, no children, merchant, owned farm.

AGEE, JOHN R.: enr. as conscript 2/23/64; assigned Co. D 3/7/64; admitted Chimborazo 8/17/64 with diarrhea - furloughed for 40 days 9/2/64; b. 7/15/1819; resident Buckingham; m. Anne Elizabeth Jones;; 1850 census – farmer – age 31 – owned $800 in real estate, father of Robert Bentley Agee.

AGEE, ROBERT BENTLY: Co. D. - took father's place in army, POW Burkeville 4/6/65 - took oath and released from Pt. Lookout 6/23/65; b. Buckingham Co. 4/23/48; florid complexion, light hair, blue eyes. 5' 7¼"; m. Adalaide Steger - 4 children; when she died, m. Leila Holman Winfrey - 16 children; farmer and carpenter, signed pension application of David Stinson 6/1904; d. Caswell Co., N.C. 5/30/1915 - bur. Providence Baptist Church, Providence, N.C.

ALCUTT, DAVID GREEN; PWL; no co. given; d. of heart trouble; m. Mary M. Adams 3/18/88 Louisa, widow applied for pension 2/13/1928.

ALEXANDER, CHURCHWELL: enl. 1/5/64 Co. H, 8th Va. Inf.; transferred Co. K. 56th Va. in exchange for Alex Morse; present 5.10/64; received clothes 10/13/64; paroled 4/24/65; applied for pension 5/14/1900 age 70 living Old Church, Hanover Co. -partial disability due to thumb lost In battle and old age - $15 approved - made pension statement 6/16/1902 age 70.

ALEXANDER. EDMOND; enl. 8/661 Co, K in Mechanicsville; AWOL from 8/31/61; discharged 9/18/61 - got substitute Robert P. Richardson, age 17 and son of William H. Richardson.

ALEXANDER, JAMES: enl. 8/6/61 Co. K in Mechanicsville; present 8/6 –

8/31/61; discharged 9/9/61 age 30; b. Hanover; fanner: sallow complexion, dark hair, 6'.

ALLEN. H. C.: Co. C, paroled Burkeville Junction 4/14 – 4/17/65.

ALLEN, JOSEPH T.; enl 7/18/61 Co. I in Richmond, age 22; discharged 8/7/61 due to disease; planter; fair complexion, dark hair, blue eyes, 5' 8 1/2"; b. Cumberland Co.

ALLISON, A.G.; enl. 2/29/64 Co. K at Chaffin's Farm; present 4/1/64 and 7/8/64.

ALLISON, JOSEPH; Co. E, POW Burkeville 4/6/65 - sent to Pt. Lookout.

AMOS, JAMES P. (A); enl. 7/26/61 CO. F in Louisa; absent with measles 7/27-8/31/61, present on rolls 9/10/61; detached service as wagoner 2/18/62-3/31/62: present 9/12,/63 and 4/1/64; 5/12/64 detached service as teamster and harness maker, surrendered by Lee at Appomattox: applied for pension 3/31/1910 age 74 living in Orchid, Louisa Co. - failing heart and arteriosclerosis - exposure during war caused health problems; b. Louisa farmer. wrote note saying never AWOL and never corrected for failing to do duty - church member 50 years - always paid taxes - $25 approved; signed George P. Hambleton's pension application 1916.

AMOS, THOMAS; PWL, Co. F - from Louisa.

AMOS, WILLIAM BARTLETT: enl 7/8/61, Co. D in Buckingham; present 7/8/61-10/61; admitted Richmond hosp. 9/24/62 with debility - furloughed 15 days 11/13/62, in Scottsville hosp. 1/8/64; 9/24/63-2/22/64 in Chimborazo with pneumonia; POW near Howlett's House 8/25/64 - sent to Pt. Lookout - exchanged 3/65, admitted Chimborazo 3/16/65 with scurvy, furloughed 30 days 3/23/65; took oath Farmville 4/28/65.

ANDERSON, DAVID W. enl. 8/6/61 Co. K In Mechanicsville; sick furlough 8/6/61-831/61; present 9/10/61; POW Ft. Donelson - sent from Camp Morton to Vicksburg for exchange; discharged 8/24/63 age 46 because over 35; carpenter; b. Hanover; 5'10", dark complexion, grey eyes; d. 1893 Old Church, Hanover Co. of apoplexy; widow Mary W. Anderson applied for pension 4/16/1900- $25 approved.

ANDERSON, JOSEPH H. (E) enl 8/19/61 Co, K in Richmond, age 45; AWOL 8/28/61; absent on furlough 9.10/61; b. Hanover: painter; sallow complexion, dark hair, 5'10".

ANDERSON, William D.: pwl, conscript assigned Co. E; KIA Gettysburg; b. about 1843 in Brunswick to Carter R. and Mary B. Anderson; sister married John F. Sadler, Co. E.

ANDERSON, GEORGE, (JR); enl: 7/10/61 Co. E in Brunswick; 7/10/61-8/31/61 sick in Richmond; POW Ft. Donelson; admitted Chimborazo 8/1/62 - furloughed 9/18/62; d. Brunswick of typhoid fever 10/13/62 while on sick furlough; death claim filed 6/19/63 by only surviving relative, brother Richard H. Anderson - owed $84.76; b. about 1837 to George and Mourning Anderson; probably never married.

ANDREWS, C. N.: pwl. Co. B, member Armistead Camp No. 26, UCV Mecklenburg 1915.

ANDREWS, JAMES H.: enr, 3/7/64 as conscript and assigned to Co. B 3/16/64; present 4/8/64; POW Burkeville 4/6/65 - sick at Pt. Lookout - took path and released 6/3/65..

APPLE, FLAVIUS J.: enl.. 8/25/62 Co. A in Mecklenburg, Cpl.; probably previously served Co. K, 20th Va. Inf. and Co. C, 59th Va. Inf. - POW Rich Mt. 7/12/61, paroled 7/1761; present Co. K 56th Va. 9/12/63. WIA near

Howlett's House 6/16/64 - left arm amputated 6/17/64 at Chimborazo - furloughed 60 days 7/21/64; 1/2765 discharged from service age 25 - unfit due to amputation of arm; b. Clarksville, Mecklenburg Co. 2/39; farmer; fair complexion, grey eyes, dark hair, 5'11"; applied for pension 5/15/1899 age 60 living Mecklenburg - $30 approved; 1900 census - living Clarksville with wife Elizabeth age 50, rn. 31 years, 8 children at home, farmer renting his farm; d. 1900 - bur. Union Cern, Rt. 738, Halifax Co,

APPLE. LEWIS C.: enl. 7/25/62 Co. A in Richmond; KIA Gettysburg - Co. reported him as '"wounded, supposed mortally" and POW, but no Federal records concerning him.

ARCHER, BENJAMIN J.: enl.. 7/10/61 Co. E in Brunswick, Pvt./Cpl.; present on all rolls; POW Ft. Donetson - sent from Camp Morton to Vicksburg for exchange; admitted to Chimborazo 2/16/63 for diarrhea; POW Fredericksburg 5/3/63 - confined Ft. Delaware; WIA Gettysburg; admitted Richmond Smallpox Hospital for variolous 4/15/64 - returned to duty 5/23/64; WIA Cold Harbor - absent wded roll 5/6/64 - lost middle finger, right hand, POW Hatcher's Run 3/31/65, took oath end released from Pt. Lookout 6/22/65; light completion, brown hair, blue eyes, 5'7": b. Mecklenburg between 1832 and 1835 to Edwin and Alethea Archer; m. Mary A. E. Parrish (age 18) 12/22/1869 - he said was 30 but probably 37 - 4 children; after Mary's death m. Virginia Hawkes 2/29/88, overseer before and after war in Brunswick, applied for pension 4/2/88 living Smoky Ordinary - approved; Brunswick pension list 1908-09, paid $24.

ARCHER, E. H.: Co. K, POW Fort Donelson - confined Camp Morton. 1916 note In CSR said his name was cancelled by pencil on Camp Morton roll.

ARNETT, JOSEPH: enl. 7/9/61 Co. C in Louisa, present 7/10/61; deserted at Richmond 11/61,

ASHBY, JOHN WASHINGTON: Field and Staff - surgeon; enl. 4/30/61 age 30 in Co. C, 7th Va Inf; Pvt - hosp. steward; relieved of duty 10/9/61; made assistant surgeon 10/11/61; promoted surgeon 4/2/62, present 9/12/63; served with 56th Va. and in hospitals in Farmville, Manassas, Orange Court House, Va. and Charlotte and Raleigh, N.C.; letter from Ashby asking for 15 day leave of absence 1/24/64 to take family to Albemarle and Halifax; appointed surgeon Raleigh, N.C. hosp. 2/25/64; b, 1828 Fauquier Co.; educated U. of Penn.; d. 1867 Miss.

ATKENSON (ADKINSON) (ATKINSON), JOSEPH P. enl. 7/26/61 Co. F in Louisa. present 7/10/61; deserted about 9/20/61; 4/1/64 and 7/64 still shown as deserted.

ATWELL, JOSIAH F. enr. 9/10/63 as conscript, assigned to Co. I 5/31/64; present on rolls 5/8/64; paroled at Farmville between 4/11 and 4/21/65.

AUSTIN, GEORGE B. enl. 7/8/61 Co. D in Buckingham; present 7/6/61-10/31/61; discharged 7/21/62 age 37 because unfit for duty for 60 days; b. Buckingham; carpenter; red complexion and hair, blue eyes, 5'9".

BABER, GEORGE W., pwl; Co. C, en.1863 - served 6 months.

BABER, JACOB A. enl. 12/1/63 Co. D at Chaffin's Farm, present 11-12/63 AWOL on roll of 4/1/64; present on rolls 5/8/64; admitted Chimborazo 3/9/65 b. Buckingham; farmer, m. Sarah F. Baker 1851 in Buckingham; applied for pension 4/21/1908 age 88 living Tucker, Buckingham Co.- disabled by old age - said served until left at Amelia Court House just before surrender, $36 approved;, d. 3/19/1910 of old age; widow applied for pension 4/12/1910 - $25 approved.

BACEY, (BAISEY) JOHN W. enl. 6/22/61 Co. B in Mecklenburg; present on all rolls 9/12/61; POW Fort Dominion - sent to Camp Morton; WIA Gaines Mill, admitted Chimborazo 9/12/63 for dysentery; admitted Chimborazo 6/5/64 for gunshot wd. of right temple and eye - furloughed 60 days 6/24/64; papers for retirement disapproved by Field Board at Chester Station and furlough recommended 12/2/64; applied for pension 8/20/1888 age 52 living South Hill, Mecklenburg Co.-owned 300 acres of land so 1st application disallowed - reapplied 1 year later - approved because auditor forgot owned land; letter from Judge W. E. Homes 3/26/94 saying auditor approved 2nd application, but Judge learned that Bacey conveyed his land to A. G. Nicholson, then got Nicholson to convey land to Bacey's minor children - conveyence was a sham - auditor also learned Bacey ablebodied; reapplied 2/21/98 - disallowed; reapplied 4/30/1900 age 63 living Forksville, Mecklenburg Co. - gunshot wd. received in eye during war caused epileptic fits - partially disabled - $30 approved; restatement 5/29/1902 - $30 approved.

BACEY, MARK A. enl. 6/22/61 Co. B in Mecklenburg; present 9/10/61; d. Ft. Donelson 2/62, death claim filed 9/19/62 by widow Margaret Bacey, - owed $63.50.

BACEY, THOMAS L.: enl. 8/22/61 Co. B in Mecklenburg; present 9/10/61; KIA Frazier's Farm - death claim filed by father Isaac Bacey - owed $119.00.

BAGBY, FRAISER SCOTT: enl. 3/15/64 Co. I at Chaffin's Farm; WIA Cold Harbor - admitted Chimborazo 6/2/64 with gunshot wd. of right aim - 7/5/64 furloughed 60 days; POW Hatcher's Run 3/31/65 - took oath and released from Pt. Lookout 6/23/65; resident of Prince Edward Co.; florid complexion, brown hair, hazel eyes, 5'7"; b. 7/45 in Va.; pension application filed 4/9/88 age 44 living in Lunenburg -could not do heavy lifting or reap grain due to gunshot wd..$15 approved; reapplied 7/20/1900 age 60 living Ontario. Charlotte Co. - $30 approved - statement made 5/24/1902 age 58 living In Lunenburg $15 worth of property - $30 approved -1900 census showed living Rehoboth District, Lunenburg with wife Martha S. Bagby age 58.

BAGBY, WILLIAM S. (T.) enl. 7/21/61 Co. F in Louisa, Sgt; 7/27-8/31/61 in Richmond hosp. with measles; present 9/10/61, discharged 10/2/62 age 36 because over 35; POW Hatcher's. Run 3/31/65 - took oath and released from Pt. Lookout 6/23/65; fair complexion, brown hair, blue eyes, 5'7"; b. Louisa Co.; applied for pension 4/28/1900 age 73 living Bumpass, Louisa Co. - partial disability due to hernia, rheumatism, and age - $15 approved - made pension statement 6/9/1902 age 75.

BAILEY, CHARLES LILBURN: enl. 7/15/61 Co. H in Albemarle; present 7/29-10/31/61; transferred 10/19/63 to Co. F. 35th Batt. Cav.; present 4/64; AWOL since 4/29/64; WIA Wilderness 5/6/64 - furloughed from Charlottesville Hosp. 7/14/64; m.12/22/66 in Albemarle; d. 1891 Ivy Depot, Albemarle Co. of consumption; widow Martha E. Bailey applied for pension 6/1/1900. not approved because married after war; reapplied 9/25/1903 - $25 approved.

BAILEY, JOHN C. pwl. Co. H; bur. Maplewood Cem., Rt. 33, Orange Co.

BAILEY, WILLIAM: enl. 8/6/61 Co. K in Mechanicsville age 22; AWOL 8/24/61; present 9/61; AWOL 10/61; POW Ft. Donelson - sent from Camp Morton to Vicksburg for exchange; furloughed 30 days 10/17/62; present on all rolls 7/63 – 8/64; b. Hanover; farmer; sallow complexion, dark hair, 5'10".

BAKER, ELIJAH W. enl. 7/8/61 Co. I in Charlotte; sick furlough 7/8/61; admitted Richmond hosp. 1/9/63 for diarrhea and chronic rheumatism - returned to duty 2/17/63, MWIA and POW Gettysburg - d. in U.S. Hosp. Camp Letterman 8/7/63 of wd. in left thigh - bur. hosp. cem. Sec. 4, Grave 22 - disinterred to Richmond 6/13/1872 Box 53 - reinterred Hollywood Cen.

BAKER, JOHN E.: enl. 7/18/61 Co. I In Charlotte; present 7/18-10/31/61; d.12/61 Richmond, bur. 1/15/62.

BAKER, PHILIP P. appointed surgeon 5/6/63; relieved of duty 8/1/63; successor - John W. Ashby.

BAKER, R. pwl. Co. I.

BAKER, THOMAS J. enl.10/64 Co. I; admitted to Chimborazo 1/30/65 - transferred to Farmville hosp. 3/14/65 with debilitas, recommended for disability discharge because of pulmonallism which he had when entered service; letter to General Cooper asking that Baker be detailed as conscript guard in Prince Edward since he was recommended for discharge - detailed as conscript guard 3/14/65 age 33; paroled Burkeville 4/19/65; b. Clarksville; farmer; fair complexion, light hair, blue eyes, 5'7".

BALLARD, JAMES M. (JOSEPH M.) enl. 7/15/61 Co. H in Albemarle, Pvt/Sgt.; present 7/29-10/31/61; probably d. 2/1/62; brother of William G. Ballard.

BALLARD, JOHN T. enl. 7/15/61 Co. H in Albemarle; present 7/29-10/31/61; POW Frazier's Farm - sent to Ft. Columbus and Ft. Delaware - exchanged at Alken's Landing 7/12/62 age 21; AWOL between 8/5/62 and 10/25/63 - listed deserter on rolls 4/8/64; paroled Columbia 5/8/65; b. 9/13/1840, blue eyes, brown hair and complexion, 5'10"; d. 11/26/1911 - bur. Moriah Cem., Rt. 614, Albemarle Co.

BALLARD, WALLACE W. enl. 7/15/61 Co. H in Albemarle; excused by governor before mustered.

BALLARD, WILLIAM G.: enl. 7/15/61 Co. H in Albemarle; absent when company mustered and still absent 9/2/61; 9/16/61 father J. J. Ballard wrote Sec. of War asking that William be discharged because both sons in army and he needed him to help support family since he was cripple.; entry cancelled, but reported to his company 9/20/61 when recovered from sickness; POW Frankfurt, Ky. 3/18/62; confined 4/4/62 Camp Chase Prison No. 3 - sent to Vicksburg to be exchanged 8/25/62 age 22 - exchanged Alken's Landing 11/10/62 - 30 day medical furlough trom Richmond 11/12/62; Co. reported him as believed POW Gettysburg, but no Federal records concerning him - probably KIA Gettysburg; b. Albemarle Co; James M. Ballard's brother, dark complexion, light hair, blue eyes, 5'81/4".

BANTON, JAMES H. (W.) enl. 7/8/61 Co. D in Buckingham; present 7/8 - 10/31/61; admitted Scottsville hosp. 7/12/63 - furloughed 30 days horn Chimborazo 11/1/63; admitted to Chimborazo 6/27/64 for diarrhea -

returned to duty 8/12/64; POW Sutherland Station 4/2/65. released and took oath at Pt. Lookout 6/23/65; dark complexion, grey hair, blue eyes, 5'9"; resident Buckingham; m. Mary Lewis 2/16/61 Buckingham; d.1/1/1889 of paralysis Buckingham; widow filed pension application 5/15/1900 - $25 approved.

BANTON, WILLIAM JAMES: enl. 7/8/61 Co. D in Buckingham (may also have been In Co. B, present 7/8 – 10/31/61; WIA Gaines's Mill and Frazier's Farm; admitted 7/13/63 Richmond hosp. - transferred Scottsville hosp.; present 9/63 – 8/64; took oath Farmville 4/25/65; 1850 census age 9 - Irving Buckingham; applied for pension 5/14/1900 age 60 - general bad health and loss of right arm In accident - land and personal property worth $335 - $30 approved; made statement 8/27/1902 age 84 - bad varicose veins from marching from Richmond to Gettysburg; d. 11/21/1919.

BARET, WILLIAM: Co, F (probably John William Barrett).

BARKER, WILLIAM N.: enl. 8/6/61 Co. K In Mechanicsville. 2nd Lt.; resigned 8/10/61.

BARNES, ASA L.: enl. 7/12/61 Co. G in Charlotte, Sgt/2nd Lt; present on all rolls; elected 2nd Lt. 12/31/63, admitted Farmville hosp. 5/9/63 for diarrhea - returned to duty 10/1/63, POW Sayler's Creek 4/6/65 - confined Old Capitol Prison 4/14/65 and Johnson's Island 4/17/65 - released and took oath 6/11/65 age 30; light complexion, dark hair, blue eyes, 5'10"; resident of Wyllesburg, Charlotte Co.

BARNES, FRANCIS CARGILL (T. C,) enl. 7/12/61 Co.G in Charlotte, Pvt/1^{st}Lt, present 7/10/61, elected 2nd Lt. 5/3/62, promoted to 1st Lt. 12/22/62; POW Gettysburg - captured at stone wall - confined Ft. McHenry 7/6/63, Johnson's Island 7/18/63, Fort Delaware 7/22/63, Old Capitol Prison 7/16/64, Hilton Head, S.C. 1/1/65 - one of the "Six Hundred" - took oath and released 6/12/65; dark complexion and hair, grey eyes, 6'; resident of Charlotte; farmer; attended 35th anniversary reunion of Gettysburg 1898 In Philadelphia; 1899 living In Chase City; member Armistead Camp No. 26 UCV; d.1/27/1910 age 73 at home near Wyllesburg, Charlotte Co.

BARNES, JAMES Co. B; POW at Pt. Lookout - released 6/10/65; resident of Baltimore, Md.; light complexion and hair, grey eyes, 5'51/2".

BARRETT, JOHN G.: pwl; enl. 7/25/61 Co. F in Louisa.

BARRETT (BARRET), JOHN WILLIAM: enl. 7/26/61 Co. F in Louisa; present on all rolls except 5/6/64 absent wded.; admitted Chimborazo 6/3/64 for gunshot wd. in right shoulder - furloughed 30 days 6/25/64; paroled Ashland 5/6/65; b. 6/18/1842 in Louisa to Alexander Maury and Sarah Starke Morrison Barret; farmer; m. Estelle Irene McGee 11/4/1885 in Fluvanna; d. 2/8/1906 in Louisa from pneumonia - bur. Hillcrest Cem. Louisa, Rt. 33; widow applied for pension 6/30/1927, owned $870 real estate - $300 personal property - husband wded. 2 times In war - $90 approved.

BARRETT, RICHARD: pwl; Co. F.

BARRETT, THOMAS O.: enl. 7/26/61 Co. F in Louisa, Cpl.; 7/27 – 8/31/61 sick in Richmond hosp. with measles, present 9/10/61; promoted 1st Cpl. 10/21/61; admitted Richmond hosp. 11/25/62 for phosphatic diathesis - discharged as unfit for military duty 1/26/63 due to kidney trouble; 9/6 – 8/64 detailed to work at Bellona Foundry, paroled Burkeville 4/24/65.

BARROW, ANDREW J.: pwl; enl., late in war Co. E; b, about 1832 to Lewis and Mary Rash Barrow in Brunswick; 1850's m, widow Mary E. Sydnor, in 1860 Irving In Dinwiddie; 2 children; bur. Dinwiddie.

BARROW, (BARRON) GEORGE A.: enl. 10/10/64 Co. E in Brunswick; dark complexion, light hair, blue eyes, 5'4"; retired 3/3/65 age 18 due to shaking palsy - developed after enlistment; b.1843 to John A. and Susan J. Dunkley Barrow in Brunswick, farmer, rn. Mary A. Finch 9/30/68 in Brunswick - 3 children; 1880 living Brunswick.

BASKET, REUBEN: enl. 8/6/61 Co. K in Mechanicsville age 38; present on all rolls; POW Ft. Donelson - sent from Camp Morton to Vicksburg for exchange; hired tor extra duty at Chaffin's Farm as wheelwright and blacksmith 10/63-5/64; admitted Chimborazo for dysentery 9/19/64 - furloughed to King and Queen 35 days 10/3/64; b. King and Queen; wheelwright; fair complexion, light hair, 5'7".

BEACH, (BEECH) (BUCH) (on county list) JOHN R..: Co. F; Issued clothing 12/30/64; admitted 3/31/65 to 2nd Division 5th Army Corps Hosp,, Army of the Potomac with bullet wd.; d. 4/2/65,

BEAL, (BEALE) WILLIAM: enl. 7/8/61 Co. A in Mecklenburg; admitted Richmond Hosp. 8/3/63 - transferred to private quarters; present 11/63-8/64; lived in Richmond before being admitted Lee Camp Soldiers' Home 10/16/1908 age 70 for old age and general debility; d. 12/3/1910 - bur. Mount Calvary Cem. Richmond.

BEASLEY, JAMES W.: enl. 7/8/61 Co. D in Buckingham; present 7/8-10/31/61; admitted Lynchburg Hosp. 9/2/63 for phthisis pulmonalis; discharged 9/27/63 for disability age 20; b. Buckingham; farmer; light hair and complexion, blue eyes, 5'9".

BEASLEY, JOHN: enr. as conscript 2/23/64 Co. D, present 4/64-8/64; d. in POW Hospital No.10626 of chronic diarrhea on 6/8/65; Number 2068 in POW Graveyard, Pt. Lookout.

BEASLEY, WILLIAM D.: enl. 7/8/61 Co. I in Charlotte, Pvt./Cpl.; present on all rolls; admitted Chimborazo 2/26/63 with Pneumonia - returned to duty 4/16/63; WIA Gettysburg; POW Hatcher's Run 3/31/65 - took oath and released 6/23/65 from Pt. Lookout; light complexion, brown hair, grey eyes, 6'1 1/4"; applied for pension 5/15/1900 age 56 living in Drake's Branch, Charlotte Co. - wded. in right leg and breast during war - totally disabled - $15 approved; signed William Woodson Berkley's pension application t906.

BEDDER, (BEDOW or BETTER) NASHVILLE enl. 7/15/61 Co. H in

Albemarle; present 7/29-10/31/61; admitted CSA General Hospital 11/25/62 for burn of the foot - sent to Colony 11/29/62; deserted 3/6/63 and listed as AWOL on all rolls after then; admitted Richmond hosp. 1/1/64 with bronchitis - sent to Castle Thunder 1/9/64; deserted and shot according to H. H. Hardesty.

BEDELL, R. S.: Co. F; paroled Columbia 5/65.

BELEW, JOHN R.: enl. 7/15/61 Co. H in Albemarle; present 7/29/61-10/61; d. of disease at Winchester 2/28/62; death claim filed by father William M. Belew 3/3/62 - owed $69.00.

BELEW, WILLIAM T.: enl. 7/15/61 Co. H. in Albemarle; discharged from service 8/20/61 because unfit for service.

BELL, ALEXANDER P.: enl. 7/961 Co. C in Louisa; d. 8/15/61.

BELLAMY, WILLIAM F. (J): enl. 7/9/61 Co. C in Louisa; sick furlough 7/61-8/61; present 9/61-10/61; admitted Chimborazo 8/11/62 with typhoid fever - furloughed 8/26/62 Tolersville, Va. - name not returned by ward master.

BENNETT, SILAS J.: enl. 6/22/61 Co. B in Mecklenburg, preset 9/61-10/61; POW Fort Donelson - sent to Vicksburg from Camp Morton for exchange; POW Gettysburg - exchanged from Fort Delaware 7/31/63: present 9/63-12/63 and 4/1/64; admitted Chimborazo 6/564 for diarrhea – d. 6/12/64 of typhoid fever.

BENTON, EDWARD: pwl; Co. D

BERKLEY, WILLIAM WOODSON: enl. 7/18/61 Co. I in Charlotte, Cpl/Sgt.; sick with typhoid pneumonia 11/61; present on all rolls; WIA Gaines's Mill- admitted Charlottesville hosp, with wd. of side 9/14/62 -transferred Lynchburg Hosp. 9/15/62, admitted Chimborazo 9/24/64 - returned to duty 10/15/64; POW Amelia Court House 4/5/65 - took oath and released from Pt. Lookout 6/23/65; b. Charlotte; farmer, dark complexion, light hair, brown eyes, 5'3"; b. 7/1/1838 Charlotte; m. Samantha Carolyn Holt (John Lee Holt's sister) 10/2366 Campbell Co; farmer; applied for pension 8/6/1906 age 68 living in Randolph, Charlotte Co. - became overheated during war and as result had stomach cramps and dizziness - $15 approved: d. 8/27/1924 - bur. Bethel Baptist Church, Charlotte Co.

BERNARD, JOHN: enl. 5/3/62 Co. H in Richmond; on rolls of 7/12/63 as deserter.

BERRICK, (BENICK), A. H: Co. B, surrendered by Lee at Appomattox.

BEVEL, JAMES T. enl. 8/29/61 Co. A in Richmond; present 9/61-10/61; AWOL 9/63-10/63; absent sick 11/63-12/63 and 5/8/64; admitted Chimborazo 6/17/64 for chronic diarrhea - furloughed 30 days 6/23/64; d. Mecklenburg - death claim filed 11/17/64 in Mecklenburg by widow Susan M. Bevel.

BIBB, ALFRED B.: enl. 7/9/61 Co. C at Louisa, Cpl/Pvt.; present 7/9/61-10/61; POW and d. 3/12/62 in 4th Street Hospital, St. Louis, Missouri of typhoid fever - where captured unknown; bur. St Louis.

BIBB, ANDREW J. enl. 7/9/61 Co. C in Louisa; AWOL 9/61-10/61.

BIBB, HENRY F.: enl. 7/9/61 Co. C in Louisa; present 7/9-8/31/61; sick furlough 9/61-10/61; discharged with debility 11/2/61 age 25; reenlisted 7/9/63 In Louisa; present 9/63-10/63; on detached service as shoemaker In C.S. Clothing Depot, Richmond 11/63-12/63; admitted Chimborazo 1/28/64 for debility - returned to shoe factory 3/24/64; absent sick 5/64-8/64; shoemaker, blue eyes, light hair and complexion, 5'11"; b. Louisa; d. 6/17/1909 age 77.

BIBB JAMES: pwl, Co. D; from Nelson Co.

BIBB, JAMES H. enl. 7/9/61 Co. C in Louisa; present 7/9/61.10/31/61; reported deserted at Richmond 8/2/62, on rolls of 9/63-12/63; WIA severe arm wd, 6/1-6/464 - absent wded. on rolls 5/64-8/64.

BIBB. JOSEPH F. enl 7/9/61 Co. C in Louisa, Sgt/2nd Lt, present 7/9/61-10/31/61; elected 2nd Lt. 5/3/62, KIA Gaines's Mill age 24; b. Louisa; light hair and complexion, blue eyes, 5'10".

BILBO, EDWIN: enl. 7/26/61 CO. F in Louisa: present 7/27/61-8/31/61; discharged 9/26/61 age 44 - unfit for duty because of eruption of skin; b. Hanover, carpenter, light hair and complexion, blue eyes, 5'7".

BINGHAM, ALLEN (ALAN) WILEY: enl. 5/3/62 Co. B in Richmond, Pvt./Sgt; Court Martial AWOL 2/23/63 - guilty of specification and charge - reduced to ranks and forfeited 2 months pay, transferred to Co. K 56th Va. 6/26/64 in exchange for Wm. E. R Thomason; paroled Charlottesville 5/18/65; applied for pension 7/9/1900 age 65 living Charlottesville -general debility from age and disease - $15 approved.

BINGHAM, JOHN S.: Co. K; POW Harpers Farm 4/6/65 - took oath and released from Pt Lookout 6/23/65; resident Appomattox; light complexion, brown hair, grey eyes, 5'614".

BIRDSONG, NATHANIEL A.: enl. 7/10/61 Co. E Brunswick; present on all rolls; WIA Gaines's Mill 6/27/62, POW Burkeville 4/6/65 - took oath and released from Pt. Lookout 6/23/65; resident Brunswick, light complexion, dark hair, grey eyes, 5'91/4"; b. 5/1/1840 to Nathaniel and Sarah Short Birdsong; brother of Thomas M; m. Martha Ann Young 12/18/66 in Brunswick - at least 3 children; farmer, d. 12/26/1903 Brunswick - bur. Mt. Carmel Methodist Church.

BIRDSONG, THOMAS E. (M.) enl. 2/9/63 Co. E in Brunswick Co.; present 9/63-12/63, AWOL 3/31/64-9/16/64 for which time pay was withheld; admitted Chimborazo 3/19/65 for dysentery - POW captured in Richmond hosp. 4/3/65 - admitted Jackson Hospital 4/7/65 and turned over to Provost Marshal at hosp. 4/14/65 - transferred to Libby Prison and then to Newport News 4/23/65 – took oath 7/1/65; resident Brunswick, light complexion, dark hair, blue eyes, 5'6"; b. about 1835 Brunswick - brother of Nathaniel A., m. Indianna P. Harris 1/21/1858 - 1 daughter - both wife and daughter d. during war, 2/1/1870 m. Maria L. Lucy - probably had 3 children.

BIRDWELL, SELL.ERS enr. as conscript 1/25/64 - assigned Co. A. 3/11/64; admitted Chimborazo 8/3/64 for chronic diarrhea - furloughed 60 days 8/6/64.

BISHOP, ELIJAH: enl. 5/3/62 Co. B in Richmond; 9/63-12/63 rolls listed as missing since Boonsboro.

BISHOP, EUGENE: enl. 7/16/61 Co. H. in Albemarle; sick furlough 9/2/61; d. 10/28/61.

BISHOP, JAMES ALEXANDER ("SANDY") enl. 7/10/61 Co. E in Brunswick, Pvt./Sgt, present on all rolls; POW Ft. Donelson - sent from Camp Morton to Vicksburg for exchange; POW Burkeville. 4/6/65 - took oath and released from Pt. Lookout 6/23/65; florid complexion, dark hair, hazel eyes, 5'10 1/4"; b. Dinwiddie Co. about 1834 to William and Susan J. Bishop; farmer; m. Mary S. Judd 3/31/1857 in Brunswick - 5 children; 1900 census - living Red Oak District, Brunswick Co. with wife Mary age 63 and son Charles Oris b. 12/78; after wife's death m. Anna Cheely (daughter of Robert L Cheely of Co. E) 12/20/1905; attended Lawrenceville reunion of CV 1908, applied for pension 4/26/1909 age 74 living Brunswick - totally disabled due to age and rheumatism - $24 approved; second application 5/29/1916 age 82 - lost original pension when land reappraised for $1300 - $50 approved, d. 6/7/1918 Rawlings of cancer - $25 paid for funeral expenses by state - bur. family cem. on his farm near Lebanon Methodist Church; widow Anna C. Bishop applied for pension 12/19/1930 - $10 approved.

BISHOP, JAMES J.: Co. B, WIA Gaines's Mill - d. from wounds in Richmond hosp. 7/12/62 - left no effects.

BISHOP, ROBERT THOMAS: enl. 4/20/64 Co. E at Chaffin's Farm; 4/20/64-9/1/64 absent sick - admitted Chimborazo 6/21/64 for chronic diarrhea.- furloughed 30 days 7/23/64; POW Farmville 4/6/65 - took oath and released from Pt. Lookout 6/23/65; florid complexion, dark hair, hazel eyes, 5'9 3/4"; b. 6/1846 to William and Susan J. Bishop in Dinwiddie; brother of James Alexander, farmer, m. Augusta P. House (daughter of John E. House of Co. E) 12/16/1874 Brunswick - 2 children as of 1880; m. Rosa Virginia Howerton 1/6/1897 after death of Augusta; 1900 census - living Red Oak District, Brunswick with wife Rosa age 43 and son Arthur H. age 24; attended Lawrenceville reunion of CV 1908; applied for pension 8/11/1910 living Brunswick - partially disabled due to age and stomach trouble; d. 3/11/23 Brunswick of influenza - bur. Frank Snead's farm near Lebanon Methodist Church; widow applied for pension 8/26/1932 - $90 approved.

BISHOP, WILLIAM J. enl 7/8/61 Co. D in Buckingham; present on all

rolls;
POW Ft. Donelson - sent from Camp Morton to Vicksburg for exchange - listed as sick; admitted Scottsville hosp. 11/62 - furloughed 30 days 11/11/62, admitted Va. hop. 7/16/63; KIA Cold Harbor.

BISHOP, WILLIAM O.: enl. 7/15/61 Co. H in Albemarle; present 7/29/61-10/31/61.

BLACKWELL, JAMES W.: enl. 7/15/61 Co. H in Albemarle, CpL/Orderly Sgt., present 7/29-10/31/61; WIA Gaines's Mill, WIA and POW Gettysburg - admitted West's Buildings Hosp. 7/26/63 age 23 with gunshot fracture in right humerus - paroled from hosp. 8/23/63, 9/63-10/63 absent wded.; furloughed 12/2/63; in hosp. in Staunton and Richmond 2/8/64-8/23/64 with flesh wd. of right arm; provost guard duty in Salem 9/64-2/65, post war list showed lost arm Hatcher's Run; resident of Staunton; d. 1906 Albemarle,

BLACKWELL, ROBERT B. (B. B.) enl. 5/3/62 Co. H in Richmond; in Richmond hosp. 8/18/62, WIA and POW Gettysburg - paroled from West's Buildings Hosp. 9/25/63 - on list of exchanged prisoners at Camp Lee; WIA 6/17/64 while on picket duty near Howlett House - admitted Chimborazo 6/19/64 - left arm amputated at shoulder point - furloughed 60 days 7/9/64; transferred to Co. F 35th Va. Batt. Cav. 7/27/64; admitted Charlottesville hosp. 1/11/65 - returned to duty 2/10/65; discharged 3/1/65 age 28 due to loss of arm - given no duty because uneducated man; b. Albemarle; farmer; fair complexion, light hair, blue eyes, 5'8", applied for pension 3/2/88 age 51 living Brown's Cove, Albemarle Co. - $30 approved.

BLAKE, E. H.: enl. 5/8/62 Co. K in Richmond; 7/63-10/31/63 AWOL and dropped from rolls by orders of General Garnett.

BLAKE, JOHN T.: enl. 7/12/61 Co. G in Charlotte; present 7/12-10/31/61, 5/8/63 and 9/12/63; admitted Danville hosp. 9/4/63 *for* debilitas - returned to duty 9/15/63; present 4/8/64;10/15/64 roll listed as absent since last mustered.

BLAND, THEODORE: :Co. E, WIA Hatchet's Run; POW Famville 4/6/65 - in hosp. at Pt. Lookout with chronic diarrhea - took oath and released 6/23/65, discharged from service 7/1/65; resident Prince George; dark hair and complexion, grey eyes, 5'.

BLANKENSHIP, ABRA (ABEL) L: Co. G; POW Rice's Station 4/6/65 - took oath and released from Pt Lookout 6/16/65, resident Franklin Co.; light complexion, brown hair, hazel eyes, 5'5 7/8"..

BLANKENSHIP, JOEL L: enl. Co. I; discharged 8/16/61 age 34 by surgeon's certificate, paid $32 for services and uniform; b. Campbell Co.; blacksmith; light hair and complexion, blue eyes, 5'6"; d. during *war*.

BLANKENSHIP, RICHARD: pwl, Co. I; d. in service.

BLANKENSHIP, SAMUEL O.: enl. 7/18/61 Co. I in Charlotte; absent on sick furlough beyond time 9/2/61 - William J. Morrison, Richard Ledbetter, and H. F. Lester detailed to go to Mosingford, Charlotte Co. to bring him to Richmond - put in guard house because thought lo be deserting, but soon released when mistake found; present 9/10/61; present Ft. Donelson; b. Charlotte; d. 3/62 Atlanta, Ga. - death claim filed 9/5/62 by father Joel H. Blankenship - owed $62.00.

BLANKENSHIP, SILAS: enr. 2/3/64 as conscript - assigned to Co. C 4/19/64; in Smallpox Hospital with variola 4/19/64 - age given as 14;

admitted Chimborazo 7/18/64 with dropsy - returned to duty 8/22/64; admitted Chimborazo 9/10/64 with fever convulsions - furloughed 60 days 10/2/64; POW Burkeville 4/6/65 - admitted Newport News Prison Hospital with diarrhea 5/29/65, took oath 6/14/65 - readmitted hosp. 6/17/65 with debilitas - d. 6/26/65 Newport News Prison Hospital - bur. Greenlawn Cem, Newport News; resident Botetourt; dark complexion, light hair, blue eyes, 5'6".

BLANKENSHIP, THOMAS G.: enl. 10/15/63 Co. G in Richmond; present on all rolls; POW Rice's Station 4/6/65 - look oath and released from Pt. Lookout 6/23/65; resident of Franklin Co.; dark complexion, brown hair, hazel eyes, 5'9 ½".

BLANKS, WILLIAM J: enl. 7/10/61 Co. E in Brunswick, present 7/61-8/61; admitted Lovingston Hosp, Winchester 9/8/62 for diarrhea - returned to duty 9/20/62; admitted Richmond hosp. 10/4/62, returned to duty 10/22/62; discharged due to disability 9/9/62, b. about 1814; m. Sarah P. Mitchell 1/15/38 in Brunswick - 1850 census - 3 children; d. before 1870.

BLICK, GEORGE R: enl. 2/9/63 Co. E in Brunswick Co., Pvt./Cpl, present 11/63-12/63, absent 4/1/64 on furlough of indulgence; present 5/64-8/64; POW Hatcher's Run 3/31/65 - took oath and released from Pt. Lookout 6/23/65; resident of Brunswick, light complexion, brown hair, grey eyes, 5'8 ½"; b. about 1842 to Elijah Hiarn H. and Margaret Blick - brother of Joseph A. and William R; m. Martha A. Cornelia Lucy 1/3/65 - 9 children; living in Brunswick1906 - signed William M. Abemathy's pension application.

BLICK, JOSEPH A: pwl; Co. E, Cpl./Lt,. - believed enlisted *7/10/61* and served to end of war; elected Lt.; b. about 1836 - brother of George R. and William A.; physician and farmer after war - 1866 living in Greensville Co.; m. Lucy E. Trotter (her brother Isham E. Trotter, Co. E) 6/6/66 in Brunswick - 1880 census - 9 children; after Lucy's death m. Rosa J. Parrish 12/18/84 - still practicing medicine in Brunswick.

BLICK, WILLIAM A.: enl. 7/10/61 Co. E in Brunswick, Pvt./Lt.; present 7/61-8/61, elected 2nd Lt. 5/3/62; KIA Gettysburg; b. about 1839 - brother of George R. and Joseph A. Blick of Co. E; m. Martha E. Short (sister of John, Richard, end William Short) 12/19/60. In 1861 owned 2 slaves and owed $7.70 in taxes.

BOOKER, HORACE: pwl; Co. I; discharged early in war.

BOOKER, ROBERT STANARD (STANHOPE) enl. 7/18/61 Co. I in Charlotte, Cpl./Pvt, present 7/61-10/61; admitted to Farmville hosp. 8/20/62 - returned to duty 11/7/62; rolls of 7/63-12/63 and 5/62-8/64 showed absent on detached service as provost guard; paroled Farmville 4/11-4/21/65.

BOOTH, HILLERY A.: enl. 7/12/61 Co. G in Charlotte, 2nd Lt.; d.12/61 near Richmond from fever contracted in service - had been left in Richmond to care for sick in regiment when others went to Abingdon; death claim flied by widow Mary B. Booth 6/562 -owed $96.67; widow applied for pension 5/8/88. m. 5/53 In Charlotte - $30 approved.

BOOTH, (BOOTHE) JAMES EDWARD: enl. 7/12/61 Co. G in Chalrlotte; present 7/12/61-10/61.

BOSWELL, THOMAS TAYLOR: enl. 7/8/61 Co. A in Mecklenburg, Capt; present 7/8/61-10/61; dropped as Capt. 5/5/62 much against his wishes; asked for job as clerk in 2nd Auditor's office 8/26/62 because over age for military duty and had pulmonary disease; became Capt. Co. A 1st Va.

Reserves 4/25/64, promoted Lt. Col. 8/12/64; held Staunton River Bridge in Charlotte against Federal raiding force of 10,000 cavalry - promoted to Col. as result - paroled by U.S. VI Corps 5/13/65; b. 1828; resident of Mecklenburg, grad of Randolph Macon; m. Martha Nelson; d. 1887.

BOSWELL, WILLIAM NELSON: pwl, drummer boy for his father Thomas Boswell for entire war - insisted on following his "dad"; 11 years old at start of war.

BOWEN, ALEXANDER (SANDY) L.: enl. 7/8/61 Co. A in Mecklenburg; absent sick with measles 9/61-10/61; served 4 years; on Halifax pension list.

BOWEN, HUGH FERDINAND: enl. 2/17/63 Co. B in Richmond, present 9/63-12/63 and 4/164; absent sick 5/64-8/64; admitted Chimborazo 6/27/64 with disease - transferred to Lynchburg Hosp. 7/9/64; admitted Chimborazo 8/6/64 - furloughed 30 days 8/16/64; POW Farmville 4/6/856 - took oath and released 6/23/65 from Pt. Lookout; resident of Brunswick; dark complexion, dark brown hair, black eyes, 5'7".

BOWEN, JAMES (JOSEPH) A: enr. as conscript 8/15/62 Co. H in Charlottesville; admitted Chimborazo 8/31/62 for debilitias - returned to duty 9/162, admitted Charlottesville hosp. 3/18/63; discharged 3/18/64 age 24 due to imbecility; b. Charlottesville; farmer; dark hair and complexion, blue eyes, 6'.

BOWEN, LEVI (LEROY) G.: enr. as conscript 3/1/64. assigned to Co. B. 5/9/64; present 4/1/64 and 5/64-8/64; POW Burkeville 4/6/65 - admitted US Jackson Hospital 4/7/65 - turned over to provost marshal 4/21/65 - took oath and released from Pt. Lookout 6/23/65; resident of Mecklenburg; light complexion, brown hair, grey eyes, 5'6 1/2".

BOWEN, LUCIUS M.: enL. 7/15/61 Co. H in Albemarle; absent when company mustered and refused to report to his company - entry cancelled; reenL. 5/3/62 In Richmond, POW 9/16/62 Hagerstown, Md. - delivered to Aiken's Landing for exchange 10/6/62, admitted Richmond hosp. 10/12/62 - returned to duty 11/1/62 - fuloughed 40 days 11/19/62, admitted Charlottesville hosp, 2/13/63 with chronic rheumatism - returned to duty 2/16/63, POW Gettysburg - confined Ft. Delaware 7/12/63 – Pt. Lookout 10/26/63 - exchanged 3/14/65; POW in Jackson Hosp. 4/3/65 - paroled 5/8/65.

BOWLES, CHESTERFIELD: enl. 7/12/61 Co. G in Charlotte, present 7/26/61 – 10/31/61.

BRANCH, CURTIS N. (IM): enl. 7/8/61 Co. D in Buckingham; present on all rolls; wded. by log falling on back while building fortifications at Ft. Donelson; WIA Gaines's Mill - shot in leg; reenl. 8/11/62; docked days wages by court martial sentence in period 7/64-8/64; POW Southside Railroad 4/2/65 - received Injury of right shoulder at Pt. Lookout – took oath and released from PL Lookout 8/23/65; b. 1/1840, resident of Buckingham; dark complexion, brown hair, hazel eyes, 5'8 3/4"; applied for pension

12/9/1895 age 56 living in Buckingham - disallowed - reapplied 5/21/1900 age 60. $15 approved; rerated 4/15/1908 -$30 approved; 1900 census showed living James River District, Buckingham Co. with wife Eliza A. age 60, 3 sons and daughter.

BRANCH, WILLIAM L.: enl. 7/8/61 Co. D in Buckingham; present 7/8/61-10/61; discharged 5/13/62 age 20 for pulmonary lesions; b. Buckingham 7/1842; farmer; dark complexion, black hair, blue eyes, 5'2"; applied for pension 5/21/1900 age 58 living Manteo, Buckingham Co. - infirm health and injuries - owned no property - $30 approved; 1900 census - living alone.

BRANHAM, JOHN (1): enl. 7/9/61 Co. C in Louisa; sick furlough 7/9/61-8/31/61; present on all rolls; transferred to Co. H, 22 Btn, Va. Vol.. 7/28/64.

BRANHAM, JOHN (2) pwl, Co. C.

BRANHAM, NATHANIEL, JR: enl. 7/9/61 Co. C in Louisa; present 7/29/61-10/61; WIA and POW Gettysburg - in Gettysburg hospital with gunshot wd. of leg listed as POW on all other muster rolls - believed killed but no Federal records concerning him.

BRANSFORD, (BRANFORD) PLEASANT A: enl. 7/8/61 Co. D in Buckingham, Cpl./Sgt.; present 7/8/61-10/61; WIA Gaines's Mill; reenl. 8/11/62; in Richmond hosp. 1/30/63, d. 1/31/63 of acute bronchitis - left $3.50 and sundry effects.

BRAUNN, N. pwl; Co. C.

BREEDLOVE. JOHN W.: enl. 7/18/61 Co. I in Charlotte; present 7/18/61-8/3/61; absent on furlough 9/61-10/61; WIA Gettysburg - admitted Farmville Hosp. 7/24/63 with gunshot wd. in forearm injuring muscles of hand and fingers - furloughed 30 days; absent wded. 7/12/63 and 4/8/64; retired 5/24/64 for 6 months due to wd. - recommended for detail as clerk and ordered to report to military station in Danville; living Baltimore, Md. in 1902

BREWER, WYLEY (WILEY) T.: enl. 7/8/61 Co. A in Mecklenburg; sick with measles 9/61; present 9/61-10/61; admitted Richmond hosp. 9/1/62 with fever - returned to duty 9/14/62; discharged 10/1/62.

BRIDGER, MONROE M.: enl. 10/10/63 Co. K in Isle of Wight; present 9/63-12/63 and 4/64-8/64; on list of deserters 2/19/65.

BRIGHTWELL, CHARLES A.: enl. 8/8/61 Co. I in Charlotte; absent on sick furlough beyond time 7/18/61-8/31/61; present 9/61-10/61; admitted 8/13/62 to Richmond hosp. with erysipelas - furloughed 60 days 8/19/62 - discharged 8/16/62 age 26 due to stiff elbow joint of left arm caused by severe attack of erysipelas; b. Charlotte; shoemaker; fair complexion, dark hair, blue eyes, 5'2"; d. 1/10/1890 of consumption In Charlotte; rn. 11/22/57 in Charlotte; widow M. A. Brightwell applied for pension 5/5/1900 - $25 approved.

BRIGHTWELL , WILLIAM: pwl; Co. I; discharged 1861; d. after war.

BRISTOW, SAMUEL: pwl; enl. 1862 Co. B; served 3 years.

BRITTON, DAVID BURRUS: Co. G; POW Farmville 4/6/65 - took oath and released from Pt. Lookout 6/23/65; resident of Charlotte; dark complexion, brown hair, blue eyes, 5'4".

BROCKMAN, JOHN: enl. 7/9/61 Co. C in Louisa: 7/9/61-8/31/61 furloughed; present on all other rolls; on list of casualties and missing at Gaines's Mill.

BRONDER, WILLIAM J.: enl. 7/10/61 Co. E in Brunswick; present 7/10/61-8/31/61.

BROOCKS (BROOKS) EDWIN S.: enl. 7/12/61 Co. G in Charlotte, Sgt; present 7/61-10/61; discharged 9/29/62 age 39 because over 38; b. Charlotte; dark complexion and hair, blue eyes, 5'9".

BROOKER, (BOOKER) JAMES H.: enl. Co. I, discharged 8/28/61 age 18 with heart disease that prevented active exercise; b. Prince Edward; teacher; fair complexion, black hair, grey eyes, 5'7".

BROOKS, (BOOKS) JAMES A: enl. 7/26/64 Co. A in Mecklenburg; present 7/64-8/64; furloughed from Chimborazo 3/27/65; POW Jackson Hosp. 4/3/65 - turned over to provost marshal 4/14/65 - sent to Libby Prison and then Newport News 4/23/65 - took oath and released 6/14/65; resident of Halifax; dark hair, black eyes, 5'9"; m. 12/2/52 in Halifax; d. 7/65, brought home sick from prison and never left his bed; widow Maria P. Brooks applied for pension 1029/1890 living Vernon Hill, Halifax Co., disallowed because husband not in service when died.

BROOKS, JOHN KENDALL: enl. 1/7/64 Co. E at Chaffin's Farm; WIA Petersburg siege; present 4/64-8/64; POW Farmville 4/6/65 - took oath and released from Pt. Lookout 6/23/65; resident of Brunswick, fair complexion, light hair, blue eyes, 5'8 ¼"; b. about 1836 in Brunswick to Beverly and Patience Brooks; m. Virginia E. Hampton 4/29/1868 in Brunswick - at least 5 children; no information after 1880 census when living in Brunswick next door to his parents.

BROOKS, JOHN R.: enl. 7/8/1861 in Co. A Mecklenburg, Pvt/2nd Lt; present on all rolls; McPhail requested that he be appointed enrolling officer in Mecklenburg 12/9/1862 elected 2nd Lt. 8/2/1864.

BROWDER, JOHN RICHARD: pwl, exempted from service 3/62 because of "lameness"; conscripted later and assigned Co. E.: b. about 1838 to Joseph and Frances Johnson Browder; carpenter before war; rn. widow Virginia E. Delbridge Harrison 1/4/65 in Brunswick, after her death m. Ann V. Stone 2/21/89; mechanic in 1880's; applied for pension 6/3/1901 age 64 living in Edmund's Store, Brunswick Co. - dislocated hip partial disability - $15 approved; made pension statement 8/21/1902 age 65 - rheumatism - disability came from exposure during war, member Bethel Methodist Church; d. 1/19/1906 age 70 - bur. family graveyard, Brunswick.

BROWDER, WILLIAM JOSEPH: pwl; enl. Co. E 1861; discharged 1864;

b. about 1818 - brother of John Richard Browder, Co. E; m. Mary E. Scoggin 11/19/1849; 1860 census - 4 children; after wife's death m. Maryland T. Ellis 3/24/1881; miller; applied for pension 5/21/1900 age 80, physical disability nearly total - $15 approved, made pension statement 8/26/1902 age 82 living Edmund's Store, Brunswick Co.

BROWN, BENJAMIN FRANK (probably Frank Brown): enl 7/8/61 Co. D in Buckingham; present 7/61-10/61.

BROWN, CHARLES THOMAS: enl. 7/15/61 Co. H in Albemarle; entry cancelled by governor before muster; enl. 5/3/62, discharged 5/27/62 age 34 due to bad ankle joint; b. Albemarle; graduate UVA - attended 1849, 1850, 1855; teacher Hanover Co.; fair complexion, hazel eyes, grey hair; living Georgia 1863; wrote Sec. of Treasury, CSA 1/15/63 asking for clerk's job and asking pay of $1250-$1500: b. 2/5/1828 d.1/2/1890 - bur. Mt. Morlah Cem., Rt. 614, Albemarle Co.

BROWN, EZRA M.: enl. 7/15/61 Co. H in Albemarle, Sgt; medical discharge 8/28/61,

BROWN, FRANK: pwl; Co. D (see Benjamin F. Brown).

BROWN, JAMES E.: enl. 7/18/61 Co. G in Charlotte; listed as deserted 5/12/63 on all rolls given.

BROWN, JOHN F: enl. 7/10/61 Co. E in Brunswick; sick furlough with measles 7/10/61- 8/31/61; m. Mary Elizabeth Pritchett 2/27/61 - 1 son; d. 1863 In Brunswick - bur. there.

BROWN, JOHN R.; enl 7/8/61 Co. D in Buckingham; present on rolls 7/10/61 and 9/10/63; reenl. 8/11/62, furloughed for general debility and anemia 11/63-12/63, AWOL 4/8/64; paroled Farmville 424/65; b.1/1831 In Va.: 1850 census - age 20, living Buckingham Co.; laborer; applied for pension 5/15/1900 age 69 living Centenary, Buckingham Co. - disability due to age and sickness - $30 approved - made pension statement 8/11/1902 age 73; 1900 census living Slate River District, Buckingham Co. with son Charles S. age 23, daughter-in-law, 2 grandchildren.

BROWN, JOSEPH AUGUSTUS: enl. 7/15/61 Co. H in Albemarle, entry cancelled by governor before company mustered; 1870 census listed J. A. Brown as farmer, age 46, living Albemarle, personal estate of $300 - wife and 7 children in home.

BROWN, L K. (M): company unknown - probably Co. B or K, received clothes 10/13/64; POW in Richmond 5/4/65, turned over to provost marshal.

BROWN, MATHEW (MATTHEW) WASHINGTON: enl. 7/8/61 Co. D in Buckingham, Sgt./Lt; present 7/8/61-10/61; promoted 2nd Lt. 10/28/61; elected 1st Lt. 5/3/62; George B. Austin's papers showed Brown commanding Co. D 7/18/62; on register of payments to discharged soldiers 10/28/62, WIA Gettysburg; absent due to wds. 9/63-12/63; retired from army 7/6/64; assigned to Comdt. of Conscripts In Va.-letter asked that assignment be revoked because needed for baling - request granted 8/84; b. 9/20/1834 In Va.; 1880 census - living Huguenot District, Powhatan Co. with wife Edmonia age 30, 4 daughters, 2 sons - oldest in school; farmer, d. 10/18/1893 Powhatan - bur. St. Luke's Episcopal Church, Powhatan.

BROWN, NATHANIEL: Co. E; MWIA and POW Gettysburg, leg amputated - d. Gettysburg hospital 7/11/63 - bur. Gettysburg - reinterred Hollywood Cem.

BROWN, NEWTON M.: enl. 7/8/61 Co. D in Buckingham, Cpl; present 7/8/61-10/61; d. 12/31/62 Buckingham of consumption - death claim filed 1/8/64.

BROWN, PATRICK W.: enl 8/6/61 Co. K in Mechanicsville; never mustered in - rejected by surgeon.

BROWN, REUBEN R.: enl, 8/8/61 Co. D in Buckingham; present 7/8/61-10/61; admitted Richmond hosp. - 5/26/62 - transferred to Farmville or Lynchburg 5/27/62; WIA Frazier's Farm; reenl. 8/11/62; WIA and POW Gettysburg - shot in neck, head, and shoulders attacking Cemetery Ridge - DeCamp Hosp. 7/63 - paroled - admitted Farmville hosp. 8/30/63- furloughed 60 days 9/8/63; admitted Chimborazo 1/29/64 - returned to duty 1/30/64; applied for pension 4/9/1888 age 48 living in Buckingham - $15 approved -rerated 3/16/1904- hemorrhoids and right side of head and right shoulder hurt from wds. - $30 approved; d. 1906 in Buckingham from effects of age and gunshot wds.; widow filed pension application 4/2/1907 - m. 1881 in Buckingham, $25 approved.

BROWN, RICHARD: pwl. Co. D, KIA Ft. Donelson.

BROWN, RICHARD H.: enl. 7/8/61 Co. D in Buckingham. Pvt./Sgt,; present 7/8/61-10/61; reenl. 8/11/62 Court Martial for desertion 8/14/63 - found guilty of AWOL - reduced to ranks, forfeited 4 month's pay and had to perform 1 month's had labor, POW Gettysburg - in Ft. Delaware and Pt. Lookout 10/26/63 - exchanged 2/13/65.

BROWN, RICHARD H. (M): enl. 7/23/61 Co. D in Buckingham, present 7/8/61-10/61, 9/63-10/63; absent on furlough 11/63-12/63; present 4/1/64, 5/64-8/64; paid bounty as 4th Cpl..; POW Gettysburg - received Ft. Delaware 7/7/63-12/63 - paroled DeCamp Gen. Hosp., N.Y. 8/24/63; clothing for 11/63-12/63 paid 1/9/64.

BROWN, RICHARD T.: enl. 7/15/61 Co. H in Albemarle; present on all rolls; admitted Charlottesville hosp. 10/1/63 - returned to duty 10/5/63; surrendered by Lee at Appomattox.

BROWN, THOMAS W: enl. 7/15/61 Co. H in Albemarle, Pvt./Cpl.; present 7/29/61-10/61; death claim filed 7/22/62 – due $85.35 coffin and burial record 3/12/62 - Manuscript No. 1761.

BROWN, WILLIAM GARRISON: enl. 5/3/62 Co. H in Richmond; present on all rolls; admitted Charlottesville hosp. 8/19/63 with debilitas - returned to duty 8/27/63; post war letter from Henry C. Michle to Garrison's daughter said he was shot in head at Gettysburg; paroled Charlottesville 5/19/65; b. 1836 Brown's Cove, Albemarle Co.; 1870 census - farmer age 35 living Albemarle with wife Susan Pitimore age 29 - 4 children; d. 7/22/1898 Albemarle.

BROWN, WILLIAM R.: enl 7/8/61 Co. D in Buckingham; present 7/8/61-10/61; AWOL all rolls of 1863 and 1864 except for 11/63-12/63; on roll of Richmond hosp. 6/16/63 - sent to Castle Thunder 6/17/63; absent in arrest 7/64-8/64; admitted Chimborazo 12/25/64 with chronic dysentery - bur. Oakwood Cem.; m. about 1853 Staunton Shops, Buckingham Co.; d. 2/17/65 of camp fever, pension application filed by widow Nancy Elizabeth Brown 4/9/1888 Buckingham - $30 approved.

BRUCE, JAMES HENRY: entered service in Southall's Battery; enl. 5/3/62 Co. H, 56th Va. in Richmond; Sgt.; absent sick 7/62-8/62; WIA Sharpsburg - absent wded. 9/62-10/62 with leg wd.; admitted Charlottesville hosp. 1/9/63 - transferred Lynchburg hosp. 9/21/63 -transferred Richmond hosp. 12/10/63; 4/1/64 AWL; 5/64-8/64 absent detached service; assigned as general agent in employment of Walter Coles A.A.G., Lynchburg 2/17/65; paroled Albernarle 5/19/65; b. Maryland 1836; applied for pension 5/3/1900 age 64 living Boonsville, Albemarle Co. - totally disabled with consumption - $30 approved; made pension statement 5/8/1902 age 66; d. 6/1902 of lung trouble Boonsville; widow Frances A. Bruce applied for pension 4/28/1903 - $25 approved

BRUMEL, (BRUMWELL) ADONIRUM (ADOMIUM) D.: enl. 7/8/61 Co. A in Mecklenburg; present 9/61-10/61; KIA Boonsboro

BRYANT, GEORGE W.: enl. 5/3/62 in Co. D at Fulton Hlll; from Nelson Co.

BRYANT, HENRY: enl. 7/8/61 in Co. D in Buckingham; present 9/61-10/61; discharged 10/23/62 age 47 because over 35; b. Buckingham; farmer, dark hair, complexion and eyes, 6'.

BRYANT, JAMES: enl. 7/23/61 Co. D in Buckingham; present 9/61-10/61 (may be son of James Henry Bryant.)

BRYANT, JAMES HENRY: enl. 7/23/61 Co. D in Buckingham; present 9/61-10/61; AWOL 9/63-12/63 and 4/64-8/64 admitted Chimborazo 7/2/64 with fistula in ano - returned to duty 10/6/64 - admitted Chimborazo 10/7/64 - deserted from hosp. 12/7/64; applied for pension 5/22/1900 age 81 living Glenmore, Buckingham Co. - infirmed by age and blindness - totally disabled; reapplied 8/11/1902 - blindness in right eye due to discharge of gun cap into eye - $30 approved: rerated 10/5/1906 age 88 – totally blind - owned no land or personal properly - $100 approved; d. 1907 Buckingham of old age; widow Mildred A. Bryant applied for pension 4/6/1908 - m. Buckingham "long before the war"; son James, Jr. wrote Va. pension board in 1910 asking for mother's funeral expanses because mother did not receive pension since State ran out of money before it got to her name - family paid 1909 pension of $25 In lieu of funeral expenses.

BUCK, FLEMING N.: Co. B; MWIA Gaines's Mill - d. 7/12/62 in Chimborazo from gunshot wd. in side - bur. Oakwood Cem; m. Albemarle about 1855; widow Authella E. Buck applied for pension 6/4/1888 - $30 approved.

BUGG, JOHN R.: enl. 7/12/61 Co. G, Sgt; present 9/61-10/61; also on roll of Co. D 1st Va. Batt.; enl. 1/1/64 3rd Co. Va. Art.; POW Spotsylvania 5/10/64 - took oath and released from Ft. Delaware 6/14/65; b. 1837 Charlotte; bookkeeper, applied for pension 2/3/1911 age 72 living in Chase City, Mecklenburg Co. but applied from Florida — age and hernia kept him from working - $24 approved; d. 1917 - bur. Old City Cem. Jacksonville, Fla.

BUGG, ROBERT H.: enl. 7/10/61 Co. B in Mecklenburg; present 9/61-10/61; in hosp. Russellville, Ky. 2/4/62; POW Ft. Donelson; d. Camp Morton Prison Hosp. 3/8/62 of typhoid fever - bur. Green Lawn Cemetery - reinterred Crown Hill Cem.

BUGG, WATKINS MERRITT: enl. 6/22/61 Co. B in Mecklenburg, Musician/Pvt.; POW Ft. Donelson — sent to Vicksburg from Camp Morton for exchange - admitted Richmond hosp. 10/22/62 with spinal disease - deserted hosp. 11/1/62 - readmitted hosp. 11/12/62 - transferred to Danville hosp. 12/28/62 age 32; readmitted Danville hosp. 6/19/63 with spinal disease - deserted hosp. 7/8/63 - furloughed 7/14/63; discharged from service 7/26/63; on roll of Blacks and Whites Hosp. 11/63 with pneumonia; b. 1831; farmer, d.. 1921 Basham.

BUNCH, (BURCH) ANDERSON H. (A): enl. 5/3/62 Co. B in Richmond; assigned to detached supply team duty near Chester for war; admitted Charlottesville hosp. 1/12/64 with bilious colic - returned to duty 1/26/64; b. Albemarle; d. 7/19/1909 age 78.

BURNLEY, (BRUMELY) CHARLES F.: enl. 7/12/61 Co. G in Charlotte; discharged 10/1/61 age 19 by furnishing substitute James R. Roach; b. Charlotte Co.; farmer; dark hair, eyes, and complexion, $5^1 3"$.

BURTON, J. R.: pwl; Co. B; served 4 years.

BURTON, JOHN T.: enl. 6/10/61 Co. E in Brunswick, 2nd Lt; elected 2nd Lt. 5/3/62; MWIA and POW Gettysburg - d. from gunshot wd. in face in POW hospital, Gettysburg; b. about 1839 to John A. and Harriet J. Burton.

BURTON, ROBERT H.: enl. 7/8/61 Co. D in Buckingham; discharged 8/28/61 from Medical College of Va.; 9/61-10/61 sick furlough for indefinite time; post war list recorded KIA Ft. Donelson.

BURTON, THOMAS JEFFERSON: enl. 6/22/61 Co. B in Mecklenburg present 9/61-10/61; WIA and POW Ft.. Donelson - admitted USA Gen. Hosp, Mound City, III. 2/20/62 with thigh wd. - exchanged from POW prison at Alton, Ill, 5/17/62; present 9/63-11/63 and 4/1/64; 6/30/64 sent to hosp. with fever - furloughed 2 months 8/10/64 - certificate recommending extension of furlough 10/12/64 and 12/1/64 because of paralysis that made arms and one leg almost useless; applied for pension 4/15/1888 age 45 living Black's Ridge, Mecklenburg Co. - never regained use of leg as result of wd. at Ft. Donelson - $15 approved rerated 5/17/1897 age 60. - $30 approved; member Armistead Camp No. 26, UCV 1898.

BUSH, ALEXANDER S.: enl. 5/3/62 Co. B at Fulton Hill; discharged 5/9/62 age 25 because of deformity of left hand caused by past wound; b. Augusta Co.; merchant; fair complexion, black eyes, black hair, 5'7 1/2".

BUSH, JOHN D.: enl. 5/3/62 Co. B in Richmond; present on all rolls.

BUTLER, JOHN G.: enl. 7/26/61 Co. F in Louisa; resident of Hanover, present 9/61-10/61; d. 4/15/62 of disease In Atlanta, Ga. - bur. Oakland Cem., Atlanta, Row 3, No. 17 - left widow and female child.

CALAHAM, JAMES R.: enl. 7/8/61 Co. A in Mecklenburg, Pvt/Cpl; appointed Cpl. 11/20/63; POW Hatcher's Run - took oath and released from Pt. Lookout 6/24/65; resident of Mecklenburg; light complexion, dark brown hair, grey eyes, 5'9".

CALHOUN, ADAM N. (M.) enl. 7/18/61 Co. I in Charlotte; sick furlough 9/2/61 and 11/7/61; present 10/24/63, 11/20/63, and 1/64; admitted Chimborazo 7/21/64 with nephritis - furloughed 35 days 9/3/64 - still sick In hospital 10/24/64; POW Farmville - paroled 4/11/65 – 4/21/65; applied for pension 6/5/1900 age 60 living Jennings Ordinary, Nottoway Co; disabled due to piles from hard marching, indigestion during war, and infirmities of age - couldn't perform manual labor - $30 approved.

CALHOUN, JOHN L (C.): enl. 7/18/61 Co. I in Charlotte; certificate of disability for discharge 9/26/61 age 24; b. Augusta Co.; farmer; light complexion and hair, grey eyes.

CAMERON, (CAMERSON) THOMAS: pwl; Co. D.

CAMMICK, JAMES: enl. 4/29/62 Co. K in Richmond; AWOL and dropped from rolls by order of Gen. Garnett.

CANADA, JOHN M.: enl. 7/12/671 Co. G. in Charlotte; admitted Charlottesville hosp. 8/26/62 for debility - sent to Lynchburg hosp. 8/27/62; present 11/63-12/63, 7/64-10/64, and 4/1/64; wagon master on list of 6/30/64.

CANADA, O. T.: enl. 10/15/63 Co. G in Richmond; present 11/20/63.

CANADA, WILLIAM F. (D): enl. 7/12/61 Co. G in Charlotte; present 11/1/1861; d. in Halifax Court House hosp. of typhoid fever 8/7/62; death claim fled by widow Rebecca Canada 1/29/63 - 3 children.

CARDWELL., WYATT H.: enl. 10/14/61 Co. A., in Richmond age 17; Pvt/Sgt; POW and released Warrenton 9/29/62 - Lynchburg hosp. 1/63; discharged from service 1/20/63 because of permanent stiffness of leg due to gunshot wd. received at 2nd Manassas; 6/17/63 applied for job as clerk to CSA Sec. of War because unfit for military duty; had job in Dept. of Field Transportation from which he withdrew without giving resignation since he thought he was hired on monthly basis; 4/11/64 wrote Surgeon Gen. L P. Moore - said discharged from army against his protests and wanted to be reinstated as Sgt.; name appeared on receipt roll for clothing 9/64; on report of POWS paroled 5/18/65 in Richmond; b. Mecklenburg;

wrote letter to Maj. John McPhail 2/21/81 saying he didn't have job - needed $10 or $15 for suit - had discarded liquor.

CAREY, WILLIAM R.: Co. G; POW Burkeville 4/6/65 - took oath and released from Pt Lookout 6/24/65; resident of Charlotte Co.; fair complexion, brown hair, hazel eyes, 5'8 3/4".

CARLTON, M.: Co. K. Lt.; admitted Richmond hosp. with chronic dysentery 3/20/65; POW Richmond 4/3/65 - took oath 4/17/65.

CARPENTER, JAMES C.: enl. 7/26/61 Co. F in Louisa; discharged and entry cancelled 9/28/61 age 43 because of badly set fracture of rt. leg; b. Louisa; painter, dark complexion, black hair, grey eyes, 5'6 ½".

CARROLL, JAMES: Co .K; on list of Confederate deserters and POWS confined in Post Guard House, Clarksville, W.Va. 4/14/65; took amnesty oath and released 4/14/65 age 21; resident of Augusta Co.; farmer; fair complexion, light hair, blue eyes, 5'10".

CARROLL, JOSEPH J. enl. 6/22/61 Co. B in Mecklenburg; deserted 8/20/62 and still absent 10/31/63.

CARROLL, WILLIAM: enl. 9/5/61 Co. B in Richmond; Manuscript 1400 1/15/62 burial record.

CARROLL. WILLIAM H.: pwl; enl. Co. D in Buckingham - served 4 years; WIA Dutch Gap - bullet broke end of rt. thumb and shell cut rt. shoulder causing bone to break and severing muscles; b. Nelson; applied for pension 7/11/1892 age 69 living in Buckingham - disability due to useless right arm - $15 approved; admitted Lee Camp Soldiers' Home 8/25/1894 age 71 due to age and wds.: d. 6/14/1895 - bur. Hollywood Cern. - No. 118 West

CARTER, ARCHER LEE: enl. 7/8/61 Co. A in Mecklenburg; WIA Gaines's Mill - right leg amputated on battlefield 6/2762; discharged 8/9/62 because of leg amputation; applied for artificial limb 7/22/64.

CARTER, EDMUND T.: enl. 7/8/61 Co. A in Mecklenburg, Cpl.; present 7/8/61-10/61; d. in Richmond 6/15/62 of typhoid fever; bur. Sec. M No. 128 Hollywood Cem.

CARTER, HILLIARD W.: enl. 5/12/61 Co. E, 14th Va. Inf., Sgt; discharged from 14th Va. 8/12/61 age 26 by promotion to 3rd Lt. In Co. A, 56th Va.; enl. 8/4/61 Co. A in Mecklenburg, 3rd Lt. - asst, quartermaster, present 7/8/61-10/31/61; appointed 2nd Lt. 3/25/62 and asst quartermaster 5/3/62; b.12/35; merchant, light complexion and hair, blue eyes; d. 7/24/63 in service - cause unknown.

CARTER, JAMES B.: enl. Turner Artillery, Sgt; discharged 9/62 because over 35; later Joined Co, F, 56th Va.; admitted Chimborazo 11/21/64 with dyspepsia - furloughed 60 days 12/1/64; fought at Hatcher's Run - POW Farmville 4/6//65 - took oath and released from Pt. Lookout 6/10/65; resident of Goochland Co.; fair complexion, auburn hair, hazel eyes, 6'1 1/2"; teacher, d. 10/1892 - bur. in yard of home in Carter family cem. in Goochland - descendant of Shirley Carters of which Robert E. Lee's mother was one.

CARTER, JAMES DELK: enl. 7/8/61 Co. A in Mecklenburg; present on all rolls given; admitted Richmond hosp. 7/14/63 - furloughed 30 days 7/25/63; POW Pt. Lookout - took oath and released 6/24/65; resident of Mecklenburg; dark complexion, black hair, grey eyes, 6"; m. 1865 in Charlotte; d. 9/84 Mecklenburg of tumor and wd. in rt. limb; widow Bettie J. Carter applied for pension 4/22/1919 - $50 approved.

CARTER, JAMES THOMAS: pwl; Co. D.
CARTER, LEMUEL KNIGHT: pwl; Co. F.; entered service at 16; on list as Cpl. of those receiving clothes Co. A. 2nd Va. Batt. 10/13/64; paroled Dover Mines 5/3/65 - in Co. F, 56th Va.; b. 1/8/1846; d. 12/19/1918 Goochland.
CARTER, MONROE A: Co. F; POW Burkeville 4/6/65 d. of fever Pt. Lookout 5/5/65 - bur. POW graveyard #1670 Pt. Lookout Conf. Cem.; m. 1852 in Louisa; widow Mary E. Carter applied for pension 4/16/1898 living Goochland - $30 approved.
CARWELL JAMES W.: enl. 10/21/63 Co. K at Chaffin's Farm; present on all rolls; in Chimborazo 9/2/64; POW at Atheneum Prison, Wheeling, W. Va. 4/15/65; took oath at Clarksville, W.Va.; resident of Augusta Co.
CASPER, L J.: Co. K.; POW Ft. Donelson - sent from Camp Morton to Vicksburg for exchange.
CATTERTON, ELIJAH R.: enl. 7/15/61 Co. H in Albemarle; present 7/29/61-8/31/61; detailed agriculturalist in Albemarle Co.; pay due him for 9/61-10/61 to be paid his substitute Benjamin McAlister.
CHADWICK, WILLIAM THOMAS: pwl; Co. K.
CHAFFIN, JOHN THOMAS: enl. 7/12/61 Co. G In Charlotte, 2nd Ll/1st Lt. - Assist Q. M.; present 7/26/61/10/61; appointed 2nd Lt 7/26/61; elected 1st Lt 5/3/62; resigned 12/23/62 due to irritability of urethra; signed oath of allegiance 8/65; b.1837 in Charlotte to William T. and Sally Chaffin; m. Mary Jennings Jeffress (niece of Thomas D. Jeffress, Co, G) 6/1/68 in Charlotte; merchant's clerk in Richmond after war; about 1870 moved to Cheyenne, Wyoming; d. 1903 in Cheyenne of "broken heart" six months after wife's death.
CHAMBERS, S. G: enl. Co. C. age 28; discharged 7/20/61 due to heart disease and curvature of spine; light complexion and eyes, blue eyes. 5'10".
CHAMBERS, WILLIAM THADEUS: enl. 4/12/64 Co. G; absent sick 5/64-6/64; present 7/64-8/64; admitted Chimborazo 8/3/64 with acute dysentery - furloughed 30 days 8/13/64; admitted Farmville hosp. 9/64 - returned to duty 9/16/64; admitted Farmville hosp. 4/8/65; paroled Farmville 4/11/65-4/25/65.
CHAMBLISS., GEORGE F.: enl. 7/10/61 Co. E in Brunswick; absent on sick furlough with measles 7/10/61-8/31/61; discharged 10/30/61 due to severe case of measles; b. about 1825 to Thomas A. and Evelina B. Smith Chambliss in Smoky Ordinary, Brunswick; m. 3/12/56 to Agnes P. Baird in Brunswick; moved from Brunswick after war and no further record found,
CHANDLER, JAMES P.: enl 3/5/64 Co. A in Mecklenburg; present 5/64-8/64; on clothing rolls of 10/64 and 12/64.
CHANDLER, JOHN: enl. 7/8/61 Co. A in Mecklenburg, Cpl./Pvt; present 7/61-10/61; POW Burkeville 4/6/65 - released from Pt Lookout 6/5/65.
CHANDLER, MATTHEW L. enl. 7/21/61 Co. A in Mecklenburg; present 7/61-10/61; WIA and POW Boonsboro· confined Ft. McHenry· sent to Ft. Monroe for exchange 10/17/62; admitted Chimborazo 10/23/62 with wd. of left hip received at Boonsboro -bullet not removed; furloughed 35 days 11/6/62; WIA Gettysburg. admitted Richmond hosp. 7/14/63 with chronic rheumatism and wd. in right shoulder received at Gettysburg; furloughed

30 days 7/25/63; absent 9/63-12/63 due to wd.; 5/64-8/64 detached for light duty due to wd.; 2 letters indicate that he was "very honorable man" . none of "old soldier" in him; m. 2/19/63 in North Carolina; d. 12/25/69 In Mecklenburg of blood poisoning from wds. received during war; widow Mollie H. Chandler applied for pension 4/30/1900 - $25 approved.

CHAPMAN, RICHARD M.: enl. 3/10/64 Co. I at Camp Lee; present 5/64-6/64; transferred Co. K 32nd Va Inf. Regt.; 7/64-8/64 absent in arrest; 11/64-12/64 present; POW with Gen. Lee; committed Old Capitol Prison 4/29/65 to be called as witness in case of B.G. Harris; on list of rebels who took oath of allegiance to U.S. 4/28/65 and given transfer to Jersey City 5/9/65.

CHAPPELL, HENRY: enl. 8/6/61 Co. K in Mechanicsville - never mustered in - did not appear.

CHEELY, ANDREW JACKSON: applied for exemption, but it was rejected *3/10/62;* conscripted and assigned Co. E; admitted Chimborazo 3/15/65 with acute dysentery; POW at Richmond hosp. 4/3/65 - transferred from Libby Prison to Newport News - took oath 6/15/65; light hair and complexion, grey eyes, 5'10"; b. about 1834 in Brunswick to John and Margaret Judd Cheely; bonded to marry Martha J. Scoggins in Brunswick *11/27/54;* 6 children; 1860 census listed as shoemaker in Brunswick; m. Martha F. Laird *3/4/1874* after death of first wife; his estate inventoried by Brunswick County Court 1877.

CHEELY, JAMES W. D. (N.W); enl. 7/10/61 Co. E in Brunswick; absent with measles 7/61-8/61; POW Ft. Donelson 2/16/62; d. Camp Morton 3/31/62 of typhoid pneumonia; bur. Green Lawn Cemetery· reinterred Crown Hill Cern.; b. Brunswick about 1833 to Joseph and Diana J. Chambliss Cheely; farmer.

CHEELY, NEEDHAM S.: pwl; conscripted and assigned Co. E; brought home sick from army and lived only short time. d. 1863
bur. Smokey Ordinary, Brunswick Co.; b. about 1829 - probably brother of William W. Cheely; m. Julietta C. Short 10/27/1852 - 3 children; clerk for merchant; widow filed pension application 4/2/1888 In Brunswick - $30 approved.

CHEELY, ROBERT LENOIR; enl. 6/10/61 Co. E in Brunswick. Cpl./Pvt.; 7/61-8/61 absent with measles; POW Ft. Donelson 2/16/62 sent from Camp Morton to Vicksburg for exchange; dropped from roll on Hunton's orders between 9/63-10/63; may have been because 37 years old; b. 2/9/1828 to Robert and Julia Hobbs Cheely; bonded to marry Maria A. Bishop 5/2718/52 - 13 children; member Lebanon Methodist Church; d. 5/20/1903 - bur. Cheely Cem. near Route 642, Brunswick.

CHEELY, WILLIAM W.: enl. *7/10161* Co. E in Brunswlck; present 7/61-8/61; assigned duty as wagoneer, discharged 10/8/62 age 42 because over 35; light hair and complexion, blue eyes; b. about 1824· may have been brother of Needham S. Cheely and son of Thomas W. and Louisa A. Smith Cheely; farmer, bonded to marry Mary F. Cheely (sister of Andrew Jackson Cheely) *1/7/1848 i*n Brunswick; 7 children; daughter Lucy m. George W. House. of Co. E.

CHILDRESS, BENJAMIN M.: enr. as conscript *3/1/64* in Richmond· assigned Co. B; admitted Chlmborazo 8/24/64 with diarrhea; furloughed 40 days 7/12/64; d. at home while on furlough of disease contracted In service.

CHILDRESS, GEORGE W.: enl. 7/1/63 Co. D in Buckingham. Pvt./Cpl.; present on all rolls; assigned duty as teamster, Court Martial 3/6/63 AWOL – guilty of specification and charge; reduced to ranks and forfeited 3 months pay; b. Campbell Co.; lived Richmond for time after war; admitted Lee Camp Soldiers Home I/13/1918 age 79 due to old age - discharged 12/12/1918 for refusing to return from furlough - readmitted 11/1919; d. 2/25/1926 age 87 - bur. Hollywood Cem., East 603.

CHILDRESS, JESSE D.: enl. 7/23/61 Co. D in Buckingham, Pvt./Cpl.; present *7/61-10/61;* reenl. *8/11/62.*

CHILDRESS, JOHN Q.: .enl. 10/8/64 Co. F at Dutch Gap; admitted Chimborazo *11/21/64* with spinal disease - still there 12/64; took oath 5/5/65; named in the act of the Virginia General Assembly entitled "An Act for relief of John G. Childress, a Confederate Soldier" approved March 3, 1898, Chapter 795, page 807 - Acts of Assembly 1897-98 - on Goochland Co. pension list.

CHILDRESS, JOSEPH D.: pwl; Co. D. (probably Jesse D. Childress)

CHRISTMAS, WILLIAM JACKSON: Co. F; POW Hatcher's Run 3/31/65 - took oath and released from Pt. Lookout 6/24/65; resi· dent of Louisa; dark complexion. black hair. hazel eyes. 5'9 1/2".

CLAIBORNE, ALPHEUS S.: enl. *10/19/64* Co. E in Brunswick; admitted Chimborazo 12/2/64 with abscess in left groin - returned to duty 1/17/65; in hosp. 3/8/65· returned to duty 3/21/65: surrendered by Lee at Appomattox; returned to TN after war; took oath Nashville, TN *7/12/65;* resident Davidson Co. Tenn.; light complexion and hair, blue eyes, 5'11".

CLARK, ALEXANDER: enl. 8/15/62 Co. A in Mecklenburg; present on all rolls; WIA and POW Gettysburg - admitted DeCamp Hosp. *7/17/63-7/24/63* - paroled 8/24/63; admitted Chimborazo *7/20/84* for debilitas - furloughed 30 days 7/23/64 -letters recommending extension of furlough; admitted Chimborazo 11/28/64 with acute diarrhea - furloughed 60 days 12/9/64 to Clarksville; POW Hatcher's Run 3/31/65· took oath and released from Pt. Lookout 6/26/65; resident of Granville Co., N.C.; dark complexion. brown hair, blue eyes. 5'10 1/2".

CLARK, ELIJAH LEWIS: enl. 7/18/61 Co. I in Charlotte; Pvt./2nd Lt.; present 7/61-10/61; elected 2nd Lt. 5/3/62; resigned 11/21/62 to join Goochland Light Artillery because his office rendered a sinecure since Co.

below minimum number. Charles A. Brightwell signed his discharge papers; enl. 3/24/63 in Goochland Light Artillery as Pvt.; promoted to Sgt. and Lt.; POW Ft. Harrison 9/30/64 - paroled and exchanged from Pt. Lookout 2/15/65; b. 1838; d. 1916.

CLARK, HENRY: pwl; Co. E; post war lists indicate transferred to 18th Va. Cav. since could provide horse.

CLARK, JAMES (JOHN): enl. 7/20/61 Co. A in Mecklenburg; discharged *8/20/61* age 25 by order of surgeon because of heart disease; b. Granville Co., N.C.; farmer; sallow complexion, light hair, blue e*yes.* 5'11".

CLARK, JOHN S.; pwl; Co. I; mustered into reserves before 18; transferred into Co. I in Jan. or Feb. 1865 at Petersburg and stayed until end of war; b. Charlotte and lived there all lIfe; applied for pension 2/18/1921 age 74; owned real estate worth $850 and $800 in bank - Income $150 per year; too feeble to work - $100 approved.

CLARK, RUFUS: enl. 7/8/61 Co. A in Mecklenburg; present 7/8/61-10/31/61; WIA Cold Harbor; admitted Richmond hosp. 9/6/62 with gunshot wd. of left hand; furloughed 20 days 9/11/62; present 9/63-12/63; admitted Chimborazo 6/2/64 age 26; furloughed 60 days 6/6/64; surrendered by Lee at Appomattox.

CLARK, WILLIAM C.: enl. 7/8/61 Co. A in Mecklenburg: present 7/61-10/61; WIA Gaines's Mill; entered Farmville. hosp. and returned to duty 4/9/63; WIA and POW Gettysburg; admitted DeCamp Hosp. 7/22/63 with wd. in thigh; paroled 8/24/63; present 11/63-12/63 and 5/64-8/64; surrendered by Lee at Appomattox.

CLARK, WILLIAM F.: Co. E; admitted Farmville hosp. 3/27/63 with rheumatism - returned to duty 4/9/63 - alive in Chase City, Mecklenburg 1912.

CLARK, WILLIAM H.: enl. 7/18/61 Co. I in Charlotte; present 7/61-8/61;
d. 9/14/61 in Richmond - left $7.75 and sundry effects - had never received any pay; death claim filed by father Publius Clark - owed $31.13, resident of Charlotte.

CLARKE CHARLES J.: enl. 7/18/61 Co. I in Charlotte, Pvt./Capt.; present on all rolls; elected 3rd Lt. 11/61; sick in private home in Atlanta after Ft. Donelson; elected 1st Lt. 5/3/62; went to enroll conscripts 8/62; promoted Capt. 8/4/62; severely WIA Gettysburg - admitted Charlottesville hosp. with wd. 7/12/63 - transferred to Farmville hosp. 7/13/63; admitted Richmond hosp. 6/27/64 with diarrhea - returned to duty 7/7/64; b. 1839; m. 1860 - several sons and daughters; returned to his farm when war over; 1895 opened hotel at Charlotte Court House - later moved to Lynchburg; Lt. Commander of H. A. Carrington Camp, UCV; d. 1/11/1902 or 6/12/1902 Lynchburg age 62 - bur. Presbyterian Cem., Lynchburg.

CLARKE, ELIJAH W.: enl. 7/18/61 Co. I in Charlotte; absent sick with measles 7/61-8/61 and absent sick 9/63-10/63: present 11/63-12/63 and

5/64-6/64; admitted Chimborazo with dysentery 10/20/64 - furloughed 60 days 10/22/64; d. 1864 - death claim filed 2/27/65.

CLARKE, WILLIAM T.: enl. 8/61 Co. K in Mechanicsville; transferred to Capt Binford because deserted from him 8/20/61; (a William T. Clarke enl. 3/10/62 In Co. H, 23rd Va. Inf. in Richmond; WIA Fredericksburg 12/4/62; absent 1/63-2/63; present 3/63-12/63; sick in hosp. 1/64-2/64; deserted 8.10/64) may be same man.

CLARKE, WOODSON FLOYD: enl. 7/18/61 Charlotte in Co. I, Pvt./2nd Lt; sick with measles 8/61; very sick 2/62 and left in Bowling Green, Ky. when Regt. went to Donelson; present on all rolls; admitted Episcopal Church hosp. with chronic diarrhea 5/1/63 - returned to duty 5/29/63; elected 2nd Lt. 11/4/64; POW Hatcher's Run 3/31/65 - confined Old Capitol Prison 4/3/65 - received Johnson's Island 4/11/65 - took oath and released 6/18/65; resident Mossingford; dark complexion and hair, blue eyes, 5'9"; member Armistead Camp No. 24, UCV 1898.

CLARY, CHARLES H. enl. 7/2/61 in Co. G. 21st Va. Inf. - discharged on surgeon's certificate 4/13/62; reenl. Co. B, 56th Va.; receipt roll for clothing 12/3/64 and 12/30/64; POW Amelia 4/6/65. took oath and released from Pt. Lookout 6/26/65; resident of Brunswick; light hair and complexion, blue eyes. 5'8 3/4"; 1880 census farm laborer; 1870 census store clerk Meherrin District, Brunswick Co.; m. Sarah Lynch 11/9/70; She is believed to have died soon thereafter; m. Eveline Wright 12/6/76 in Brunswick - 7 children; bur. private graveyard near residence of Lewis M. Wright, Route 46, Brunswick.

CLARY, RICHARD; enl. 8/10/64 Co. I at Camp Lee - served 8 months - left army because of afflictions; present 7/64-8/64; receipt roll for clothing 9/27/64, 10/19/64, and 12/30/64; m. about 1856 in North Carolina; applied for pension 5/21/1900 age 74 living Ebony, Brunswick Co. - partially disabled due to infirmities of age - $15 approved - made statement 7/29/1902 age 76 - no property; d. 2/8/1915 in Brunswick of old age; widow Caroline J. Clary applied for pension 2/7/1916.

CLARY, WILLIAM BYRD: pwl; Co. B; farmer; d. about 1870 of heart trouble in Brunswick; m. 1839 in Brunswick - 4 children; widow Emily F. Clary applied for pension 8/23/1902 - said served his country faithfully and not wounded seriously - $25 approved.

CLAYBORNE, WILLIAM: enl. 1864 Co. A; POW Harper's Farm 4/6/65 - took oath and released from Pt. Lookout 6/26/65; resident of Mecklenburg; light complexion, dark hair, grey eyes, 6'; b. 6/17/27; d. 1/15/1920 - bur. Oakhurst Cem., Clarksville.

CLAYTON, JOHN K.: enl. 7/10/61 Co. E in Brunswick. Pvt./Sgt; present 7/61-8/61; WIA Gaines's Mill; furloughed 2/8/63 -2/28/63; believed KIA Gettysburg - Co. reported him POW as of 11/21/63 but no Federal or Confederate records concerning him; b. about 1836 to John and Harriet

Creath Clayton.

CLEATON, CHARLES L. enl. 6/22/61 Co. B; Cpl./Pvt.; present on all rolls; admitted Charlottesville hosp. 8/26/62 with debility - transferred Lynchburg hosp. 8//27/62; admitted Chimborazo 8/8/64 with chronic dysentery - furloughed 40 days 8/16/64; POW Hatcher's Run 3/31/65 - took oath and released from Pt. Lookout 6/24/65; resident of Mecklenburg; fair complexion, brown hair. hazel eyes, 5'9".

CLEATON, E. S.: (CSR filed under Charles L Cleaton's name.): Co. B; entered service in Richmond - served 4 years; had chronic diarrhea and typhoid fever during war; admitted Chimborazo 1/23/65 with chronic rheumatism; b. Brunswick; applied for pension 4/21/1906 age 84 living Black Ridge, Mecklenburg Co. where had lived 70 years - disabled due to old age and general debility - $30 approved.

CLEATON, THOMAS J.: enl. 6/22/61 Co. B in Mecklenburg, Cpl.; furloughed 9/61-10/61; on register of payments to discharged soldiers 11/22/61.

CLEATON, THOMAS P.: enl. 7/10/61 Co. B in Mecklenburg; present 9/61-10/61; d. in Atlanta, Ga. 2/25/62; death claim filed 9/19/62 by heirs George, Delphi C. and Mary W. Cleaton - owed $67.16 - no wife or child.

CLEATON, WILLIAM D.: enl. 6/22/61 Co. B in Mecklenburg; present 9/61-10/61; living La Cross, Va. in 1911.

CLINE, WILLIAM; Co. H; POW Petersburg 9/25/64 - in Military Prison, Louisville, Ky. - sent to Camp Chase 10/24/64 - took oath and released 5/13/65; florid complexion, dark hair, grey eyes, 57˝.

CLOPTON, PATRICK H. enl. 8/6/61 Co. K in Mechanicsville, Sgt/2nd Lt.; present 8/6/61-10/61; appointed 1st Sgt. 9/28/61; appointed 2nd Lt. 10/15/61; POW Ft. Donelson - confined Camp Chaps 3/1/62 -transferred to Johnson's Island 4/10/62 - sent to Vicksburg for exchange 9/1/62; resigned 5/5/63 age 31; dark brown hair and eyes, 5'9".

COBBS, ROBERT A.: enl. 7/8/61 Co. D in Buckingham; present 7/18/61 - 10/61; POW Gettysburg - confined Ft. Delaware 7/12/63 - transferred to Pt. Lookout 10/26/63 - sent to City Pt. for exchange 4/27/64; admitted Chimborazo 5/1/64 with chronic diarrhea -furloughed 30 days 5/17/64; absent sick 4/64-8/64; POW Burkeville 4/6/65 - took oath end released from Pt. Lookout 8/10/65; resident of Buckingham; dark complexion, dark black hair, brown eyes, 5'5 3/4".

COCKE, THOMAS E (O.): enl. 7/26/61 Co. F in Louisa; present on all rolls 7/61-12/63; WIA Boonsboro; assigned duty as teamster 1/64-3/64; WIA Petersburg 6/16/64 age 32 - admitted Chimborazo 6/17/64 with contused wd. of right leg - returned to duty 9/12/64; farmer, applied for pension 4/21/1900 age 68 living in Louisa - partially disabled - $15 approved - made pension statement 5/12/1902 age 70 - pension disallowed because property valued at $753.

COFFE, (COFFEY) ALEXANDER: pwl; Co. D

COFFE, (COFFEY) ANDREW JOSEPH: enl. 7/1/61 Co. D in Buckingham; reenl. 8/11/1862; deserted to enemy 9/63.

COFFE, (COFFEY) HESKIAH (HESIKIAH): enl. 8/11/62 Co. D in Fulton Hill; from Nelson Co.

COGBILL, JOHN: pwl Co, H,

COLE, ISAAC B.: enl. 6/22/61 Co. B in Mecklenburg; d. 11/19/61 in Richmond - body sent home to Mecklenburg - death claim filed 9/19/62 by father John R. Cole - owed $29.21.

COLE, JAMES H.: Co. G; on receipt rolls for clothing 10/19/64, 11/14/64, and 12/28/64; POW Farrnville 4/6/65 - took oath and released from Pt. Lookout 6/10/65; resident of Charlotte; fair complexion, light blue eyes, dark red hair, 5'6 ½".

COLE, JOSEPH: pwl; Co. G.

COLE, THEODERICK N.: enl. 7/12/61 Co. G in Charlotte; present 7/26/61-10/61; KIA Ft. Donelson 2/15/62 age 41; b. Charlotte; farmer, light complexion, dark hair, blue eyes, 5'2"; death claim filed by widow Martha C. Cole - owed $54.

COLEMAN, C. A: enr. as conscript 3/1/64 - assigned to Co. A 3/9/64; present 5/64-6/64; admitted Chimborazo with debilitas 7/22/64 - d. in hospital 8/4/64.

COLEMAN, DABNEY C.: enl. 5/3/,62 Co. H; discharged 8/14/62 age 30 with spinal disease; b. Albemarle; farmer, fair complexion, light hair, blue eyes, 5'11".

COLEMAN, THOMAS H.: enl. 7/10/61 Co. E; present 7/61-8/61; power of attorney given at Camp Lee 11/4/61; transferred to Co. I, 3rd Va. Cav.; b. about 1832; m. Elisabeth J. ? after war started - 9 children; d. 9/6/1899 - bur. Cheely Cem. near Rt. 642 Brunswick

COLEMAN, WILLIAM G.: enl. 5/3/62 Co. H in Richmond; WIA Gaines's Mill - admitted Chimborazo 6/28/62 with hand wd. - immediately returned to duty; admitted Charlottesville hosp. 1/5/63 with gunshot wd. - returned to duty 1/6/63; on detached detail on all rolls 1863 and 1864 - reported to Col. Tallaferro, comdg. conscripts; 1870 census - farmer age 35 with wife and 2 children ages 8 and 14 - $400 in personal estate.

COLLIER, BENJAMIN J.: enl. 6/14/61 Co. G in Charlotte; d. 3/19/62 age 27 - owed $66.44; b. Charlotte; farmer; dark complexion, light hair, blue eyes, 5'2".

COLLIER, JOHN: enl. 7/8/61 Co. A in Mecklenburg; present 7/61-10/61; WIA Gaines's Mill - admitted Richmond hosp. with wd. 7/462 - on furlough 7/5/62; absent 9/63-12/63 - missing since Boonsboro.

COLLINS, ANDREW J.: enl. 5/3/62 Co. B in Richmond; admitted Chimborazo 6/23/62 with diarrhea - transferred Scottsville 6/23/62 - admitted Charlottesville hosp. 7/9/62 with chronic rheumatism - returned to duty 7/22/62; present 9/63-12/63 and 4/1/64; AWOL 5/64-8/64; admitted

Charlottesville hosp. 5/20/64 with contusion of knee joint; deserted hosp. 7/18/64; readmitted hosp. 10/20/64 with chronic rheumatism - furloughed 2/11/65; m. 12/31/56; d. 12/11/1910 of cerebral hemorrhage in Albemarle; widow Martha A Collins applied for pension in Albemarle 2/25/1911 - $25 approved.

COLLINS, BENJAMIN J.: enl. 7/12/61 Co. G in Charlotte; present 7/61-10/61.

COLLINS, EDWARD: enl. 8/6/61 Co. K in Mechanicsville; discharged 8/17/61 - got substitute George Deakin.

COLLINS, JAMES D.: Co. A; issued clothing 12/28/64; POW Burkeville 4/6/65 - took oath and released from Pt. Lookout 6/26/65; b. 6/14/1833; resident of Mecklenburg; light complexion, brown hair, dark grey eyes, 5'5"; applied for pension 4/30/1900 age 67 living in Skipwith, Mecklenburg Co. - partially disabled due to double hernia - $15 approved; made statement 7/29/1902 property worth $464 - rerated 4/16/1906 - infirmities of old age, hernia, defective vision - $30 approved; d. 12/1/1910; bur. Wood, Collins, and Harris Family Cem., Rt. 688, Mecklenburg Co.

COLLINS, JOHN C.: pwl; Co. G; enl. 8/4/64 in Hanover, d. 6/22/85 of brain fever in Charlotte; widow Annie M. Collins applied for pension 5/11/1900 in Hanover - $25 approved.

COLLINS, THOMAS J.: enl. 7/12/61 Co. G in Charlotte; present 7/26/61-10/61; b. Charlotte; d. 3/10/62; death claim filed 5/21/62 in behalf of mother Elizabeth S. Collins - owed $63.16.

COLLINS, WILLIAM HENDERSON: enl. 7/8/61 Co. A; present 7/61-10/61; Court Martial 1/20/63 desertion - found not guilty of specification but guilty of AWOL, forfeited 4 months' pay and on detail to cut wood for Co. and Regt. until 4/1/63; POW Leesburg 5/4/63 - exchanged at Ft. Monroe 5/14/63; admitted Episcopal Church Hosp. Williamsburg 5/14/63 with catarrh - returned to duty 5/22/63; present 5/64-12/64; POW Burkeville 4/6/65 - took oath and released from Pt. lookout 6/26/65: light hair, dark complexion, hazel eyes, 5'9 1/4"; b. Halifax; m. 1863 in Mecklenburg; member Armistead Camp No. 26, UCV; applied for pension 4/26/1900 age 71 living Hanford, Mecklenburg Co. – disability due to blindness - $30 approved - made pension statement 7/25/1902 age 73; d. 10/7/1903 from stroke in Mecklenburg; widow Martha Rebecca Collins applied for pension 7/14/1904 - $25 approved.

COLLINS, WILLIAM T.: Co. G - from Charlotte; on receipt roll for clothing 10/13/64 and 10/14/64; paroled Farmville 4/11-4/21/65.

COOK, JAMES M.: enl. 7/9/61 Co. C in Louisa; present 7/62-10/682.

COOKE, W. J.: enr. as conscript 2/23/64 - assigned to Co. I 12/24/64.

COOPER, EDMUND: enl. 6/22/61 Co. B in Mecklenburg; in Medical College of Virginia 8/5/61 – 8/21/61; present 9/61-10/61; d: 11/17/61 in

Richmond - body sent home to Mecklenburg; heir was mother Martha Cooper - due $28.23 from CSA

CORKER, JAMES HENRY: enl. 7/26/61 Co. F in Louisa; present 7/27/61-10/61; admitted Charlottesville hosp. 8/26/62 with debility - transferred to Lynchburg hosp. 8/27/62 - returned to duty 10/12/62; transferred to Co. H - 25th Va. 9/9/63; present 5/64-8/64; on clothing receipt rolls 10/13/64, 10/19/64, and 12/3/64; took oath 4/25/65; resident of Hanover.

CORKER, THOMAS J.: enl. 7/25/61 Co. F in Louisa; WIA Frazier's Farm; present 9/63-12/63; sick furlough 3/1/64-6/30/64; admitted Chimborazo 8/25/64 with pneumonia - furloughed to Louisa 30 days 8/30/64; on clothing receipt roll 12/28/64.

CORKER, WILLIAM J.: enr. 7/23/64 as conscript - assigned Co. F 7/24/64; present 7/64-8/64; admitted Petersburg hosp. 4/11/65 with gunshot wd. right thigh - lower third of leg amputated in hosp.; POW in hosp. 4/15/65 - d. 4/29/65 from gunshot wd. - bur. hosp. cem.

CORLEY, MATTHEW A.: pwl; conscript, enr. Co. F at Petersburg - served until end of war; b. Louisa; miller. m. 7/30/85 in Louisa: applied for pension 5/24/1917 age 74 living at Vontay, Hanover Co. where had lived for 26 years - $50 income, 51 acres of land worth $500, and $25 personal property - weak, nervous and senile - $50 approved; d. 10/11/1928 in Rockville, Hanover Co. of old age; widow Alice S. Corley applied 11/16/1928 - $100 approved.

COSBY, THOMAS W.: enl. 7/26/61 Co. F, 2nd Lt; present 7/27/61-8/31/61; AWOL 9/61-10/61; 10/1761 received $170.66 for service in army 7/27/61-9/30/61.

COX, CHARLES B.: enl. 5/1/62 Co. K in Richmond; admitted Chimborazo 8/11/62 with continued fever - returned to duty 9/2/62; on furlough 7/63-8/63; present 9/63-10/63; present 11/63-12/63; exchanged for J. H. Hundley 4/4/64.

COX, ISHAM: enr. as conscript 2/20/64 - assigned to Co. C 2/25/64; present 4/1/64.

CRAFTON, J. E.: pwl; Co. G.

CRAFTON, ROBERT G. Co. G - transferred from Co C 25th Batt.; POW Farmville 4/665 - took oath and released from Pt. Lookout 6/24/65; resident of Charlotte; light complexion. light brown hair, grey eyes, 6'1".

CRAIG, JOHN M. enl. 8/15/62 Co. H in Gordonsville; WIA and POW Gettysburg - admitted Gettysburg hosp. 10/22/63 with wd. in thigh - paroled DeCamp Hospital - admitted Charlottesville hosp. 10/28/63 - returned to duty 12/17/63.

CRAIG, ROBERT F.: enl. 5/3/62 Co. H in Richmond; POW Sharpsburg - released, n. d.; present 7/63-1263; roll of 7/64-8/64 shows exchanged for man In Co. D, 46th Va. Regt..

CRAWLER, LEONIDAS J.: Co. D; POW Burkeville 4/6/65, took oath and released from Pt. Lookout 6/10/65; resident of Appomattox; dark complexion, dark brown hair, blue eyes, 5'101/4".

CRAWLEY, JOHN: pwl. Co. G.

CRAWLEY, WILLIAM W.: Co. I; POW Burkeville 4/6/65 - took oath and released from Pt. Lookout 4/15/65.

CREASY, JOHN: pwl; Co. I - from Charlotte, Pvt./Lt..; described as "a gallant man, promoted to Lt., and WIA and POW at Gettysburg."

CREASY, (JAMES) FRANKLIN.: enl. 7/8/61 Co. I in Richmond; discharged 8/30/61 age 30 - incapable of performing duties of soldier because of dislocation of left clavicle and diseased lungs; b. Bedford; overseer, fair complexion, light hair, blue eyes. 6'2".

CRENSHAW, JAMES N.: enr. as conscript 2/16/64 age 23 - assigned Co. I; b. Charlotte; farmer; dark hair, blue eyes, 5'9".

CRENSHAW, WYATT THOMAS: enl. 3/62 Co. G in Charlotte; POW Hatcher's Run 3/31/65 - took oath and released from PL Lookout 6/24/65; b. Lunenburg; resident of Charlotte; farmer, dark complexion, dark hair, blue eyes, 5'71/2"; applied for pension 5/1/1915 age 84 living in Keysville, Charlotte Co. - totally disabled due to age - $320 real estate - $75 personal property - $43.20 approved.

CREWS, HIRAM GEORGE: served as chaplain in Richmond hospitals and Huguenot Springs Hospital in Powhatan; appointed chaplain 56th Va. 5/2/63 - declined; also declined appointment 5/10/64; went to Washington, D.C. and Baltimore under appointment of Educational Committee of Soldiers' Orphan and Children's Fund after war; b. 7/31/1831; d. 7/29/1917 in Scottsburg.

CRONIN, STEPHEN D.: enl. 8/1/61 Co. I in Richmond, Pvt./1st Lt.; present 7/18/61-10/61; elected 2nd Lt. 5/3/62; WIA Gaines's Mill - admitted Richmond hosp. 6/28/62 with wd.; promoted 1st Lt. 1/10/63; POW Gettysburg - in Gettysburg hosp. - confined Ft. Delaware 7/14/63 and Johnson's Island 7/27/63 - transferred to City Point for exchange 2/24/65 - paroled and took oath 5/2/65.

CROSS, WILLIAM B.: enl. 7/125/61 Co. F in Louisa; present on all rolls until 4/1/64 listed as deserted to enemy since mustered for pay; received 2/10/65 by provost marshal, Army of the Potomac - took oath at City Point 2/12/65; dark complexion and hair, grey eyes; 5'8"

CROSS, WILLIAM T.: en. 7/10/61 Co. E in Brunswick; admitted to Petersburg hosp.4/1/62 for bronchitis - returned to duty 5/7/62,

CROWDER, H. C. (probably Henderson Crowder): enl. 7/15/61 Co. B in Richmond; POW Ft. Donelson - sent from Camp Morton to Vicksburg for exchange - in Richmond hosp. 8/31/62; discharged from service 1/23/63 age 27 due to pneumonia; b. Mecklenburg; farmer, light complexion, dark hair, blue eyes, 5'10".

CROWDER, HENDERSON: enl. 6/22/61 Co. B in Mecklenburg; present 9/61-10/61; b. Mecklenburg; d. Lynchburg hosp. - bur. Lynchburg Cem. Row 2, Grave 10 - death claim filed by executor 2/27/63. (Charles Thomas wrote of Henderson Crowder being in hosp. 1/10/63 and hadn't heard from him.)

CROWDER, HOWELL: enl. 6/22/61 Co. B in Mecklenburg; absent - at home on furlough 9/61-10/61.

CROWDER, JULIUS L.: enl. 6/1/61 Co. B in Mecklenburg; discharged from service 8/16/61 age 34 because not recovered from disease; b. Brunswick; farmer; dark complexion, light hair, blue eyes, 5'10".

CRUTCHFIELD, JOHN R: enl 6/22/61 Co. B in Mecklenburg; POW Ft. Donelson - d. 2/28/62; death claim filed by father 6/25/62 - due $58

CRUTCHFIELD, THOMAS A.: enl. 8/25/62 Co. B in Richmond; present on all rolls; admitted Petersburg hosp, 5/6/63; returned to duty 7/12/63; admitted Petersburg hosp. 7/13/63 - transferred lo Smallpox Hosp. 7/16/63: receipt roll for clothing 9/30/63 at Gen. Hosp. Blacks and Whites, Va.; m. 12/11/61 in Mecklenburg; d. 4/2/76 in South Hill, Mecklenburg Co. of strangulated hernia caused from wd. received in war; widow Eliza G. Crutchfield applied for pension 1900 - $25 approved.

CUMBY, (COMBEY) JOHN J.: enl. 7/1/61 Co. I in Charlotte; sick in hosp. 7/18/61-8/31/61; discharged from service 1863.

CUNNINGHAM, JAMES, JR.: pwl; Co. A, 3rd Lt.; b. 2/5/1835; d. 7/31/61, bur. family cem. - Dodd St., Chase City.

CUNNINGHAM, ROBERT R.: pwl; Co. D; wded. in foot later part of 1864 by ax while discharging night duty under detail in trenches at Howlett's Farm - lost 4 toes; applied for pension 1/1/1897 age 70 living In Norwood, Buckingham Co. - disallowed.

CUNNINGHAM, VALENTINE HYLTON: enl. 7/1/63 Co. D in Buckingham, Cpl.; present on all rolls; POW Hatcher's Run 3/31/65; sick at Pt. Lookout - took oath and released from Pt. Lookout 6/3/65; from Nelson Co.

CURD, FRANCIS E.: enl. 7/3/61 Co, D in Buckingham; reenl. 8/11/62 in Richmond; admitted Scottsville hosp. 3/17/63; on receipt roll for clothing Scottsville hosp. 8/25/63; admitted Gen. Hosp. Charlottesville with wd. 10/1/63 - returned to duty 10/3/63; m. 4/29/67 in Buckingham; d. 11/1/1895 from pneumonia in Nelson; widow Pauline E Curd applied for pension 6/19/1901 - $25 approved.

DAMERON, D.: pwl; Co. D.

DAMRON, (DAMERON) JAMES D.: enl. 7/1/63 Co. D in Buckingham; present on all rolls; POW Hatcher's Run 3/31/65 - released from Pt. Lookout 6/26/1865.

DAMRON, THOMAS B. (or DAWSON, ROBERT B.): enl. 7/1/61 Co. D in Buckingham; WIA and POW Gettysburg - admitted West's Buildings Hosp. 7/4/63 with gunshot wd. of shoulder and back - paroled 9/25/63 - admitted Chimborazo 9/28/63 - furloughed 30 days 10/10/63 and 30 days 12/3/63 - readmitted 1/28/64 with gunshot wd. of right shoulder - furloughed 35 days 2/5/64; present 4/1/64; AWOL 5/64-6/64; present 7/64-8/64.

DANIEL, GEORGE C.: enl. 6/15/61 Co. I in Charlotte; present 7/18/61-8/31/61; sick furlough 9/61-10/61; sick In Bowling Green, Ky. - detailed as nurse there 2/62; admitted Danville Hosp. 7/30/62 with rheumatism - returned to duty 10/22/62; WIA Gettysburg; - admitted Richmond Hosp. 8/5/63 - furloughed 30 days; POW Howlett's House 8/25/64 - confined Ft. Monroe and Pt. Lookout 8/28/64; d. of chronic diarrhea 4/17/65 - buried POW grave.

DANIEL HAL S.: Co. I; unfit for field service so detailed as clerk 11/24/64; wrote requesting duty near his home so could help mother with plantation.

DANIEL JOHN C.: enl. 2/1/64 Co. I at Chaffin's Farm; present 5/64-8/64; admitted Chimborazo 7/20/64 with chronic diarrhea - returned to duty 8/25/64 - readmitted for same reason 11/15/64 - retumed to duty 11/22/64; POW Hatcher's Run 3/31/65- took oath and released from Pt. Lookout 6/11/65; resident of Charlotte; light complexion, dark brown hair and eyes, 5'7"; applied for pension 5/5/1900 age 57 living Charlotte - severe rheumatism - $15 approved.
DANIEL SAMUEL pwl; Co. I: KIA near Chester Station.
DANIEL STID G.: Co. A; POW Burkeville 4/6/65- took oath and released from Pt. Lookout 6/11/65; resident of Halifax; dark complexion, black hair, dark brown eyes, 6' 1/2".
DANIEL ZACHARIAH Y.: enl. 7/8/61 Co. A in Mecklenburg; present on all rolls; admitted Richmond hosp. with typhoid fever 9/24/62 - returned to duty 11/1/62; admitted Richmond hosp. with chronic rheumatism 7/14/'63 - furloughed 30 days 7/25/63; POW Harper's Farm 4/6/65 - on list of sick POWS at Pt. Lookout - took oath and released from Pt. Lookout 6/3/65; m. 2/1/66 in North Carolina; d. 6/8/1904 Nelson Co. as result of internal bleeding of wd. received at Gettysburg; widow Emily Ann Daniel applied for pension 12/18/1908.
DAVIS, ANDREW JACKSON: enl. 6/25/61 Co. B in Mecklenburg; discharged 11/26/61 because of age - brother George W. Davis signed him up with understanding that he would be discharged if Randolph Macon College convened - at time of discharge had typhoid fever, later enl. as 1st Lt. in Gen. Joseph E. Johnston's army in N.C. with regt. of "mercenaries" (Yankee POWS who preferred fighting for enemy to being in prison); b. Mecklenburg; matriculated age 16 from Randolph Macon to VMI Class of 1866 - attended 1 year 9 months but considered graduate because fought at New Market; Adj. Joseph E. Johnston Camp, UCV; Magistrate-at-Large Chesterfield Co.; d. Grace Hosp., Richmond 10/5/1915 age 70.
DAVIS, BENJAMIN J.: enl. 7/22/61 Co. B in Mecklenburg; present 9/61-10/61.
DAVIS, D. E.: pwl; Co. D.
DAVID, EDWARD D.: enl. 8/25/62 Co. B in Richmond; present on all rolls; admitted Farmville hosp. with debilitas 5/8/63 - transferred to Gen. Hosp. Blacks and Whites, Va. 5/13/63; admitted Chimborazo 9/29/64 with dysentery - furloughed 30 days 10/8/64 to Mecklenburg; m. 1863 in Boydton; d. *3/1/1877* Brunswick of consumption; widow Elvira J. Davis applied for pension 4/7/1905 - $25 approved.
DAVIS, ELIJAH (J.): pwl; Co. H (probably Elijah Johnson Dunn).
DAVIS, GEORGE W.: enl. 6/22/61 Co. B in Mecklenburg, Capt.; detailed Quartermaster duty 11/1/61; led regiment at Ft. Donelson; recommended for promotion for gallantry but Floyd's suspension prevented papers from reaching Secretary of War; dropped as Capt. 5/5/62; appointed Q.M.

11/4/63 - roster of 4/25/64 said no order ever received assigning him to Q.M. duty; field Q.M. until 8/64 when ordered to post at Danville to relieve Maj. W. T. Sutherlin; 8/3/64 sick Richmond hosp. with internal fever and general debility - furloughed 30 days 8/15/64 to Salmon Springs, Mecklenburg Co.; went with Gen. Lomax to Greensboro, N.C. to Gen. Johnston's army; b. Mecklenburg; applied for pension 4/11/1911 age 79 living In Goodes Ferry, Mecklenburg Co.; farmer and merchant until 7/28/1910 when adjudged bankrupt - after then no occupation - left arm amputated 1909 because of spider bite received 2 years before - also rheumatism - brother supporting him - $36 approved.

DAVIS, IRA L.: pwl; Co. H (probably Ira Dunn).

DAVIS, JOHN JAMES: enl. 7/3/61 Co. D in Buckingham; present 7/8/61-10/31/81; POW Ft. Donelson - sent from Camp Morton to Vicksburg for exchange; WIA and POW Gettysburg – wded. in right hip charging up Cemetery Heights - paroled and transferred from West's Buildings Hosp. to City Pt. 11/12/63- admitted Chimborazo 11/18/63 with gunshot wd. - furloughed 60 days 11/2063; name on list dated 3/6/65 of Co. H 59th Ga. at Hanover Court House of those missing for year 1864; admitted Chimborazo 3/5/65 with gunshot wd. of groin and hips; took oath 5/4/65 in Mechanicsville; b. 11/8/1842; m. 1866 In Buckingham; applied for pension 4/3/1888 age 45 living In Paynes Landing, Buckingham Co. - $15 approved; d. 1903 in Buckingham of pneumonia; widow Martha Jane Davis applied for pension 3/16/1904 - $25 approved.

DAVIS, LILBOURNE LUCIEN: enl. 7/26/61 Co. F in Louisa; present 7/27/61-10/31/61; MWIA and POW Boonsboro; d. Boonsboro, Md. 10/15/62.

DAVIS, M. P.: pwl; enl. Co. H 5/3/62 - discharged little later as over 35 - returned to Co. H 7/63 or 8/63 and remained until end of war; applied for pension 5/29/1900 age 80 and 8 months, living in Albemarle - total disability due to old age and asthma; made statement 5/8/1902 age 83 - $462 personal property; d. Free Union 7/1906 age 88.

DAVIS, PETER L.: pwl; Co. H; b. Albemarle 9/23/1843; d. Henrico 2/26/1915.

DAVIS, WILLIAM G. (E.): enl. 7/10/61 Co. E in Brunswick; sick furlough - measles 7/10/61-8/31/61; power of attorney given Camp Lee 11/4/61; bonded to Ann E. Drummond 5/16/1835 in Brunswick (Burwell B. Wilkes, Jr. of Co. E, her uncle); 1850 census - farmer age 39 with 5 children; bur. Wilkes' Family Cem., Rt. 644.

DAWSON, A. J.: Co. B; WIA Gaines's Mill; name on list of payments to discharged soldiers 9/171862.

DEAKIN, GEORGE enl. 8/1/61 Co. K in Richmond - substitute for Edward Collins; deserted 8/27/61.

DEAN, ALEXANDER (SANDY): enl. 7/10/61 Co. E in Brunswick; b. about

1834 to Anderson and Lucy Rebecca Lanier Dean in Brunswick; m. Prudence M. Daniel 6/11/1857 In Brunswick; POW Ft. Donelson; d. 3/16/1862 Indianapolis, Ind. of typhoid fever -bur. Green Lawn Cem. - reinterred Crown Hill Cem.; death claim filed 3/12/63 for widow; due $74.86.

DEAN, JAMES H.: Co. E; b. about 1834 in Brunswick- brother of Alexander Dean of Co. E; m. Allsey Lanier (sister of Charles H. Lanier of Co. E) 11/25/1856 in Brunswick; POW Amelia Court House 4/6/65; d. of rheumatism 4/25/65 at Pt. Lookout bur. POW graveyard.

DEDMAN, JOHN H.: enl. 4/10/63 Co. A in Mecklenburg; WIA and POW Gettysburg - leg amputated on field 7/5/63 by Dr. B. C. Harrison of 56th Va. - paroled from West's Buildings Hosp. to City Pt. /25/63 - admitted Chimborazo 9/28/63 - furloughed 60 days 10/8/63; requested artificial limb 3/9/64; admitted Charlottesville hosp. 5/7/64 with leg wd. - furloughed 8/16/64; resident of Mecklenburg; filed pension application 4/16/88 age 55 living Mecklenburg - $30 approved.

DEDMAN, THOMAS J.: enl. 7/8/61 Co. A in Mecklenburg, Pvt./Cpl.; present 9/61-10/61; POW of Army of Potomac on roll dated 10/3/62; d. of wds. In Maryland 10/1/62.

DEDMAN, WILLIAM H.: enl. 7/8/61 Co. A in Mecklenburg; sick with measles 7/61-8/31/61; admitted Richmond hosp. with wd. of middle finger, left hand 9/10/62 - furloughed 9/10/62; KIA Gettysburg - claim filed by Amanda Dedman 2/21/1865.

DELBRIDGE, JAMES KNOX POLK: pwl; at beginning of war in Co. H, 12th Va. Inf.; discharged for unknown reason; conscripted and assigned Co E 1864; in service 12 months - left at surrender, b.1843 to Benjamin and Lucy Welton Delbridge in Brunswick (one sister married Edward R. Abernathy and another married Marcellus Abernathy of Co. E); farmer and laborer; age 40 m. Susan Clerks 2/3/85; filed pension application 11/7/1908 age 63 living Triplette, Brunswick Co. - almost totally disabled due to kidney and bladder trouble and eye cancer - $24 approved; d.10/8/1909 of cancer, widow applied for pension 1930 - approved.

DENTON, JOHN T.: enl. 7/1/61 Co. D in Buckingham; reenl. 5/3/62; admitted Richmond hosp. with remittent fever 10/13/62 - furloughed 20 days 10/28/62 MWIA and POW Gettysburg - admitted Camp Letterman Hosp. 7/29/63 with gunshot wd, of left lung - d. 8/2/63 age 30 - bur. grave 4, 2nd Section, Gen. Hosp., Gettysburg - disinterred to Richmond 613/72 In Box #52 and bur, Hollywood Cem.; resident Nelson Co.; m. 12/3/56 in Buckingham; widow Susan E. Denton applied for pension under 1900 act - $30 approved.

DENTON, L. J.: pwl; Co. D; from Dinwiddie.

DEY (DAY) JOHN M.: enr. as conscript 2/3/64 - assigned to Co. C 2/25/64; admitted Chimborazo 5/23/64 with swollen ankle joint - transferred to Petersburg Hosp. 5/27/64 - transferred to Kittrell Springs Gen. Hosp., N,C. 6/18/64; POW Burkeville 4/6/65 - took oath and released 6/12/65; resident of Forsyth Co., N.C.; light complexion, brown hair, blue eyes. 5'7".

DICKERSON, DRURY L.: enr. as conscript 2/16/64, assigned to Co. I 2/23/64; present 5/64-8/64; d. of heart disease in Rollins Hills, Charlotte Co. n.d.; widow Catherine H. Dickerson living in Charlotte filed for pension 1900 - $25 approved.

DICKERSON, JOHN J.: enl. 7/18/61 Co. I in Charlotte; present 7/61-10/61; WIA Ft. Donelson; discharged 9/9/62 age 38 because over 35; farmer; b. Charlotte; dark complexion and hair. 5'3"; m. 11/14/1844; d. in Charlotte of dropsy, n. d.; widow Matilda J. Dickerson applied for pension 4/14/1900 - $25 approved.

DICKERSON, JOSEPH RICHARD: enl. 7/18/61 Co. I in Charlotte; present 7/61-10/61; d. at Emory and Henry College 4/27/62 age 21 or 23; father Robert R. Dickerson filed death claim 9/6/62 - owed $82.76; b. Charlotte; farmer, blue eyes, dark hair, fair complexion, 5'8"

DICKERSON, PETER C.: enl. 7/12/61 Co. G in Charlotte; present on all rolls; extra duty as teamster 7/63-10/63 and 1/64-3/64; surrendered by Lee at Appomattox.

DICKERSON, ROBERT P.: enl. 7/12/61 Co. G in Charlotte; present 7/61-10/61; b. Charlotte; coffin obtained 3/18/62, death claim filed 7/3/62; owed $65.

DICKERSON, WILLIAM D.: enl. 7/12/61 Co. G in Charlotte; present 7/61 10/61; death claim filed 7/3/62 - owed $60.97; b. Charlotte.

DICKINSON, ROBERT POLLARD: enl. 7/9/61 Co. C in Louisa, Cpl./Capt.; 9/61-10/61 absent furlough; POW on rolls 9/63-12/63 and 5/64-8/64; elected 2nd Lt.; promoted 1st Lt.; promoted Capt. 12/31/63; paroled Beaver Darn 5/9/65; b. 2/26/1839 Louisa to Charles M. and Christiana G. Hester Dickinson; farmer; m. Josephine D. Smith 8/5/1867 Louisa; d. 4/4/1902 Louisa age 66 of heart failure - survived by widow, 2 sons, and daughter, Mrs. O. E. Driscoll of Charlottesville - bur. Mt. Pleasant Methodist Church, Louisa; widow applied for pension 6/5/1918 living in Albemarle - owned part of 81 acres of land - $50 approved.

DISHMAN, BAKER: Co. H; deserter - took oath at Bermuda Hundred 1/30/65; sent to Washington, D.C. 2/2/65; admitted Balfour U.S.A. Gen. Hosp. 2/8/65 with pneumonia - returned to duty 3/13/65.

DIXON, GEORGE H: enl. 2/10/64 Co. I at Chaffin's Farm; present 5/64-6/64; d. 8/25/64.

DIXON, JOHN T.: enl. 7/18/61 Co. I in Charlotte; 7/18/61-8/31/61 sick furlough; present 9/61-10/61; admitted Richmond hosp. 11/14/62 returned to duty 11/29/62; present 7/63-12/63; WIA 6/16/64 age 29; admitted Chimborazo with wd. of right leg - furloughed 40 days 6/22/64 - furlough extended 30 days 7/29/64; took oath 4/23/65; farmer, on roster of H. A. Carrington Camp, UCV 5/15/1922.

DOGGET, BURNET (DOGGETT, BURNETT): Co. A; not mustered in.

DOGGETT, ASA DAVID: enl. 7/18/61 Co. A in Mecklenburg, Pvt./2nd Lt.; 7/61-8/61 present; 9/1961-10/9/61 sick with measles; elected 2nd Lt. 5/3/62; MWIA Boonsboro - d. 12/27/62 at home age 37 from wds. - bur. Bethel Baptist Church Cem. Hwy. 609, Chase City; death claim filed 7/23/63 by mother Mary Doggett - owed $62.10; b. Mecklenburg; farmer, light complexion, blue eyes, dark hair, 5'6".

DOGGETT, DURRELL (DOT) D.: enl. 7/8/61 Co. A in Mecklenburg; present sick with measles 7/8/61-8/31/61; discharged 5/15/62 age 27 due to loss of left arm from wd. received Ft. Donelson; farmer; fair complexion, dark hair, grey eyes, 5'8"; bur. Bethel Baptist Church Cem, Chase City.

DOGGETT, JUDSON B.: enl. 10/7/61 Co. A in Richmond; served 4 years - left at Lee's surrender; b. Mecklenburg; farmer, member Armistead Camp No. 26, UCV; applied for pension 11/20/1908 age 82 living Skipwith, Mecklenburg Co. - disabled due to old age and rheumatism - $36 approved; d. 6/29/1918 - state paid $25 for funeral expenses.

DOLEN, (DOLAND) JOHN MAJOR: enl. 7/8/61 Co. D in Buckingham; present on all rolls; reenl. 5/3/62; WIA Gaines's Mlll and Frazier's Farm - first man in company wded.; $1 taken from pay by court martial on roll 7/64-8/64; paroled Farmville 4/11/65-4/21/65; applied for pension 12/12/98 age 64 living Buckingham - disabled due to wd. in left shoulder received at Ft. Donelson; reapplied 5/14/1900 age 66 - $15 approved; d. 12/21/1915 - state paid $25 for funeral expenses.

DORTCH, JAMES D.: enl. 6/22/61 Co. B in Mecklenburg; present on all rolls; POW Ft. Donelson - sent from Camp Morton for exchange; WIA Gettysburg - admitted Chimborazo with wd. 7/13/63 - furloughed 40 days 7/18/63; on clothing receipt lists of 10/19/64 and 11/15/64; m. 12/22/1853 in Mecklenburg; applied for pension 10/15/1888 living South Hill, Mecklenburg Co, - total paralysis of right side due to minie ball wd. received Fredericksburg 12/13/63 and still in side - $30 approved; d. 7/4/1891 Mecklenburg of paralysis; widow Martha J. Dortch filed pension application 4/30/1900 - $25 approved.

DOSWELL. LEMUEL; enl. 7/15/61 Co. H in Albemarle; absent when Co. mustered; discharged 9/7/61 - working for S. G. Atkins who had contract with CSA to supply artillery harnesses.

DRAKE. JOEL T.: enl. 7/10/61 Co. E in Brunswick: 7/10/61-8/3/61 sick in Richmond; present on all other rolls; admitted Chimborazo 7/28/62 with continual fever - furloughed 9/28/62; readmitted Chimborazo 10/22/62 with hemorrhoids - returned to duty 1/17/63; surrendered by Lee at Appomattox; b. 1833 to John D. and Mary P. Foster Drake; bonded to marry Nancy A. Hammonds 12/26/53 in Brunswick - 3 children; d. 1865 in Dinwiddie of rheumatism; widow applied for pension 4/28/1900 living Chesterfield Co. - $25 approved.

DRISCOLL., (DASHILL) LARKIN R.: Co, I; MWIA and POW Gettysburg - admitted USA Gen. Hosp. Chester, Penn. with gunshot wd. of foot - d. 7/28/63 from pyemia - bur. grave 63, Chester, Penn. Cem..- later moved to

Philadelphia Nat Cem.; death claim filed 3/1/65.
DRUMMOND, WILLIAM E. conscripted 2/9/63 and assigned Co. E; deserted 5/8/63; 7/64-8/64 absent on furlough; 9/24/64 on receipt roll for clothing; detailed with special orders 3/24/65; b. 1827 to Allen B. and Mary B. Wilkes Drummond in Brunswick m. Rebecca *Jane ? 1840's* outside of Brunswick - 14 children; farmer, d. 1870's in Brunswick.
DRUMWRIGHT, CLAIBORNE: enl. 6/22/61 Co. B in Mecklenburg; discharged by surgeon's cert. 10/26/61 age 45; b. Mecklenburg; 6'3"
DRUMWRIGHT, RICHARD C.: enl. 6/22/61 Co. B in Mecklenburg; WIA Frasier's Farm; discharged 9/13/62 age 17 because under 18; b. Mecklenburg; farmer; fair complexion, blue eyes, light hair, 6'2".
DRUMWRIGHT, WILLIAM R. enl. 6/22/61 Co. B in Mecklenburg; present on all rolls; admitted Richmond hosp. 9/1/62 with typhoid fever - returned to duty 9/13/63.
DUDLEY, NELSON PELT: enl. 7/15/61 Co. H in Albemarle; present 7/29/61-10/31/61; POW Ft. Donelson - sent from Camp Morton to Vicksburg for exchange - admitted Charlottesville hosp. for debilitas 10/7/62 - returned to duty 10/7/62.
DUFFER, WILLIAM G: enl. 10/15/63 Co. G in Richmond present 9/63-12/63.
DUKE, THOMAS: enl. 4/15/64 Co. H in Albemarle; AWOL 5/64-8/64.
DUNCAN, LUKE: Co. E; POW Burkeville 4/6/65 - took oath and released from PL Lookout 6/5/65; applied for pension 4/18/1901 age 70 living Childress, Montgomery Co. - totally disabled as result of wd. in left arm received on skirmish line 5/64 - $15 approved.
DUNCAN, ROBERT H.: enl. Co. D 1864 in Richmond; POW Hatcher's Run 3/31/65 - took oath and released from Pt Lookout 6/11/65; b. Buckingham; farmer; light complexion and hair, grey eyes, 5'9 1/4"; applied *for pension 4/2/1907* age 62 living Scottsville, Buckingham Co. - disability due to useless right arm from effects of vaccination during *war* - $15 approved; rerated 4/25/1917 age 75 living in Albemarle - totally disabled due to old age and poor health - $35 approved.
DUNFORD, FRANK: *enr.* as conscript 2/11/64; assigned Co. C 2/25/64 at Chaffin's Farm; deserted near Richmond 3/64.
DUNFORD, JAMES: enr. as conscript 2/11/64 - assigned to Co. C 2/25/64; deserted near Richmond 3/64.
DUNN, ELIJAH JOHNSON: enl. 5/3/62 Co. H in Richmond; present 7/63-12/63 and 4/64-8/64; admitted Charlottesville hosp. 5/28/63 with pneumonia - returned to duty 9/30/63; deserted from Chimborazo 6/23/64; POW Hatcher's Run 4/2/65 - paroled at Charlottesville 5/17/65; b. near Nortonsville 7/11/1830 or 1839; m. Susan Ann Sandridge 1861; farmer and justice of peace; d. 9/21/1911 In Charlottesville - bur. Riverview Cem., Charlottesville.
DUNN, GEORGE M.: enl. 5/3/62 Co. H in Richmond, Pvt./Cpl.; admitted

Chimborazo 6/24/62 with bronchitis - transferred to Lynchburg 6/26/62; admitted Charlottesville hosp. 5/18/63 with chronic diarrhea; transferred Farmville hosp. 5/17/63; returned to duty 7/16/63; present 7/63-12/63; admitted Chimborazo 8/10/64 with chronic diarrhea - furloughed 40 days 9/2/64 to Ivey Depot, Albemarle Co.; post war list showed d. 9/64 from injuries received in service.

DUNN, HENRY M.: Co. H; WIA Gaines's Mill - admitted Chimborazo 7/28/62 with remittent fever; d. 8/24/62 of typhoid fever - death claim filed by mother Elizabeth Dunn 2/25/64.

DUNN, HENRY T.: Co. H; admitted Chirnborazo with constant fever 10/20/64 - furloughed 60 days 10/22/64; admitted Richmond hos p. 1/18/65 - returned to duty 1/19/65; paroled Charlottesville 5/18/65; d. 1894 near Nortonsville, Albemarle Co. from disease; widow applied for pension 6/1/1900 living Brown's Cove, Albemarle Co. - $25 approved.

DUNN, IRA: enl. *5/3/62* Co. H in Richmond; present 7/63-12/63; transferred from Farmville hosp. to Charlottesville hosp. 6/9/63 with chronic diarrhea - returned to duty 8/28/63; admitted Richmond hosp. 9/25/63 - returned to duty 9/26/63; 7/64-8/64 absent sick - furloughed to Albemarle 9/30/64 from Chimborazo - readmitted to Charlottesville hosp. 11/2/64 with chronic diarrhea - returned to duty 1/18/65.

DUNN, JOHN T.: enl. 7/15/61 Co. H in Albemarle; present 7/61-10/61; admitted Charlottesville hosp. 10/12/62 with debility – sent to Colony 10/17/62 - returned to duty 11/6/62; present 7/63-12/63 and 4/64-8/64; POW Dinwiddie Court House 3/3/65 - confined Old Capitol Prison - deserted to enemy and released on oath of allegiance 6/6/65.

DUNN, THOMAS W.: enl. 5/3/62 Co, H in Richmond; resident of Albemarle; admitted Chimborazo 6/24/62 with neuralgia - transferred Lynchburg hosp. 6/26/62; admitted Chimborazo 5/16/63 with debility - returned to duty 5/27/63; KIA Gettysburg; death claim filed 11/4/63 - owed $57.63.

DUPRIEST, JOHN N.: enr. as conscript 3/7/64 - assigned Co. G 3/16/64; present *4/1/64;* absent sick 5/64-8/64; admitted Chimborazo 6/5/64 with dyspepsia - furloughed 30 days 6/25/64 - furlough extended 30 days 7/26/64; 8/26/64 ordered to report to his command by Farmville Medical Board; admitted Chimborazo 12/29/64 with acute dysentery - furloughed 30 days 2/5/65; POW Burkeville 4/6/65 - took oath and paroled from Pt. Lookout 6/11/65; resident of Lunenburg; florid complexion, dark brown hair, hazel eyes, 5'81/2'.

DURRETTE, JAMES T., M.D.: enl. 7/15/61 Co. H., Sgt. - promoted hosp. steward and acting asst. surgeon at Chimborazo; present *7/29/61-10/31/61*; detailed 2/19/62 by Sec. of War to Chimborazo as druggist until end of war; age 22 on roll 9/63; applied to U. S. authorities for parole at Chimborazo 4/17/65; b.10/21/1840 in Albemarle, son of Thomas Durrette,

Jr. and Mary E. Early; m. Susan A. Gaines of Prince William - d. childless; m. Mary M. Moon 9/12/1871 in Washington, D.C. - 2 boys and girl; 1884 - practicing medicine in Earlysville, Albemarle Co. and cultivating his estate in Rivanna district.

DUTTON, W. C.: Sgt.; POW paroled Richmond 5/1/65.

EADES, JAMES H.: enl. 7/8/61 Co. D in Buckingham; broke arm at Gettysburg; present on all rolls until discharged 7/15/64; applied for pension 5/14/1900 age 72 living in Centenary, Buckingham Co. - disability due to old age - received $30; made pension statement 8/11/1902 age 74 - no property; in Mexican *War.*

EARLY, GEORGE W.: enl. 7/15/61 Co. H in Albemarle, 2nd Lt.; appointed 2nd Lt. 7/29/61; present 7/61-10/61; dropped 5/5/62

EARNEST. HENRY CLAY: enl. 8/6/61 Co. K in Mechanicsville, Cpl./Pvt; POW Ft. Donelson - sent from Camp Morton to Vicksburg for exchange; present on all rolls until 7/64-8/64 when roll showed reduced to ranks; received clothing 9/27/64 and 10/13/64; POW Burkeville 4/6/65 - took oath and released from Pt. Lookout 6/11/65; resident of Hanover, light complexion and hair, blue eyes, 5'103/8".

EARNEST, VICTOR: enl. 7/9/61 Co. E in Louisa; got substitute and deserted 5/14/62.

EAST, WILLIAM T. (Y.): Co. K; POW Farmville 46/65; d. of pneumonia Pt. Lookout 5/3/65 - bur. POW graveyard.

EDMUNDS, NICHOLAS EVERETT: enl. 7/10/61 Co. E in Brunswick absent on sick furlough with measles 7/10/61-8/3/61; WIA Gaines's Mill - admitted Chimborazo 6/28/62 with wd. in head; 9/63-10/63 roll shows dropped by order of Gen. Hamilton; joined Co. B, 32nd Va. Cav.; elected Lt; b. 4/6/1839 to Nicholas Sterling and Martha Harrison Edmunds (maternal grandfather Captain James Junkin Harrison famous for his racing thoroughbreds and member Virginia Senate 1845); graduate Hampden. Sydney 1858; worked for father operating farm, store, foundry and making harnesses *and saddles*; 1871 went to Mississippi and then Texas where taught school; m. Sarah Wilkinson; lived rest of life in Bell County, Texas; 7 children; d. 4/6/1920 age 81 - bur. Wilkinson Cem. in Wilkinson Valley, Bell Co., Texas - after Stillhouse Hollow Reservoir built, cem. was moved to Cedar Knob Cem. Belton, Texas.

EDWARDS, David D.: enr. 8/4/63 as conscript - assigned 2/23/64 to Co. C; present 5/6-8/64; on clothing roll 10/64.

EDWARDS, WILLIAM E.: enl. 6/22/61 Co. B in Mecklenburg, Musician/Pvt; POW Ft. Donelson - sent from Camp Morton lo Vicksburg for exchange.

ELAM, JOHN W.: Co. I; POW Hatcher's Run 3/31/65 - released *and* took oath 6/4/65; signed J. W. Pollard's pension application 1/20/1913. Probably Billy Elam mentioned in John Holt's letters.

ELDER, JOHN W.: enl. as conscript 2/16/64; assigned to Co. G 2/25/64; present on all rolls until deserted to enemy 1/6/65 - took oath of rebel deserter at Bermuda Hundred 1/8/65 - sent to Washington, D.C. 1/11/65 - then to Henderson, Ky.

ELLINGTON, BRANCH A.: enl. 7/18/61 Co. I in Charlotte; admitted Richmond hosp. 12/24/62 with debility; furloughed 60 days 2/13/63; present on all rolls until 6/1/64; MWIA Cold Harbor - admitted Chimborazo shot through left lung - d. 7/2/64 - left $1 and sundry effects - bur. Oakwood Cem.

ELLIOTT, ALEXANDER: enl. 7/8/61 Co. A in Mecklenburg; present 7/61-10/61 and 9/63-10/63; absent on detached duty as shoemaker at C.S. Clothing Depot in Richmond 11/63-12/63 and 1/64-8/64; POW near Howlett's House 8/25/64 - confined at Bermuda Hundred, Ft. Monroe, and Pt. Lookout 8/27/64 - paroled and transferred Aiken's Landing for exchange 3/14/65 - admitted Chimborazo 3/17/65 with chronic diarrhea - furloughed 60 days *3/24/65.*

ELLIOTT, JOHN: enl. 7/8/61 Co. A in Mecklenburg; present until died in Richmond hospital 9/13/61.

ELLIOTT, M. D.: pwl; Co. H.

ELLIOTT, ROBERT: enl. 7/18/61 Co. I in Charlotte; present 7/61-10/61; KIA Gettysburg.

ELLIOTT, THOMAS C.: enl. 7/12/61 Co. G in Charlotte; Cpl.; present 7/61-10/61.

ELLIS, ROBERT STAPLETON, JR. (Dr."'TUMP" nickname for Robert): enl. 7/9/61 Co, C in Louisa, 2nd Lt./Lt./Capt; absent since 8/4/61 *for* unknown reason; present 9/61-10/61; appointed 2nd Lt. 7/9/61; elected 1st Lt. 5/3/62; KIA Gettysburg; b. Ellis Plantation in Orange Co. to Robert S. and Emily Sneed Ellis; attended University of Pennsylvania Medical School - graduated from Woodlawn Academy (now Medical College of Virginia).

ELLIXSON, JAMES B.: enl. 7/8/61 Co. A in Mecklenburg; Cpl.; admitted Richmond hosp. 7/13/62 with dysentery - returned to duty 7/23/62; WIA Gettysburg - Co. later reported "wded., supposed mortally," but no Federal records concerning him.

ELMORE, JAMES R.: enl. 7/10/61 Co. E in Brunswick Co.; 7/61-8/61 absent on sick furlough with measles; power of attorney signed 11/4/61; deserted 4/23/63 - amnesty oath 10/31/64 - forwarded to Ft. Monroe 11/1/64 - confined at Military Prison, Camp Hamilton, Va.; released by Federals 11/15/64 - went to Norfolk which was in Federal hands - no record found to indicate he returned to Brunswick; dark complexion, brown hair, grey eyes, 5'10"; b. 1837 to John T. and Jane E. Wilkes Elmore in Brunswick.

ELSOM, RICHARD S.: enl. 7/1/63 Co. D in Buckingham; listed as AWOL 9/63-12/63; from Nelson Co.

EPPERSON, DAVID J.: enl. 3/11/62 in Lunenburg Rebel Artillery in Richmond; discharged for disability 8/9/62; enl. 2/9/63 Co. E in Brunswick; present 9/63-10/63; absent sick 11/63-12/63; admitted Episcopal Church Hosp. Williamsburg 3/21/64 with vulnus incision; absent sick 4/64-8/64; on roll of CSA Hosp. Danville 10/10/64 with debilitas - returned to duty 10/11/64; in Chimborazo 12/12/64; letter saying he should be furloughed because unfit for duty due to ulcer of toe; portion of nail removed 12/15/63; b.1828 probably son of David end Patsey Moore Epperson; m. Susan R. Epperson daughter of James and Martha Pritchett Epperson - 4 children; d before 1880 of T. B. in Surry Co.; widow applied for pension 1900 living near Walthall's Store - approved.

EPPERSON, JAMES E.: enl. 2/9/63 Co. E in Brunswick; POW Gettysburg - sent to Ft. Delaware 7/7/63-7/12/63 - Chester Hosp., Gettysburg 8/10/63 - Pt. Lookout 10/2/63 - d. at Pt. Lookout 12/24/63 - bur. Pt. Lookout Confederate Cem. - death claim filed 9/21/64 by widow; b. about 1829 in Brunswick to James and Martha M. Pritchett Epperson (James's sister married David J. Epperson of Co. E).; m. Jane Lewis 1/7/63 in Brunswick; wrote will 2/10/63..

ESTES, JAMES E.: enl. 6/18/61 Co. G in Charlotte; POW Gettysburg - confined Ft. McHenry and Ft. Delaware - on list of POW's who joined 1st Connecticut Cavalry 10/4/63; b. Dinwiddie.

ESTES, JOHN H.: Co. C; admitted Chimborazo 3/21/65 with rubeola - POW Richmond hosp. 4/3/65 - sent to Jackson Hosp. 4/8/65, Libby Prison, and then Newport News 4/23/65; took oath 6/15/65; resident of Orange Co., light complexion, dark hair, blue eyes. 5'5".

ESTES, LITTLETON E .: enl. 5/3/62 Co. H in Richmond; admitted Charlottesville hosp. 1/5/63 with wd. - returned to duty 1/13/63; present 7/63-12/63; admitted Chimborazo 6/4/64 with flesh wd. of right hand - furloughed 60 days 6/9/64; admitted Charlottesville hosp. with hand flesh wd. 8/19/64 - furloughed 30 days; receipt roll for clothing 10/13/64 and 11/3/64; applied under 1888 pension act in Albemarle - paid $36 in 1909.

ESTES, ROBERT G.: enl. 7/15/61 Co. H in Albemarle; present 7/61-10/61; POW on all rolls after 7/63 and believed KIA Gettysburg, but no Federal records concerning him.

ESTES, W. JOE: enl. 5/3/62 Co. H in Richmond; transferred Salisbury, N.C. 10/10/62 admitted C.S.A. General Hospital 10/12/62 - sent to Colony 10/17/62 - returned to duty 10/24/62; KIA Gettysburg, but no Federal records concerning him.

ESTIS, THOMAS B. (J. B.): enl. 9/1261 Co. C. ; Pvt/Sgt; present 9/61-10/61; WIA Frasier's Farm; MWIA Gettysburg; admitted Richmond hosp. 7/19/63 with gunshot wd. of shoulder - d. of wds. 8/8/63 - left pocketbook containing $76.05; bur. Sec. T, No. 301 Hollywood Cem. 8/9/63; death claim filed 1/19/64 - owed $133.97; b. Louisa.

EUDAILEY, FRANCIS C.: enl 7/21/61 Co. G in Charlotte; present on all rolls; furloughed from Richmond hosp. 9/21/62; admitted Chimborazo 9/11/63 with fever - returned to duty 9/23/63; receipt roll for clothing 12/28/64; b. Charlotte; lived In Amelia before admitted R. E. Lee Camp Soldiers' Home 3/1/1909 age 73 because of old age and infirmities; d. 1/10/1911 *age* 75 - bur. Hollywood Cem. East Section,
EUDAILEY, JOHN T.: enl. 7/12/61 Co. G in Charlotte, Pvt./Cpl.; present on all rolls; admitted hosp. 10/9/62 with debility - returned lo duty 10/23/62; POW Hatcher's Run 3/31/65 - took oath end released from Pt Lookout 6/12/65; resident of Charlotte; farmer, light complexion, dark brown hair, blue eyes, 6'1".
EUDAILEY, SAMUEL P.: enl 7/12/61 Co. G in Charlotte; present 7/61-10/61; believed KIA Gettysburg - death claim filed 6/18/64.
EVANS, EDWIN P.: Co. G; permission to go home to his tannery and other business granted 11/14/64 and 12/10/64; POW Farmville 4/6/65 - took oath at Newport News; resident of Appomattox; dark hair, complexion, and eyes, 5'11".
EVANS, JOHN L.: enl. 6/22/61 Co. B in Mecklenburg; Pvt./Cpl.; admitted Chimborazo 1/22/63 with debility - returned to duty 3/25/63; present on all rolls - temporarily on detached quartermaster service baling hay 4/64-5/64; admitted Sub Depot Field Hosp. Army of Potomac in Burkeville with gunshot wd. of right knee 4/16/65 - POW paroled Burkeville 4/14/65-4/17/65.
EVANS, ROBERT M.: Field and Staff - Asst Surgeon/Surgeon; appointed Asst. Surgeon 10/16/61 in Tenn.; assigned 59th Va. 1/30/61; appointed Asst. Surgeon 56th Va. 5/3/62; Appointed Surgeon 7/18/62; relieved from 56th Va. 5/15/63 and ordered to report for new assignment.
EVANS, WILSON E.: enl. 8/25/62 Co. B in Richmond; POW Gettysburg - d. Ft. Delaware 11/4/63 of intermittent fever - bur. Finns Point National Cem., N.J.
EZELL, BENJAMIN J:. Co. B; d.10/23/62 of typhoid fever at Winchester - death claim filed *2/2/63* by mother Elizabeth Ezell - owed $79.30.
EZELL, JOHN W.: pwl; Co. B; came home sick during war and died week later of typhoid fever contracted In service; m. 9/21/1853 in Mecklenburg; widow Mary T. Ezell applied for pension 4/21/1888 living South Hill, Mecklenburg Co. - $30 approved.

Chapter 15

Roster 56th Virginia Regiment, F thru L

FAISON, JAMES H.: enl. 8/7/63 Co. K at Hicksford; present 9/63-12/63 and 4/64-6/64; admitted Chimborazo 6/14/64 with bronchitis, - returned to duty 6/28/64; admitted Chimborazo 11/5/54 - d. of pneumonia 11/8/64.

FALLEN, JAMES: pwl; Co. I.

FALLEN, LAFAYETTE H.: enl. 10/1/64 Co. I in Dutch Gap; admitted Chimborazo with pneumonia 11/23/64 - returned to duty 1/17/65; MWIA and POW Battle of Hatcher's Run; admitted Fair Ground Hosp. Petersburg 4/11/55 with gunshot wd. of right thigh - d. 4/20/65 bur. Fair Ground Hosp. Cem.; m. 2/11/1851 in Appomattox; widow Mary A. Fallen applied for pension 5/10/1888 living in Appomattox - $30 approved.

FARLEY, HENRY (HARVEY): pwl; Co. G.

FAULKNER, A. H.: Co.G; admitted Chimborazo 11/4/64 with chronic cystitis; admitted Farmville hosp. with chronic rheumatism 2/25/65 - granted leaves 3/15/65 and 4/4/65; paroled Farmville 4/11/65-4/21/65.

FEILD, (FIELD) DR. JOHN ALEXANDER: enl. 7/10/61 Co. E in Brunswick, 2nd Lt.; POW Ft. Donelson age 27 - received Camp Chase 3/1/62 - transferred lo Johnson's Island 4/10/62 - sent to Vicksburg for exchange 9/1/62; dropped as 2nd Lt. 5/5/62; reentered army as Surgeon to Stonewall Brigade where served until end of war, born in Brunswick 1835; son of Dr. John and Mary Harriet Bolling Feild (brother was Dr. Hume Feild, Assistant Surgeon CSA - another brother William Meade Feild was Lt Col. CSA); graduated Hampden-Sydney 1852; attended UVA 1854-1855; received medical degree from University of New York -practiced in Brunswick before war and 5 years after war - moved to Greenville Co. where practiced until 1/1880; dark brown hair, 5'10"; m. Maria E. Tucker of Brunswick 11/6/1867 - 1 Son.

FEILD, (FIELD) RICHARD V.: enl. 7/10/61 Co. E in Brunswick, Sgt.; 12/9/62 McPhail requested that Feild be enrolling officer in Brunswick; WIA Gettysburg - admitted DeCamp Gen. Hosp. with hip wd. 7/17/63 - paroled from DeCamp 9/16/63; WIA Petersburg siege 1864; took oath in Richmond 5/23/65; b. about 1835 to Richard W. and Ann Catherine Wyatt Feild; 1850 census - living in home of Methodist minister John G. Claiborne and attending school conducted in his home; m. Louisa C. Flournoy 5/30/66 (3 of her brothers in Co. E) - 9 children; moved to California after marriage and lived there rest of life; d. 4/28/1904 age 69 in Tulana Co., Calif.

FERGUSON, JAMES P.: enl 7/8/61 Co. D in Buckingham; 2nd Lt./Lt.; present 7/61-10/61; KIA Ft. Donelson; survived by mother, 2 sisters, and brother - owed $243 by C.S.A.

FERGUSON, THOMAS E.: enl 7/8/61 Co. D in Buckingham; present 7/61-10/61; AWOL on all other rolls; b. Buckingham; applied for pension 5/14/1900 age 75 - disability due to old age and general debility - $15 approved.

FIELDS, JOHN A.: enl. 8/6/61 Co. K in Mechanicsville; present 7/61-10/61; WIA and POW Gettysburg - admitted Gen. Hosp. Gettysburg with heel wd. 7/12/63 - sent to Ft. McHenry. Ft. Delaware. and Pt. Lookout -paroled 2/18/65; on list of POWS in U.S. Military Prison (Libby) 4/10/65; b. Hanover Co.; admitted Lee Camp Soldiers' Home temporarily 1/27/1900 age 67 for general debility - admitted permanently 3/8/1900; received Soldiers' Cross of Honor 1/12/1912; d. 4/30/1913 age 80 – bur. East, No. 206 Hollywood Cem.

FINLEY, GEORGE WILLIAMSON: enr. as Capt (Capt. George Finley's Co. Clarksville Blues) 5/12/61 Co. E 14th Va. Inf. age 22 - not reelected Capt at reorganization 5/6/62; Appointed 1st. Lt. and adjutant 5/27/62; resigned 11/10/62 because called home by order of civil court to help widowed mother settle his father's involved estate; elected Lt. of Co. K 56th Va. Inf. 4/63; POW Gettysburg at stone wall - confined Ft. Delaware, Johnson's Island 7/18/63, Pt. Lookout 4/22/64 (admitted Hammond U.S. Hosp. at Pt. Lookout with chronic dysentery), Ft. Delaware 6/25/64, and Hilton Head 8/20/64 - one of the "Six Hundred" sent for retaliation - sent back to Ft. Delaware 3/12/65 where took oath and paroled 5/14/65; light complexion, brown hair, hazel eyes, 5'10"; b. 12/1/1838 in Caswell Co, N.C. son of Augustus Clemens Finley and Anne Edwards Williamson Finley; raised in Clarksville, Mecklenburg Co.; attended Clarksville Academy and Dan River Academy, Yanceyville, NC.; entered Hampden-Sydney - was graduated from Washington College (now Washington and Lee)1858; discount clerk in Clarksville bank - after 4 months became manager of bank; m. Margaret Elizabeth Booker of Charlotte 5/4/1859; decided to become minister while POW - entered Union Theological Seminary 1866 - took only partial course load due to poor health from prison life - minister In Springfield. W.Va. - 1890 appointed evangelist for Abingdon Presbytery, 1903 pastor of Tinkling Springs Presbyterian Church, Augusta, Va. and chaplain of 3rd Brigade, Va. Division UCV; trustee of Hampden-Sydney, UTS, Davis and Elkins College, and president of Board of Trustees Mary Baldwin; received honorary Doctor of Divinity from Washington and Lee 1899 member Phi Kappa Psi fraternity; 14 children; d. 4/23/1909 in Staunton leaving 5 sons and 4 daughters - bur. Tinkling Springs church yard.

FLETCHER, JAMES D.: enl. 7/9/61 Co. C in Louisa; present on all rolls; paroled Louisa Court House 5/24/65; b. 1/18/1824; d. 12/1/1917 - bur. McNew Family Cem., Mabe.

FLOURNOY, JACOB MORTON: enl. 7/10/61 Co. E in Brunswick,

Pvt./Cpl.; WIA and POW Ft. Donelson - sent from Camp Morton to Vicksburg for exchange; WIA Gettysburg – furloughed from Richmond hosp. 60 days 8/10/63 to Lawrenceville due to wd. of right forearm and pneumonia - absent on sick furlough 9/63-12/63 and 4/1/64 - present 5/64-8/64; POW Hatcher's Run 3/31/65; released from Pt. Lookout and took oath 6/12/65; light complexion, light brown hair, light blue eyes, 5'11-3/8"; b. about 1844 in Charlotte Co, to Thomas, and Frances M. Venable Flournoy; farmer, m. Mildred Carrington - 4 children; after her death m. Mary Virginia Merritt 1/4/1888; Commander of Brunswick Camp CV - attended last reunion in Lawrenceville in 1908; applied for pension 5/28/1925 age 82 living in Charlie Hope, Brunswick Co. - totally disabled by old age - $140 approved; bur. Union Church Cem. on Route 656 in Brunswick - Confederate tombstone.

FLOURNOY, NATHANIEL ABRAHAM; enl. 7/10/61 Co. E in Brunswick age 21; 1st. Lt./Capt.; appointed 1st Lt. 7/15/61; POW Ft. Donelson – confined Camp Chase 3/1/62 and Johnson's Island 4/10/62; sent to Vicksburg for exchange 9/1/62; 5/5/62 dropped as 1st Lt.; 3/29/63 promoted to Captain Co. K, 56th Va.; admitted Richmond hosp. 5/7/63; 7/63-8/63 absent on detached service - present 9/63-12/63, 4/1/64. and 5/64-6/64 - absent sick 7/64-8/64; admitted Richmond hosp. 9/24/64 with diarrhea - furloughed 10/1/64 - admitted Farmville hosp. 10/5/64 with fever and chronic diarrhea - furloughed 30 days; admitted Richmond hosp. with chronic diarrhea 3/15/65 - returned to duty 3/18/65; 6' tall; b, 1839 in Charlotte (Jacob Morton Flournoy's brother); graduate Hampden-Sydney 1858; attended UVA 1859; taught school in Miss. before war, m. Laura E. Lewis 12/21/64 - 4 children; moved to TN after war and opened school; d. 1870's TN.

FLOURNOY, WILLIAM VENABLE: pwl; enl. Co. E latter part of war; b. 1846 Charlotte (brother of Jacob Morton and Nathaniel Abraham Flournoy); went to TN and Calif. after war where taught school; acquired a lot of land in Tulare Co., Calif.; returned to Va..; attended Lawrenceville reunion 1908; never married; d. 3/31/1929 Brunswick - bur. Union Church Cem. with Confederate marker.

FLOYD, EDWARD A.: enl. 6/22/61 Co. B in Mecklenburg; Charles Thomas's letters indicated he was cook for company; furloughed 4/11/62-5/1/62; present 9/63-12/63 and 4/64-8/64; admitted Chimborazo 2/25/65 with acute diarrhea; surrendered by Lee at Appomattox.

FORD, JAMES M.: enl. 2/17/61 Co. B in Richmond; admitted Chimborazo 5/16/63 with debility - furloughed 30 days 6/7/63 - returned to duty 7/30/63; present 9/63-12/63, 4/1/64, and 5/64-8/64; POW Farmville 4/6/65 - released 6/2/65.

FORD, WILLIAM JACKSON: enr. as conscript in Richmond 3/14/64, assigned to Co. B 3/21/64; present 4/1/64 and 5/64-/8/64 - improperly absent since mustered for pay 6/30/64; POW Burkeville 4/6/65 - took oath and released from Pt. Lookout 8/12/65; light complexion, brown hair, dark blue eyes. 5'61/2"; b. North Carolina - but moved to Brunswick before war. m. Mollie Manning 1861 in Warren County, N.C. - 10 children; overseer before war; farmer in Brunswick after war, d. 3/16/1905 - bur. Prospect United Methodist Church, Ebony - tombstone says in Co. G, 21st Inf. Regt.

FORE, ROBERT McD.: enl. 10/1/64 Co. G in Farmville; discharged age 33 due to surgical double hernia; b. Campbell Co.; miller, black eyes and hair, dark complexion, 5'7".

FOSTER, R. B.: Co. A; received clothing 12/28/64; POW in Richmond - took oath and released 4/17/65.

FOSTER, W. B.: pwl; enl. 1862 Co. K.; applied for pension 5/5/1900 age 63 living Drake's Branch, Charlotte Co. - disabled due to liver disease, rheumatism, and general debility - not approved; reapplied 5/12/1902 age 65 - $15 approved.

FOSTER, WELLINGTON W.: enr. as conscript 1/8/64 at Chaffin's Farm - assigned to Co. C 1/11/64; admitted Chimborazo 7/25/64 with acute dysentery - returned to duty 8/18/64; POW near Howlett's House 8/25/64 - confined Bermuda Hundred, Ft. Monroe, and Pt. Lookout 2/10/65 - exchanged 2/10/65; admitted Chimborazo 2/15/65 - furloughed to Louisa 60 days 3/9/65; POW Louisa - took oath and released 5/22/65; applied for pension 4/28/1900 age 68 living Trevillans, Louisa Co. - partially disabled due to heart disease - $15 approved; made pension statement 5/12/1902 age 70.

FOSTER, WILLIAM L.: Co. E; POW Burkeville 4/6/65 - took oath and released from Pt. Lookout 6/12/65; resident of Brunswick; dark hair and complexion, grey eyes, 5'101/8"; lived Brunswick 1850's; 1860 census age 33 living San Marino, Dinwiddie Co. with wife Mildred and 7 year old son; 6 children; farmer and wheelwright; d. about 1881.

FOWLER, W. J.: Co. I; POW at Fair Ground Post Hosp. Petersburg 4/3/65; d. in hosp. 4/20/65; from Lunenburg.

FOWLKES, (FOLKES) W. E. (W. T.): enl. 7/18/61 Co. I in Charlotte age 30 - substitute for James R. Hill; POW Ft. Donelson – sent from Camp Morton to Vicksburg for exchange; d. 2/15/63 in Gen. Hosp. Lynchburg from diabetes - bur, Lynchburg Cem. Section 106, Row 4, Grave 1; resident of Lunenburg; dark complexion, black hair, 6'.

FOX, SAMUEL A. (H.): enl. 7/1/61 Co. D in Buckingham; reenl. 8/11/62; admitted Charlottesville hosp. 8/26/62 with debility - sent Lynchburg hosp. 8/27/62; POW Gettysburg - confined Ft. Delaware and Pt. Lookout 10/26/63 - admitted U.S.A. Smallpox Hosp. at Pt. Lookout with smallpox 11/24/64 - exchanged 3/14/65; admitted Chimborazo 3/17/65 with Scorbutus; POW in hosp. 4/3/65 - confined Jackson Hosp. 4/7/65 – paroled 5/15/65; b. Albemarle; farmer, applied for pension 2/6/1903 age

59 living in Nelson where lived 44 years; partially disabled due to rheumatism, scurvy, and smallpox contracted while POW - $75 approved; c. 1908 age 64 living in Nelson Co.

FOX, THOMAS W.: pwl; Co. D.

FRASER, FRANCIS RIERS (sic): enl. 4/15/64 Co. E at Chaffin's Farm; absent sick 5/64-6/64; admitted Chimborazo 6/27/64 with remittent fever – transferred to Lynchburg 7/9/64; took part in adventure with Freeman W. Jones; POW Farmville 4/6/65; took oath and released from Pt. Lookout 6/12/65; dark complexion, dark brown hair, blue eyes, 5'3 3/4"; b. about 1846 in Brunswick to Edwin Fraser and his 2nd wife Mary Chieves Rives; farmer; m. Jennie G. Haskins 6/17/1869 in Brunswick - at least 4 children.

FRASER, JOSEPH (JOSIAH) A. (Sandy): enl. 7/10/610 Co. E in Brunswick, Sgt./Capt.; present 7/10/61-8/31/61; elected 1st Lt 5/3/62; promoted Capt. 11/15/62; sick in private house - returned to duty 8/20/62; POW Gettysburg at stone wall - confined Ft. McHenry, Ft. Delaware 7/12/63, and Johnson's Island 7/18/63 - exchanged 2/24/65; b. 3/25/1832 in Brunswick to Edwin and Dolly W. Cheely Fraser (half brother of Francis R. Fraser of Co. E); m. Hester A. Belville 9/8/1868 - 2 children; d. 3/7/1906 of paralysis in Dinwiddie - bur. Butterwood Methodist Church Cem. Dinwiddie; widow applied for pension in Blackstone, Nottoway Co. 1927.

GAIN, THOMAS E.: Co. unknown; POW and paroled in Richmond 4/26/65.

GAINES, JOHN C.: enl. 7/18/61 Co. I in Charlotte, Pvt./Sgt.; 7/18/61-8/31/61 absent on furlough; present 9/61-10/61, 7/63-12/63, 4/64-8/64; POW Hatcher's Run 3/31/65 - took oath and released from Pt. Lookout 6/12/65; resident of Charlotte; light complexion, brown hair and eyes, 5'7"; member of Zollicoffer Camp UCV, St. Petersburg, Fla. where lived for 20 years - drew pension No. 06137 in Fla.; never married; elder in St. Petersburg Presbyterian Church; d. 11/14/1918.

GAINES, WILLIAM B.: enl. 7/18/61 Co. I in Charlotte; on furlough 7/18/61-8/31/61; present 9/61-10/61; WIA Sharpsburg 9/17/62, admitted Richmond hosp. 9/28/62 - furloughed 60 days 10/6/62; admitted Chimborazo 1/9/63 with gunshot wd. of hand - furloughed 1/22/63; admitted Chimborazo 4/17/63 with debility - discharged 4/17/63; discharged from army 4/9/65 age 21 due to gunshot wd. of right hand - assigned to light duty by medical board - wrote letter to Capt. Richard V. Gaines to see if could be assigned to him 2/19/65; b. Charlotte; farmer, dark hair and complexion, brown eyes, 5'6"; surrendered by Lee at Appomattox; applied for pension 4/2/1888 age 44 living Smithville, Charlotte Co. - disabled due to gunshot wd. of hand causing stiff fingers - $15 approved; amended 2/5/1894 age 49, increased to $30; admitted to Lee Camp Soldiers' Home 10/22/1890 age 49 due to infirmities - discharged at own request 6/11/1891; readmitted age 65 for wds. and

infirmities 7/19/1906; d. 12/27/1908; bur. Hollywood Cem.
GALAWAY, (GALLOWAY) WILLIAM A.: enl. 7/23/61 Co. D in Buckingham; present 7//61-8/61 & 10/61; reenlisted 5/3/62; MWIA Gaines's Mill - d. 7/4/62 in Richmond from wds. - death claim filed by mother Frances Galloway 8/24/63.
GARDEN, ALEXANDER: enl. 7/12/61 Co. G in Charlotte; present 7/26/61 - 10/31/61; discharged 7/17/62 age 29 due to heart disease; detailed as guard Petersburg hosp. 12/17/64; b. Charlotte; farmer; blue eyes, light complexion, dark hair, 5'8"; admitted Lee Camp Soldiers' Home 8/10/97 age 64 for general debility - sent to Asylum 5/11/98; d. 8/9/1909.
GARDNER, DAVID: pwl; Co. H.
GARDNER, IRA T.: enl. 5/3/62 Co. H in Richmond; present 7/63-12/63; 5/64-6/64 absent sick; d. 7/19/64 at Chaffin's Farm Hosp.
GARNER, ALFRED HENRY: enl. 7/8/61 Co. A in Mecklenburg, Sgt.; present on all rolls except 9/63-10/63 absent - wded.; WIA Gaines's Mill - admitted Richmond hosp. with wd. 7/4/62 - furloughed 7/5/62; admitted Richmond hosp. 7/14/63 with chronic diarrhea - furloughed 30 days 7/25/63; reported wded. as of 11/20/63; POW, took oath and released 6/27/65 from Pt. Lookout; resident of Mecklenburg; light complexion, brown hair, blue-grey eyes, 5'9"; m. 10/24/1869 in Mecklenburg; d. 4/20/1918 in Mecklenburg of T.B. and pleurisy - bur. Bethel Baptist Church Cem., Chase City; widow Rose C. Garner applied for pension 3/4/1924.
GARNER, DAVID N. (M.): enr. as conscript 3/1/64 - assigned to Co. A 3/9/64; 5/64-8/64 absent sick; admitted Richmond hosp. 6/2/64 - furloughed 60 days 7/9/64 - furlough extended 9/6/64 because unfit for service due to chronic dyspepsia; paroled Appomattox 4/9/65 but not present with command; signed Emily Daniels widow's pension application 9/19/1908; bur. Bethel Baptist Church Cem., Chase City.
GARNER, (GARDNER) JAMES A.: enl. 7/8/61 Co. A in Mecklenburg, Sgt./1st Lt.; present 7/8/81-10/31/61 and 9/63-12/63; elected 2nd Lt. 5/3/62; furlough of 20 days requested 1/8/64 to visit home in Mecklenburg; MWIA Frazier's Farm - admitted 6/17/64 Richmond hosp. with leg wd. - d. 6/23/64 age 32 - bur. Oakwood Gem.- death claim filed by father Lewis Garner 12/7/64 - owed $458.66.
GARNER, THOMAS M.: enl. 6/28/61 Co. G, 14th Va. Inf. in Mecklenburg, Sgt./2nd Lt.; present 7/62-12/62; elected 2nd Lt. 7/30/62; present 3/63-4/63; absent sick 5/63-6/63; present 7/63-10/63; declined promotion to Lt. 8/8/63; refused to appear before examining board 11/17/63 - resigned 11/26/63 - in letter Garner said he resigned from 14th Va. because he did not make a good officer, but would make good Pvt. in 56th Va. where had brothers and friends; letter 12/9/64 from his father Lewis Garner requesting that Thomas Garner be exempted from service - said that one son died of disease in 1863 and another one was killed in battle In June, 1864 - also a

son-in-law died while in the service - 23 people left who Lewis Garner (age 64) must care for -Thomas has three children and feeble, delicate wife - Thomas granted exemption in 1863, but now called to Co. A 56th Va. Inf.; received clothing 12/3/64.

GARNETT, THOMAS M.: enl. 7/26/61 Co. F in Louisa, Pvt./2nd Lt.; present 7/27/61-10/31/61 &11/63-12/63, absent wded. 5/64-6/64, present 7/64-8/64; elected 2nd Lt. 12/31/63; letter from him 2/18/64 asking leave of absence to move his family from Louisa to Caroline Co. because father dead and only brother in service; wded. and in hosp. at time of inspection report near Howlett's House 8/9/64; admitted Richmond hosp. 12/19/64 with syphilis - returned to duty 3/7/65; admitted Richmond hosp. 3/9/65 with acute diarrhea - returned to duty 3/21/65; paroled Columbia 5/65; m. 1860 in Louisa; d. 4/29/1875 Louisa of typhoid pneumonia; widow America C. Garnett applied for pension 6/28/1904 living Orange Co. - $25 approved.

GARRETT (GARNETT), HENRY: enl. 7/26/61 Co. F in Louisa; present 7/27/61-10/61; b. Louisa; discharged 10/2/62 age 46 because served one year and over 35; carpenter; light complexion, dark black eyes, 5'10".

GARRISON, BENJAMIN C.: enl. 7/15/61 Co. H in Albemarle; present 7/26/61-10/31/61; father Clifton Garrison wrote Sec. of War 9/6/61 and 9/21/61 requesting Benjamin's discharge so he could come home and take care of him - needed him to raise crops and build his fires - 3 sons in army -2 in Michie's Co. and 1 in Southall's; d. 2/25/62 under 21 years of age; death claim filed by father - owed $67.16.

GARRISON, (GARSON) HENRY WHITE: enl. 7/10/61 Co. H in Albemarle; present on all rolls; paroled Charlottesville 5/18/85.

GARRISON, JOHN R.: enl. 7/18/61 Co. I in Charlotte; present on all rolls; payment made to him as discharged soldier 6/15/62; WIA near Chester Station; clothing receipt for 9/27/64, 10/13/64, and 10/19/64; POW Amelia Court House 4/3/65 - took oath and released from Pt. Lookout 6/13/65; resident of Charlotte; fair complexion, light brown hair, greyish eyes, 5'5 3/4".

GARRISON, JOSEPH WILLIAM: enl. 7/18/61 Co. I in Charlotte; 7/18/61-8/31/61 absent on sick furlough beyond time; present 9/61-10/61; Court Martial 2/23/63 AWOL - guilty of charge and specification - forfeited 2 months pay and had to cut wood and bring water until 4/1/63; admitted Richmond hosp. 6/63 - transferred Chimborazo 8/19/63 with debilitas - furloughed 8/29/63 30 days; WIA Gettysburg - examined at Farmville 11/11/63 for wd. received 7/3/63 of left lower leg; 7/63-10/63 absent wded.; 11/63-12/63 present; 5/64-8/84 absent wded.; WIA 6/16/64 - furloughed 7/21/64 30 days from Farmville hosp. with gunshot wd. of right forearm - furlough extended 40 days 8/23/64; admitted Chimborazo 10/3/64; POW Amelia Court House; sick at Pt. Lookout, released and took oath 6/3/65; admitted Jackson Hosp. 6/5/65 - took oath 6/11/65.

GARRISON, REUBEN R.: enl. 8/16/64 Co. I at Camp Lee; admitted Chimborazo with intermittent fever 10/2/64 - returned to duty 10/14/64; admitted Chimborazo 11/4/64 with rubeola; in army until left on Howlett line; b. Montgomery Co.; farmer; applied for pension 5/5/1900 age 55 living in Charlotte - disabled due to deep cold that settled on lungs when had measles during war - $15 approved; 1902 dropped from pension roll because property assessed at more than $500; rerated 1/30/1917 age 72 - annual Income $100 - real estate $610- personal property $90 - $50 approved; member H. A. Carrington Camp, UCV 5/15/1922.

GARTHRIGHT, (GARTHWRIGHT) JOHN EDWARD: enl. 6/26/62 Co. K in Richmond, Pvt./Sgt.; POW Gettysburg - confined Ft. Delaware 7/12/63, Pt. Lookout 10/26/63 - exchanged 5/3/64; present 5/64-8/64; took oath in Ashland 4/27/65.

GARTHRIGHT, JOSEPH ALPHEUS (ALLIE): Co. K; KIA Gaines's Mill.

GARTHRIGHT, PHILIP T.: enl. 8/6/61 Co. K in Mechanicsville; present on all rolls; on receipt roll for pay as foot scout 10/29/63, 12/15/63, and 12/26/63; received clothing 7/17/63, 9/27/64, 10/13/64, 10/19/64, 12/30/64; b. Henrico Co.: admitted Camp Lee Camp Soldiers' Home 8/28/1914 age 75 for infirmities of age - previously lived In Maryland; sent to Eastern State Hospital 1/21/1920.

GARTHRIGHT, BENJAMIN W.: enl. 8/6/61 Co. K in Mechanicsville; discharged 8/20/61 age 37 with heart disease; b. Hanover, carpenter; dark complexion and hair, hazel eyes, 5'11".

GEARY, RICHARDSON O.: Co. C.; no rank given; admitted Chimborazo 12/26/64 with rheumatism - transf. 12/26/64 to 6th Street between Cary and Canal Streets for treatment; POW Richmond - took oath 4/12/65; carpenter.

GEE, BENJAMIN C.: enl. 6/22/61 Co. C in Mecklenburg, Sgt/Pvt.; present 9/61-10/61; POW Ft. Donelson - sent to Camp Morton; 30 day furlough given 10/28/62 by Dr. W. P, Palmer; POW Gettysburg and according to muster roll probably KIA, but no Federal records concerning him.

GEE, LEONIDAS J: enl. 6/22/61 Co. B in Mecklenburg, Sgt; present 9/61-10/61; admitted Chimborazo with mini ball wd. of hand 6/28/62 - sent to pvt. quarters; MWIA and POW Gettysburg - admitted U.S. II Corps Hosp. Gettysburg with gunshot wd. of arm and leg - leg amputated - d. 7/17/63 - bur. Yard D, Row 2 of hosp. cem. in Jacob Schwarz's cornfield on Rock Creek; disinterred to Richmond 6/13/1872 with 110 others in 10 large boxes labeled "S" - reinterred Hollywood Cem.

GEE, WALTER A.: enl. 8/25/62 Co. B in Richmond; Pvt./Cpl.; present 9/63-12/63, 4/1/64, and 5/64-8/64; WIA Hatcher's Run 3/31/65 - POW Fair Ground Post Hosp. 4/3/65 - transf. Petersburg Gen. Hosp. 4/7/65 with severe minie ball wd. of left shoulder; transferred hosp. Point of Rocks

4/9/65; applied for pension 4//16/1888 age 44 living South HIII, Mecklenburg Co. - disabled due to minie ball lodged left side - $15 approved.

GENTRY, ABNER C.: enl. 7/26/61 Co. F in Louisa; present 7/27/61-10/61; receipt roll for pay as wagoneer 2/18/62 and 3/31/62; WIA Gaines's Mill; on detached service as provost guard stationed in field on rolls 9/63-12/63, 4/1/64, and 5/64-8/64; admitted Chimborazo 6/18/64 with intermittent fever - returned to duty 7/9/64; applied for pension 1/8/1898 age 62 living Louisa - disabled due to war wds. - disallowed; reapplied 4/28/1900 age 65 - partial disability due to 2 wds. and feeble health - $15 approved; made pension statement 6/9/1902 age 67.

GENTRY, BENJAMIN: pwl; enl. 1863, Co. C - served 1 year.

GENTRY, JAMES G.: Co. H; didn't report until 9/5/61; discharged - got substitute Michael Stuart 9/25/61.

GEORGE, LEWIS W.: enl. 10/19/62 Co. B at Leetown; present 7/64-8/64; POW 4/6/65 - took oath and released from Pt. Lookout 6/13/65; resident Mecklenburg; fair complexion, sandy hair, hazel eyes. 5'1$^{1}/4$".

GEORGE, M. W.: enl. 6/61 Co. B in Mecklenburg; discharged 7/28/61 age 22 due to stiffness of thumb joint and right hand; b. Mecklenburg; farmer, dark complexion, dark blue eyes, light hair.

GEORGE, WILLIAM A.: enr. as conscript 3/1/64 - assigned Co. B 3/10/64; admitted Chimborazo 5/23/64 with dysentery - furloughed 60 days 6/1/64; 7/64-8/64 present; 8/5/64 sent by officer to Farmville hosp. with debility following pneumonia attack 5/64 - scrofulous enlargement of clavicle glands on left side - furloughed 30 days; discharged 5/31/64 age 29 due to pneumonia and enlarged clavicle; admitted Chimborazo 10/27/64 with scrofula; furloughed 60 days 11/3/64; POW paroled and took oath in Richmond 5/10/65; b. Mecklenburg; farmer; fair complexion, hazel eyes, dark hair.

GIBSON, BIAS P.: enl. 7/9/61 Co. C in Louisa. Pvt./Sgt.; absent sick furlough 7/6/61-8/31/61; present 9/61-10/61 and 9/63-12/63; admitted Richmond hosp. 3/8/64 - remarks - well; admitted Richmond hosp. 5/3/64 - returned to duty 5/5/64; d. Chimborazo hosp. 6/18/64 age 26 of wd. to abdomen received 6/13/64 (one roll said d. of disease); farmer.

GIBSON, LINNEAR CHURCHWELL (CHAMBERWELL): enl. 7/9/61 Co. C in Louisa; present 7/9/61-10/31/61; absent wded. 9/63-12/63; admitted Richmond hosp. 3/6/64 - returned to duty 3/7/64; present 5/64-8/64; received clothing 10/13/64 and 10/19/64; applied for pension 5/23/1900 living Madison Run, Orange Co. - partially disabled due to wd. received Gettysburg - ball passed through one leg and then the other - knee shattered; POW Cold Harbor, $15 approved; d. 3/29/1917 of T. B. Madison Run; widow Rosa B. Gibson applied for pension 5/15/1922 - m. 8/26/1875 Madison Run.

GIBSON, GEORGE W.: enl. Co. C in Louisa; 7/9/61-8/31/61 sick furlough; present 9/61-10/61.

GIBSON, GRANVILLE R.: enl. 7/9/61 Co. C in Louisa; 7/9/61-8/31/61 sick furlough; present 9/61-10/61; admitted Chimborazo 7/29/62 with continued fever; may have been WIA Gettysburg; present 9/63-12/63; 7 day furlough 3/7/64 and then 30 day furlough; present 5/64-8/64.

GIBSON, HENRY T.: Co. H; admitted Chimborazo 6/24/62 with catarrh - returned to duty 8/10/62: MWIA and POW Gettysburg - admitted West's Buildings Hosp. 7/25/63 with gunshot wd. of humorous and right chest - d. 8/19/63 age 27 - bur. Confederate Lot, Grave A-13, Loudon Park, Baltimore, Md.; death claim filed 11/4/63 - owed $175.43; resident of Albemarle; unmarried.

GIBSON, JESSE: pwl; Co. H.

GIBSON, JOHN L: enl. 7/9/61 Co. C in Louisa; present 7/9/61-10/31/61.

GIBSON, MERRIMAN: enl. 3/18/62 Co. H; admitted Chimborazo 12/15/64 with acute diarrhea; POW Hatcher's Run 3/31/65; took oath and released Pt. Lookout 6/27/65; resident of Albemarle; fair complexion, *dark* brown hair, blue eyes, 6' 1/2"; d. 1904 Boonesville, Albemarle Co. of pneumonia; widow Mary J. Gibson filed pension application 1/15/1915; m. Boonesville and for 65 years.

GIBSON, PETER: pwl; enl. 3/18/672 Co. H; may have been discharged because over age or may have served 3 years.

GIBSON, PHILIP S.: enl. 7/9/61 Co. C in Louisa; present 7/9/61-10/31/61; on 9/63-12/63 rolls listed as POW Murfreesboro, TN.

GIBSON, PITMAN: pwl; Co. H (may be Peter Gibson.)

GIBSON, RILEY: enl. 10/5/61 Co. C as substitute for C. T. Poindexter: MWIA Gaines's Mill – d. Richmond 8/6/62 - had applied for discharge before death - discharged 7/21/62 due to amputation of right leg from wd. received at Gaines's Mill.

GIBSON, SANDY: pwl; enl. 1862 Co. H - served 2 years.

GIBSON, WILLIAM C.: enl. 5/3/62 Co. H in Richmond; present 7/63-12/63, 4/1/64 and 5/64-8/64; received clothing *9/27/64* and 10/13/64; had malaria during war; left service when Lee surrendered; b. 1842 Albemarle; farmer; applied for pension 11/9/1916 age 74 living Free Union, Albemarle Co. - disability due to old age, rheumatism, and Bright's disease; $50 approved.

GIBSON, WILLIAM W.: enl. 5/3/62 Co. H in Richmond; admitted Richmond hosp. 10/7/62 - returned to duty same day; present 7/63-12/63; POW Gettysburg - confined Ft. Delaware 7/7/63 - exchanged sick with tonsillitis 8/1/63 and admitted Episcopal Church Hosp., Williamsburg - returned to duty 8/11/63; in Chaffin's Farm Hosp. 2/12/64 with chronic hepatitis - 30 day furlough to Albemarle 4/1/64; absent on detached service 5/64-6/64; buried University of Va..

GILLESPIE, ALEXANDER (SANDY): pwl; Co. A; widow Mary A. E. Gillespie applied for pension 5/24/1902 living in Chase City, Mecklenburg Co.; husband d. 1/1867 of fever; married 1857 In Mecklenburg.

GILLESPIE, GEORGE W.: enl. 7/8/61 Co. A in Mecklenburg; present 9/61-10/61; discharged 9/9/62 age 32 - served one year and over 35; carpenter, dark complexion and eyes, light hair, 5'11".

GILLESPIE, RICHARD O.: pwl; Co. A.

GILLIAM, JAMES: pwl; Co. G.

GILLIAM, JOHN M.: Co. G; resident Prince Edward Co.; POW Harper's Farm 4/6/65 - took oath and released from Pt. Lookout 6/13/65; fair complexion, brown hair, blue eyes, 511".

GLASSCOCK, EZRIAH B.: enl. 10/22/61 Co. A in Richmond; present 9/61-10/61; discharged 3/18/62; enlisted Co. K 14th Va. 9/18/62 in Halifax; AWOL 11/17/62; present 1/63-4/63; Court Martial 4/9/63; AWOL 5/25/63; present 9/63-12/63; AWOL 2/27/64-3/18/64 and 6/23/64; present in arrest 9/64-10/64 - forfeited 6 months pay by order of court martial; POW Petersburg - took oath and released from Pt. Lookout 6/12/65; resident of Mecklenburg; fair complexion, brown hair, grey eyes, 5'11 7/8".

GLASSCOCK, THOMAS B.: enl. 7/8/61 Co. A in Mecklenburg; present 7/61-10/31/61; d. 3/1/62 age 19; death claim filed by father Sanford Glasscock - owed $69.36; b. Clarksville; farmer.

GLOVER, GEORGE D.: enl. 7/8/61 Co. D in Buckingham; present 7/61-10/31/61; reenl. 5/3/62; AWOL 9/63-10/63; absent on furlough 11/63-12/63; AWOL 4/64-6/64; d. 7/64.

GODSEY, WILLIAM HENRY: enl. 6/22/61 Co. B in Mecklenburg; present 9/61-10/61; POW Ft. Donelson - sent from Camp Morton to Vicksburg for exchange; 30 day furlough 11/12/62; admitted Richmond hosp. 11/25/62 - returned to duty 11/29/62; WIA Gettysburg - admitted Charlottesville hosp. 7/12/63 with wd. - transferred Lynchburg hosp. 9/21/63 - sick in hosp. 9/63-10/63; on detached service as hosp. guard 11/63-12/63; present 4/64-8/64; POW and WIA Burkeville 4/6/65 - took oath and released from Pt. Lookout 6/13/65; b. Powhatan Co.; resident of Mecklenburg before war and Brunswick afterward; light complexion, brown hair, grey eyes, 5"8 ¾"; applied for pension 9/24/1895 age 58 living in Ebony, Brunswick Co.- disallowed; reapplied 3/29/1898 age 60 - partial paralysis due to wd. below knee received Amelia Courthouse - $15 approved.

GOLD, (GOULD) PLEASANT: enl. 7/28/61 Co. A in Mecklenburg; present 7/8/6-10/31/61; discharged 9/9/62 age 45 - served one year and over 35; farmer, fair complexion, dark hair, grey eyes, 5'11"; d. about 1877 Mecklenburg from consumption; widow Pamela J. Gould applied for pension 5/30/1900 - m. about 1857 - $25 approved.

GOODE, EDWARD BRANCH: Field and Staff; drill master for volunteers at Camp 4/61-7/61; appointed adjutant 56th Va. 10/61; name appeared on requisition for supplies dated 10/15/61; name appeared on morning reports at Bowling Green, Ky. 1/12, 1/13, and 1/17/62 name last appeared on morning report of 2/3/62 near Russellville; at Ft. Donelson - escaped before surrender with Gen, Floyd - had attack of typhoid fever so stayed in Ky. few months within Federal lines - reported as "dead" to war department - had many narrow escapes from capture - ran 200 mile blockade to reach Confederate lines at Chattanooga 7/4/62: appointed 1st. Lt.. and Adj. of 34th Va. 10/14/62; WIA in trenches Petersburg; surrendered by Lee at Appomattox; b. 11/8/39 "Wheatland", Boydton, Mecklenburg Co. to William O. (Congressman in 1850's) and Sarah Massie Goode; mother died when he was 4; attended boarding school at 11; matriculated VMI 9/17/58 - received no demerits 1860 -graduated 10th in class of 35 12/12/61: brother was Col. J. Thomas Goode; m. Lucy Tanny Watkins 1/25/65 - 11 children; planter, mill owner, lawyer, and Virginia legislator; member St. James Episcopal Church, Boydton - vestryman, junior and senior warden, and representative at Diocesan Council; helped organize L. A. Armistead Camp, UCV; d. 10/15/1920 age 81 "Wheatland" - survived by 4 daughters and 3 sons - bur. St. James's churchyard.

GOODE, JOSEPH: enl. 7/8/61 Co. D in Buckingham; present 9/61-10/61; d. 12/16/? during war at Warren Ferry; widow applied for pension 4/9/1888; m. Willis's Mountain, Buckingham Co. 1853.

GOODE, THOMAS: pwl; Co. D.

GOODMAN, W. B.: Company unknown; name appears on list of rebel deserters received at Camp Hamilton from White House, Va. 3/25/65 - sent to Provost Marshal at Bermuda Hundred and then to Col. T. Ingraham 3/29/65.

GOOLSBY, ALEXANDER C.: enl. 7/8/61 Co. D in Buckingham, Pvt./Lt.; present 7/8/61-10/31/61; reenl. 8/11/62; elected Lt. 9/14/63; MWIA and POW Petersburg hosp. 4/3/65 with wd. in leg received Sayler's Creek – d. 4/10/65 of gunshot wd. - bur. in cem. attached to hosp.

GOOLSBY, GUSTAVUS ROSE: enl. 7/1/61 Co. D in Buckingham; WIA Gaines's Mill - admitted Richmond hosp. with gunshot wd. 6/62; AWOL 9/63-10/63; furloughed 11/63-12/63; AWOL 4/64-8/64; frorn Nelson Co.; d, Talcot, W. Va. of pneumonia - n.d.; widow Martha J. Goolsby applied for pension 4/11/1910 living Albemarle Co. - rn. 12/24/1857 - $25 approved.

GORDON, ALEXANDER: pwl; Co. G; from Charlotte; d. 8/9/1909.

GORDON, R.: Pvt. - Co. unknown; POW and paroled 5/12/65 in Richmond.

GORDON, WILLIAM SAMUEL: Co. A; POW Hatcher's Run 3/31/65 in Pt. Lookout Hosp. with chronic diarrhea; took oath and released from Pt. Lookout 6/28/65; b. 10/15/1830; resident of Mecklenburg; dark complexion, brown hair, blue eyes, 5'10"; d. 2/6/1897; bur. State Line Assembly Cem. – end Hw. 721 near Clarksville, Mecklenburg Co.;

survived by wife Lonie A. Gordon and daughter Lizzie.
GRADY, GEORGE W: enl. 7/9/61 Co. C in Louisa; sick furlough 7/9/61 – 8/31/61; present 9/61-10/61; listed as deserter 12/3/62 on all other rolls.
GRADY, JAMES T.: enl. 7/9/61 Co. C in Louisa; present 7/9/61-10/31/61; MCV Hosp. 8/6/61—8/14/61; on list of POWS paroled by Army of Potomac 10/3/62; admitted Richmond hosp. 10/23/62 with wd. of left side; furloughed 20 days 11/6/62; WIA and POW Gettysburg - confined Ft. Delaware and Pt. Lookout - paroled and exchanged 2/18/65; admitted Gordonsville hosp, 3/25/65 with gonorrhea simplex; b. Louisa; admitted Lee Camp Soldiers' Home 6/16/1927 age 96; 100th birthday celebrated in Harrisonburg in 1931.
GRAVES, EDWARD: enl. 7/8/61 Co. A in Mecklenburg; rejected - too young
GRAY, ROBERT: enl. 2/9/63 Co. E in Brunswick; discharged 7/3/63 age 27 for general imbecility; enr. as conscript 3/14/64 and assigned Co. E 3/21/64; sick in hosp. 6/12/64-12/19/64 - acute diarrhea and fever, name on list of prisoners in E.D.M. prison who volunteered in Winder Legion for defense of Richmond against Sheridan's Raid in 1864 in return for pardon by President Jefferson Davis; b. about 1837 to William H., Sr. and Mary Gray in Brunswick; farmer; m. Alice Louise Crowder 2/5/1872; 4 children: applied for pension 5/21/1900 age 68 living Gholsonville, Brunswick Co. - partial disability due to weakness - $15 approved; d. 1900 of heart trouble; widow applied for pension 10/10/1929 - $120 approved.
GRAY, WILLIAM H. (JR): enl. 7/10/61 Co. E in Brunswick; absent 7/10/61-8/31/61; discharged for physical disability 11/1/61 age 29; reenl. 29/63; absent POW on all rolls from 9/63-10/63; d. in prison - believed MWIA Gettysburg but no Federal records concerning him; b. 1830 in Brunswick; brother of Robert Gray of Co. E; farmer; light complexion, dark hair, blue eyes, 5'10".
GREEN, REV. H. G.: pwl; Chaplain.
GREEN, WILLIAM EDWIN: enl. 7/18/61 Co. I, Capt./Col.; elected Major 9/17/61; 30 day sick furlough 6/11/63; appointed Lt. Col. 7/31/63; sick furlough 6/10/64; appointed Col. of 56th Va. 6/13/64; took oath to U.S. 4/65; b. "Greenwood," Mossingford, Charlotte Co. *2/5/1827;* graduate of Hampden-Sydney and UVA *1846;* m. Jennie Elliott Boylan; owned plantation in Miss. during war; owned large farm in Charlotte Co. and practiced law; d. "Greenwood" 12/12/1891.
GREEN, WILLIAM GRESSET: enr. as conscript 3/7/64 in Lunenburg - assigned Co. G 3/16/64; absent sick 5/64-8/19/64; POW Petersburg hosp. 4/3/65; farmer, applied for pension 5/18/1900 age 60 living Lunenburg - partial disability due to weak back caused by diseased kidney - $15 approved; made statement 7/14/1902 age 62 - rheumatism contracted during war - owned $210 property.

GREEN, WILLIAM T.: enl. 7/18/61 Co. I in Charlotte; present 7/18/61-8/31/61; sick in hosp. 9/61-10/61; d. in Richmond - death claim filed 5/19/62.

GREGORY, A. B.: enr. as conscript 10/1/63 - assigned to Co. A; discharged 11//27/63.

GREGORY, CHARLES G.: enl. 7/12/61 Co. G in Charlotte; present on all rolls; admitted Richmond hosp. with debility 6/18/64 - returned to duty 7/14/64; admitted Farmville hosp. 4/8/65 with neuralgia; paroled Farmville 4/11/65-4/21/65; b. Mississippi about 1842 - moved to Va. *1849;* hotel clerk; applied for pension 2/23/1903 age 61 living Burkeville, Nottoway Co. - disability due to palsy since 1884, rheumatism, and partial blindness - $15 approved.

GREGORY, JAMES A. (G.): enl. 7/8/61 Co. A in Mecklenburg; present 7/8/61-10/31/61; discharged 9/10/62 age 18 due to arghylosis of joints; b. Mecklenburg 12/9/1842; dark complexion, brown hair, blue eyes, 5'9"; new member of Armistead Camp, UCV 8/25/1898; d. 3/14/1904.

GREGORY, JAMES BENNETT: enl. 7/20/61 Co. A in Mecklenburg; present 7/8/61-10/31/61; conscripted 8/16/64 Co. G, 9th Va. Cav.; b. 11/6/33 in Charlotte; m. Anne Smith; son Ernest T. Bennett; became minister; d. 3/13/1908 age 75 - bur. New Hope Baptist Church Cem., Skipwith, Mecklenburg Co, - CSA marker says, "Another Confederate soldier of undaunted courage has answered the last roll call and passed over the river."

GREGORY, JOHN W.: Co. B; POW Harper's Farm 4/6/65 - took oath and released from Pt. Lookout 6/13/65; b. Mecklenburg; dark complexion, brown hair, hazel eyes, 5'9 1/2".

GREGORY, WILLIAM H.: Co. B; received clothing 12/30/64; admitted Richmond hosp. 2/25/65; surrendered by Lee at Appomattox; resident of Mecklenburg; d. 4/10/1920 - $25 paid toward funeral expenses under 1900 act.

GRIMES, WILLIAM B.: pwl; Co. I; b. Charlotte Co; resident Lee Camp Soldiers' Home; d. 12/29/1908 age 67; bur. East No. 79 Hollywood Cem.

GROOM, (GROOME) GEORGE W.: enl. 7/9/61 Co. C in Louisa; present 7/9/61-10/31/61; believed KIA Boonsboro; widow Martha A. Groom applied for pension 4/9/1888 living Louisa - $30 approved; m. 5/10/1859 Louisa.

GRUBBS, FREDERICK J.: enl. 7/26/61 Co. F in Louisa; present 7/27/61-10/31/61; admitted Richmond hosp. with rheumatism 7/29/62; present 9/63-12/63 and 4/1/64; absent sick 5/64-8/64; furloughed 1/1/64-2/29/64; paroled Louisa 5/19/65; farmer; applied for pension 4/9/1888 age 51 living Shannon Hill, Louisa Co.; lost left eye Gaines's Mill -pension disallowed as not given for lost eye; reapplied 7/14/1902 age 70 living Quall, Louisa Co. - dislocated shoulder and chronic nephritis - $15 approved; d. 1/11/1911 Louisa of lung complications contracted during war and consumption; widow Sallie A. Grubbs applied for pension 5/9/1911; m. 9/3/1857 on Southanna River; she owned 2 cows and 1 horse - $25 approved.

GRUBBS, WILLIAM E. (J.): enl. 7/9/61 Co. F in Louisa, Pvt/Sgt.; present on all rolls; WIA Gaines's Mill; admitted Petersburg hosp. 5/6/63 with catarrh - returned to duty 5/22/63: admitted Richmond hosp. 12/28/63 - returned to duty 12/29/63; admitted Richmond hosp. 10/2/64 with intermittent fever - returned to duty 10/24/64; paroled Louisa 5/13/65.

GUILL, JOHN R.: enl. 7/18/61 Co. I in Charlotte; court martial for AWOL 2/23/63 - guilty of charge and specification - forfeited 2 month's pay and on detail to cut wood and bring water for Co. and Regt. until 4/1/63; absent on furlough 7/18/64-8/31/64; present on all other rolls; admitted Richmond hosp. 11/15/64 with chronic diarrhea - returned to duty 11/22/64; admitted Richmond hosp. 3/26/65.

GUILL, JOSEPH: enl. 7/18/61 Co. G in Charlotte; present on all rolls; POW Frederick, Md. 9/12/62 - exchanged from Ft. Delaware 10/2/62; 30 day furlough 11/262; admitted Richmond hosp. 6/22/63 with chronic dysentery - furloughed 30 days 7/11/63; received clothing 9/27/64,10/13/64,10/19/64, 11/14/64, and 12/2/64.

GUILL, WILLIAM M.: enl. 7/12/61 Co. G in Charlotte; absent 7/26/61-8/31/61; present 9/61-10/61; admitted Charlottesville hosp. 8/26/62 with debility; admitted Richmond hosp. 10/11/62 - wded. Chaffin's Farm - deserted hosp. 11/12/62.

GUILL WILLIAM T.: enl. 7/18/61 Co. I in Charlotte Co., Cpl./Color Guard; present 7/8/61-8/31/61; absent sick 9/61-10/61; deserted 5/12/62; admitted Charlottesville hosp. 9/4/62 with wd. of hand - transferred Lynchburg hosp. 9/5/62; Court Martial AWOL 2/23/63; guilty of charge and specification - reduced to ranks and forfeited 2 months pay; was Color Guard and KIA Gettysburg.

GUNTER, J. T.: pwl; Co. D.

GUNTER, RICHARD B. (R.): enl.. 7/23/61 Co. D in Buckingham; present 7/8/61-8/31/61; discharged due to disability 9/11/61; d. 1891; m. 1870; widow Mary A. Gunter applied for pension under rights of 1st husband George W. McFadden who d. during war.

GUNTER, THOMAS J.: enl. 7/23/61 Co. D in Buckingham; present 7/8/61-8/31/61 and 9/63-10/63; absent furlough 11/63-12/63; present 4/1/64; AWOL 5/64-8/64; POW age 28 surrendered by Lee at Appomattox; b. Buckingham Co.; farmer for 50 years; fair complexion, 5'8"; applied for pension 10/10/1905 age 72 living Buckingham - disability due to infirmities of old age - $30 approved.

HACKETT, F. M.: pwl; Co. D (probably Francis Marion Hackett).

HACKER, FRANCIS MARION: enl. 7/23/61 Co. D in Buckingham; present 7/8/61-1031/61; d. Williamsport. Md.; death claim filed 9/23/63 by

widow Mary F. Hackett saying he died of sickness; probably KIA Gettysburg; widow applied for pension 5/19/1908; m. Buckingham 1845.
HAINS, JOSEPH H.: enl. 7/10.61 Co. E in Brunswick; discharged for disability 9/2/61.
HALL, ANDERSON A.: enl. 2/17/63 Co. B in Richmond; present 9/63-12/63 and 4/64-8/64; on receipt roll for clothing 12/20/64; b. about 1829 to Amos and Margaret Hall; blacksmith before war; m. Louisa J. R. 1855 - 7 children; farmer and blacksmith after war; applied for pension 5/21/1900 age 71 living In Brodnax, Brunswick Co. - partial disability because overheated at Gettysburg and rheumatism contracted during war - $15 approved; made pension statement 8/23/1902 age 75.
HALL, BENJAMIN F.: enl. 7/9/61 Co. C in Louisa; in Medical College of Va. 8/6/61-8/12/61; admitted Chimborazo for debility 4/12/63 - returned to duty 4/12/63; 5/64-8/64 rolls say absent wded. since 5/63; paroled Louisa 5/22/65.
HALL, EDMUND (EDWARD) N. (E. B.): enl. 7/26/61 Co. F in Louisa; present on all rolls through 8/64; on list of deserters 3/21/65; received from Gen. Sheridan at City Point - sent to Lt. Col. McEntee at Norfolk for examination – to be sent to Washington, D.C.
HALL, GEORGE W.: enl. *7/12/61* Co. F in Louisa; present 7/27/61 - 10/31/61; WIA Gaines's Mill - admitted Chimborazo 6/29/62 with gunshot wd. of leg; POW Gettysburg - d. Ft. Delaware 10/6/63 - bur. Finns Pt. Nat. Cem., N.J.
HALL, J. M.: enr. as conscript 1/10/64 in Campbell Co. - assigned to Co. K 1/15/64; KIA assault Petersburg 6/16/64 - death claim filed by widow Frances A. Hall 8/22/64.
HALL, JAMES C. (G.): enl. 7/26/61 Co. F in Louisa; sick furlough from 7/20/61; discharged 5/8/62 age 24 due to scrofula; b. Louisa; farmer; florid complexion, red hair, blue eyes, 6'.
HALL, JAMES F.: enl. 5/3/62 Co. H in Richmond; POW Gettysburg - confined Ft. Delaware 7/12/63 and Pt. Lookout 10/26/63 - exchanged 2/18/65 at Camp Lee; d. 5/23/1927 UVA Hosp. of pneumonia; widow Mary Hall applied for pension 5/21/1927 - m. 1882 Staunton; $90 approved.
HALL, NATHANIEL: pwl; Co. F (may be Edmund N. Hall).
HALL, RICHARD D.: enl. 7/9/61 Co. C in Louisa; d. 8/21/61 - death claim filed 3/24/64; owed $36.08.
HALL, TIMOTHY T.: enl. 7/26/61 Co. F in Louisa; present on all rolls; admitted Chimborazo with debilitas 10/2/64 - returned to duty 10/14/64; paroled Columbia 5/8/65.
HALL W. A.: Co. I, Sgt; furloughed from Chimborazo 10/19/63 by S.O. 278 Dept of Henrico.
HALL, WILLIAM: Co. A; deserted 4/10/65 and look oath at Louisville, Ky. 4/13/65; told to remain north of river during war, resident of Lee Co.; fair

complexion, light hair, blue eyes, 5'6".

HAMBLETON, (HAMILTON) BENJAMIN L.: enl. 7/26/61 Co. F in Louisa; present 7/27/61-10/31/61; deserted at Snickers Gap 6/26/63; paroled Beaver Dam 5/8/65; farmer.

HAMBLETON, GEORGE P.: enl. 7/26/61 Co. F in Louisa: absent with measles 7/27/61-8/31/61; present 9/61-10/61; deserted 6/26/63 at Snickers Gap; POW Burkeville 4/6/65 – took oath and released from Pt Lookout 6/13/65; b. Jackson; resident Henrico Co.; farmer; fair complexion, black hair, blue eyes, 5'8 ¾"; applied for pension 1/24/1916 age 75 living Bumpass, Louisa Co.; too feeble to make living due to old age and rheumatism - $265 personal property - $359 real estate - $50 approved; admitted Lee Camp Soldiers' Home age 83, 8/11/1923 due to old age; d. *8/27/1923* - body taken by relatives.

HAMBLETT, (HAMLET) EDWARD W.: enl. 7/18/61 Co. I in Charlotte; present 7/18/61-10/31/61; detailed as nurse in Jackson Hosp. 7/63-12/63; WIA Gettysburg; furloughed 15 days 10/16/63; present 5/64-8/64; admitted Jackson Hosp. 3/20/64 with wd. of rt. Leg; applied for pension 5/15/1900 age 73 living in Abell, Charlotte Co. - $30 approved; d. 11/5/1905 of dropsy, Charlotte; widow Mary L Hamlett applied for pension 5/5/1907 – m. 1852 - $75 approved.

HAMBLETT (HAMLET) JESSIE WESLEY: enl. 7/18/61 Co. I in Charlotte; present on all rolls; name on pay roll of paroled and exchanged prisoners paid at Richmond 10/2/62; slightly WIA 6/1/64-6/4/64; farmer; applied for pension 5/15/1900 age 66 living in Charlotte - disabled due to head swimming and heart palpitations - $15 approved; rerated 2/28/1914 age 78 - $43.20 approved d. 8/1914 near Rough Creek, Charlotte Co. of old age and paralysis; widow Sallie A. Hamlett applied for pension 4/14/1915 - m. 1865; $30 approved.

HAMBLETT, (HAMBLET) THOMAS PLEASANT: enl. 2/12/63 Co. I at Guinea Depot; present 7/63-12/63 and 5/64-8/64; admitted Chimborazo 3/8/65; d. 5/1/1918 Roanoke City of heart trouble; widow Lucy A. Hamlett applied for pension 2/21/1921- m. 1870 Charlotte - $60 approved.

HAMERSLEY, JAMES C. (S. E.):, enr. as conscript 12/13/63 - assigned to Co. I at Camp Bruce, Wilmington, S.C. by Capt. Paris; present 5/64-6/64; sick in hosp. 7/64-8/64 - admitted Chimborazo *8/27/64* with hepatic derangement - furloughed 35 days 9/6/64 - furlough extended 30 days 10/11/64 due to scorbutus, debility and emaciation – 11/15/64 ordered to his command; POW Hatcher's Run 3/31/65 - took oath *and* released from Pt. Lookout 6/13/65; resident of Charlotte; fair complexion, light hair, blue eyes, 5'10 1/2".

HAMERSLEY, (HAMMERLY) WILLIAM RICHARD: enl. 9/3/62 Co. I in Charlotte; received clothing at Gen. Hosp. Lynchburg 6/11/63; WIA and POW Gettysburg - confined Ft. McHenry 7/6/63, Ft. Delaware 7/12/63, and Pt. Lookout 10/26/63 - exchanged 2/18/65; d. 9/5/1917 Charlotte of uremia; widow Martha W. Hamersly applied *for* pension 8/22/1923 - m. 11/23/1970 Charlotte - $76 approved.

HAMILTON, JOHN B.: enl. 9/3/62 Co. I in Charlotte Co.; deserted 9/62 - never paid.

HAMILTON, (HAMBLETON) JOSEPH: pwl; Co. F.

HAMLIN, JOHN R.: enl. 3/15/63 Co. I in Petersburg; present 7/64-8/64; admitted Richmond hosp. 3/18/65 with debility - furloughed 60 days 3/31/65.

HAMMOND, (HAMMONDS) JAMES TURNER (F.): enl. 7/1061 Co. E in Brunswick; present 7/10/61-8/31/61; POW Ft. Donelson - sent Camp Morton to Vicksburg for exchange; discharged from Co. E; 2/13/63; enl. Co. H, 53rd Va. - substitute for John S. Kelley, present 1/63-8/63: admitted Chimborazo 7/13/63 - transferred Petersburg 7/19/63; 15 days pay deducted by order of court martial 7/28/63; AWOL 9/6/63-12/16/63; admitted Chimborazo 4/2764 - consitipation - transferred Farmville - 30 day furlough 5/14/64; admitted Farmville hosp. 7/8/64 with debility; POW Farmville hosp. 4/65 - paroled 4/11/65-4/21/65; b. about 1821; m. Mary Jane Floyd in Brunswick 1841; m. Ann Elizabeth Martin 1856; 1860 census one son age 2.

HAMNER, (HAMMER) ROBERT M.: enl. 6/22/61 Co. B, 2nd Lt; elected 2nd Lt. 5/3/62; present 9/63-12/63; POW near Howlett's House 8/25/64 - confined Ft. Monroe, Pt. Lookout *8/27/64,* Old Capitol Prison 9/1/64, and Ft. Delaware 9/19/64; took oath & released from Ft. Delaware 6/17/65; resident of Albemarle; dark complexion, light hair, brown eyes, 5'10".

HANCOCK, MARTIN B.: Co. G; received clothing 12/28/64; surrendered by Lee at Appomattox; b. Appomattox Co. 6/22/1838.

HANKS, WILLIAM ROBERT: pwl; conscript assigned Co. E; POW probably along route of retreat; b. about 1833 to Thomas R. and Nancy Reece Hanks in Brunswick; m. Maria L Elmore *2/26/1856;* 1860 census overseer with 5 children; 1870 laborer; believed moved to Petersburg.

HANNA, BENJAMIN CARTER: enr. as conscript 4/4/64; assigned Co. K 4/6/64; absent sick 4/1/64 and 5/64-6/84; admitted Richmond hosp. 5/27/64; present 7/64-8/64; forfeited 2 months pay by order of court martial; received clothes 9/64, 10/64, and 12/64.

HARDIMAN, (HANDMAN) JOHN ED: enl. 7/18/61 Co. I in Charlotte, Pvt./Cpl.; sick in Richmond hosp. 9/2/61; present 9/61-10/61; WIA Gaines's Mill; WIA and POW Gettysburg - admitted DeCamp Hosp. with gunshot wd. of thigh 7/22/63 - paroled and exchanged at Camp Lee 8/31/63; applied for pension 4/2/1888 age 48 living Charlotte - disabled due to wd. Gaines's Mill - shot through body from left to right breaking piece of back bone - $30 approved - paid $36 in 1909.

HARLOW, JAMES S.: pwl;; Co. H; d. 1892 Gilberts, Albemarle Co. of dropsy; widow Margaret C. Harlow applied for pension 5/30/1900 - m. 1860 Albemarle - $25 approved.

HARLOW, SAMUEL (J.) (J. S.): enl. *7/29/61* Co. H in Albemarle; present 9/61-10/61; reenl. 5/3/62; WIA Gaines's Mill; AWOL 7/63-8/63; present 11/63-12/63 but pay kept back because AWOL; present 4/1/64; AWOL 5/64-6/64; present 7/64-8/64 but 3 months' wages deducted for AWOL and indebted to CSA for cartridge box, bayonet, and shoulder belt; received clothes 9/27/64. (may be James S. Harlow)

HARLOW, WILLIAM JAMES (JAMES W.): enl. 2/64 Co. C at Chaffin's Farm; admitted Richmond hosp. 6/17/64 age 26 with gunshot wd. of left hip - furloughed 60 days 6/28/64; farmer; paroled Louisa 5/15/65; b. 1838; applied for pension 4/9/1888 age 51 living Louisa - disabled due to gunshot wd. of left hip received at Chester Station 6/16/64 - $15 approved; bur. 2 miles west of Ferncliff, Route 250, 1st State Road, Butler Family Cem.

HARLOW, WILLIAM L. (J.): enl . 2/15/64 Co. H at Chaffin's Farm; AWOL 5/64-6/64; present 7/64-8/64 but 3 months pay deducted because AWOL and indebted to CSA for cartridge box, shoulder belt, bayonet, and bayonet scabbard; received clothes 9/64, 10/64, and 12/64; b. 1847; d. 1928 - bur. Riverview Cem., Charlottesville.

HARPER, JAMES H.: enl. 7/26/61 Co. F in Louisa; present 9/61-10/61; MWIA and POW Ft. Donelson - admitted U.S. General Hosp., St. Louis, Missouri 3/4/62 - d. gunshot wd. 3/16/62 - bur. St. Louis.

HARRIS, ADDISON S.: enl. 4/15/62 Co. H in Charlottesville; admitted Charlottesville hosp. 6/3/62 with chronic rheumatism; discharged due to rheumatism 10/30/62 age 19; b. Albemarle; blacksmith; dark complexion and hair, black eyes, 5'10".

HARRIS, CHARLES T. (F.): Co. F; received clothes 12/28/64; admitted Chimborazo 3/22/65 with pneumonia; POW Richmond hosp. 4/3/65 transferred Jackson Hosp., Libby Prison and Newport News - took oath and released 7/1/65; resident of Goochland; fair complexion, dark hair, blue eyes, 5'8".

HARRIS, GEORGE T.: pwl; enl. 7/25/61 Co. F; (probably Charles T. Harris).

HARRIS, JAMES JR.: pwl; Co. A.

HARRIS, JAMES L.: enl. 7/26/61 Co, F in Louisa; present 7/27/61-10/31/61; MWIA and POW Gettysburg - admitted U. S. 2nd Corps hosp. with gunshot wd. of leg - leg amputated - d. in hosp. 7/16/63 - bur. Yard D, Row 3 of hosp. cem. in Jacob Schwartz's cornfield on Rock Creek; body reinterred and bur. in mass grave at Hollywood Cem.

HARRIS, JAMES W.: enl. 7/9/61 Co. C in Louisa; present 7/9/61-10/31/61; POW Gettysburg while serving as nurse 7/5/63 - admitted West's Buildings Hosp. 7/25/63 - sent from Pt. Lookout for exchange 3/6/64; admitted Richmond hosp. 10/2/64 with intermittent fever - returned to duty 10/24/64; paroled Ashland 5/2/65; applied for pension 4/21/1900 age 66 living Mineral City, Louisa Co. - totally disabled due to paralysis - $30 approved; made pension statement 5/17/1902 age 68.

HARRIS, JOHN R.: Co. B; WIA and POW Burkeville age 17 - admitted Lincoln U.S. General Hospital, Washington, D.C. 4/19/65 - took oath 6/12/65; resident of Mecklenburg; light complexion, auburn hair, blue eyes, 5'7".

HARRIS, JOSEPH H.: enl. 7/10/61 Co. E in Brunswick; discharged 9/3/61 ape 23 due to physical disability; b. 1837 Brunswick to Robert H. and Martha M. Howell Harris; farmer; dark complexion and eyes, black hair, 5'9 "; d. of disease in service.

HARRIS, RICHARD: pwl, Co. A.

HARRIS, S. J.: enl. 5/3/62 Co. H in Richmond, Cpl./Pvt.; listed as AWOL or deserter on all rolls.

HARRIS, SAMUEL T. (SLIM O.) enl. 7/8/61 Co. A in Mecklenburg; d. in Clay Street Hosp., Richmond 7/28/61 of measles; death claim filed 10/22/63.

HARRIS, WILLIAM H.: enl. 7/8/61 Co. A in Mecklenburg; furloughed 8/27/61-9/2/61; present 9/61-10/61.

HARRIS, WILLIAM H.: enl. 5/2/62 Co. H in Richmond; returned to duty from Richmond hosp. 8/17/62; AWOL on rolls 7/63-12/63; in arrest 4/1/64 and 5/64-6/64: admitted Smallpox Hosp. 4/23/64 age 29 with rubeola 60 day sick furlough from Chaffin's Farm Hosp. due to dysentery 5/28/64; deserted 7/64-8/64.

HARRIS, ZACHARIAH P. (P. P.): enl. 5/3/62 Co. H in Richmond; in Richmond hosp. and returned to duty 8/17/62; admitted Richmond hosp. 11/12/62 - returned to duty 11/19/62; AWOL 7/63-12/63 and 5/64-6/64; deserter on rolls 4/1/64 and 7/64-8/64.

HARRISON, B. C.: Field and Staff, Asst. Surg./Surg.; appointed Asst. Surg. 5/27/63; WIA and POW Gettysburg while attending wded. - in Gettysburg hosp. sick and wded. - confined Ft. Monroe, Ft. Norfolk, and Ft. McHenry - paroled and exchanged 11/63; POW paroled Richmond 4/28/65.

HARRISON, DABNEY CARR: enl. 8/6/61 Co. K in Mechanicsville, Capt.; detailed for court martial duty 11/1/61; appointed Capt. 8/6/61; d. on way to Nashville from wds. received at Ft. Donelson - will dated 1/3/62 left $500 in Confederate bonds, books, and furniture to wife after his debts were paid; widow Sally B. Harrison filed death claim - owed $329.33; b. 9/12/1830 in Albemarle, son of Peyton Harrison; relative of President William Henry Harrison; entered Princeton age 15; studied law at UVA 1849-t850 and with relative In Martinsburg - entered law practice In Martinsburg; decided lo enter Union Seminary in Prince Edward Co. 1852 - taught 2 years there replacing one of his professors who died; minister at

First Presbyterian Church in Lynchburg; appointed Chaplain UVA age 27 for 2 years; accepted call from Bethlehem Church, Hanover; organized Co. K when war started; member Beta Theta Pi; widow wrote Confederate *Veteran* in 1896 from 1619 17th St., NW, Washington, D.C. asking if anyone knew where her husband was buried - all she knew was he was carried on boat from Ft. Donelson to Nashville.

HARRISON, WILLIAM (G.): enl. 6/256/63 Co. K in Dublin; present 4/1/64 and 5/64-6/64; absent sick 7/64-8/64; admitted Richmond Hosp. with conjunctivitis 8/3/64 - furloughed 45 days 8/30/64,

HART, FRANKLIN: enr. as conscript 7/15/63 in Dublin - assigned to Co. K 1/15/64; present 4/1/64; absent sick 5/64-8/64; admitted Richmond hosp. 6/7/64 with chronic diarrhea - transferred Lynchburg hosp. 7/9/64.

HARVEY, JESSE R.: transferred to Co. I 10/62 - originally enlisted in Georgia; absent sick 9/63-10/63; d. 11/5/63 - bounty due.

HARVEY, NATHAN BARKSDALE: enL 11/6/63 Co. I at Camp Lee - paid $50 bounty; present 11/63-12/63 and 5/64-8/64; received clothes 9/27/64, 10/13/64, 10/19/64, and 12/30/64; b, 5/3/1829; d. 3/1/1896 - bur. Greenhill Cem, Danville, Plot D 12.

HARVEY, R. H.: Co. G; admitted Richmond hosp. with gunshot wd, of right thumb - furloughed 60 days 12/26/64 to Prince Edward; admitted Farmville hosp. 2/21/65 with chronic bronchitis - returned to duty 3/1/65; paroled Farmville 4/21/65.

HARVEY, S. W.: pwl; Co. I; applied for pension 4/1/1901 age 66 living at Vincent's Store, Charlotte Co. - catarrh of throat, blind in 1 eye, kidney trouble - "Dead" written across application.

HARVEY, THOMAS (S.): enl. 7/18/61 Co. I in Charlotte Co.; present 7/18/61-10/31/61; WIA Ft. Donelson; d. 12/30/1896 Aspenwall, Charlotte Co.. of gangrene of foot; widow Nancy Harvey applied for pension 5/5/1900; m. 3/5/1844 Charlotte - $25 approved.

HARVEY, WILLIAM D. (HERVEY, W. G.), enl.. 7/18/61 Co. I in Charlotte Co.; present 7/18/61-10/31/61 and 7/63-12/63; sick in hosp. 5/64-6/64; furloughed 7/64-8/64; WIA Gaines's Mill 6/27/62; admitted Richmond hosp. 5/23/64 - furloughed 30 days 7/8/64; furlough extended 40 days 8/5/64 - returned to duty 9/16/64; paroled Farmville 7/65; d. Smithville from chills and fever; widow Elizabeth S. Harvey applied for pension 5/2/1900 - m. 12/11/1850 near Rice Depot - $25 approved.

HARVEY, WILLIAM H.: enl. 6/62 Co. I in TN.; present 7/63-12/63 and 5/64-8/64; detached duty as teamster 6/63-7/63; transferred from Richmond hosp. to Appomattox 2/165; paroled Farmville 4/25/65; m. 10/3/1849 Charlotte Co.; d. 10/7/1893 of general debility and paralysis; widow Sarah K. Harvey applied for pension 4/1/1895 living Skippers, Greensville, Co. - disallowed because Harvey died 28 years after war.

HARVEY, WYATT C.: enl. 7/18/61 Co. I in Charlotte; present 7/18/61-

10/31/61; pay roll receipts indicated detached as waggoner 2/62—3/62 and teamster 1/63-9/63; present 7/63-12/63; absent wded. 5/64-6/64; present 7/64-8/64; admitted Richmond hosp. with ear wd. 6/3/64; returned to duly 7/1/64; received clothing 10/64 and 12/64.

HASKINS, EDWARD L.: enl. 7/12/61 Co. G in Charlotte; Orderly Sgt./2nd Lt.; present 7/26/61-10/31/61; WIA Ft. Donelson; elected 2nd Lt. 5/3/62; WIA Gaines's Mlll - surgeon wrote 11/4/62 that he would not be fit for duty for 8-12 months due to gunshot wd. of leg; Haskins wrote 11/20/62 letter of resignation due to injury and because his company had 15 efficient men to be officers - resigned 12/10/62; resident of Red Oak Grove, Charlotte Co.

HASS, G. conscript enrolled 2/13/64; assigned to Co. C 2/24/64; present 4/1/64.

HATCHEL., JAMES: enl. 6/28/61 Co. B in Mecklenburg; discharged age 26 by surgeon's certificate 10/31/61; b. Mecklenburg; laborer, dark complexion and hair, blue eyes, 5'6".

HAWKES, (HAWKS) BURWELL (BERTHIER) BOTT (HAWKINS, B. B.): enl. 2/9/63 Co. E in Brunswick; had been exempted 3/18/62 due to injury of right hand; admitted Richmond hosp. 6/16/63 with chronic diarrhea - returned to duty 7/19/63; present 9/63-12/63; WIA Cold Harbor age 21- admitted Richmond hosp. 6/21/64 with gunshot wd. causing partial paralysis of right arm and shoulder - furloughed 30 days 6/28/64; b. 8/6/1841 to John A. and Mary A. Abernathy Hawkes; m. Martha Beryl Kirkland 2/28/1867 - 9 children; farmer, applied for pension 4/2/1888 age 47 living Wagna, Brunswick Co. – phlebitis caused loss of leg - $15 approved; d. 9/6/1921 - bur. Hawkes section Warfield Cem., Brunswick - Confederate marker.

HAWKS, ROBERT: pwl; Co. E

HAWTHORN, (HAWTHORNE or HAWKINS) PETER W.: enl.. 7/25/62 Co. G in Lunenburg; present 5/64-6/64; detailed as nurse at Chester 7/64-8/64; POW Garrett Station 4/2/65 - took oath at Hart's Island, New York Harbor 6/20/65: resident of Lunenburg; light complexion and hair, grey eyes, 6'.

HAY, GEORGE W. enl. 8/6/61 Co. K in Mechanicsville, Cpl./2ndLt.; present 8/6/61-10/31/61; appointed 2nd Lt. 11/30/61; POW Ft. Donelson - confined Camp Chase 3/1/62 and Johnson's Island 4/10/62 age 35 - sent to Vicksburg for exchange 8/5/62; resigned 2nd Lt. 5/5/62; light brown hair, blue eyes, 6'.

HAYES, JOHN H.: enl. 7/28/61 Co. A in Mecklenburg; AWL 8/20/61-9/2/61; discharged 10/9/61 age 30 because furnished substitute; b. Mecklenburg; dark hair and complexion, grey eyes, 5'10".

HAZELWOOD, J.: Co. I; paroled Burkeville 4/65.

HAZELWOOD, WILLIAM G.: enl. 6/1/61 Co. B in Mecklenburg;

discharged 7/30/61 age 24 due to poor health; b. Mecklenburg; dark complexion, dark sandy hair, blue eyes, 5'11".

HEATH, LOGAN (W.) (N. W. or S. W): enl. 8/6/61 Co. K in Mechanicsville; present 8/6/61-10/31/61; POW Ft. Donelson - sent from Camp Morton to Vicksburg for exchange; furloughed by Medical Directors Office 30 days 10/24/62; WIA and POW Gettysburg - paroled from West's Buildings Hosp. 8/24/63 - admitted Petersburg hosp. 8/24/63 with gunshot wd. of thigh - furloughed 50 days; admitted Richmond hosp. 6/28/64 with Intermittent fever - still there 12/2/64; paroled Amelia 4/2/65.

HENDERSON, ROBERT: enl. 7/26/61 Co. F in Louisa, Pvt./Cpl.; present 7/27/61-10/31/61, 9/63-12/63, 4/1/64 and 5/64-8/64; WIA Gaines's Mill; deserted to enemy and sent to Washington, D.C. from Norfolk 3/21/65.

HENDERSON, W.: enl. 4/25/62 Co. K in Richmond; AWOL 7/63-8/63 - dropped from rolls by order of Gen. Garnett.

HENKLE, (HINKLE) JOHN: enl. 5/3/62 Co. H in Richmond; admitted Charlottesville hosp. with internal fever 10/62 - returned to duty 10/24/62; absent prisoner on rolls 7/63-12/63 - believed KIA Gettysburg. but no Federal records concerning him.

HENRY, THOMAS STANHOPE: enl. 7/18/61 Co. I in Charlotte, 1st Lt./Capt.; present 7/18/61-10/31/61; appointed Capt. 9/1/61 - elected Capt. unanimously 10/3/61; resigned 11/1/61 due to hemorrhage of lung; b. 7/20/1833 Red Hill, Charlotte Co. son of John and Elvira McClelland Henry; matriculated VMI 7/22/1850. age 17 from Brookneal, Charlotte Co.; letter written March 8, 1910 by Henry to Joseph R. Anderson relating he was appointed color bearer at VMI but owing to some dissatisfaction of Major Gilharn, Com. Corps, was reduced to ranks July, 1852 - in fall of 1852 suspended by Cadet Philips - taken sick and resigned 10/25/52 on surgeon's recommendation; grandson of Patrick Henry; m. Mary Gaines of Charlotte 1/20/1858 - 2 sons and 1 daughter, farmer before war - physician after war, d. 11/11/1912 age 80 Red Hill, Charlotte.

HENSHAW, PLEASANT J: enl. 7/26/61 Co. F in Louisa; 7/27/61-8/31/61 in Richmond hosp. with measles; present 9/61-10/61; deserted summer of 1862; POW paroled Ashland 5/1/65; b. Louisa; farmer: applied for pension 3/6/1911 age 74 living Jackson, Louisa Co. - disability due to heart trouble - $24 approved.

HERRING, B. FRANKLIN: enl. 7/15/61 Co. H in Albemarle; present 7/29/61-8/31/61: absent sick 9/61-10/61; admitted Charlottesville hosp. with chronic rheumatism 2/21/62 - returned to duty 3/18/62 - to Colony 5/5/62; WIA Frazier's Farm; admitted Charlottesville hosp. 12/1/62 with debilitas - returned to duty 12/21/62; present 7/63-10/63; on detached service 11/63-12/63; present 4/1/64 and 5/64-8/64; on detached duty as wheelwright and ambulance driver most of 1864.

HERRING, BLAND (HERRON, BLAN): enl. 5/3/62 Co. H in Richmond;

WIA Gaines's Mill; AWOL 7/63-12/63, 4/1/64, and 7/64-8/64; listed as deserter on roll 7/64-8/64; paroled Charlottesville 5/24/65; d. 5/14/1897 of paralysis in Albemarle; widow Catherine M. Herring applied for pension 5/3/1900 - m. 3/1849 in Green Co. - $25 approved.

HERRING, CHARLES: pwl; enl. 1/15/63 Co. F, 35th Batt. Va. Cav.; POW 6/9/63 Beverly Fords - paroled Old Capitol Prison. 6/25/63; transferred Co. H, 56th Va. 7/27/64; d. in service.

HERRING, GEORGE E.: enl. 7/15/61 Co. H in Albemarle; d. 9/12/61; death claim filed by father James Herring - owed $41.50.

HESTER, ELIJAH: enl. 10/20/61 Co. C; admitted Farmville Hosp. 5/8/63 with fever - furloughed 30 days 6;/5/63 - general debility following measles.

HESTER,. GEORGE T. B.: enl. 10/20/61 Co. C; admitted Richmond hosp. 12/25/62 - d. 1/1/63 of typhoid pneumonia.

HESTER, JAMES H.: enl. 7/9/61 Co. C in Louisa; discharged 8/19/61 age 28 with varicose veins of thigh; b. Louisa; farmer, light complexion, brown heir, grey eyes, 5'9".

HIGGASON, (HICKERSON or HIGGERSON) WILLIAM B.: enl. 7/26/61 Co. F in Louisa; present 7/27/61-10/31/61 and 9/63-10/63; recommended for furlough 11/11/63 due to general debility and anemia; absent sick 11/63-12/63, 4/1/64 and 5/64-6/64; present 7/64-8/64; POW Hatcher's Run 3/31/65 - released from Pt. Lookout and took oath 6/13/65; resident of Louisa; farmer; fair complexion, brown hair, hazel eyes, 5'9 3/4"; applied for pension 3/29/1911 age 71 living Orchid, Louisa Co. - total disability due to feet being frost bitten during war and shortness of breath caused by exposure during war - grist mill worker for previous 2 years - doctor said senile - owned no property - $24 approved; admitted Lee Camp Soldiers' Home 6/26/1912 age 72 d. 9:00 p.m. 4/12/1915 - bur. Hollywood Cem.

HIGGINS, M. A.: pwl; Co. K; detailed to work on bridges during war, applied for pension 6/7/1900 age 62 living Quinton, New Kent Co. - partial disability due to rupture - $15 approved.

HIGGINS, WILLIAM F.: pwl; Co. K; b. New Kent Co.; lived in Richmond prior to entry into Soldiers' Home 8/15/1894 age 70; d. 9/11/1896 – bur. West 134, Hollywood Cem.

HILL, JAMES R.: enl. 8/1/61 Co. I in Richmond; present 7/18/61-.8/31/61; got substitute W. E. Fowlkes.

HITE, GEORGE W. (H.): enl. 7/8/61 Co. A in Mecklenburg; present and sick with measles 7/8/61-8/31/61; present 9/61-10/61; 9/63-12/63 and 5/64-8/64 on detached service as provost guard in field; paroled Burkeville 4/14/65-4/17/65.

HOFF, OLIVER: Field and Staff - Assistant Surgeon; assigned to 56th 6/30/62 - relieved 5/25/63; paroled Gen. Hosp., Thomasville, N.C. 5/1/65.

HOFFMASTER, LOUIS: pwl; Co. B; d. 1/11/65 at Camp Chase - bur. Camp Chase Confederate Cem. - grave 742

HOGAN, GEORGE W.: enl. 8/6/61 Co. K in Mechanicsville age 28; sick furlough 8/6/61-8/31/61; present 9/61-10/61; POW Ft. Donelson - sent sick from Camp Morton to Vicksburg for exchange; discharged 10/31/62 enrolled as conscript 1/4/64 and assigned Co. K 1/7/64; discharged 5/5/64 age 31 due to insanity; b. New Kent; carpenter, dark complexion, hair, and eyes.

HOLLINS, GEORGE T. (W.): enl. 7/25/61 Co. F in Louisa; in hospital with measles 7/27/61-8/31/61; present 9/61-10/61; WIA Gaines's Mill; present 9/63-12/63 and 4/1/64; WIA Cold Harbor - admitted Richmond hosp. 6/3/64 - furloughed 60 days 6/28/64; applied for pension *4/9/1888* age 48 living Old Town, Louisa Co. - disability due to arm wd. received Cold Harbor - $15 approved - still living 3/31/1916.

HOLLINS, WILLIAM C.: enl. 7/25/61 Co. F in Louisa; present 9/63-12/63 and 4/1/64; WIA Chester Station 6/16/64 - admitted Richmond hosp. 6/17/64 age 20 with gunshot wd. of right side - furloughed 30 days 6/22/64 - present 7/64-8/64; received clothing 11/64; applied for pension 4/8/1912 age 68 living in Shelfar, Louisa Co. - paralyzed on left side - WIA Gettysburg and Chester Station - entered service at Chaffin's Bluff and left three days prior to surrender because incapacitated physically from starvation and service and saw no hope for the cause - said looking out for himself - had no intention of deserting; real estate $418 and personal property $130 - $36 approved; d. 5/30/1920 - funeral expenses of $25 paid by state of Va.

HOLT, BURWELL (BERKLEY on pension app.) NICHOLAS M. ("NICK"): enl. 7/18/61 Co. I in Charlotte; present 7/18/61-10/31/61; had jaundice 9/61; sick 7/62; WIA Frazier's Farm; WIA and POW Gettysburg - exchanged from Chester, Penn. hosp. - admitted Richmond hosp, with gunshot wd. of hip 7/13/63; absent wded. 7/63-10/63; present 5/64-8/64; received clothing 10/13/64; brother of John Holt; b. 4/3/1836 Campbell Co.; farmer, m. Charlotte Elizabeth East 11/16/1865 - 5 children; d. 7/20/1922 of old age in Charlotte - bur. Bethel Baptist Church Cem, Charlotte; widow applied for pension 12/29/1922 - $76 approved.

HOLT, JAMES PASCHAL (PASCAL): enl. 7/18/61 Co. I in Charlotte; present 7/18/61-10/31/61; had measles 8/61: had jaundice 9/61; WIA Fort Donelson - sick in private home Atlanta, Ga.; selected by Lt. Charles Clark 8/62 to help him enroll conscripts; WIA and POW Gettysburg - in Chester, Penn. hosp. - exchanged 8/63; absent wded, 9/63-10/63; admitted Farmville hosp. *2/9/64* with gunshot wd. of abdomen received at Gettysburg - furloughed 30 days 2/9/64 - furlough extended 30 days 3/11/64 and 20 days 4/12/64. application for extension refused 5/3/64 and ordered to report to command; KIA Drewry's Bluff 6/20/64 - claim for deceased soldier filed 3/1/65; brother of John Holt; m. Adella E. Mason 10/16/1851 Campbell Co. - 3 sons and daughter.

HOLT, JOHN LEA (LEE): enl. 7/18/61 Co. I in Charlotte; present 7/18/61-10/31/61; had measles 8/61; in Empire Hospital, Atlanta 3/62-mid 4/62; went with wded. brother Meredith to Winchester hosp. after Boonsboro; employed as nurse at Old School Presbyterian Church and Market House Hospitals, Winchester 9/20/62-11/1/62; admitted Richmond hosp. with diarrhea 11/26/62 - returned to duty 12/11/62; KIA Gettysburg, but no Federal records concerning him - Co. reported him as "supposed to be prisoner" 10/24/63 -1/19/64; death claim filed 3/1/65; b. 5/31/1829 Campbell Co. son of James F. Holt and Sara Mason Holt; tobacco grower and school master, m. Ellen Elizabeth Lawson 1/19/1859 Hat Creek, Campbell Co. - had son and daughter, widow applied for pension 5/16/1888 living Campbell Co. - $30 approved.

HOLT, M C.: enl. 8/22/61 Co. I in Richmond; present 7/18/61-8/31/61 - name cancelled on roll. (may be Marcellus Holt, brother of John Holt - joined Montgomery's Co. Light Artillery).

HOLT, R. J. (I.): Co. I - discharged 8/24/61; may have reenl. - post war records indicate MWIA Gaines's Mill.

HOLT, RICHARD MEREDITH: enl. 7/18/61 Co. I in Charlotte; present on all rolls; sick furlough 4/62-6/62; slightly wded. Frazier's Farm; WIA Boonsboro - in Old School Presbyterian Church Hospital - sick furlough 10/62-5/63; admitted Virginia State Hosp. 1/9/63; received clothing 10/13/64, 11/14/64, 12/2/64 and 12/30/64; John Holt's brother; b. Campbell Co.; m. 8/21/1854 Sarah Elizabeth (Betty) Frances Berkley, sister of William Woodson Berkley who married Holt's sister Samantha; school teacher and overseer.

HOLT, ROBERT A.: enl. 7/18/61 Co. I in Charlotte, Pvt./Sgt; present 7/18/61-10/31/61; admitted Richmond hosp. with wd. in side 9/6/62 - furloughed 40 days 10/3/62 - returned to duty 3/1/63; admitted Richmond hosp. with hernia 8/5/63; returned to duty 10/20/63; on detail at Richmond arsenal 10/63-12/63 and 5/64-8/64.

HOLT, W. THOMAS: enl. 7/18/61 Co. I in Charlotte, Pvt./Sgt.; present 7/18/61-10/31/61; sick in Bowling Green, Ky. 2/62; MWIA Gaines'. Mill; d. 7/3/62 - death clam filed by father Robert Holt 12/5/62 - owed $97.36; b. Campbell Co.; John Holt's cousin.

HOUSE, ALEXANDER W.: enl. 7/15/61 Co. B in Mecklenburg; d, 8/10/61 Richmond - death claim filed 11/13/61 by mother Frances House - owed $14.67.

HOUSE, GEORGE M.: pwl; Co. E (may be George W. House)

HOUSE, GEORGE W.: enl. 2/63 Co. E in Petersburg; POW Hatcher's Run 3/31/65; took oath and released from Pt. Lookout 6/5/65; b. 10/24/1845 in Brunswick to John E. and Mary Elizabeth Quarles House; farmer; m. Lucie Ann Cheely 12/22/1875 - 5 children; applied for pension 6/30/1922 age 76 living Rawlings, Brunswick Co.- totally disabled due to blindness and hernia; $130 approved; d. 12/22//1926 of paralysis and old age Brunswick - bur. Lebanon Methodist Church, Brunswick; widow applied for pension 3/4/1927 - $90 approved.

HOUSE, JOHN E. enl. 7/10/61 Co. E in Brunswick; present 7/10/61-8/31/61; POW Ft. Donelson - sent from Camp Morton to Vicksburg for exchange; discharged 10/4/62 age 46 because of physical disability; dark complexion and hair, blue eyes, 5'6"; b. about 1821 Brunswick; mechanic and wheelwright; m. Mary Elizabeth Quarles 1842 Brunswick - 7 children (father of George W. House. Co. E); age 69 and living Brunswick 1880; bur. Lebanon Methodist Church, Brunswick

HOUSE. (JOHN) JAMES: enl. 7/2/61 Co. G, 21st Va. Inf. - discharged 10/23/61 for disability; conscripted and assigned Co. E 2/9/63 in Brunswick; POW Gettysburg; confined Ft. Delaware and Pt. Lookout; d. 1/24/64 Pt. Lookout from chronic diarrhea; effects, given to friends before death; bur. graveyard Pt. Lookout; son of Jordan and Martha J. Mason House; brother of Philip House of Co. E.

HOUSE, MARCELLUS: enl. 3/14/64 Co. B in Richmond; present 4/1/64; admitted Chimborazo 6/24/64 with remittent fever - d. *6/27/64* of disease.

HOUSE, PHILIP E.: pwl; conscripted late in war in Brunswick and assigned Co. E; brother of John James House, Co. E.

HOUSE., RICHARD J.: enl. 6/22/61 Co. B in Mecklenburg 9/64-10/64 furloughed to home; discharged 10/31/61 - no reason given.

HOWARD, MARION: pwl; Field and Staff - surgeon of 56th at beginning of war.

HOWELL. JAMES D.: pwl; Co. E (may be John H. M. Howell).

HOWELL, JOHN H. M.: enl. 7/10/61 Co. E in Brunswick; absent sick with measles 7/10/61-8/31/61; discharged 12/17/61 due to severe case of measles; b. 1820 to Spencer and Elizabeth M. Talley Howell; wheelwright; m. about 1852 - wife probably Mary Harris - 3 children in 1860 census; d. 1870's.

HUDNALL, BENJAMIN A.: enl. 7/8/61 Co. D in Buckingham; present 7/8/61-8/31/61; d. of measles - n. d. g.

HUDSON, (HUTSON) JAMES ALFRED: enl. 7/12/61 Co. G in Charlotte; present 7/16/61-10/31/61; KIA Frazier's Farm age 22; death claim filed by father Grief Hudson - owed $41.50; b. Charlotte; farmer; light complexion and hair, blue eyes, 5'6".

HUDSON, (HUTSON) JOHN P.: Co. B; admitted Chimborazo 2/25/65 with fever, POW 4/3/65 in hosp. – sent to Libby Prison, Jackson Hosp., and Newport News; took oath 7/1/65; resident of Mecklenburg; dark complexion and hair, blue eyes;. 5'.

HUDSON, (HUTSON), JOHN T. enl. 7/12/61 Co. G in Charlotte; KIA Frazier's Farm; claim filed by father 7/3/62 - owed $65.73; b. Charlotte.

HUDSON. (HUTSON or HUTTON) MARTIN: enl. *7/8/61* Co. A in Mecklenburg; present 7/8/61-10/31/61; admitted Richmond hosp. 8/29/62 with rheumatism - furloughed 20 days 12/8/62; present 9/63-12/63 and 5/64-6/64; absent sick 7/64-8/64; admitted Chimborazo 10/2/64 and 2/24/65 with rheumatism - furloughed 2/28/65; applied for pension 5/30/1900 age 66 living Clarksville, Mecklenburg Co.; contracted rheumatism during war -$15 approved; made pension statement 5/31/1902.

HUDSON, THOMAS J.: enl. 7/1/61 Co. D in Buckinharn; admitted Richmond hosp. 5/15/62 with rubeola – returned to duty 6/12/62; POW Boonsboro 9/15/62 - sent for exchange from Ft. Delaware to Aiken's Landing 10/2/62; present 9/63-12/63, 4/1/64 and 5/64-8/64; admitted Richmond hosp. 4/4/64 - furloughed 5 days 4/5/64; POW Burkeville - took oath and released from Pt Lookout 6/14/65; b. Amherst Co.; farmer and teacher at Harewood School; resident of Nelson Co.; fair complexion, brown hair, blue eyes; 6' 1 3/4"; applied for pension 4/1/1901 age 63 living Claypool, Nelson Co. - partially disabled due to rupture; $15 approved; rerated 9/27/1909 age 72 living Roseland, Nelson Co. - totally disabled due to age; $36 approved.

HUDSON, WESTON: pwl; enl. 7/61 Co. A - served for entire war.

HUGHES, JAMES H. pwl; Co. D; lost right arm in battle.

HUGHES, WILLIAM H.: enl. 8/6/61 Co. K in Mechanicsville; never mustered in because did not appear.

HUGHSON, (HUGSON) AUBREY: enl. 7/25/61 Co. F in Louisa; Pvt./Sgt; present on all rolls; admitted Chimborazo 7/16/64 with dysentery; returned to duty 8/864; POW Hatcher's Run 3/31/65 - took oath and released from Pt. Lookout 6/13/65; b. Louisa and lived there all life; farmer; dark complexion, blonde hair, hazel eyes; 5' 7 ½"; applied for pension 3/13/1911 age 67 living Poindexter, Louisa Co.; no property or income -totally disabled by old age and general debility - $24 approved; signed pension application of Frederick Grubb's widow 1911; d. of heart failure in Poindexter, n. d.; widow Bettie L Hughson applied for pension 8/30/1926; m. 10/28/1873 in Louisa - $90 approved.

HUGHSON, CLEON ABNER: enl. 9/2/61 Co. F; present 9/61-10/61; admitted Chimborazo 5/16/63 with bronchitis - transferred 6/16/63 to Danville hosp.; bur. St. John's Episcopal Church. Green Springs, Louisa Co.

HUMPHREY, (HUMPHRY) JAMES P.: enr. as conscript 1/18/64 - assigned to Co. C 2/23/64; present 4/1/64 and 5/64-8/64; received clothing 10/64, 11/64, and 12/64.

HUMPHREYS,(HUMPHREY or HUMPHRIES) NATHANIEL H.: enl. 7/9/61 Co. C in Louisa; present 7/9/61-10/31/61; WIA Boonsboro and POW Sharpsburg - sent from Ft. McHenry 10/17/62 to Aiken's Landing for exchange; admitted Chimborazo 10/24/62 with gunshot wd. of left shoulder - furloughed 40 days 11/5/62; present 9/63-10/63; on detached service in distillery in Salisbury, N.C. and as hosp. guard in Charlotte, N.C. 11/63-12/63, 5/64-8/64, and 11/64-12/64; paroled at Salisbury, N.C. 5/3/65; applied for pension 4/23/1888 age 60 living Ft. Defiance, Augusta Co., shot through left shoulder al Boonsboro; arm and hand totally disabled - $15 approved.

HUMPHRIES, (HUMPHREYS), McDONALD (MAC K. DONALD): enl. 7/8/61 Co. A in Mecklenburg; AWL 8/23/61-9/2/61; detached duty as waggoner 3/62 and 1/63-5/63; POW Gettysburg - confined Ft. Delaware 7/12/63; admitted Chimborazo 6/18/64 with debility; deserted 7/8/64; POW Amelia Court House 4/5/65 - took oath and released 6/13/65; resident of Mecklenburg; dark complexion, brown hair, blue eyes, 6'1/4"; was on N.C. pension list until his death In 1911 of heart trouble; widow Sallie A. Humphreys applied for pension 6/11/1925 living in Nelson, Mecklenburg Co. - m. 1852 in N. C. - $80 approved.

HUNDLEY, CHARLES: pwl; Co. I; discharged 1861.

HUNDLEY, J. H.: enl. 10/19/63 Co. K at Chaffin's Bluff; present 5/64-8/64; received clothes 9/64 and 10/64.

HUNT, (HURT) R. T.: Field and Staff - Asst. Surgeon; relieved 12/19/64; POW remaining in Richmond and paroled at Appomattox - residence Union Street, Richmond.

HUNTER, WILLIAM H.: enl. 6/22/61 Co. B in Mecklenburg; present 9/61-10/61; POW Ft. Donelson - sent from Camp Morton to Vicksburg for exchange; admitted Richmond hosp. 5/12/62 - furloughed 10/24/62; present 9/63-12/63 and 4/1/64; admitted Chimborazo 7/16/64 with dysentery - furloughed 40 days 7/26/64; d. 8/64 - no cause or place given.

INGLES, JAMES L.: enl. 5/18/62 Co. D at Chaffin's Bluff; discharged 8/12/62 age 31 due to deformity of hand from wd.; b. Buckingham; carpenter; dark complexion, auburn hair, blue eyes, 6'; d. at home on Church Hill, Richmond 1/63; death claim filed by widow America Ann Ingles 1/19/63 - owed $48.75.

INGRAM, WILLIAM: enl. 8/6/61 Co. K in Mecklenburg age 23 - sick furlough 8//6/61-8/31/61; present 9/61-10/61; POW Ft. Donelson; sent from Camp Morton to Vicksburg for exchange; admitted Richmond hosp. 10/12/62 with internal fever - transferred to pvt. quarters 1/2/63; present 7/63-12/63, 4/1/64, and 5/64-6/64; AWOL since last muster on roll 7/64-864; b. Caroline Co -; farmer; dark complexion, light hair and eyes. 5'8".

IRVINE, POWHATAN J.: enl. 7/18/61 Co. I in Charlotte; present 7/18/61-10/31/61; discharged 9/24/62 age 46 because over 35; carpenter; dark complexion and hair, grey eyes.

JACKSON, GEORGE: enl. 5/8/62 Co. K in Richmond; AWOL and dropped by order of General Garnett.

JACKSON, JETHRO (JOSEPH) W.: pwl; enl. 3/2/62 2nd Co., 12th Inf. Regt. in Brunswick, age 36; discharged on surgeon's certificate 7/62; 5'8", dark complexion, blue eyes, light hair; conscripted 2/9/63 - assigned Co. E; deserted 3/4/63; b. 1826 to Asberry and Sally Doyle Jackson; 1880 census shows Jethro (34) living near Benton Post Office, Brunswick Co. with wife Martha (36) and son John J. (2).

JACKSON, JOSEPH A.: pwl; conscripted in Brunswick and assigned Co. E; surrendered by Lee at Appomattox; b. about 1835 probably in DInwiddie; laborer.

JACKSON, THOMAS - alias PATRICK COLLINS: enl. 8/3/61 Co. K in Richmond; present 8/6/61-10/31/61; POW Ft. Donelson; sent from Camp Morton to Vicksburg for exchange; left Richmond 10/28/62 for Petersburg with passport in name of Patrick Collins; arrested while attempting to get passport to Wilmington, N.C. - confined Castle Thunder - admitted he deserted and asked for discharge 1/22/63; present 7/63-12/63; admitted Chimborazo 12/29/63 - may have been for duty; present 4/1/64 and 5/64-6/64; WIA Chaffin's Farm 9/29/64 - right arm amputated - admitted Chimborazo 10/22/64 - furloughed 60 days 11/12/64; discharged 2/22/65 age 26; b. in Westmoreland Co., England; sailor or soldier; came to United Slates 3 years before war; fair complexion, brown hair, blue eyes, 5'8".

JACKSON, WILLIAM G.: enl. 6/28/61 Co. B in Mecklenburg; released by furnishing substitute 9/12/61.

JACKSON, WILLIAM N.: enl. 7/26/61 Co. F in Louisa; 7/27/61-8/31/61 sick at home with measles; present 9/61-10/61; discharged 10/2/62 no reason given.

JEFFRESS, JAMES W. (H.): enl. 7/12/61 Co. G in Charlotte; present 7/26/61-10/31/61; KIA Ft.. Donelson 2/15/62 age 18 – got through Yankee lines far in advance of his command; killed by ball in forehead - members of 17th Illinois laid him "tenderly away" - found picture on him but no name; Thomas D. Jeffress identified him in the *Confederate Veteran* in 1912 - death claim filed by father Tanner W. Jeffress 6/6/62 – owed $54.00; b. Charlotte; farmer; light complexion, dark hair, black eyes, 5'.

JEFFRESS, THOMAS DANIEL: enl. 7/12/61 Co. G in Charlotte – appointed Captain 7/26/61; elected Captain 5/3/62; served In Kanawha Valley Campaign 1861 and at Ft. Donelson; WIA Gaines's Mill; detached for recruiting duty In Mecklenburg and provost marshal in Lynchburg under Major General G. W. Smith; commandant of Libby Prison for 3 months; resigned 12/29/62; took up farming to end of war; b. 2/8/1840 in Charlotte to Jennings M. and Susan Finch Jeffress; educated at Columbia University - PHD 1858; m. Alice Rebecca Overby 1862 - 3 sons and 2 daughters; after war merchant and editor of Clarksville's "Virginian"; studied law and admitted to bar 1876; mayor of Chase City 12 years and member town council 10; Commander of L A. Armistead Camp, No. 26, UCV of Mecklenburg Co. 4 years; chairmen of Pickett's Division Association many years - made speech at Gettysburg 1906 when General Armistead's sword was returned by Philadelphia Brigade; d. 3/11/1914 Chase City; bur. Overby, Holt, Shelton, etc. Family Cem., Mecklenburg.

JEFFRIES, JARARD (HENRY GERARD): enl. 8/6/61 Co. K in Mecklenburg, Cpl.; present 8/6/61-10/31/61; MWIA Gaines's Mill - admitted Richmond hosp.; d. 10/19/62 of leg wd. and chronic diarrhea; left effects totaling $101.

JENKINS, ANDREW JOSEPH: enl. 8/6/61 Co. K in Mechanicsville; POW Ft. Donelson - sent from Camp Morton to Vicksburg for exchange; admitted Richmond hosp. 10/10/62 - deserted hosp. 12/4/62; AWOL 7/63-8/63 - dropped from roll by Gen. Garnett's order; d.12/6/1888 of pneumonia Hanover; according to widow Lucy Ann Jenkins, Jenkins joined Marion Hill Heavy Artillery after return from Ft Donelson - lived on farm "South Wales" owned by Edward P. Winston; widow applied for pension 8/22/1902; m. 1859 in Hanover - $25 approved.

JENKINS, LEWIS: enr. as conscript 1/27/64 – assigned to Co. C 2/24/64; admitted Richmond hosp. 4/27/64 - returned to duty 4/28/64; present 5/64-8/64; received clothes 10/64 and 12/64.

JENKINS, SOL B.: enl. 8/6/61 Co. K in Mechanicsville; discharged 8/19/61 age 20 due to enlarged spleen and tendency to dropsy; b. Hanover; laborer; sallow complexion, light hair, grey eyes.

JERSEY, J. C.: Company unknown; POW paroled in Richmond 5/13/65.

JETER, ROBERT SAMUEL: enl. 3/3/63 Co. K at Chaffin's, Farm; present 4/1/64 and 5/64-8/64; received clothes 9/64 and 10/64; d. 9/7/1911 of T. B. Hanover; widow Louise Adeline Jeter applied for pension 1/22/1926 - according to application her husband volunteered at 18 and served 3 years - m. 9/28/1872 King William Co. - $90.10 approved.

JETT, E. S.: pwl; Co. E; surrendered by Lee at Appomattox.

JOHNSON, CLEM: pwl; Co. I; discharged 1861.

JOHNSON, DELAWARE C.: enl. 7/25/61 Co. F in Louisa; enrolled as conscript 3/8/64 and assigned Co. F 4/28/64; POW near Howlett's House 8/25/64 - confined Bermuda Hundred, Ft. Monroe and Pt. Lookout; paroled at Pt. Lookout and sent to Aiken's Landing for exchange 3/14/65; paroled Ashland 4/25/65.

JOHNSON, F. J.: Co. F; paroled Columbia 5/65.

JOHNSON, G. (J.) R.: pwl; Co. A; served 2 years; Amherst pension list.

JOHNSON, GEORGE W.: Co. E; received clothes 12/28/64; POW in fighting around Petersburg 1864; POW paroled in Richmond 5/8/65; resident of Brunswick.

JOHNSON, HENRY: enl 7/12/62 Co. B in Richmond; deserted 7/22/62.

JOHNSON, J. R.: pwl; Co. I; d. 1861.
JOHNSON, JAMES J.: enl. 7/22/61 Co. G in Charlotte; present 7/26/61-8/31/61; d. 10/20/61 age 17; owed $22.53 - mother sole survivor; b. Mecklenburg; farmer; light complexion, dark hair, blue eyes, 5'4".
JOHNSON, JERRY Y.: enl. 7/8/61 Co. A in Mecklenburg; present 7/8/61-10/31/61.
JOHNSON, JOHN: enl. 5/3/62 Co. B in Richmond; deserted 5/14/62 or 5/14/63.
JOHNSON, PETER B.: enl. 2/9/63 Co. E in Brunswick; admitted Williamsburg hosp. 4/26/63 - transferred Blacks and Whites hosp. - returned to duty 5/22/63; admitted Chimborazo 6/12/64 with dysentery - transferred Lynchburg hosp. 7/5/64 - furloughed 40 days 8/13/64 - ordered to report to command from Farmville hosp. 9/4/64; present 9/64-12/64; probably son of Amos Johnson of Lunenburg.
JOHNSON, RICHARD: enl. 7/9/61 Co. C in Louisa; admitted MCV 8/6/61 - returned to duty 8/12/61; present on all rolls; POW paroled Richmond 5/4/65.
JOHNSON, RICHARD A.: enl. Co. E 7/10/61; transferred to Co. H, 53rd Va. Inf. 8/6/62; transferred 9/20/64 Co. I, 9th Va. Cav. to be with brother Nathaniel E. Johnson; b. about 1827 to John H. and Lucy Johnson; worked in Petersburg before war; m. Virginia A. Ewell 10/5/1866; applied for pension 5/1900 living Brunswick - approved; d. 10/24/1904 Prince George Co.
JOHNSON, THOMAS J.: enl. 7/26/61 Co. F in Louisa; present 7/27/61-10/31/61; WIA Ft. Donelson; WIA Gainse's Mill 6/29/62; on other rolls listed as absent - disabled; detailed 10/24/64 to Surgeon McCaw at Chlmborazo; paroled and took oath at Columbia 5/8/65; applied for pension 4/9/1888 age 47 living Louisa - total disability due to wds. of knee and ankle received in war - $15 approved; rerated 5/13/1889 - $30 approved; d. of blood poisoning from leg wd. received in war; widow Julia T. Johnson applied for pension 7/14/1902 - owned 1 acre and $12 income per year - $25 approved.
JOHNSTON, R. (REUBEN) C.: enl. 7/18/61 Co. I in Charlotte; present 7/18/61-10/31/61; d. 6/12/62 Charlotte from disease,
JOHNSTON, W. J.: enl. 7/18/61 Co I in Charlotte; sick in hosp. 7/18/61-10/31/61; sick furlough 9/61-10/61.
JONES, BENJAMIN CRAWLEY: enl. 7/10/61 Co. E in Brunswick, 2nd Lt./Capt.; elected Capt. 5/3/62; WIA Gaines's Mill - leg amputated 6/28/62 - admitted Farmville hosp. 8/18/62 - private quarters 9/9/62; in 1862 lived in Dinwiddie; resigned 11/15/62 because permanently disabled from wd.; on register of beneficiaries of Association for Maimed Soldiers; wrote Dr. William A. Carrington 4/23/64 requesting artificial leg; b. Brunswick 9/14/1840 to Hon. Francis F. Crawley and Sallie Green Thweatt Jones;

brother of Francis G., Freeman W., George Washington, and Thomas Thweatt Jones of Co. E; graduated with BA Hampden-Sydney 1859; studied law UVA 1859-1860; practiced law Brunswick; m. Mildred Bolling Field at beginning of war; d. of wds. *2/18/66* in Brunswick; son Benjamin Crawley Jones, Jr. became a highly respected physician.

JONES, CHARLES S. (JR.).: enl. 7/9/61 Co. C in Louisa; 2nd Lt.; present 7/9/61-10/31/61; appointed 2nd Lt. 7/9/61 - dropped 5/5/62; b. about 1829 son of Charles S. and Sarah Cowherd Jones - father was gentleman of "large estate;" matriculated VMI *7/7/1846* age 17 from Louisa Court House - dropped 10/25/1847; practiced law before war; farmer on mother's farm Louisa Co. after war and then moved with her to Cumberland; never married; d. 1898 - bur. near Hoopers Rock, Cumberland Co.

JONES, CHARLES W.: enl. 7/1/61 Co. B in Mecklenburg; present 9/61-10/61; bur. Woodlawn Cem., Chase City – CSA marker, no dates given.

JONES, FRANCIS: enl. 6/22/61 Co. B in Mecklenburg; present 9/61-10/61; POW Williamsport, Md. 9/15/62; sent from Ft. Delaware to Aiken's Landing for exchange 11/10/62; possibly WIA Gettysburg; received clothing in Richmond Hosp. 7/20/63; present on all other rolls.

JONES, FRANCIS GREEN: enl. 7/10/61 Co. E in Brunswick, Sgt./1st Lt.; elected 2nd Lt. 9/3/61; POW Ft. Donelson - sent from Camp Morton to Vicksburg for exchange; furloughed 30 days by Dr. Palmer 10/22/62; WIA Gettysburg - admitted Petersburg hosp. 7/13/63 – transferred to Richmond hosp. 7/14/63; promoted 1st Lt. 9/24/63; requested 20 day furlough of indulgence from Chaffin's Farm to go to Brunswick 2/20/64; WIA near Howlett's House 6/16/64 - furloughed 40 days to San Marina, Va.; on list of those not present, but surrendered by Lee at Appomattox - may have *been in* command of Co. at surrender; b. about 1838; brother of Benjamin C., Freemen W., George W. & Thomas T. Jones of Co. E; m. Emma Field after war - 6 children; d. 12/11/1898 - bur. Concord Presbyterian Church, Brunswick.

JONES, FREEMAN WARD: enl. 4/15/64 Co. E at Chaffin's Farm, age 17; took part in Battle of Cold Harbor; WIA 7/24/64 in skirmish with enemy's picket line on Bermuda Front, Chesterfield Co. - admitted Chimborazo 8/25/64 - furloughed to Dinwiddie 8/26/64 - on morning report at Richmond hosp. 11/4/64; volunteered for expedition against enemy under Capt. Charles W. Reed - failed because deserter apprised enemy of object.; POW Hatcher's Run 3/3165 - took oath and released from Pt. Lookout *6/14/65;* b. Brunswick 8/7/1846 to Francis F. and Sallie Green Thweatt Jones - youngest of 5 brothers in Co, E; fair complexion, brown hair, blue eyes, 5'9"; farmer for 2 years after war, decided to go to California but stopped in Texas - engaged in cattle grazing In San Patricio; after few months returned to Va. on horseback with companion and drove of horses - returned to farming in Brunswick; 1870 elected Sheriff of Brunswick - held post 9 years; m. Harriett Randolph Morrison 10/23/1872 - 4 children; 1/1880 accepted appointment as sampler of tobacco at Centre Warehouse, Petersburg and held office until abolished; 1888 elected Sergeant of Petersburg for 2 *years;* 1892 became tobacco merchant with C. A. Pope and Co. of Centre Warehouse in Petersburg; d. 11/3/1903 - bur. Blandford Cem., Petersburg.

JONES, GEORGE WILLIAM (WASHINGTON): enl. 7/10/61 Co. E in Brunswick,; Sgt.; sick furlough 7/10/61-8/31/61; discharged 9/11/681 age 26 due to delicate nature caused by severe attack of typhoid fever; light complexion, black hair, blue eyes, 5'6"; b. about 1835 in Brunswick to Francis F. and Sallie Green Thweatt Jones - oldest of 5 brothers in Co. E; farmer; m. Nannie B. ? 1857 - 5 children; 1880 living Nottoway Co.

JONES, ISHAM (CHAM) H.:. enl. 7/12/61 Co. G in Charlotte; present on all rolls; WIA Gettysburg - admitted Chimborazo 7/12/63 with gunshot wd. right arm - furloughed 30 days *7/23/63;* received clothes 10/64; applied for pension 5/2/1900 age 60 living Hugh, Charlotte Co.; partial disability due to hernia and eye infirmity . $15 approved,

JONES, J. B. (BENJAMIN): Co. D, Sgt.; POW Spotsylvania 5/12/64 - sent to Elmira, N.Y. 8/2/64; d. 5/10/65 of pneumonia.

JONES, JAMES E. enl. 8/6/61 Co. K in Mechanicsville, Sgt.; present 8/6/61-10/31/61; d. 1/3/62 in Abingdon; death claim filed 3/19/63 - not due money because not in service 6 months.

JONES, JAMES W.: enl. 7/12/61 Co. G in Charlotte, Pvt./Cpl.; present on all rolls; admitted Chimborazo 7/16/64 with remittent fever - returned to duty 8/8/64; POW Farmville - took oath end released from Pt. Lookout 6/28/65; resident of Charlotte; fair complexion, light brown hair, hazel eyes, 5'10"; applied for pension 1/4/1927 age 84 living in Charlotte - left army 3 days before Lee surrendered - annual Income $350 - real estate $2940 - personal property $360 - totally disabled due to old age $150 approved; member H. A. Carrington Camp, UCV.

JONES , JOHN *(A.):* enl. 7/15/61 Co. H in Albemarle, Pvt./Sgt.; present 7/29/61-10/31/61; POW Gettysburg - confined Ft. Delaware and Pt. Lookout 10/26/63 - paroled and exchanged 2/18/65.

JONES, JOHN L.: enl. 7/12/61 Co. G in Charlotte, Cpl./Sgt.; present 7/26/61-10/31/61; POW Gettysburg - confined Ft. Delaware and Pt. Lookout 10/26/63 - paroled and exchanged 2/13/65; member H. A. Carrington Camp, UCV 5/15/1922.

JONES, JOHN PETER (G. P.): enl. 7/8/61 Co. D in Buckingham, 3rd Lt./Capt.; present 7/8/61-10/31/61; elected Capt.. 5/3//62; WIA Gaines's Mill 6/27/62 - admitted Richmond hosp. - transferred Buckinharn; POW Gettysburg - confined Ft. McHenry, Ft. Delaware, Johnson's Island - paroled and sent to Pt. Lookout for exchange 3/14/65; wife wrote letter to

CSA Treasury asking for his pay while he was at Johnson's Island; member John Bowie Strange Camp, UCV; bur. Charlottesville.
JONES. JOHN R.: enl. 7/12/61 Co. G in Charlotte; sick furlough 7/26/61-8/31//61; present 9/61-10/61; may have d. Atlanta Medical College Hosp. 4/1/62 - bur, Oakland Cem. Atlanta, Row 4, Grave 14.
JONES, JOHN W. : enl. 7/29/61 Co. B in Richmond, Pvt./Capt. furlough 9/61-10/61; present on all other rolls; WIA Frazier's Farm - commended for bravery and daring in John B. Strange's report on battle; promoted Capt. 1/9/63; captured at stone wall at Gettysburg; asked tor 1st furlough of indulgence 9/23/63; asked 20 day furlough 1/26/64; furloughed 15 days 12/64; surrendered by Lee at Appomattox - commanding regiment at time - property consisted of horse and personal baggage - paroled and took amnesty oath 6/6/65 Richmond; resident of Mechanicsville,
JONES, MOSIAS H, (JR.): Co. H; admitted Chimborazo 7/8/62 - transferred Lynchburg 8/7/62; d. 9/17/62 of chronic diarrhea Lynchburg hosp. - bur. Lynchburg Cem., Section 179, Row 2, Grave 7; death claim filed by widow Susan M. Jones 11/10/62 - owed $126.33.
JONES, ROBERT T. (C.): Co B; POW High Bridge 4/6/65 - took oath and released from Pt. Lookout 6/14/65; resident Mecklenburg; light complexion, brown hair, blue eyes, 5'4 3/4".
JONES, SAMUEL B.: enl. 7/8/61 Co. D in Buckingham, Pvt./Sgt.; present on all rolls; furloughed 6/30/63-8/31/63; admitted Richmond hosp. 7/31/64 with wd. of left leg; admitted Richmond hosp. 4/65 - POW in hosp. 4/3/65; d. 4/27/65 in Jackson hosp. of gunshot wd. of left leg - bur. West 180, Hollywood Cem.
JONES, THOMAS T.: enl. 4/25/62 Co. K in Richmond - AWOL 7/63-8/63; dropped from roll by Gen. Gamett's order.
JONES, THOMAS THWEATT: enl. 7/10/61 Co. E in Brunswick, Cpl./Sgt. Major; said to be smallest man in company˙, present 7/10/61-8/31/61; POW Ft. Donelson – sent from Camp Morton to Vicksburg for exchange; admitted Petersburg hosp. 7/13/63 - transferred to White Oak Hosp., Dinwiddie 7/14/63 - discharged from service 8/13/63 on surgeon's certificate; elected to Va. Senate 1863; 1864 led 6-8 old men against 32 Yankee raiders in Brunswick and captured them; b. 8/23/1836 to Francis. F. and Sallie Green Thweatt Jones; m. Margaret Ann Bolling before war - 11 children; studied for ministry became minister of Concord Presbyterian Church 1874-1903 - longest pastorate in Concord's history; he and his wile operated Sunnyside School; d. 5/25/1903 - bur. Concord Church Cem.
JONES, WALLER H.: Co. H; d. 6/12/62 at Chaffin's Farm of measles - death claim filed by father Mosias Jones 10/15/62 - owed $89.30 - probably brother of Mosias Jones, Jr.
JONES, WILLIAM EDWARD: enl. 7/8/61 Co. D in Buckingham, Sgt./2nd Lt.; present 7/8/61-1-/31/61; elected 2nd Lt. 5/3/62; WIA Gaines's Mill;

reenl. 8/11/62; believed KIA Gettysburg, but no Federal records concerning him.

JONES, WILLIAM J.: Co. B; surrendered by Lee at Appomattox.

JONES, WILLIAM THOMAS: enl. 7/12/61 Co. G in Charlotte; present on all rolls; WIA Gaines's Mill; WIA Frazier's Farm; admitted Richmond hosp. 12/10/64 with chronic diarrhea - returned to duty 12/13/64; POW Burkeville 4/6/65 - took oath and released from Pt. Lookout 6/28/65; resident of Charlotte; fair complexion, light brown hair, hazel eyes, 5'9 1/2"; d. 9/1/1879 near Wylliesburg – widow Ellen M. Barnes (remarried after Jones died) applied for pension 9/20/1923; m. 12/20/1860 in Halifax - $76 approved.

JORDAN. J. (JOHN) WESLEY: enl. 7/15/61 Co. H in Albemarle, present 7/29/61-10/31/61; d. 6/1/62 of fever in Albemarle.

JOYCE, ROBERT: Co. E; d. 6/22/63 of chronic diarrhea in Lynchburg hosp.- bur. Lynchburg Cem, Section 192, Row 3, Grave 10 - left $26; b. 7/30/1827; m. Caroline F. Thomas of Mecklenburg about 1855; 1860 census living Brunswick with 3 children.

KEASTER, L B.: enl 5/3/62 Co. H in Richmond; present on all rolls; admitted Richmond hosp. 9/12/63 - returned to duty; received clothes 10/64 and 12/64.

KEENE, LEVI O. (OSCAR): enl.10/19/61 Co. C. 2nd Batt. N.C. Inf.; POW Roanoke Island 2/8/62 - paroled Elizabeth City, N.C. 2/21/62 present 2/28/62-6/3062; Company became part of another Co. 11/15/62; POW Farmville 4/6/65 and listed as Co. A, 56th Va. - took oath and released from Pt. Lookout 6/14/65; resident of Mecklenburg; fair complexion, brown hair, blue eyes, 5'6 3/4"; signed Emily Davis's pension application 9/19/1908; bur. Keene Family Cem., Highway 737 on hill in Mecklenburg; CSA marker - grave #3.

KEETON, (KEYTON) JAMES H.: enr. as conscript 3/7/64 at Lunenburg - assigned Co. G. 3/16/64; admitted Chimborazo 5/22/64 with nephritis - transferred Farmville hosp. 5/28/64 - furloughed 7 days 6/3/64 and 6/20/64 and 60 days 10/21/64; discharged 1/17/65 age 24 because of injury of spine caused by fall from height of 30 feet while in line of duty as Sgt, of guard - caused paralysis of lower extremities; b. Lunenburg; farmer; fair complexion, light hair, grey eyes, 6'.

KEETON, (KIETON) JAMES P.: enl. 7/9/61 Co. C in Louisa; present 7/9/61-10/31/61; POW Ft. Denison – on POW roll at Camp Douglas 8/1/62; POW Gettysburg - on roll 7/64-8/64 Co. reported as absent wded. since 7/3/63 - believed MWIA Gettysburg, but no Federal records concerning him.

KIERSON, ARCHER L.: enl. 7/8/61 Co. A in Mecklenburg; present sick with measles 7/8/61-8/31/61; present 9/61-10/61; WIA Gaines's Mill - admitted Richmond hosp. with gunshot wd. 7/1/62; present 9/63-12/63 and

5/64-6/64; absent sick 7/64-8/64; admitted Chimborazo 9/16/64 with acute diarrhea.; furloughed 35 days 10/13/64; POW High Bridge 4/6/65 - took oath and released from Pt. Lookout 6/26/65; resident of Mecklenburg; light complexion, brown hair, hazel eyes, 5'9 ½"; member Armistead Camp, UCV 1898.

KELLEY, (KELLY) EDWARD WASHINGTON: enl. 8/6/61 Co. K in Mechanicsville; present 8/6/61-10/31/61; POW Ft. Donelson - sent from Camp Morton to Vicksburg for exchange; admitted Richmond hosp. 1/17/63 - still in hosp. 4/3/63; POW and WIA Gettysburg - gunshot fracture of left elbow joint - arm amputated by Surgeon J. M. G. McGuire, CSA - paroled from West's Buildings Hosp. 9/25/63 and exchanged at City Point 9/27/63; admitted Richmond hosp., 9/27/63 - furloughed 60 days 10/7/63 - readmitted 12/7/63 - furloughed 60 days 12/16/63; retired 9/5/64 age 23 - in invalid corps; b. Hanover 4/30/1840; farmer; light complexion and hair, gray eyes; merchant after War; d. 10/17/1926 Richmond.

KELLEY, (KELLY) HENRY P.: enl. 8/6/61 Co. K in Mechanicsville; present 8/6/61-10/31/61; POW Ft. Donelson - sent from Camp Morton to Vicksburg for exchange; furloughed 10/24/62-11/24/62; in Officers Quarters hosp. - returned to duty 3/2/63; present 7/63-12/63, 4/1/64 and 5/64-8/64; paroled Burkeville 4/14/65 – 4/17/'65

KELLEY, (KELLY) JOHN: enl. 6/18/61 Co. G in Charlotte; deserted 5/12/62.

KELLY, BARNEY: enl. 9/26/63 Co. K.; present 9/63-12/63; listed as substitute; present *4/1/64;* AWOL 5/64-8/64.

KELLY, B. F.: enl. 2/4/64 Co. K at Chaffin's Farm; paroled Ashland 5/1/65; farmer; (may be Barney Kelly)

KELLY, JOHN S.: enl. 5/4/61 Co. H, 53rd Va. Inf. - got substitute James Turner Hammonds 2/13/63; later returned to army and enl. Co. E, 56th Va.; admitted Richmond hosp. *2/3/65* with gunshot wd. of left arm - furloughed 60 days 3/17/65; POW Hatcher's Run 3/31/65 - took oath and released from Pt. Lookout 6/14/65; light complexion, dark brown hair, grey eyes, 5'10 1/2"; b. 3/13/1836 to Samuel D. and Mason Abernathy Kelly in Brunswick; *8/4/64* m. Indiana M. Griffin (father was Capt. Sabal Griffin, Commander Co. C, 4th Battalion, Va. Reserves) - no children; Justice of Peace Sturgeon District, Brunswick; d. 1909 of paralysis - bur, private cem. several miles west of Dophin, Va; widow applied for pension 1926.

KENNON, CHARLES M.: enl. 7/9/61 Co. C in Louisa; present 10/31/61.

KENNON, GEORGE W.: enl. 79/61 Co. C in Louisa; discharged 7/27/61 age 18 due to heart disease; reenlisted 4/1/64 at Chaffin's Farm; deserted since last muster on 7/64-8/64 roll; received clothes 9/27/64, 10/13/64 and 10/19/64; on list of deserters turned over to provost marshal to be examined and sent to Washington, D.C.; b, Goochland; farmer; light

complexion, dark grey eyes, 5'8"; d. 1880 of consumption Louisa; widow Ann E. Kennon applied for pension 12/3/1915 - m. 2/67 Louisa - $400 real estate - $50 personal property - $33 approved.
KENNON, JAMES: pwl; enl. 7/9/61 Co. C.
KENNON, JOSEPH FRANKLIN: enl. 7/961 Co. C in Louisa; in MCV hosp. 8/6/61-8/18/61; present on all rolls; admitted Richmond hosp. 4/4/64 - furloughed 7 days; readmitted hosp. 6/12/64 - deserted hosp. 6/18/64; POW Hatcher's Run 4/1/65; took oath and released from Pt. Lookout 6/10/65; light complexion, brown hair, grey eyes, 5'11 1/4"; b. 3/24/1845; farmer, applied for pension 4/30/1914 age 73, living Mineral, Louisa Co. - wded. twice during war - total disability due to chronic rheumatism and general debility - doctor said senile - no property or income - $43.20 approved; d. 11/30/1922 of arterial sclerosis, Mineral - bur. Rt. 644, Mineral; widow Lucy J, Kennon applied for pension 12/5/1922 - m. 7/19/1875 Louisa - $100 approved.
KENNON, NATHANIEL M.: enl. 7/9/61 Co. C in Louisa; present 7/9/61-10/31/61; discharged 3/25/62
KENNON, ROBERT W.: enl. 7/26/61 Co. F in Louisa; present 7/27/61-10/31/61; present in arrest 9/63-12/63; prevent 5/64-6/64; admitted Richmond hosp. 6/18/64 with gunshot wd. of right knee - d. 8/4/64.
KENNON, WILLIAM M.: enl. 7/9/61 Co. C in Louisa; present 7/9/61-10/31/61; absent sick 9/63-10/63 - surgeon's letter of 10/31/63 said he should have furlough due to acute rheumatism in right knee; deserted on rolls 7/6-8/64; turned over to U.S. Provost Marshall in Norfolk for examination - sent to Washington, D.C. 3/21/65.
KERRENCE, JOHN: enl. 6/18/61 Co. G in Charlotte - discharged 8/1/62.
KERSEY, CHARLES J.: pwl; enl. 1882 Co. A; served 3 1/2 years.
KERSEY, JAMES: enl. 7/26/61 Co. F in Louisa; present 7/27/61-10/31/61; KIA Gaines's Mill.
KERSEY, JOHN R.: Co. I; d. 8/4/61 of fever in Richmond.
KERSEY, THOMAS F.: enl. 7/25/61 Co, F in Louisa; admitted Chimborazo 6/23/62 with catarrh - transferred Danville hosp. 6/26/62 - Danville register lists as deserted 7/9/62; on detached service as ordnance guard in the field on rolls of 9/63-12/63, 4/1/64, and 5/64-8/64; surrendered by Lee at Appomattox; b. Louisa: admitted Lee Camp Soldiers' Home 3/14/1890 age 52 for rheumatism; d. 4/1/1891.
KESTER, W. J.: pwl; Co. C; from Louisa.
KEYTON, (KEATON) S. FRANKLIN: enl. 7/15/61 Co. H in Albemarle; present 7/20/61-10/31/61: WIA and POW Gettysburg - paroled from DeCamp Gen. Hosp. and received at City Point for exchange 9/16/63; absent wded. 5/64-6/64; absent on detail 7/64-8/64; paroled Staunton 5/1/65 age 24; dark complexion, black hair, blue eyes, 5'7
KIDD, ALLEN B.: enl. 6/22/61 Co. B in Mecklenburg, Pvt./Cpl.; present

9/61-10/671; furloughed 5/8/62-5/16/62; WIA Boonsboro left shoulder; present 9/63-12/63, *4/1/64,* and 5/64-8/64; WIA Sayler's Creek - fingers of rt. hand broken; surrendered with Co. at Appomattox; applied for pension 1/20/1896 age 57 living in Mecklenburg - conflict over interpretation of whether disability was total - application amended 4/19/1897 - no work with left arm and practically none with right hand - $15 approved; d. 11/20/1903 in Dinwiddie - shot in an altercation and killed instantly; widow Margaret Kidd applied for pension 8/3/1912 – m. 1866 in Mecklenburg - $25 approved.

KIDD, EDWARD R.: enl. 6/22/61 Co. B in Mecklenburg; on Richmond hosp. roll 8/31/62 and 10/13/62 - furloughed 10/20/62; furloughed 10/20/63 - 11/19/63; furloughed 1/1/64-4/30/64; admitted Chimborazo 6/17/64 age 41 with gunshot wd. of rt. foot received 6/16/64 - furloughed 30 days 6/22/64; farmer.

KIDD, JOHN J.: pwl; Co. D; d. 10/30/1900 in Rose Mills, Nelson Co. of heart trouble; widow Lucinda C. Kidd applied for pension 3/3/1901 – m. 10/20/1850 - $25 approved.

KIDD. WILLIAM T.: enl. 6/22/61 Co. B in Mecklenburg; present 9/61-10/61; furloughed 20 days 1/24/63-2/3/63; present 9/63-12/63, 4/1/64 and 5/64-8/64; POW Burkeville 4/6/65 - took oath and released from Pt. Lookout 6/28/65; light complexion, brown hair, hazel eyes, 5'8 1/2"; b. Mecklenburg; moved to Brunswick 1874; m. Frances ? - 8 children; applied for pension 9/22/1902 living Brunswick age 66 - totally disabled due to nervousness and rheumatism - $30 approved.

KING, THOMAS: enl. 4/26/62 Co. K in Richmond; AWOL and dropped from rolls by Gen. Garnett's order 10/24/63.

KIRBY, JAMES HENRY: enl. 6/15/61 Co. H in Albemarle; sick furlough 7/20/61-8/31/61; present 9/61-10/61; discharged from service for general debility 12/15/62 age 32; enr. as conscript 2/13/64 - assigned Co. H 2/23/64; absent wded. 5/64-6/64; admitted Charlottesville hosp. 8/5/64 with gunshot wd. of right forearm - furloughed 9/5/64; received clothes 12/300/64; b. Albemarle; cook; light complexion and hair, blue eyes, 6'1"; applied for pension 4/15/1900 living Albemarle age 70 - wd. in right arm left with no strength - $15 approved; made pension statement 5/15/1902 age 72.

KIRKLAND, W. J.: pwl; enl. 1862 Co. B; served 3 years.

KNAUFF, GEORGE T. (F.): enr. as conscript 2/1/64 - assigned to Co. A 3/10/64; admitted Richmond hosp. 3/25/64 with gunshot wd. of finger; on detached duty as guard and messenger in war department on rolls 4/64-8/64.

KNIGHT, DAVID: pwl; Co. G; KIA Hatcher's Run.

KNIGHTON, ALBERT: enl. 7/9/61 Co. C in Louisa; present 7/9/61-10/31/61; WIA Gettysburg - admitted Richmond hosp. with wd. 7/13/63 -

returned to duty 8/19/63; readmitted 12/23/63 with diarrhea - furloughed 40 days 12/24/63; d. at home 12/31/63 of chronic diarrhea; death claim filed by father Thomas M. Knighton - owed $173.98.
KNIGHTON, GEORGE WILLIAM: enl. 7/9/61 Co. C in Louisa; present 7/9/61-10/31/61; Court Martial AWOL 2/23/63 - found guilty of specification and charge – forfeited 2 months pay and had to cut wood and bring water for Co. and Regt. until 4/1/63; WIA and POW Suffolk - admitted Chesapeake U.S.A. Hosp., Ft. Monroe 5/7/63 - d. 6/2/63.
LAFFOON, JOSEPH H.: enr. as conscript 1862 - exempted due to injury; conscripted later and paid $500 for substitute; enl. Co. E late in war; paroled Burkeville 4/21/65; grandson said Joseph told him he realized war was lost so set his gun down by tree and surrendered; b. 9/16/1836 to Simon and Mildred Laffoon; carpenter; moved to Texas after war; m. Martha Rainey 1870 in Waco, Texas - 2 children; d. 1/19/1892 in Eastland, Texas - bur. Eastland Cem.
LAMBERT, ANDREW J.: enl. 6/22/61 Co. B in Mecklenburg; on roll of Medical College of Virginia 8/5/61-8/14/61; d. 8/31/61 - death claim filed by father Baxter Lambert - owed $24.30.
LAMBERT, GEORGE D. (W.): enl. 7/1/61 Co. B in Mecklenburg; Pvt./Sgt.; on roll of Medical College of Virginia 8/6/61-8/14/61; present 9/61-10/61; WIA Gettysburg - admitted Chimborazo with gunshot wd. 7/12/63 - furloughed 8/26/63-9/11/63; present on rolls 5/64-8/64; admitted Chimborazo 6/9/64 with debilitas - returned to duty 6/30/64; readmitted 10/1/64 - furloughed 60 days 10/12/64 due to gunshot wd. of left hand.
LAMBERT, MARTIN VAN BUREN ("JACK"): enl. 7/8/61 Co. B; surrendered by Lee at Appomattox; b. 12/27/1846 to Martin Foster and Mary Carroll Lambert In Mecklenburg; farmer before and after war; m. Minerva Adeline Pearson 12/5/1866 Brunswick - 9 children; moved to Brunswick 1884; d. 8/25/1901 Brunswick - was plowing lot, got hot, ate some watermelon and died from the effects of it - bur. Canaan United Methodist Church Cem.. near Broadnax, Va.; widow filed for pension 7/14/1914 - $30 approved.
LAMBERT, ROBERT B.: enl. 6/22/61 Co B in Mecklenburg; present 9/61-10/61; POW Ft. Donelson - sent from Camp Morton to Vicksburg for exchange – declared exchanged at Aiken's Landing 11/10/62.
LAMBERT, WILLIAM: enl. Co. B; received clothes 12/30/64; paroled and took oath 5/27/65 at Statesville, N.C.
LANDIS, L H.: pwl; enl. 1861 Co. A; served entire war; Greenville pension list. (may be L H. Lester)
LANE (LAYNE) ADDISON H.: enl. 7/8/61 Co. D in Buckingham; present 7/8/61-8/31/61; sick furlough 9/61-10/61; reenl. 5/3/62; on list of payments to discharged soldiers 11/17/62.
LANE, ALONZA:: pwl; Co. H.

LANE, EDWARD V. (B.): Co. G; resident of Charlotte; received clothes 12/28/64; POW High Bridge 4/6/65 - took oath and released from Pt. Lookout 6/26/65; light brown hair, fair complexion, hazel eyes, 6'4 ½"..

LANE, (LAYNE) JOHN H.: enl, 5/3/62 Co. H in Richmond, Pvt../Cpl..; present 7/63-12/63, 4/1/64, and 5/64-8/64; received clothes 9/64,10/64, and 12/64; POW Hatcher's Run 3/31/65 - took oath and released from Pt. Lookout 6/14/65; resident of Albemarle; light complexion, brown hair, dark blue eyes, 5'8 3/4".

LANE, RICHARD R.: enl. 7/12/61 Co. G in Charlotte; present 7/26/61-10/31/61; admitted Chimborazo 6/22/62 with diarrhea - transferred Danville hosp. 7/3/62; discharged 9/8/62 age 36 at Hagerstown, Maryland because over 35 - going to Staunton; admitted Chimborazo 12/17/64; returned to duty 12/24/64; b. Charlotte; farmer; light complexion and hair, blue eyes, 6'.

LANE, THOMAS EDWARD: pwl; enl. Co. H age 20 at beginning of war; fought with Co. H until captured Roanoke Island - POW and later paroled; joined Co. A, 19th Va. Inf.; fought at 2nd Manassas, Boonsboro, and Sharpsburg (haversack shot from body but was not wded.); rejoined 56th. Co. H when returned to Va. 1863 - served until end of war; d. 10/1870 of consumption near Peakes, Va.; widow Margaret E. Lane applied for pension 9/7/1914 living Hanover - $400 real estate; $60 personal property, $50 income - $30 approved.

LANIER, CHARLES H.: enl. 7/10/61 Co. E in Brunswick; present 7/10/61-8/31/61; POW Ft. Donelson - sent from Camp Morton to Vicksburg for exchange - furloughed 30 days 10/22/62; furloughed 8/25/63 – 9/25/63; WIA Cold Harbor - letter written from Chester 2/24/65 by surgeon who found him incapable of performing duty in field due to wd. that caused contraction of tendons of left middle finger - recommended light duty - another letter said his light duty could be catching deserters if he could mount horse; b. about 1838 to Samuel H. and Margaret Saunders Lanier; plasterer and mason; m. Julia Ann Melton in Greeneville Co. 1/12/1870; no children; lived Dinwiddie after war; applied for pension 1900 - loss use of left hand due to war wd. - $15 approved; rerated 5/26/1911 - property worth $140 - $32.40 approved: d. Dinwiddie.

LANIER, LEGRAND H.; enl. 7/10/61 Co. E in Brunswick, Pvt./Sgt; present 7/10/61-8/31/61; admitted Chimborazo 7/28/62 with continual fever - furloughed 8/28/61-10/3/62; WIA and POW Gettysburg - confined Ft. Delaware 7/12/63 and Pt. Lookout 10/26/63; paroled from Pt. Lookout 2/18/65 - received with 3038 prisoners at Boulwares and Cox Wharf on James River 2/20/65-2/21/65; b. about 1838 to Richard and Sarah Gibbs Lanier, Brunswick; overseer before war; m. Leila E. Howell 1/3/1870; 1880 census - 3 children, farmer, and living Greensville Co.

LANIER, WESLEY H.: enl. 7/10/61 Co. E in Brunswick; present 7/10/61-

8/31/61; POW Ft Donelson - sent from Camp Morton to Vicksburg for exchange; admitted Richmond hosp. - 11/25/62 - also 5/63-6/63; WIA Gettysburg - admitted Richmond hosp. 7/20/63 with gunshot wd. of thigh - furloughed 30 days 7/28/63 to residence in Smoky Ordinary, Va.; listed as AWOL on 9/63-10/63 roll; absent wded. 11/63-12/63, 4/1/64, and 5/64-8/64; discharged middle 1864; b. 1842; brother of Legrand Lanier, laborer and farmer, m. Sarah E. Rideout 12/21/64, Greensville Co.

LAWSON, PEYTON R.: enl. 7/18/61 Co. I in Charlotte, Sgt./Pvt.; sick furlough beyond time 7/18/61-8/31/61; present 9/61-10/61; sprained ankle and got sick furlough 12/1/61; on 7/63-12/63 rolls shown as absent - supposed to be prisoner and missing since 9/14/62; KIA Boonsboro.

LAWSON, THOMAS G. enl. 7/18/61 Co. I in Charlotte; sick furlough 7/18/61-10/31/61; guarded baggage in Greensville, N. C.: POW and WIA Gettysburg - confined DeCamp Hosp. 7/22/63 with gunshot wd. of left groin - paroled and exchanged 8/24/63; admitted Farmville hosp. 8/30/63 - deserted hosp. 9/3/63; admitted Chimborazo 6/28/64 with remittent fever - transferred Lynchburg 7/9/64; received clothes 10/64 and 12/64.

LAYNE, (LANE) N. (NEHEMIAH): enl. 3/18/62 Co. H in Charlottesville; admitted Richmond hosp. 6/24/62 with intermittent fever; transferred to Danville 6/26/62 with syphilis - returned to duty *8/28/62;* Court Martial AWOL 2/23/63 - found guilty of specification and charge - forfeited 2 months pay; present 7/63-12/63; admitted Richmond hosp. 3/18/64 - remarks – well; given 7 day furlough; present 4/1/64 and 5/64-8/64; POW paroled Richmond 4/22/65.

LAYNE, (LANE) ROBERT CARSON: enl. 7/15/61 Co. H in Albemarle; present 7/29/61-8/31/61; reported as POW by Co. and later KIA Gettysburg, age 29, but no Federal records concerning him; death claim filed by widow Cordella A. Lane 2/18/64; owed $104.63; b. Albemarle; farmer; fair complexion, dark hair, blue eyes. 5'9".

LAYNE, T. E.: enl. 4/15/61 Co. H in Charlottesville; present 7/64-8/64; admitted Chimborazo 11/20/64 with chronic diarrhea - deserted hosp. 12/3/64.

LEDBETTER, RICHARD T.: enl. 7/18/61 Co. I in Charlotte; present 7/18/61-10/31/61; detailed to go to Charlotte; received clothes 12/30/64,

LENTON, JOHN F.: enl. 8/11/63 Co. D in Richmond.

LESTER. HARTWELL F.: enl. 7/18/61 Co. I in Charlotte; on sick furlough beyond time 7/18/61-8/31/61; present on all other rolls; furloughed 3/9/63-3//24/63 and 6/30/63-10/31/63; detailed to Charlotte; paroled Farmville 4/11/65-4/21/65; carpenter; applied for pension 4/14/1900 *age* 65 living in Charlotte - disability due to broken right arm during war and stomach trouble - $15 approved; rerated 5/8/1911 age *77;* on roster of H. A, Carrington Camp, UCV 5/15/1922, signed Martha Hamersly's pension application in 1923; d. Halifax - n. d.; widow Susan H. Lester applied for

pension 12/10/1930 - m. 12/1890 Charlotte - $120 approved.
LESTER, LEROY H. (M.): enl. 10/1/63 Co, A at Chaffin's Farm; present 9/63-12/63; WIA skirmish near Howlett's House 8/29/64 - admitted Chimborazo 8/29/64 with gunshot wd. of hand - furloughed 60 days 9/22/64; readmitted 12/24/64; discharged from service 1/30/65 age 44 - disabled as result of gunshot wd.; on list of those paroled 5/65 by Headquarters 6th Army Corps; b. Halifax; farmer; dark complexion, gray hair, blue eyes. (may be L H. Landis).
LESTER, THOMAS PARKER: enl. 7/18/61 Co. I in Charlotte; present 7/18/6-10/31/61; d. 1881 Charlotte of pneumonia; widow Sarah A. Lester applied for pension 5/3/1900 - m. 1857 Charlotte; $25 approved.
LESTER, WILLIAM TAL: enl. 7/18/61 Co. I in Charlotte; present 7/18/61-10/31/61; admitted Farmville hosp. 5/3/63 with chronic diarrhea - furloughed 30 days 5/13/63 to Mossingford, Va. - returned to duty 6/23/63; furloughed 1/7/64-3/29/64; present 7/64-12/64; admitted Chimborazo 6/5/64 with intermittent fever - readmitted with chronic diarrhea 7/16/64 - furloughed 30 days 7/20/64; paroled Farmville 4/11/65-4/21/65; applied for pension 4/14/1900 age 69 living Reeses, Charlotte Co. - total disability due to spinal trouble - $15 approved - made statement 5/12/1902 age 71.
LEWIS, HAMBLIN H.: enl. 7/10/61 Co. E in Brunswick; present 7/10/61-8/31/61; POW and WIA Ft. Donelson - wded. in thigh and arm; brought from Ft. Doneleon to Mound City, Ill 2/19/62 on USA steamer Chancellor - admitted USA hosp.; d. 2/19/62 - bur. Illinois; dropped from roll by Hunton's orders 11/1/63 because believed dead; b. about 1823; m. Antoinette Wells 1850 Dinwiddie; overseer before war, 1860 census living Sturgeonville with wife and daughter age 7.
LEWIS, JAMES (JOSEPH) F.: pwl; Co, E.; entered service 4/64 at Belfield in reserves - in service 1 year; POW 4/6/65 - came home 2 months after surrender; b. Brunswick to James and Susan Lewis; farmer; m. Mary Jane Vaughan 8/16/1871 - 5 children: applied for pension 4/10/1916 age 70 living Brunswick - disabled due to asthma, rheumatism, and heart trouble - $50 approved; d. 1923.
LEWIS, JAMES WASHINGTON: enl. 9//2/63 Co. E in Brunswick present 9/63-12/63, 4/1/64, and 5/64-8/64; POW Burkeville 4/6/65; took oath and released from Pt. Lookout 6/14/65; dark complexion, dark brown hair, hazel eyes, 5'7 3/4"; b. about 1825 Brunswick; farmer; m. Martha Wray 1848 Brunswick - 6 children; living Red Oak District, Brunswick 1860 census.
LEWIS, JOHN W.: enr. as conscript 2/16/64 - assigned Co. I 12/23/64; admitted Chimborazo 6/3/64 with wd. of abdomen and right index finger - furloughed 40 days 8/27/64; POW Hatcher's Run 3/31/65 - took oath and released from Pt. Lookout 6/14/65; resident of Charlotte; light complexion, brown hair, grey eyes, 5/7 1/2".

LEWIS, PHILIP JAMES: enl. 7/10/61 Co. E in Brunswick; present 7/10/61-10/31/61; WIA Gettysburg; admitted Richmond hosp. 7/14/63 with chronic diarrhea - furloughed 7/25/63; present 9/63-12/63, 4/1/64, and 5/64-8/64; received clothes 10/13/64, 10/19/64, 12/3/64, and 12/2/164;
b. 8/17/1842 in Brunswick to Frederick A. and Almira B. Kelly Lewis; farmer & merchant; m. Eduella Jane Rawlings 5/9/1866; 7 children; d. 1/11/1918 Lawrenceville age 76; bur. Lewis Family Cem., Charlie Hope, Va.

LEWIS, WILLIAM A.: enl. 1864 Co. A - served 6 months; received clothes 12/28/64.

LIPFORD, WILLIAM A.: enl. 7/12/61 Co, G in Charlotte; present 7/26/61-10/31/61.

LIPSCOMB, EDWARD T.: enl. 7/12/61 Co. G in Charlotte; present on all rolls; furloughed 7/1/63-8/31/63; received clothes 10/13/64 and 12/28/64.

LIPSCOMB, GEORGE A.: enr. as conscript 2/16/64 - assigned to Co. G 2/23/64; present 4/1/64 and 5/64-8/64; admitted Chimborazo 3/8/65 with chronic bronchitis - POW in hosp. - confined Jackson Hosp., Libby Prison, and Newport News 4/23/65: took oath and released from Newport News 5/1/65; resident of Charlotte; fair complexion, light hair, blue eyes, 5'7".

LIPSCOMB, PLEASANT T.: enl. 10/63 Co. I at Chaffin's Farm; received clothes 10/19/64, 12/2/64, and 12/30/64; POW paroled Farmville 4/11/65-4/21/65; farmer; applied for pension 4/18/1912 age 67 living Randolph, Charlotte Co. - no income or real estate - personal property $112 - partial disability due to infirmities of old age; on roster of H. A Carrington Comp, UCV 5/15/1922 d. 6/14/1934 of cancer Chase City - bur. Salem United Methodist Church Cem., Hwy. 47 East - 5 miles from Chase City; widow Luella D. Lipscomb applied for pension 7/24/1934 - m. 6/25/1873 Charlotte - $120 approved.

LITTLE, ROBERT O.: enr. as conscript 2/20/64 - assigned Co. C 2/25/64; KIA Howlett's Farm 6/16/64 - death claim filed by widow Harriet W. Little - owed $102.66; b - Campbell Co.

LIVESAY, WILLIAM M.: enl. 8/6/61 Co. K in Mechanicsville; sick furlough 8/6/61-8/31/61; discharged 9/10/61 - got substitute T. J. Truman.

LLOYD, ROBERT H.: enl. 7/9/61 Co. C in Louisa; present 7/8/61-10/31/61; WIA Gettysburg; AWOL 9/63-12/63; deserted on roll 5/21/64.

LOAFMAN, GEORGE W.: enl. 7/18/61 Co. A in Mecklenburg; sick with measles 7/8/61-10/31/61; d. Bowling Green, Ky. 1/15/62 - death claim filed by father William Loafman 5/2/63.

LOAFMAN, JAMES H.: enl. 7/12/61 Co. G in Charlotte; present 7/26/61-10/31/61 and 9/63-10/63; discharged 1/16/64 age 33 because of disease of flesh; b. Mecklenburg; fair complexion, dark hair, hazel eyes. 5'2";
d. 9/5/1875 Mecklenburg of consumption contracted in war; widow Nannie E. Loafman applied for pension 5/1/1900 - m. 5/5/1855 Mecklenburg - $25 approved.

LOCKE, A. J.: enl. 4/2/64 Co. G at Chaffin's Farm; admitted Chimborazo 8/8/64 - d. 8/16/64 of internal fever.

LOCKE, JAMES W.: enl. 7/12/61 Co. G in Charlotte; present 7/26/61-10/31/61; WIA, Gaines's Mill; WIA Gettysburg - admitted Richmond hosp. 7/21/63 - gunshot flesh wd. of right leg - furloughed 30 days to residence in Drakes Branch, Va. 8/4/63; WIA Bermuda Hundred 6/16/64, age 24 - admitted Chimborazo 6/17/64 - gunshot wd, through left knee joint and left hip - furloughed 40 days 7/1/64; furloughed 60 days 8/5/64 by Farmville hosp.; extra duty as shoemaker in Richmond 9/64-12/64; b. Charlotte; carpenter; applied for pension 4/17/1888, age 44 living Chatham - disallowed because not totally disabled; reapplied 7/11/1894 living Danville - $15 approved; admitted Lee Camp Soldiers' Home 11/20/1911 age 71 for old age and blindness; d. 7/30/1925, age 85 - bur. Hollywood Cem. East 585.

LOCKE, WILLIAM S.: enl. 7/12/61 Co. G in Charlotte; present 7/26/61-10/31/61; discharged 9/8/62 because over 35; farmer, dark complexion, hair, and eyes; d. from injuries received in service - n. d.; widow E.J. Locke applied for pension 3/3/1898 - $15 approved.

LOCKETTE, MARCELLUS: pwl; Co. G.

LOCKETT, ROYAL (ROZALL): enl. 7/26/61 Co. G in Charlotte; present 7/26/61-10/31/61; WIA Frazier's Farm - gunshot wd. in right foot - commended for bravery and daring by Col. John B. Strange, 19th Va. Inf.; discharged 1/14/63 age 21 due to gunshot wd.; b. Mecklenburg 1842; farmer; fair complexion, light hair, dark eyes, 5'8"; d. 6/1867 in Mecklenburg.

LOCHART, JAMES ASHBURN: enl.7/25/61 Co. F in Louisa; present 9/63-12/63; furloughed 1/1/64-2/29/64; present 4/1/64; absent sick 5/64-8/64; b.. Louisa; farmer, well digger, and miller; applied for pension 4/1/1903 age 74 living Locust. Creek, Louisa Co.; partially disabled - treated for cancer 1900 in Richmond - had dropsy during war - $15 approved.

LONGAN, EDMOND: enl. 8/6/61 Co. K in Mechanicsville, Pvt../2nd Lt.; present 8/6/61-10/31/61; elected 2nd Lt. 5/3/62; WIA Gaines's Mill; d. 7/11/62 at his home of typhoid fever or wds. - carried there by William E. Talley, 3rd Lt. 56th Va. - death claim filed 10/4/62 - owed $226.

LOVING, JAMES H.: enl. 10/18/61 Co. C.

LOWELL, J. J.: Co. F; paroled Farmville 411/65-4/21/65.

LOWRY, WYATT D.: enl. 8/8/61 Co. F in Louisa; present 7/27/61-10/31/61; WIA Frazier's Farm; discharged 10/2/62 age 46 because over 35; must have reenlisted - roll listed as deserted 5/1/64; paroled Ashland 4/27/65; b. Hanover; farmer, dark complexion, blue eyes, 5'10".

LOYALL, PARSONS B.: enl. 7/26/61 Co. F in Louisa; in hosp. with measles 7/27/61-8/31/61; sick furlough 9/61-10/61; AWOL since 9/11/62;

discharged 11/4/62.
LUCEY, JOHN J., JR.: enl. 7/10/61 Co. E in Brunswick; sick furlough with measles 7/10/61-8/3/61; admitted Chimborazo with typhoid fever 7/28/62; d. 8/1/62; born 1840 to John J. and Margaret B. Moore Lucey.
LUTTON, S. A.: pwl; Co. B; from Mecklenburg; on roster of Armistead Camp No. 25 UCV 8/15/1914.
LYLE, SAMUEL A. (J.): enl. 7/12/61 Co. G in Charlotte; discharged 8/12/61, age 19 due to hernia and division of tibula in right leg by cut; b. Mecklenburg; farmer; light complexion, dark hair and eyes, 5'6".
LYNCH, ROBERT: enl. 2/5/63 Co. G in Fredericksburg; admitted Richmond hosp. with typhoid fever – furloughed to Burgess Store 30 days 6/23/63; present 9/63-10/63; furloughed due to rheumatism 10/31/63-12/31/63; absent sick 4/1/64 and 5/64-8/64; furloughed from Danville hosp. 6/7/64; present 7/64-8/64; POW Farmville 4/6/65 - took oath and released from Pt. Lookout 6/14/65; resident of Pittsylvania; florid complexion, auburn hair, grey eyes, 5'10".
LYNCH, THOMAS JEFFERSON, SR: enl. Brunswick Artillery 3/1/62; discharged 11/12/62 due to diseased heart; enl. 2/17/63 Co. B in Richmond; present 9/63-12/63, 4/1/64 and 5/64-8/64; admitted Chimborazo with contusion 9/30/64 - returned to duty 10/8/64; POW Hatcher's Run 3/31/65 - took oath & released from Pt. Lookout 6/28/65; dark complexion, dark brown hair, hazel eyes, 5'10"; b.1846 to James Madison and Arlan F. Fenn Lynch in Brunswick; farmer, m. Tabitha R. Kirkland 10/11/65 - 6 children; d. 4/6/1900 of pneumonia, Brunswick - bur. private cem. between Rte. 626 and Pea Hill Creek, west of Gasburg – CSA marker; widow applied for pension 8/15/1902 - m. 10/11/65 - $25 approved.

Chapter 16

Roster 56th Virginia Regiment, M thru R

MADISON, GEORGE H.: enl. 7/9/61 Co. C in Louisa; present 7/9/61-10/31/61

MADISON, JAMES: pwl; Co. H; d. in service.

MADISON, WILLIAM H.: enl.. 2/4/64 Co. K at Chaffin's Farm; admitted Richmond hosp. 5/31/64 with debility - returned to duty 7/18/64; detailed as hosp. guard 7/15/64 - unfit for duty in field due to enlarged spleen; deserted according to hosp. roll 8/2/64; admitted Chimborazo 10/5/64 with debilitas – ret. to duty 12/8/64; POW Richmond 4/20/65; resident of King William Co.

MAITLAND, HARTWELL J.: enl. 7/10/61 Co. E in Brunswick; present 7/10/61-8/31/61; POW Ft. Donelson - sick; sent from Camp Morton to Vicksburg for exchange; admitted Richmond hosp. 10/12/62 - returned to duty 10/3/62 - readmitted 10/21/62 - furloughed 7 days 11/7/62; sick furlough 3/4/63-3/24/63; WIA repulsing Butler's advance R and P Railroad (Bermuda Hundred) 6/16/64 - admitted Chimborazo age 35 6/17/64 with gunshot wd. of right arm - furloughed 30 days 6/24/64; b. 1830 to Samuel and Martha Lewis Maitland; farmer; m. Mary Elizabeth Hawks 9/15/1852 Brunswick - she d. 7/18/1853; remarried 1857 Dinwiddie - 3 children; applied for pension 4/2/1888 age 59 living Brunswick - $15 approved; d. 10/16/1901 of paralysis (also senile) Brunswick; widow Frances A. Maitland applied for pension 9/22/1902 -.$25 approved.

MAITLAND, JAMES COLEMAN: enl. 7/10/61 Co. E in Brunswick ; present 7/10/61-8/31/61; POW Ft. Donelson - sick ; sent from Camp Morton to Vicksburg for exchange; admitted Richmond hosp. 10/12/62 - furloughed 20 days 10/22/62; d. Richmond hosp. of typhoid fever 10/28/62 - death claim filed by widow Sarah Ann Maitland - owed $181.26; b. 1829; brother of Hartwell Maitland; m. 1851 Brunswick - 4 children; wife applied for pension 4/22/1889 - $20 approved.

MAITLAND, JAMES M.: enl. 7/10/61 Co. E in Brunswick; present 7/10/61-8/31/61; POW Ft. Donelson - sick; sent from Camp Morton to Vicksburg for exchange; sick furlough 30 days 10/22/62; present 9/63-12/63, 4/1/64, and 5/64-8/64; received clothes 9/27/64, 10/13/64, 12/3/64, and 12/28/64; b. about 1836 to Michael and Roda Lewis Maitland; m. Anne E. Maitland, sister of Hartwell Maitland and James Coleman Maitland - 3 children.

MAITLAND, RURAL (RUEL) ("SONK"): enl. 7/10/61 Co. E in Brunswick: present 7/10/61-8/31/61: discharged 9/8/62, age 40 because served one year and over 35; admitted Richmond hosp. 10/16/62 -

returned to duty 10/23/62; farmer, probably James M. Maitland's brother; dark complexion and hair, grey eyes, 5'6"; bonded to marry Martha Lewis 9/3/1849 - 4 children.
MAITLAND, WILLIAM HENRY: enl. 7/10/61 Co. E in Brunswick.; present 7/10/61-8/31/61; POW Ft. Donelson - sent from Camp Morton to Vicksburg for exchange; admitted Richmond hosp. 12/9/62 - deserted hosp. 12/28/62; admitted Chimborazo 6/27/64 with chronic diarrhea - transferred Lynchburg hosp. 7/8/64; b. about 1839 - brother of James C. and Hartwell Maitland; laborer; m. Rebecca M. Williams 1/1/1868 in Brunswick - had at least 1 daughter.
MAITON, (MAYTON) WILLIAM ROBERT: enl. 2/9/63 Co. E in Brunswick; WIA Gettysburg - admitted Richmond hosp. 7/15/63; in hosp. 9/63-12/63 wded.; 4/1/64 AWOL; WIA Cold Harbor - admitted Richmond hosp. 6/9/64 with gunshot wd. of left arm - returned to duty 11/6/64; took amnesty oath 5/29/65 at Headquarters Provost Marshal, Defenses South of the Potomac; resident of Alexandria; fair complexion, light brown hair, brown eyes, 6'; b. about 1834 to David and Elizabeth Grant Mayton; m. Mary Catherine Manly 12/22/1852 – 8 children; moved from Brunswick to Nottoway Co.; applied for pension 1888 age 60 living near Blackstone; d. 2/6/1903 Nottoway - bur. Lakeview Cem.; widow applied for pension 4/1903 - she listed him as Co. G, 3rd Va.. Inf.
MAJOR(S.) (MAYO) HENRY: Co. G, Col's. servant - Negro slave; d. Camp Morton Prison Hosp. 3/24/62 - bur. Green Lawn Cem.
MAJOR (S.), WILLIAM E.: enl. 7/12/61 Co. G in Charlotte, Cpl.; present 7/26/61-10/31/61; d. 4/11/62 of typhoid fever Chattanooga, TN.
MALLORY, JOHN W.: enl. 7/26/61 Co. F in Louisa; present 7/27/61 - 8/31/61; discharged 10/22/61 age 37 - Daniel W. Snyder substitute; b. Hanover; light complexion, dark hair, blue eyes, 5'9".
MALONE, ROBERT: enl. 7/1/61 Co. B in Mecklenburg; discharged because unfit for duty 9/21/61 age 36; b. Brunswick; farmer; dark complexion, dark grayish hair, hazel eyes, 5'7".
MANTLO, CORNELIUS M.: enl. 8/6/61 Co. K in Mechanicsville - never mustered in.
MANTLO, JOHN E: enl. 8/6/61 Co. K in Mechanicsville - discharged 8/19/61 - substitute Joseph E. Anderson.
MARCEY, J. S.: Co. B; POW at Fair Ground Post Hosp. Petersburg 4/3/65 - transferred Gen. Hosp. 4/22/65.
MARQUISS, (MARCUS) ALBERT: enr. as conscript 1/11/64 in Madison Co. - assigned Co. K 1/15/64: admitted Chimborazo 6/13/64 with typhoid fever, b. 10/7/1830 in Madison Co.; admitted Lee Camp Soldiers' Home 11/17/1909 age 79 due to old age - sent to Eastern State Hosp. for the insane 3/26/1910 - d. 1/21/1912 - bur. Cedar Grove Cem. Williamsburg.
MARSH, JOHN CABEL: enl. 3/6/63 Co. H in Petersburg, Pvt./Cpl.;

present 7/63-12/63; admitted Chimborazo with gunshot wd. of hand 6/4/64 - deserted hosp. 6/23/64; received clothes 10/19/64, 11/3/64, 11/14/64; b. Greene Co.; farmer and miller; applied for pension 8/4/1903 age 72 living Proffits, Albemarle Co. - partial disability due to chronic bronchitis, diseased lungs, and hernia; said enlisted 1862 and served 3 years - $15 approved; d. 7/13/1911 Albemarle from old age and fall; widow Louisa M. Marsh applied for pension 5/24/1913 - m. 1860 Standardsville, Greene Co.

MARSH, WILLIAM FRANKLIN: enl. 5/3/62 Co. H in Richmond; WIA Frazier's Farm; POW and WIA, Gettysburg - admitted West's Buildings Hosp. with gunshot wd. of thigh; on roll of paroled and exchanged prisoners at Camp Lee 8/31/63; present 5/64-8/64; received clothes 9/27/64 and 12/30/64; applied for pension 4/16/1900, age 60 living Albemarle - $15 approved; made statement 5/24/1909, age 60 - property $20; d. 5/18/1912 of old age Albemarle - bur. there; widow Mary C. Marsh applied for pension 8/27/1924 - m. 9/10/1882 Albemarle - $80 approved.

MARSHALL, BENJAMIN F.: enl. 8/6/61 Co. K in Mechanicsville, Pvt./Cpl.; present 8/6/61-10/31/61; POW Ft. Donelson - sent from Camp Morton to Vicksburg for exchange; furloughed 10/24/62-11/24/62; present 7/63-12/63; made Cpl. 10/1/63; present 4/1/64 and 5/64-8/64; paroled Ashland 5/1/65; farmer, resident of Henrico.

MARSHALL, BENJAMIN W.: pwl; Co, I; applied for pension 5/11/1900 age 80 living Madisonville, Charlotte Co. – disabled due to paralysis of both legs - $30 approved - "DEAD" written across application.

MARSHALL, C. H.: enl. 5/6/62 Co. K in Richmond; admitted Charlottesville hosp. with chronic diarrhea 8/26/62 - returned to duty 9/4/62; AWOL 7/63-8/63; dropped from roll by Gen. Garnett's order.

MARSHALL, R. V.: Co. I; detailed for extra duty at Richmond as agent 2/20/65 – reported to Capt. Richard Gaines, Inspector Field Transportation.

MARTIN, ALEXANDER M.: enl. 8/6/61 Co. K in Mechanicsville, Pvt./Sgt.; KIA Gaines's Mill; death claim filed by father Allen M. Martin - owed $103.30.

MARTIN, JOHN D.: enl. 8/6/61 Co. K in Mechanicsville; sick furlough 8/6/61-8/31/61; present 9/61-10/61 - lost 12 days pay because AWOL; admitted Chimborazo 8/22/62 with diarrhea - returned to duty 7/6/62; d. 8/5/62 in Hanover of disease - death claim filed 12/5/62 - owed $80.83

MARTIN, RICHARD A.: enl. 7/10/61 Co. E in Brunswick; absent sick with measles 7/10/61-8/31/61; POW Ft. Donelson - sent from Camp Morton to Vicksburg for exchange; POW Gettysburg - confined Ft. Delaware; d. 10/12/63 - bur. Finn's Pt., N.J.; b. about 1840 to Henry and Ann Elizabeth Medlin Martin in Brunswick; laborer; m. Mary Jane Newton 3/10/1859;

widow applied for pension 4/2/1888 - $30 approved.

MARTIN, WILLIAM T.: enl. 8/6/61 Co. K in Mechanicsville; furloughed 8/6/61-8/31/61 - lost 10 day's pay because AWOL; discharged 8/24/63 age 46 because over 45; reenlisted 10/22/63; present 9/63-12/63 and 4/1/64; admitted Chimborazo with gunshot wd. of left hand 6/8/64 - deserted from hosp. 6/18/64; absent sick 5/64-8/64; b. Hanover; farmer; dark complexion, hazel eyes, 5'10".

MASON, ALPHEUS L: enl. 7/18/61 Co. I in Charlotte; present 7/18/61-10/31/61; d. 3/15/62 age 22 - death claim filed by father Pascal B. Mason - owed $67; b. Campbell Co.; farmer; dark complexion, black hair and eyes, 5'7".

MASON, ANDREW M. (W.): enl. 7/18/61 Co, I in Charlotte, Pvt./Sgt.; present 7/18/61-10/31/61; had measles 8/61; MWIA Gaines's Mill – d. 7/16/62, age 22 in Charlotte; 1st man in Co. I killed; death claim filed by father Oliver S. Mason; b. Campbell Co.; farmer; fair complexion, dark hair, black eyes, 5'10"; John L Holt's cousin.

MASON, BENJAMIN D. ("Big" Daniel): enl. 8/22/61 Co. I in Charlotte; present 7/18/61-10/31/61; detailed as nurse 2/62 in Bowling Green, Ky.; discharged 4/4/62. may have d. during war; John L Holt's cousin.

MASON, CLINTON (CLAIBORNE) W.: pwl; Co. I; applied for pension 5/5/1900. age 54 living Terryville, Charlotte Co. - lost use of left arm and eyesight as result of fever during war - partial disability - $15 approved; bur. Mt. Carmel United Methodist Church, Charlotte.

MASON, HILLARY M.: enr. as conscript 2/20/64 - assigned to Co. I 2/23/64; admitted Chimborazo 6/24/64 with heart palpitations - furloughed 30 days 7/12/64; readmitted 8/17/64 with fever - returned to duty 8/18/64; on roll as guard at Chimborazo 7/64-10/12/64, 2/65, and 4/65; furloughed 14 days 12/14/64; resident of Campbell Co; farmer; applied for pension 5/5/1900, age 62 living Charlotte – disability from over exertion during war, 2 hernias, and heart disease - $15 approved; rerated 4/27/1906 -.$30 approved; d. 10/23/1907 of heart disease Staunton Hill, Charlotte Co.; widow Annie E. Mason applied for pension 4/24/1908 - m. 8/15/1862 Campbell Co. - $25 approved; brother of Alpheus, Benjamin, and Samuel Mason.

MASON, JAMES H.: enl. 8/16/61 Co. K in Richmond, Sgt./Capt.; present 8/6/61-10/31/61; elected & commissioned 2nd Lt. 9/13/61; elected Capt. 5/3/62; admitted officers quarters hosp. 3/3/63; dropped or resigned 3/20/63.

MASON, JOHN R. (probably nicknamed "Tobe"): enl 7/18/61 Co. I in Charlotte; Pvt./Sgt.; present 7/18/61-10/31/61; WIA Gainse's Mill; absent 7/63-12/63 - supposed to be prisoner; believed KIA Gettysburg, but no Federal records concerning him.

MASON, SAMUEL L.: enl. 7/18/61 Co. I in Charlotte; present 7/18/61-

10/31/61; discharged 1/4/62 - had bad leg when entered - wanted to stay in army, but friends encouraged to get discharge because thought might lose leg; John Holt's cousin.

MATHEWS, JOHN H.: enl. 7/20/61 Co. C in Louisa; discharged 8/15/61 on muster roll; admitted Richmond hosp. 12/24/62 with typhoid pneumonia - furloughed 30 days 2/10/63; absent on roll 9/63-10/63 - supposed to be POW Gettysburg; believed KIA Gettysburg, but no Federal records concerning him.

MATHEWS, OHN J.: enl. 7/26/61 Co. F in Louisa; in Richmond hosp. with measles 7/27/61-8/31/61; sick furlough 9/61-10/61; discharged 6/5/62 - no reason given.

MATHEWS, NATHANIEL G.: enl. 7/10/61 Co. E in Brunswick; absent sick in city 7/10/61-8/31/61; discharged 9/27/61, age 22 due to T. B.; b. Brunswick; farmer, light complexion and hair, grey eyes, 5'6".

MATHEWS, WILLIAM: enl. 7/9/61 Co. C in Louisa; present 7/9/61-10/31/61, Pvt./Sgt.; WIA Galnes's Mill; on Invalid Corp's register - retired 4/4/63; discharged 2/15/64, age 28 - unfit for duty due to gunshot wd. of left forearm; b. Louisa; carpenter; fair complexion, dark hair, hazel eyes, 5'6".

MAUPIN, C. B. (probably CARSON BARNETT): enl. 5/3/62 Co. H in Richmond; absent prisoner 7/63-12/63 - believed KIA Gettysburg, but no Federal records concerning him.

MAUPIN, C. PRICE (probably CLIFTON PRICE): enl. 7/22/64 at Howlett's House; present 7/64-8/64; received clothes 9/27/64, 10/31/64, 11/3/64, and 12/30/64; b. 1/8/1845 son of Clifton Maupin; applied for pension 5/2/1911, living Moorman's River, Albemarle Co. - no use of 1 arm and hand – totally blind in 1 eye and almost in other -7 in family and poor - $15 approved.

MAUPIN, DAVID G.: enl. 7/15/61 Co. H in Albemarle, Pvt./Cpl.; present 7/29/61-10/31/61; WIA Gaines's Mill; supposed to be POW Gettysburg 7/63-12/63 - believed KIA Gettysburg, but no Federal records concerning him; son of Pleasant and Lucinda Wood Maupin; m. Lucy Mills.

MAUPIN, GABRIEL NICHOLAS: enl. 7/22/61 Co. H, 57th Va. Inf. in Charlottesville; WIA Gettysburg - admitted Charlottesville hosp. 7/28/63 with gunshot wd. - returned to duty 10/19/63; enrolled as conscript 2/13/64 - assigned Co. H, 56th Va. Inf. 2/23/64; admitted Charlottesville hosp. 5/6/64 with debility - returned to duty 5/14/64; admitted Chimborazo 10/1/64 with heart disease - furloughed 30 days 10/19/64; detailed as nurse in Charlottesville hosp.; POW Harper's Farm 4/6/65; took oath and released from Pt. Lookout 6/29/65; resident of Albemarle; fair complexion, brown hair, hazel eyes, 5'7"; son of Thomas and Susan Gibson Maupin; John D Maupin's brother. d. 1912 of stroke and gastritis near Free Union, Lunenburg Co.; widow Bettie F. Maupin applied for

pension 4/22/1916 living Albemarle; m. 2/14/1867 Nortonsville.
MAUPIN, J. R.: pwl; Co. A; attended Newport News reunion 11/1911. (probably James Ross Maupin).
MAUPIN, JAMES ROSS: enl. 5/3/62 Co. H in Richmond, Pvt./Sgt.; POW and WIA Gettysburg - admitted DeCarnp General Hosp. 7/17/63-7/24/63; paroled 8/24/63 - received at City Point 8/28/63; present 4/1/64 and 5/64-6/64; absent sick 7/64-8/64; tanner: applied for pension 4/26/1901 age 56 living Glendown, Albemarle Co. - disability due to war wd, and rheumatism - $15 approved - rerated 4/17/1909 age 66 - $36 approved; d. 8/8/1927 Albemarle of heart trouble and old age; widow Emma Pocahontas Maupin applied for pension 8/20/1927 - m. 12/18/1881 Albemarle - real estate 54 acres worth $430 - $100 personal property - $90 approved.
MAUPIN, JOHN D.: enl. 5/3/62 Co. H in Richmond; WIA Gaines's Mill; admitted Farmville hosp. 4/27/63 with fistula In ano – transf. Charlottesville 5/17/63 - returned to duty 7/16/63; admitted Chimborazo with debility 8/20/64 - furloughed 30 days 9/1/64; admitted Richmond hosp. 10/1/64 with dropsy - returned to duty 12/18/64; on Appomattox surrender list; m. Susan Ogg; Gabriel Maupin's brother; d. 9/14/1898 age 68 near Free Union.
MAUPIN, JOHN R. (W.): enl. 7/15/61 Co. H in Albemarle; Sgt./2nd Lt.; present 7/29/61-10/31/61; elected 2nd Lt. 1/1/64; admitted Episcopal Church Hosp. Williamsburg 4/26/63 with diarrhea; admitted Farmville hosp. 5/8/63 with chronic diarrhea - transferred to Charlottesville hosp. 5/16/63 - returned to duty 8/27/63; admitted Farmville hosp. 8/30/63 with gunshot wd. of right thigh - transferred to Charlottesville 9/4/63 - returned to duty 9/19/63; asked furlough of indulgence 2/21/64 to go home to Albemarle to find those in his Co. who are AWOL and tend to personal business; admitted Richmond hosp. 6/20/64 with rheumatism - furloughed 40 days 9/24/64; admitted to Charlottesville hosp. 11/7/64 with chronic rheumatism – ret. to duty 2/1/65.
MAUPIN, JOHN (JOSEPH) S.: pwl; Co. H.
MAXEY, CHARLES R. (H.): enl. 7/23/61 Co. D in Bucldngham; present 7/8/61-10/31/61; WIA Frazier's Farm; reenlisted 8/11/62 at Fulton Hill - paid $50 bounty; POW Gettysburg; in Ft. Delaware 7/12/63, Pt. Lookout Smallpox Hosp. 10/26/63, Pt. Lookout 11/23/63 - paroled 2/18/65; took oath Farmville 4/25/65.
MAXEY, CLAIBORNE H.: enl. 7/8/61 Co. A in Mecklenburg, Cpl.; AWL 8/26/61-9/21/61; present 9/61-10/61; furloughed 3/1/63 - 3/20/63; present 9/63-12/63; absent sick 5/64-8/64 - admitted Chimborazo 6/27/64 with chronic hepatitis; furloughed due to diseased lung 12/6/65.
MAXEY, EDWARD: enl. 7/8/61 Co. D in Buckingham; present 7/8/61-10/31/61.
MAXEY, EDWARD G.: (may be Edward L Maxey). enl. 5/3/62 Co. D.

MAXEY, EDWARD L.: enl. 7/23/61 Co. D in Buckingham; present 7/8/61-10/31/61; admitted Chimborazo 5/26/62 with diarrhea - transferred to Lynchburg hosp; detailed as teamster for much of 1862, 1863, and 1864; furloughed 6/18/62-7/3/62 and 2/1/64-2/29/64; present 9/63-12/63 and 5/64-8/64; POW Hatcher's Run 3/31/65 - took oath and released from Pt. Lookout 6/29/65; resident of Buckingham; fair complexion, dark brown hair, hazel eyes; 5'7".

MAXEY, GEORGE D.: enr. as conscript 3/8/64 - assigned to Co. I 3/9/64; furloughed 5/1/64-8/31/64; admitted Chimborazo 6/28/64 with debilitas - returned to duly 7/19/64; readmitted 9/19/64 with chronic diarrhea - furloughed to Buckingham 9/27/64 for 60 days; admitted Chimborazo 3/6/65 with chronic rheumatism.

MAXEY, HARMON C.: enl. 7/8/61 Co. D in Buckingham; present 7/8/61-10/31/61; reenlisted 2/11/62; admitted Richmond hosp. 7/24/62 - transferred to Scottsville hosp. 8/22/62; admitted Richmond hosp. 4/18/63 with dyspepsia - transferred Scottsville and Huguenot Springs; admitted Richmond hosp. 9/23/63; returned to duty 2/22/64; POW Amelia Court House 4/4/65 - took oath and released from Pt.. Lookout 6/15/65; resident of Buckingham; fair complexion, brown hair, blue eyes, 5'6 1/2"; admitted Lee Camp Soldiers' Home 10/15/1925 age 92 due to old age; d. 10/15/1926 - bur. Hollywood Cem.

MAXEY, JOHN A.: enl. 7/8/61 Co. D in Buckingham; discharged by commissioned officers in Yancey Guards because the conditions under which he joined rendered it with the officers a point of honor - signed a pension application of John C. Garrett's widow *4/29/1911;* d. 8/10/1918 - $25 paid for funeral expenses under 1902 pension act.

MAXEY, (MASSEY) PEYTON B.: enl. 9/1/63 Co. A in Mecklenburg: present 9/63-12/63; admitted Richmond hosp. 6/2/64 with gunshot wd. of hand - furloughed 6/6/64; POW near Howlett's House 8/25/64 - sent Bermuda Hundred, Ft, Monroe and Pt. Lookout - exchanged 11/1/64; on roll of hosp. in Macon, Georgia 11/15/64 with influenza - transferred to Mecklenburg 11/18/64; POW and paroled at Headquarters 6th Army Corps 5/14/65.

MAXEY, WILLIAM H.: enl. 8/64 Co. D in Buckingham; present 7/64-8/64; paroled Farmville 4/25/65; applied for pension 5/14/1900 living Well Water, Buckingham Co. - approved.

MAY, GEORGE W.: enl. 7/9/61 Co. C in Louisa, 1st Lt./Ord. Sgt.; present 7/9/61-10/31/61; dropped as 1st Lt. 5/2/62; appointed Field and Staff 3/3/63; present 11/63-12/63 and 5/64-8/64; received clothes 10/19/64, 12/3/64, & 12/30/64; brother of Isaac Newton May; 1850 census - age 8.

MAY, ISAAC NEWTON: enl. 7/9/61 Co. C in Louisa;. Sgt.; present 7/9/61-10/31/61; son of John Spearman May; 23 in 1850; graduate of UVA; taught math Baylor University, principal of Bryan Female College. Baptist minister; father left him estate "Oakland" in Louisa Co. in 1880; opened Oakland Male Academy at his home 9/1880 to prepare students for UVA or other colleges or business - food prepared by former slave Aunt Bet Payne - wife helped him with students - no liquor sold within 3 miles of school - "the moral tone of the neighborhood is such as to exert a wholesome influence on the students" - 1890 became co-educational; 2/1900 house burned to ground - students helped rebuild; d. 2/17/1913 of acute indigestion; bur. family cem. at "Oakland"; academy closed 9/1913 - burned completely 4/19/1915.

MAY, JOHN S.: enl. 7/9/61 Co. C in Louisa, 1st Sgt./Pvt.; sick furlough 7/9/61-8/31/61; present 9/61-10/61; Court Martial 2/23/63 for AWOL - found guilty of charge and specification - forfeited 2 months pay and had to cut wood and bring water for Co. and Regt. until 4/1/63; POW and WIA Gettysburg - admitted West's Buildings Hosp. 7/31/63 with gunshot wd. causing fracture of middle third right leg - transferred Gen. Hosp. 1/10/64 and then Pt. Lookout - paroled from Pt. Lookout 3/16/64; admitted Richmond hosp. 3/25/64 - furloughed 60 days - readmitted 7/12/64 - furloughed 60 days 7/30/64; retired from service and put In Invalid Corps 1/23/65 - assigned Louisa as agriculturist 3/6/65.

MAYNARD, JOHN C.: pwl; Field and Staff; Assistant Quarter-master, Captain.

MEADE, ROBERT E.: enl. 7/10/61 Co. E in Brunswick; present 7/10/61-8/31/61; POW Ft. Donelson - sent from Camp Morton to Vicksburg for exchange; discharged 10/12/62 age 45 because served one year & over 35; dark complexion, hair, & eyes, 6'1"; b. 12/11/1816 to David M. and Nancy Stith Meade in Brunswick; farmer and attorney; attended UVA 1833-35 and William and Mary Law School 1836; m. a Miss Booth; after her death m. Martha Ashby 1842; after her death m. Elizabeth S. Taylor 2/2/1852; elected to state legislature from Brunswick 1862; d. 1/21/1888 Brunswick - bur. at his home "Sandy Hook."

MEEKS, (WEEKS) WILLIAM: enl 7/9/61 Co. C in Louisa; AWOL 9/61-10/61; POW Ft. Donelson - admitted City Gen, Hosp. St. Louis. Missouri 2/27/62 with gunshot wd.; d. 3/12/62 of gunshot wd. or typhoid pneumonia; bur. St. Louis.

MELTON, CHARLES, T.: enl. 7/15/61 Co. H in Albemarle – absent when mustered in and still absent 7/29/61-8/31/61 - entry cancelled.

MELTON, JOHN H.: enl. 7/15/61 Co. H in Albemarle; absent when mustered in - entry cancelled.

MERIDITH, JAMES THOMAS (C.): enl. 7/26/61 Co. F in Louisa; present 7/26/61-10/31/61 - nurse at Medical College Hosp., Atlanta, Ga. 2/22/62-4/7/62 - removed by Gen. Floyd; admitted Chimborazo 6/24/62 with diarrhea; paroled at camp near Keedysville, Md. 9/20/62; took oath and paroled at Winchester 10/4/62; on duty Petersburg hosp. 5/22/63;

present 9/63-12/63; special orders 11/17/63 - extended 1/14/64-3/17/64; on detached service on Va. C. R. Road 4/64-6/64; present 7/64-8/64; admitted Chimborazo 3/8/65 with chronic diarrhea - deserted hosp, 3/26/65; POW Burkeville 4/6/65 - took oath and released from Pt. Lookout 6/15/65; fair complexion, light brown hair, blue eyes, 5'8 1/2"; b. Bloomingdale, Louisa Co. 3/14/1841; d, 6/8/1908 of Bright's Disease; widow Willie B. Meredith applied for pension 6/8/1916 - m. 1867 Louisa - $33 approved.

MERIDITH, JOHN W.: enl. 7/26/61 Co. F in Louisa, Sgt.; sick furlough 7/27/61-8/31/61; present 9/61-10/61; discharged 11/11/61 age 25 due to spinal disease; b. Louisa; farmer, light complexion and hair, blue eyes, 5'6".

MERIDITH, JOSEPH (JOHN) S., M. D.: enl. 7/26/61 Co. F in Louisa, Sgt./2nd Lt.; present 7/26/61-10/31/61; appointed 2nd Lt. 11/31/61 - resigned 4/12/62 due to poor health and appointed physician in 7th district.

MERRYMAN, WADKINS L.: enl. 9/1/63 Co. B in Richmond; present 9/63-10/63; detailed as shoemaker in Richmond 11/63-12/63 and most of 1864; WIA Hatcher's Run 3/31/65; applied for pension 6/11/1895 age 71 living South Hill, Mecklenburg Co, - rifle ball lodged In neck during war and could not be removed because too near brain - disability due to paralysis on left side - $30 approved; d. 6/15/1896 Mecklenburg from paralysis; widow Lucy W. Merryman applied for pension 4/26/1900 - m. 12/17/1850 - $25 approved.

MICHIE, EUGENE O.: enl. 7/15/61 Co. H in Albemarle, 2nd Lt; present 7/29/61-10/31/61; appointed 2nd Lt. 7/29/61; in camp near Murfreesboro, TN 2/25/62; dropped as 2nd Lt. 5/5/62; enl. 2nd Va. Cav., Co. K; severely WIA 1864; b. 1841; member J. B. Strange Camp UCV; d. 1895.

MICHIE, HENRY CLAY: enl. 4/17/61 in Southern Guard, Albemarle Rifles (Co. B, 19th Va. Inf.) - company of UVA students - after two weeks company was ordered back to UVA and disbanded; transferred to Co. H, 56th Va. 9/21/61, Sgt./Capt; elected 1st Lt. 5/3/62; WIA Gaines's Mill; WIA 2nd Manassas; made Capt 1863; POW and WIA Gettysburg at stone wall – confined Ft. McHenry, Ft Delaware, Johnson's Island - sent to Pt. Lookout 3/14/65 for exchange; b. Bel Air, Albemarle Co. 1/9/1842 son of James and Frances D. Michie; entered UVA 10/1860; farmer in Albemarle - estate called "The Meadows"; brother of Thomas Garth and John Augustus Michie; m. Eunice Dandridge Sykes 12/10/1867 at Lawrence, Alabama; chairman pension board Albemarle Co.; Commander of John Bowie Strange Camp, UCV, Charlottesville -1919; d. 1/29/1925 age 83 Staunton from the effects of severe fall while visiting his daughter Mrs. J. B. Catlett; survived by 3 daughters and 2 sons including Major H. C. Michie, U.S.A.; bur. Riverview Cem., Charlottesville

MICHIE, JOHN AUGUSTUS: enl. 7/15/61 Co. H in Albemarle, Capt:; received military training VMI for 4 *weeks,* spring 1861 – 35 at matriculation; appointed Capt 7/29/61; present 9/61-10/61; dropped as Capt. 5/5/62 b. Albemarle 1827; received medical degrees from UVA in 1846 and Jefferson College, PA; doctor and planter with large estate in Earlyville, Albemarle Co.; "unique character" and "hottest Republican in Albemarle"; 4 daughters and 3 sons; brother of Henry Clay and Thomas Garth Michie; d. 6/3/1902 age 75.

MICHIE, O. G.: enl. 7/15/61 Co. H in Albemarle - absent when Co. mustered; 9/61-10/61 refused to report - entry cancelled; 12/26/61 signed note asking for 1 cord of wood for Headquarters Adjt. Gen. Office, Winchester.

MICHIE, ORIN G. (may be O. G. Michie): enl. 7/15/61 Co. H in Albemarle; present 9/61-10/61; POW Boonsboro - in Camden Street Hosp., Baltimore, Md.; paroled at DeCamp Hosp. – n. d.; admitted Charlottesville hosp, 12/27/62 with gunshot wd..- returned to duty 4/4/63; POW Gettysburg and MWIA while serving as Color Bearer - exchanged from DeCarnp Hosp. 9/16/63 - d. of wds. sometime thereafter in unknown hosp. - age 24; b. 1839.

MICHIE, THOMAS GARTH: enl. 7/15/61 Co. H in Albemarle; 1st Lt.; attended VMI 4 weeks for military training, spring 1861 age 29; appointed 1st Lt. *7/29/61;* present 9/61-10/61; admitted Charlottesville hosp. 11/11/61. furloughed 10 days 11/11/61; resigned 4/19/62 due to chronic diarrhea; b. 10/20/1831 in Albemarle; attended Episcopal High School; m. Mary P. Budd 3/24/1857 - she d. 9/8/1858 leaving one child born 2/8/58; m. Sallie Jackson 10/7/1862 – 4 sons and 4 daughters; received MS 1864 from UVA; owned 652 acre farm; school trustee; son Henry Clay Michie, II killed age 32 when fell through trap door in ice house on fathers estate; applied for pension 7/21/1914 age 82 and 9 months living Ivy Depot, Albemarle Co. - totally disabled due to atrophy of spinal cord and old age; real estate previously deeded to son; $43.20 approved; d. 10/17/1916 of pneumonia at home "Oak Mills" in Batesville, Albemarle Co. - bur. Emanuel Episcopal Church, Route 250, Albemarle; widow applied for pension 7/20/1926 - $1700 in real state - $90 approved.

MILES, ROBERT: enl. 7/23/61 Co. D in Buckingham; present 7/23/61-10/31/61; POW Ft. Donelson; sent from Camp Morton to Vicksburg for exchange 8/24/621; furloughed 1/1/64-2/29/64: retired 4/30/64 to Invalid Corps; m. 8/6/1881 in Glenmore; applied for pension in Buckingham 5/14/1900 age 62 living Glenmore, Buckingham, Co. - dislocated arm and general poor health; $15 approved - statement made 8/11/1902 age 68 - cited general decline of old age and deafness brought on by exposure and hardship in service - owned no property; d. 12/1903 of heart trouble - bur. Miles Family Cem. across from Emmanuel Episcopal Church,

Buckingham; widow Lucy J. Miles filed pension application 1/31/1928 - $100 approved.

MILL, J. L.: Pvt. in Co. C; paroled Columbia 5/65.

MILLER, IRA ALLEN: enl 7/15/61 Co. H in Albemarle, Cpl./Lt.; present 7/20/61-10/31/61; elected 2nd Lt. 5/3/62; resident of Waynesboro 1862; admitted Charlottesville hosp. 11/26/62 with debility - returned to duty 12/26/62; WIA and POW Gettysburg - admitted DeCamp Gen. Hosp. with leg wd.; promoted 1st Lt 8/12/63; sent to Johnson's Island 9/18/63; paroled and sent to Pt. Lookout for exchange 3/14/65; m. 10/30/1855 Waynesboro; d. 6/25/1883 Luray of dropsy; widow Susan E. Miller applied for pension 4/8/1914 Albemarle - $25 approved.

MILLER, JAMES WEISILER: pwl; enl. 4/62 Co. D in Richmond; in service 6 months - became sick, sent home and on home duty until end of war; b. 3/31/1820 Nelson; farmer and teacher, applied for pension 2/26/1910 age 90 living Massie's Mill, Nelson Co. - disabled due to infirmities of age and blindness - $36 approved.

MILLS, JAMES T.: enl. 3/1/64 Co. B in Richmond; present 5/64/8/64; received clothes 10/13/64, 12/3/64 and 12/30/64; surrendered by Lee at Appomattox; b. Mecklenburg; wheelwright; applied for pension 2/24/1919 age 75 living Jeffress, Mecklenburg Co.; real estate $1275; personal property $500 - $160 Income annually - disability due to varicose veins and cramps with infirmities of age - $75 approved; member L. A. Armistead Camp, UCV - present 9/4/1930 at 37th reunion.

MILLS, JOHN J.: enl. 7/26/61 Co. F in Louisa, Cpl.; present 7/29/61-10//31/61, 9/63-12/63, and 4/1/64; absent sick 5/64-8/64; admitted Richmond hosp.1/16/65 with chronic ulcer, deserted 3/65.

MILLS, MARCELLIN J.: enl. 7/9/64 Co. C in Louisa; present 7/64-8/64; received clothes 10/19/64 and 12/2/64; POW and paroled at Richmond 4/26/65.

MILLS, NATHANIEL H.: enl. 7/9/61 Co. C in Louisa; present 7/9/61-10/31/61, 9/63-12/63, and 5/64-8/64; furloughed from Chimborazo 10/7/64 to Goochland; received clothes 12/28/64; b 1839; admitted Lee Camp Soldiers' Home 11/6/1917 age 78 due to old age; d. 10/15/1930 - remains taken by relatives - bur. Griffin Mills Cem., Rt. 603, Goochland.

MILLS, THOMAS M.: enl. 7/9/61 Co. C in Louisa; AWOL 9/61-10/61; received clothes 10/19/64 and 12/28/64, admitted Richmond hosp. 2/15/65 - furloughed 5 days 2/16/65; paroled Louisa 5/22/65.

MILLS, WILLIAM H.: enl. 7/9/61 Co. C in Louisa; present 7/9/61-10/31/61, 9/63-12/63, 5/64-8/64, admitted Richmond hosp. 3/11/65 - returned to duty 3/26/65; POW and paroled Richmond 4/26/65; applied for pension 2/171890 age 49 living Fife's, Goochland Co. - unfit for any business - WIA Gettysburg - shot in neck - affected eyes and partially deaf - $15 approved; bur. pvt. cem. between Rte. 608 and 673, Goochland.

MILLS, R. E. F.: Co. I; conscript; admitted Richmond hosp. 2/27/64 with variola - returned to duly 4/7/64; received clothes 4/7/64 and 12/30/64; paroled Burkeville 4/27/65.

MITCHELL, JAMES B.: enl. 10/22/63 Co. K in Henry Co.; present 9/63-10/63; AWOL 11/63-12/63; sick furlough 4/1/64; present 5/64-8/64; admitted Chimborazo 8/14/64 with scrofula - returned to light duty 9/29/64 - furloughed 9/29/64 and 10/31/64 - readmitted hosp. 12/19/64 - furloughed 1/6/65; WIA Hatcher's Run,

MITCHELL, WILLIAM H.: enl. 2/17/63 Co. B. in Richmond; present 9/63-12/63, 4/1/64. and 5/648/64; received clothes 9/28/64, 10/13/64, *10/19/64,* 12/3/64, and 12/30/64; surrendered by Lee at Appomattox; believed to be son of Bannister and Temperance Mitchell of Brunswick; m. India A. Watkins 5/7/18*73,* Greensville Co.

MODENA, BENJAMIN J.: enl. 7/9/61 Co. C in Louisa; present 7/9/61-10/31/61 and 9/63-12/63; admitted Richmond hosp. 5/6/64 - returned to duty 5/7/64; present 5/64-8/64; admitted Chimborazo 9/30/64 with concussion - returned to duty 10/17/164; paroled Gordonsville 5/23/65; living Orange 1922.

MODENA, GEORGE H.: pwl; Co. C.

MOODY, WILLIAM M.: enl. 7/8/61 Co. A in Mecklenburg, Sgt; present 7/8/61-10/31/61; paid for 10/*31/61-4/30/62,* discharged - n. d. or reason; farmer, dark complexion and hair, blue eyes; 5'6".

MOON, E. C. (C. C.): pwl; Co. G (may be E. C. Morse)

MOON, FLEMING B.: enl. 5/3/62 Co. B in Richmond; present 5/63-8/63; on Scottsville hosp. roll 4/24/63, 6/17/63, 9/18/63; admitted Chimborazo 9/22/63 with chronic diarrhea - furloughed 30 days 11/26/63 - readmitted 12/25/63 with chronic diarrhea - returned to duty 3/4/64; present 4/1/64 and 5/64-8/64; paroled Charlottesville 5/20/65.

MOON, JOHN S.: enl. 7/12/61 Co. G in Charlotte; present 7/26/61-10/31/61; Manuscript 1944 requested coffin 3/13/62 in Chattanooga; death claim filed by widow Nancy J. Moon 10/11/62.

MOON, JOHN S., JR.: pwl: Co. G - from Charlotte.

MOON, JOHN W.: enl. 7/12/61 Co. G in Charlotte; discharged 8/5/61 age 24 due to hernia resulting from blow to stomach in camp near Richmond; farmer, resident of Campbell Co.; light complexion, dark hair, grey eyes, 5'7"; applied for pension 9/4/1894 age 56 living Wylliesburg, Charlotte Co. - not able to do manual labor due to hernia - $15 approved.

MOON. PHILIP S.: pwl; Co. D; received pension Richmond; d. 1889; (probably Moore, P. S.)

MOON, T. B.: pwl: Co. B; Cumberland pension list.

MOON, WILLIAM S.: enl. 7/12/61 Co. G in Charlotte; present 7/26/61-10/31/61; discharged 5/8/62 age 44 due to debility from typhoid fever and spinal disease that left partially paralyzed; b. Charlotte; farmer: dark complexion, hair, and eyes, 5'10"; d. just before end of war in Charlotte of fever; widow Mariah A. Moon applied for pension 6/1/1891 - m. 1841 Charlotte.

MOONEY, DAVID G.: enl. 7/8/61 Co. D in Buckingham; present 7/8/61-10/31/61; POW Ft. Donelson and sick – sent from Camp Morton to Vicksburg for exchange; furloughed 30 days 11/11/62; present 9/63-12/63; absent sick 4/1/64 and 5/64-8/64.

MOONEY, JOSEPH M.: enl. 9/3/63 Co. K in Augusta; enrolled as conscript 1/9/64 - assigned Co. K 1/15/64; AWOL 4/1/64 and 5/64-8/64; received clothes at Castle Thunder 5/14/64; surrendered at Wheeling, W.Va. 12/7/64 age 30 - in Atheneum Prison in Wheeling - sent Camp Chase 12/30/64 - released on taking amnesty; resident of Augusta; dark complexion, hair and eyes, 5'8".

MOORE, (MOON, G. W.) GEORGE WASHINGTON: enr. as conscript 3/14/64 - assigned Co. B 3/21/64; present 4/1/64; admitted Chimborazo 5/14/64 with phitisis pulmonalis; absent sick in hosp. 5/64-8/64; b. about 1837 to John R. and Mary Edwards Moore in Brunswick; farmer; m. Elizabeth J. Whitley 5/9/1888; applied for pension 5/21/1900 age 67 living Brunswick - disability due to old age and general debility - $15 approved - made statement 8/20/1902 age 70 - consumption due to exposure during war, rerated 3/5/1917 age 85 - totally disabled due to rheumatism and old age - $50 approved.

MOORE, HARTWELL STEPHEN: enl. 7/23/61 Co. D in Buckingham; on MCV roll 8/16/61-8/22/61; admitted Richmond hosp. 8/9/63 with slight gunshot wd. of right arm - deserted hosp. 8/17/63 - admitted 8/23/63 with rheumatism - returned to duty 8/23/63; present 9/63-12/63 and 4/1/64; admitted Richmond hosp. 6/4/64 with gunshot wd. of middle finger right hand and dyspepsia - furloughed 30 days 6/5/64; absent wded. 5/64-8/64; received clothes 12/2/64 and 12/28/64; d. 6/22/1903 of heart trouble in Scottsville; widow Fannie A. Moore applied for pension 9/27/1927 in Albemarle - m. 11/25/1875.

MOORE, JAMES H.: enl. 729/61 Co. B in Mecklenburg, Pvt./1st Lt.; absent on furlough in Richmond 9/61-10/61; elected 2nd Lt. 5/3/62 - appointed 1st Lt 2/1/63; present 9/63-12/63; asked for 15 day furlough to see family in Mecklenburg 10/63 as only 23 in Company and 2 officers - stationed at Chaffin's Farm; admitted Chimborazo 6/27/64 with chronic diarrhea - furloughed 30 days 7/22/64; readmitted hosp. 7/15/64 with structured urethra - returned to duty 8/6/64; stationed Dutch Bend 10/19/64-12/30/64; POW Sayler's Creek 4/6/65 - confined Old Capitol Prison and Johnson's Island 4/17/65 - took oath and released 6/19/65.

MOORE, JAMES P.: enl. 6/1/61 Co. D in Buckingham; 9/63-12/63 under arrest; present 4/1/64; AWOL 5/64-8/64; b. Nelson; carpenter and wheelwright; applied for pension 3/9/1907 age 74 living Rose Mills, Nelson Co.-

said entered spring 1862 and left at Appomattox - served with Co. at first and then detailed government service - with Co. at close of war - $30 approved.

MOORE, JOSEPH E: enl. 2/17/63 Co. B in Richmond; received clothes in hosp. Blacks and Whites, Va. 7/29/83 - possibly WIA Gettysburg; present 9/63-12/63 and 4/1/64; sick in hosp. 5/64-6/64 - sick furlough 7/64-8/64..

MOORE, P.S. (PHILIP SHELTON or W. S.): enl. 6/1/61 Co. D in Buckingham - joined Co. 5/16/63; present 9/63-12/63; admitted Chimborazo 9/13/63 with hernia - returned to duty 10/26/63; employed as nurse at Chaffin's Farm Hosp. *12/28/63;* present 4/1/64 and 5/64-8/64; surrendered by Lee at Appomattox. (may be P. S. Moon)

MOORE, PLEASANT D.: enl. 8/6/61 Co. K in Mechanicsville. 2nd Lt.; resigned 8/10/61.

MOORE, ROBERT L.: enl. 7/23/61 Co D in Buckingham; present 7/8/61-10/31/61; admitted Scottsville hosp. 12/62 - may have been guard at hosp. in 1863; present 9/63-12/63: admitted Chirnborazo 6/4/64 with dyspepsia - furloughed 30 days 6/4/64 - returned to duty 8/28/64; received clothes 12/2/64; d. 1896 of dropsy; widow Mary F. Moore applied for pension 5/20/1908 living Albemarle - said married 2nd year of war - he was wded. and left service - approved.

MOORE, WILLIAM RILEY: enl. 2/9/63 Co. E at Brunswick admitted Williamsburg hosp. 4/26/63 - furloughed 5/20/63; present 9/63-12/63 and 4/1/64; detached service as ambulance driver at Chaffin's Farm 3/64-8/64; admitted Chimborazo 2/20/64 with rubeola; surrendered by Lee at Appomattox; b. about 1829 to Benjamin and Mary Finch Moore; m. Natina C. ? 1850's - 4 children.

MORGAN, WILLIAM: enl. 7/15/61 Co. H in Albemarle; absent when company mustered and still absent 7/29/61-8/31/61.

MORGAN, WILLIAM E.: enl. 7/12/61 Co. G in Charlotte; present 7/26/61-8/31/61; sick furlough 9/61-10/61; discharged 3/17/62 age 31 due to liver and heart disease; enrolled as conscript 3/1/64 - assigned Co. G 3/9/64; present 5/64-6/64; detached for light duty 8/20/64; b. Charlotte; farmer, light complexion, dark hair and eyes, 5'9".

MORRIS, DANIEL J.: enr. as conscript 3/1/64 Co. B in Richmond; present 4/1/64 and 5/64-8/64; admitted Chimborazo 8/3/64 with acute dysentery - furloughed 30 days to Mecklenburg 8/16/64; admitted Chimborazo 11/21/64 with plurisy - furloughed 30 days 1/27/65 - readmitted 3/14/65 with chronic diarrhea; surrendered by Lee at Appomattox.

MORRIS, ELIAS: enl. 7/29/61 Co. H in Albemarle - substitute for J. Morris; present 9/61-10/61; AWOL 7/63-8/63; deserter 9/63-12/63 roll.

MORRIS, JACKSON (H.): enl. 7/15/641 Co. H in Albemarle; present 7/29/61-8/31/61 - got substitute.

MORRIS, JAMES N. (M.): enl. 7/10/61 Co. B in Mecklenburg; discharged on 7/10/61 roll; enr. as conscript 3/2/64 - assigned to Co. B 3/10/64; furloughed 3/1/64-4/1/64; admitted Chimborazo 5/25/64 with phthisis pulmonalis – furloughed 60 days 5/30/64; present 7/64-8/64; admitted Chimborazo 9/24/64- furloughed 60 days 10/17/64; POW Jarrett's Station near Farmville 4/1/65 - admitted Petersburg hosp. 4/7/65 with wd. of head - transferred to Pt. of Rock's 4/22/65 - sent to Newport News where took oath and released 7/1/65 age 42; resident of Mecklenburg; farmer; dark complexion and hair, grey eyes, 6'1".

MORRIS, WILLIAM EDWARD, JR: enl. 7/10/61 Co E in Brunswick; present 7/10/61-8/31/61; WIA Frazier's Farm; present 11/63-12/63, 4/1/64, and 5/64-6/64; absent sick 7/64-8/64; received clothes 9/27/64 and 10/13/64; son of William Edward and Lucy A. Martin Morris; m. Martha Maitland 12/25/1862 - 8 children; m. Martha's sister Caroline J. 1/30/1878 - sisters of Hartwell Maitland and his brothers.

MORRIS, WILLIAM J.: enl. 7/26/61 Co. F in Louisa; present 7/27/61-10/31/61; deserted 2/14/63; 4/1/64 in arrest to be tried for desertion: prisoner in E. D. M. Prison - volunteered 8/3/64 in Winder Legion for defense of Richmond against Sheridan's Raid of 1864 - pardoned by Jefferson Davis; POW near Howlett's House 8/25/64; confined at Bermuda Hundred and Pt. Lookout - took oath and released 2/18/65; received clothes at Castle Thunder 5/14/65; pardoned Louisa 5/20/65.

MORRIS, ZACK T.: Co. A; resident of Charlotte; POW Farmville 4/6/65 - took oath and released from Pt. Lookout 6/29/65; light complexion, brown hair, grey eyes, 5'9"; applied for pension 5/5/1900 age 62 living Vincent Store, Charlotte Co. - totally disabled with rheumatism caused by exposure during war - $15 approved; made pension statement 5/12/1902 age 64; rerated 2/24/1904, $30 approved.

MORRISON, GEORGE FRANK (S.): enl. 2/15/64 Co. I at Chaffin's Bluff; 5/64-8/64 absent wded.; wded. 6/2/64 - furloughed 30 days 8/5/64 to Charlotte - gunshot wd. of posterior part of shoulder not healed so continually furloughed by Farmville hosp. through 4/14/65.

MORRISON, WILLIAM J.: enl. 7/18/61 Co. I in Charlotte; Sgt.; present 7/18/61-10/31/61; one of soldiers sent to Charlotte Co. to bring Booker Trent and Samuel Blankenshlp to Richmond 9/3/61; promoted 2nd Sgt. 1/6/62 - promoted 1st Sgt. 3/6/62; MWIA Ft. Donelson age 30; death claim filed 9/5/62 by widow Margaret I. Morrison - owed $95.56; John Holt wrote of him at his death: ", .. none knew him but to love him. A better hearted man was hard to be found, and a good soldier, always cheerful and seemingly happy under the most discouraging circumstances of a soldier's life. And what is best of all, I believe he was a true Christian... "; b. Charlotte; wheelwright;sandy hair, fair complexion, blue eyes, 5'6".

MORSE, ALEXANDER: enl. 8/7/63 Co. K at Hicksford; furloughed

11/1/63-12/21/63; present 9/63-10/63, 4/1/64, and 5/64-8/64.
MORSE, C. C.: Co. G; paroled Farmville 4/11/65-4/21/65 (may be C. C. Moon)
MORTON, JACOB WILLIAM: enl. 7/18/61 Co. I in Charlotte, Cpl./Lt.; present 7/18/61-10/31/61; furloughed 3/28/63-4/18/63; WIA and POW Gettysburg - confined Ft. McHenry, Ft. Delaware, and Pt. Lookout 10/26/63 - paroled and transferred for exchange 2/14/65; paroled Farmville 4/11/65-4/21/65; b. 9/30/1842; d. 11/11/1911.
MORTON, JOHN ALEXANDER: enl. 7/18/61 Co. I in Charlotte; present 7/18/61-8/31/61; discharged 10/1/61; d, 1894 of Bright's Disease in Texas; widow Lucy A. Morton applied for pension 7/6/1911 - m. 1847 in Charlotte -said husband in army 4 years - $25 approved.
MORTON, TIGNEL J.: elected Capt. Co. B 5/3/62; WIA Frazier's Farm; dropped as Capt. 1/9/63 because of prolonged absence; Lt. Col, commanding Camp of Instruction in Petersburg - returned to ordinary duties 2/20/63 - transferred to Mississippi; wrote war dept asking to be made Colonel of new regiment - appointed Col. age 20 of 53rd Tenn. Inf.; 10/63 WIA; in command of camp in Columbus, Miss. in spite of wds. in lungs; declared permanently disabled 10/14/64; surrendered Citronelle, Ala. 5/4/65 - paroled 6/15/65 at Mobile, age 22; fair complexion, dark eyes, light hair, 6'2"; b. "Roseland" near Boydton, Mecklenburg Co. 8/27/1843; matriculated VMI 1860 - entertained fellow students with his fiddle playing - left VMI to join army 5/3/62: m. Suzanne Davis of Ala. 1/10/1865 - 2 children; d. 1871 with consumption from effects of wds. in battle; described as "a fearless, gallant soldier, a noble Christian gentleman, aristocratic *and* cultured..."
MOSELEY, ALFRED: pwl; Co. D; d. from illness and hardship on retreat from Ft. Donelson.
MOSELEY, BENJAMIN M.: enl. 7/12/61 Co. G in Charlotte, Pvt./Sgt.; present 726/61-10/31/61; listed on payment record for 11/1/61-10/31/62; detached on forage detail 4/12/63-6/12/63.
MOSELEY, CHARLES WESLEY: enl. 6//22/61 Co. B in Mecklenburg, 2nd Lt.; present 9/61-10/61; appointed 2nd Lt. 7/15/61 - dropped 5/5/62; POW Ft. Donelson 2/16/62 - confined Johnson's Island and sent Vicksburg for exchange 9/1/62 - on list of officers captured and paroled at different times and places and exchanged 11/8/62; member Armistead Camp, UCV 1892; d. 6/1893 of disease in Boydton; widow Jennie P. Moseley applied for pension 6/20/1907 in Brunswick - m. 1865 Mecklenburg - $25 approved.
MOSELEY, JULIUS C.: enl. 4/20/64 Co. B in Isle of Wight; sick and sent to hosp. since mustered for pay on roll 5/64-6/64; present 7/64-8/64; POW High Bridge 4/6/65 - took oath and released from Pt. Lookout 6/29/65; fair complexion, dark brown hair, grey ayes, 5'51/2"; resident of Brunswick; b.

about 1845; m. Martha ? after war - *8* children; 1880 farmer in Brunswick; 1910 living Emporia.

MOSELEY, WILLIAM P.: enl. 7/12/61 Co. G in Charlotte; discharged 8/5/61 age 19 due to hernia he had since age 8; b. Halifax; farmer; light complexion and hair, blue eyes, 5'9".

MOSELEY, WILLIAM S.: enl. 7/12/61 Co. G in Charlotte; discharged 7/28/61 age 22 due to foot disease caused by burn; b. Charlotte; farmer, light complexion and hair, blue eyes, 6'.

MOSELEY, WILLIS FEARN: pwl; Co. D; at Ft. Donelson; transferred to Co. K Buckingham Cavalry – sharp shooter - considered "fearless soldier"; WIA Raccoon Ford; b. 1840 Buckingham Co., son of Robert (brother editor of "The Richmond Whig") and Virginia Boudurant Moseley; VMI class of 1861- attended 1 year & 2 months; m. Willie Harlan of Fluvanna - no children; killed in saw mill accident about 1884 or 1894 in Newark, New Jersey where had been engaged in manufacturing establishment; also farmer and lumber man.

MOSER, PETER: Co. H; resident of Monroe Co., TN; deserted at Culpeper Court House 5/18/63 - remained at home until 7/64 - was on POW list of Knoxville, TN 7/1/64 - received pass to Loudon, TN - allowed to return home on recommendation of Union citizens.

MOSES, JOHN F.: enr. as conscript 2/16/64. assigned Co. G 2/25/64 - on detached service baling forage 3/64; present 5/64-6/64.

MOSS, C. W.: enl. 5/3/62 Co. H in Richmond; 7/63-12/63 AWOL; 4/1/64 in arrest; 5/64-8/64 AWOL; 7/64-8/64 deserter.

MOSS, (MORSE) ROBERT O.: Co. B; POW High Bridge 4/6/65 – took oath and released from Pt. Lookout 6/15/65; resident of Mecklenburg; fair complexion, light hair, blue eyes, 5'9 ¾"; m. Lula Virginia; bur. Union Chapel Methodist Church Cem. Hwy. 715, Palmer Springs, Va.

MULHOLAND, H. G. (B.): pwl; Co. C - bur. plot 585 Hollywood 8/17/64.

MULLINS, L R.: enl. 8/62 Co. A; served 6 months.

MULLIN, (MULLEN) EDWARD: enl. 6/18/62 Co. E in Richmond; deserted 6/20/62.

MULUNS, (MULLEN) ABNER C.: enl. 7/12/61 Co. G in Charlotte; present 7/26/61-10/31/61; d, 3/18/62 in Atlanta Medical College – bur. Oakland Cem. Atlanta, Row 2, Number 14 - death claim filed 7/3/62 - owed $65.73

MULLINS, (MULLENS) P. R.: enl. 8/15/62 Co. A in Mecklenburg; admitted Chimborazo 11/28/63 with gunshot wd. of left hand - furloughed 45 days 12/12/63; absent wded. 5/64-8/64.

MULLINS, WILLIAM JEFF: enr. as conscript 2/16/64. assigned Co. G 2/24/64; present 4/1/64 and 5/64-8/64; received clothes 10/13/64, 10/19/64

and 12/28/64; d. 9/19/1897 Mecklenburg of stomach trouble; widow Mary J. Mullins applied for pension 11/18/1922 - said husband served 4 years and was wded. - m. 7/11/1869 - $76 approved.
MURRAY, FLEMING: enl. 7/15/61 Co. H in Albemarle; present 7/29/61-10/31/61.
MURRAY, JAMES H.: enl.. 7/15/61 Co. H in Albemarle; present 7/29/61-10/31/61; d. 1861 - coffin purchased 12/1/61 - receipt for coffin received at Abingdon 2/18/62.
MURRAY, THOMAS: enl. 7/8/61 Co. A in Mecklenburg; d. 8/31/61 of measles in Clay Street Hosp., Richmond - bur. Hollywood Cem.
McALISTER, BENJAMIN (D. or R.): Co. H; substitute for E. Catterton 9/3/61; on list of patients at Chimborazo transferred to Jackson hosp. - n. d.; received clothes 12/30/64.
McALISTER, R. N.: pwl; Co. H.
McALISTER, WILLIAM T.: enl. 5/1/61 age 24, Co. E, 19th Va.; discharged 12/14/61; fair complexion, black hair and eyes, 5'10"; enl. Co. H, 56th Va., n. d. g.: admitted Chimborazo 3/8/65 with hepatitis - furloughed 3/15/65; paroled Charlottesville 5/17/65; b. Albemarle 6/20/1838; mechanic; d. 1/24/1910; bur. Oakwood Cem., Charlottesvllle.
McCAN, REUBEN: enl. 7/8/61 Co. A in Mecklenburg; present 7/8/61-8/31/61; d. 9/29/61 in Clay St. Hosp., Richmond.
McCAULEY, ANDREW J.: pwl; Co. D.
McCAULEY, MILETUS (A.): enl 7/15/61 Co. H in Albemarle; present 7/29/61-8/31/61; admitted Charlottesvlle hosp. with measles 9/14/61 - returned to duty 10/5/61 - readmitted 11/19/61 with measles and jaundice - returned to duty 12/19/61; applied for pension 4/28/1900 age 77 living Mitchell Station, Culpeper, Orange Co. - disabled due to age - $15 approved; b. 6/26/1822; d. 10/22/1910 - bur. Laurel Hill Baptist Church, Rt. 649, Albemarle.
McCAULEY, ROBERT W. (B. W. or K. W.): enl. 5/3/62 Co. H in Richmond; furloughed 5/6/62-6/19/62; POW and WIA Gettysburg - in West's Buildings Hosp. with gunshot wd. in left arm - Union doctor performed resection of elbow joint 7/13/63; d. 8/19/64 age 31 at Pt. Lookout of chronic diarrhea - had been paroled for exchange 5/3/64 - bur. Confederate Cem., Pt. Lookout; death claim filed by widow Margaret J. McCauley 2/16/65.
McCAULY, LEANDER: enl. 7/8/61 Co. D in Buckingham; present 7/8/61-10/31/61; d. Emory and Henry Hosp., Abingdon 5/5/62 – death clam flied 9/15/63 by mother Catherine M. Glass - owed $24.93. (may be Andrew J. McCauley)
McCLARIN, (McLARIN) JAMES W.: enl. 8/1/62 Co. E in Brunswick, musician; present 9/63-12/63, 4/1/64, and 5/64-8/64; admitted Chimborazo 3/8/65 with debility - returned to duty 3/11/65; paroled Burkeville

4/14/65-4/17/65; admitted Lee Camp Soldiers' Home 12/30/1887 age 50 for hernia and loss of eye sight - d. 8/29/1923 - bur. Maury Cem. by relatives.

McDANIEL, THOMAS L.: enl. 8/29/61 Co. A in Richmond; present 9/61-10/61.

McGEHEE, ALEXANDER S.: Co, C; received clothes 10/1964; paroled at Gordonsville 5/20/65.

McGEHEE, EDWARD C.: enl. 8/22/61 Co. H in Richmond; discharged age 31 due to deafness 2/18/63; b. Albemarle; farmer, dark complexion and hair, blue eyes, 5'7".

McGEHEE, GEORGE V. (McGEE., JOSEPH V.): enl, 7/9/61 Co, C in Louisa; sick furlough *7/9/61-8/31/61;* present 9/61-10/61; WIA Gettysburg; absent wded. 8/63-12/63 and 5/64-8/64; paroled Columbia 5/65; applied for pension 5/21/1892 age 56 living Louisa Court House – disability due to many wds. received Gettysburg and rheumatism - $15 approved; d. 9/5/1900 Louisa - effects of wds. and grippe; widow Cordella V. McGehee filed for pension 3/30/1901 m. Washington, D.C. 1859 - $25 approved.

McGEHEE, H. S.: pwl; Co. C - according to pension application enlisted 10/64 in Gordonsville - left army 3/65 due to sickness; b. Louisa; farmer; applied for pension 4/8/1901 age 84 living Beaver Dam, Hanover Co.- no income - 1/12th interest in 64 acres worth $800 - totally disabled due to age, $36 approved.

McGEHEE, (McGEE) JAMES E.: enl. 9/2/61 Co, F Louisa, Pvt./Sgt.; WIA Gaines's Mill - admitted Chimborazo 6/29/62 with gunshot wd. of leg - furloughed 60 days 7/4/62 - returned to duty 9/6/62; POW Gettysburg - confined Ft. Delaware 7/12/63 - d. 8/6/63 Ft. Delaware hosp. of congestion of brain - bur. Finn's Pt., N. J. Nat Cem.

McGHEE, (McGEE) JOHN L: enl. 8/6/61 Co. K in Mechanicsville; present 8/6/61-10/31/61; POW Ft. Donelson - sent from Camp Morton to Vicksburg for exchange - declared exchanged at Aiken's Lending 11/10/62; furloughed 7/1/63-10/31/63; present 11/63-12/63, 4/1/64, 5/64-8/64; & 7/64-8/64; forfeited 2 months pay by sentence of court martial; received clothes 9/27/64, 10/13/64, and 10/19/64.

McGHEE, (MAGEE) PETER C.: enl. 8/6/61 Co. K in Mechanicsville; present 8/6/61-1/31/61; furloughed 2/12/63-2/28/63; POW Gettysburg - captured while serving as nurse – admitted West's Buildings Hosp. 7/26/63 - confined Ft. McHenry 9/12/63, Pt. Lookout 9/15/63 - paroled 2/18/65 - exchanged at Camp Lee 3/1/65.

McGHEE, WILLIAM A.: enl. 8/6/61 Co. K in Mechanicsville; Pvt./Cpl.; present 8/6/61-10/31/61; furloughed 3/7/63-3/27/63; present 7/63-11/63; furloughed 11/1/63-12/31/63; present 4/1/64 and 5/64-8/64; received clothes 9/27/64, 10/13/64, 10/19/64, and 12/3/64; b. Hanover, farmer;

admitted Lee Comp Soldiers' Home 8/4/1897 age 55 for varicose veins - discharged 4/17/1903 on his demand while under charges for AWOL; applied for pension 7/2/1910 age 69 living Hanover - said served until end of war - disabled due to old age and varicose veins - no income or property - $24 approved.

McGREGOR, ALLEN W.: enl. 8/6/61 Co. K in Mechanicsville; discharged 8/16/61 age 35 due to varicose veins left thigh and leg; b. Hanover; farmer; light complexion, dark hair, grey eyes, 6'.

McGUIRE, SAMUEL: pwl; Co. D.

McHAYNES, (McHANES) MARCELLUS: enl. 4/1/62 (or 1864) Co. C at Chaff in's Farrn; present 5/64-8/64; paroled Gordonsville 6/5/65.

McPHAIL, JOHN BLAIR II: enl 7/8/61 Co. A in Mecklenburg age 24, Lt./Lt Col.; sick furlough 8/27/61-9/2/61; present 10/1/61; elected Capt. 5/3/62; WIA Boonsboro; on detached service by order of Sec. of War as head of 5th Congressional District to enforce conscription law; present 5/64-8/64; promoted to Major 6/13/64; appointed Lt Col. 12/7/64; POW Hatcher's Run 3/31/65 - confined Old Capitol Prison and Johnson's Island - took oath and released 7/15/65 age 29; pardoned by Pres. Johnson 7/31/65; b. 1835 in Mecklenburg to John Blair and Nancy Cabell Carrington McPhail; 1856 graduate Hampden Sydney; fair complexion, black hair, hazel eyes, 5'10"; president of railroad and farmer, co-inheritor of Mulberry Hill, Charlotte: never married; d. 1904; left his share of home to brother Paul C. McPhail.

NASH, JOHN G.: enl. 6/22/61 Co. B in Mecklenburg, Sgt; present 9/61-10/61; in hosp. in Russellville, Ky. 2/4/62; POW Ft. Donelson; sent from Camp Morton to Vicksburg for exchange; discharged 10/28/62 age 28 due to disability; b. Mecklenburg; farmer; fair complexion, dark eyes, black hair, 6'2".

NASH, PHOCION E.: enl. 6/1/61 Co. B in Mecklenburg; discharged 10/26/61 age 22 because of heart disease; b. Mecklenburg; farmer, dark complexion and hair, blue eyes, 6'.

NAWILL, J. W.: Co. D, Lt.; paroled Farmville 4/11/65-4/21/65;

NEAL, GRANVILLE: Co. G; on 12/63 roll of deserters in Department of West Va. – took oath of allegiance and sent north; resident of Tazewell, W. Va.; 30 In 1863; farmer; dark complexion and hair, blue eyes, 5'10".

NEESE, HENRY H.: enl. 6/1/61 Co. D in Buckinghan; admitted Danville hosp. 6/4/62 with debilitas; reenlisted 8/11/62; admitted Charlottesville hosp. 6/6/63 with chronic bronchitis - returned to duty 8/3/63; admitted Richmond hosp. 9/12/63 with catarrh - returned to duty 11/5/63; admitted Richmond hosp. 4/3/604 - retumed to duty 4/14/64; readmitted 6/13/64 with poison oak; transferred to Lynchburg hosp. 7/9/64; admitted Charlottesville hosp. 10/7/64 with dyspepsia; discharged 2/13/65 *age* 32 due to dyspepsia; b. Nelson Co.; farmer; fair complexion, light hair and eyes, 6'; d. 1879 of cancer Nelson; widow Mary S. Neese applied for pension 2/25/1903 - m. 1857 Nelson Co. - $25 approved.

NEESE, WILLIS HARRIS: enl. 6/1/61 Co. D in Buckingham; admitted Richmond hosp. with rubeola 5/15/62 age 29 - transferred Danville 6/3/62 - returned to duty 8/31/62; reenlisted 8/11/62; POW and paroled Staunton 5/18/65; fair complexion, light hair, blue eyes, 5'9"; d. Nelson 2/26/1891 of face cancer; widow Sally Jane Neese applied for pension 5/11/1903 - m. 1/12/1862, Nelson - $25 approved.

NELSON, ADAM S.: enl. 7/9/61 Co. C in Louisa; present 7/9/61-10/31/61.

NELSON, EDWARD J. (JAMES EDMOND on pension application): Co. A; received clothes 10/19/64 and 12/28/64; POW Farmville 4/6/65 - took oath and released from Pt. Lookout 6/15/65; resident of Mecklenburg; dark complexion, brown hair, hazel eyes; 5'10"; d. 1906 of cancer in Mecklenburg - bur. Rock Springs Baptist Church, Townsville, N.C.; widow Mary S. Nelson applied for pension 8/19/1924 - m. 2/2/1872 near Clarksville - no income or property - $80 approved.

NELSON, FRANK W.: enl. 7/8/61 Co. A in Mecklenburg; 1st Sgt./Capt.; present 7/8/61-10/31/61; elected 1st Lt. 5/3/62; commanded Co. for "18 long months" while McPhail served as enrolling officer of 6th Congressional District; asked for 15 day furlough 9/18/63; present 11/63-12/63; WIA in skirmish near Chester Station 6/16/64 - admitted Richmond hosp. 6/17/64 with gunshot wd. of scrotum - furloughed to Clarksville 8/1/64 with wd. and typhoid fever; POW and paroled 5/10/65 at Headquarters 2nd Brigade, 1st Division, 6th A.C.; b 12/25/1843; resident of Lee Camp Soldiers' Home 1925; still living in 1936 age 93; one of last survivors of Pickett's Charge.

NELSON, JOHN: enl. 7/8/61 Co. A in Mecklenburg; Cpl.; present 7/8/61-10/31/61.

NELSON, JOHN E.: enl. 7/9/61 Co. C in Louisa; AWOL since 8/14/62.

NELSON, WILLIAM H.: enl. 8/8/61 Co. A in Mecklenburg, Sgt.; WIA Gaines's Mill; furloughed 6/28/62 - 7/26/62 and 10/13/62 – 11/13/62; WIA Cold Harbor; detached for duty in conscript service 3/6/65; POW at Blacks and Whites, Va. 4/20/65 - group cut off from Lee's army at time of surrender - came in and gave themselves up - paroled at Jones House, Va.; applied in Charlotte for pension 5/4/1891 age 51, but living Prince Edward Co.; disabled due to war - wd. of right arm - $15 approved; rerated 3/2/1908 - totally disabled - $30 approved - 1909 paid $36.

NEWCOMB, HENRY J.: enl. 7/12/61 Co. G in Charlotte; present 7/26/61 -10/31/61 and 7/64-8/64; received clothes 10/19/64.

NEWCOMB, (NEWCOMBE) JAMES H. (may be HENRY J. NEWCOMB): enl. 6/18/61 Co. G in Charlotte; wded. Gettysburg 7/3/63 in left hand and left side of head; admitted Richmond hosp. 7/12/63 with gunshot wd.- furloughed 8/9/63 for 30 days; present 9/63-12/63; on detached service as shoemaker at C.S. Clothing Depot, Richmond 11/63-12/63 and 2/64-8/64; furloughed 4/20/64-5/20/64; received clothes 9/27/64 and 12/28/64; b. 8/4/1830; m. Sarah Sans Robert 3/4/1861 Charlotte; applied for pension 4/18/1892 age 67 living Orgainsville, Mecklenburg Co. - $15 approved; d. 7/29/1900 from old age, dropsy, and wounds - bur. New Hope Baptist Church, Skipwith; widow applied for pension 7/31/1900.

NEWCOMB, JOHN: Co. C; received clothes at Winder 7/21/63; enl. at Howlett's House 7/64 - taken prisoner there 8/25/64 - confined Bermuda Hundred, Ft. Monroe and Pt. Lookout; d. Pt. Lookout of typhoid fever 2/12/65 - bur. POW graveyard.

NEWCOMB, SAMUEL CLAY: pwl; Co. I; b. 11/18/1846 Charlotte; d 1/7/1933 Charlotte.

NEWMAN, ROBERT J.: enl. 7/26/61 Co. F in Louisa; present 7/27/61-10/31/61; waggoner 2/18/62 – 3/62 - probably helped remove government stores from Nashville, TN; admitted Chimborazo 8/4/62 with chronic diarrhea; detached service as ambulance driver on rolls 2/63-10/63 and 1/64-8/64; paroled Columbia 5/8/65; b. 11/14/1837 Orange Co. - family moved to Louisa after 1840 and father purchased 400 acres; m. Mary C. Garnett 11/171856 - 3 children; m. Susan J. Robertson 12/29/70 – 6 children; ran mill in Louisa after war; d. 6/22/1904 on King St. Charlottesville of stomach cancer; bur. Oakwood Cem.. Charlottesville.

NEWTON, ALEXANDER: enl. 7/8/61 Co. D in Buckingham; present 7/8/61-10/31/61; furloughed from Abingdon with pneumonia 3/10/62; d. at home of brother John J. Newton in Buckingham 3/24/62; claim of deceased soldier filed 6/18/62 - owed $67.80.

NEWTON, GEORGE E.: enl. 7/8/61 Co. D in Buckingham; Cpl.; present 7/8/61-10/31/61; d. 9/27/62 age 23 in Richmond hosp. from leg wd. received Gaines's Mill; claim of deceased soldier filed by father John J. Newton 2/27/63 - owed $232.33; b. Buckingham; farmer; light complexion, dark hair, blue eyes, 5'6".

NEWTON, JOSEPH A.: enl. *7/10/61* Co. E in Brunswick; present 7/10/61-10/31/61; on detached duty as ambulance driver Chaffin's Farm 2/62-3/62, 10/6/64, 3/64, 5/64; admitted Winder 7/20/62 with remittent fever; present 11/63-12/63, 4/1/64 and 5/64-8/64; AWOL since 9/*4/64; age 36* in 1864; b. about 1832 in Brunswick to Henry and Mary Ann Newton; m. Martha Ann Lanier 2/19/1856 Brunswick; his sister m. Richard H. Martin, Co. E; farmer; light complexion and eyes, dark hair, 5'6".

NEWTON, WILLIAM BENJAMIN: enl. *7/10/61 Co.* E in Brunswick.; present 7/10/61-8/31/61; POW Ft. Donelson - sent from Camp Morton to Vicksburg for exchange; admitted Winder 10/20/62 -furloughed 11/7/62 for 20 days; b. about 1826 Brunswick; brother of Joseph A. Newton; bonded to

marry Jane C. Harrison 6/21/1852; 1860 - 5 children, living near Smoky Ordinary, and working as carpenter; 1870 census – laborer; d. 1870's.
NEWTON, WILLIAM J.: enl. 7/1/61 Co. D in Buckingham; reenlisted; POW Gettysburg - sent Ft. Delaware and Pt. Lookout - admitted Smallpox Hosp. Pt. Lookout 11/11/63 - d. 11/26/63; from Nelson Co.
NEWTON, WILLIAM P.: pwl; Co. D (probably William J. Newton).
NEWTON, WILLIAM W.: enl. 7/8/61 Co. D in Buckingham; present 7/8/61-10/31/61; POW Ft. Donelson - sent frorn Camp Morton to Vicksburg for exchange; admitted Winder 10/15/62 with remittent fever - deserted 10/21/62 present 9/63-12/63, 4/1/64, and 5/64-8/64 - forfeited one month pay by order of court martial; wded. 6/16/64 age 23 - admitted Richmond hosp, 6/19/64 with wd. of scrotum and penis - returned to duty 6/25/64; paroled Farmville 4/11/65-4/21/65; farmer, applied for pension 7/9/1888 age 47 living Curdville Buckingham; wded, Dutch Gap 3/10/65 by shot in lower bowel causing double rupture - $15 approved; paid $36 1909.
NICHOLAS, LORENZO D. enl. 7/8/61 Co. D in Buckingham; discharged 8/2/61 - no reason given; reenlisted 8/11/62; absent on detached service working near Chester on rolls of 9/63-12/63, 4/1/64, and 5/64-8/64; admitted Chimborazo 8/8/64 with vulvus incisium; returned to duty 8/25/64: paroled Farmville 4/28/65.
NICHOLAS, ROBERT CARTER: enl. 7/8/61 Co. D in Buckingham, 1st Lt./A.C.S.; present 7/8/61-8/31/61; listed as Captain on receipts in 1861 and 1862; appointed A. C. S. 5/3/62; admitted Charlottesville hosp. 7/26/63 with primary syphilis - returned to duty 8/7/63; b. Virginia Mills, Buckingham Co. to Robert Carter and Orrilla A. Bigelon Nicholas; matriculated VMI 8/24/1857; left because mistreated by older students; attended Hampden-Sydney; never married; procurement merchant of firm Thaxton and Nicholas in Richmond after war, d. on route to Virginia Springs in railroad train 7/7/1881.
NICHOLAS, WILLIAM HENRY: enl. 7/8/61 Co. D in Buckingham; present 7/8/61-10/31/61; on roll of MCV 8/13/61-8/22/61; discharged 10/26/61 - no reason given; admitted Chimborazo 5/26/62 with debilitas – transferred 5/27/62 to Lynchburg; reenlisted 8/11/62; AWOL 9/63-12/63 and 5/64-8/64; listed as deserter 4/1/64; paroled Farmville 4/28/65.
NICHOLSON, ACRE: enr. as conscript 1/27/64 - assigned to Co. C 2/24/64; absent sick 5/64-8/64; admitted Chimborazo 7/15/64 with debility - furloughed 8/11/64 for 30 days.
NOEL, JOHN: Co. F; originally filed under *Co. F*, 50th Va. Inf.; POW near Spotsylvania Court House 5/12/64 – sent to Elmira, N.Y. 7/30/64; d. 10/14/64 of hosp. gangrene - no effects - was to have been exchanged 11/15/64.
NORRIS, JAMES A.: pwl; enl. 1862 Co. H; served 3 years. (probably James Henry Norris)

NORRIS, JAMES BARNARD: pwl; Co. H; d. 4/17/1910 as result of fractured skull suffered in accident involving runaway horse - bur. Oakwood Cem., Charlottesville.

NORRIS, JAMES HENRY: enl. 5/3/62 Co. H in Richmond from 88th Militia Regt. of Albemarle; POW Gettysburg *7/6/63;* sent Ft Delaware and Pt. Lookout 10/27/63; took oath and released 6/15/65; dark complexion, black hair, grey eyes; 5'4 1/2"; b. 1/7/1844, son of William and Mary S. Gibson Norris in Earlysville, Albemarle Co.; farmer; 4 children; attended 50th Gettysburg reunion 7/3/1913; applied for pension 9/13/1918 age 75 in Boonesville, Albemarle Co. - owned 101 acres worth $1028 and $375 personal property - totally disabled due to age - $75 approved; m. Virginia L. ? 1869 - *4* children – she d. between 1880 and 1891; m. Matilda Shiflett 12/31/1891 in Albemarle; d. age 78 - bur. Charlottesville.

NORTHCROP, R. W.: pwl; Co. F.

NORVELL, THOMAS BURTON (BENTON): enl. 7/8/61 Co. D in Buckingham, Pvt./Sgt.; present 7/8/61-10/61; reenlisted 8/11/62; admitted Scottsville hosp. 2/7/63 - still there 6/30/63; present 9/63-12/63, 4/1/64, and 5/64-8/64; furlough 7/64-8/64; POW Hatcher's Run 3/31/65 - took oath and released from Pt. Lookout 6/15/65; b. 8/13/1840; resident of Buckingham; light complexion, dark brown hair, grey eyes, 5'4 1/2"; committed suicide at home 1/22/1897; widow Mary E. Norma applied for pension 4/12/1907 - m. near Glenmore, Buckingham Co. 3/1/66 - $25 approved.

NORWOOD, JESSE: enl. 7/8/61 Co. A in Mecklenburg; present sick with measles 7/8/61-8/31/61; sick furlough 9/61-10/61; KIA Gaines's Mill; claim of deceased filed 8/7/63 - owed $20.90 - heir widow Harriett Norwood; pension application filed by widow 1888: m. *4/4/1860* In Granville, N.C.; $30 approved.

OAKS, P. H.: enl. 2/25/62 Co. H in Richmond; discharged 5/17/62 age 23 due to disability; b. Albemarle; farmer; fair complexion, dark hair, hazel eyes, 5'7".

O'HARA, JAMES: enl. 6/18/62 Co. B in Richmond; deserted 6/18/63; shown on rolls 9/63-12/63.

OSBORNE, H.: Co. C; paroled Burkeville 4/14/65-4/17/65.

OTEY, WALTER HAYS: entered war as 1st Lt. P. A. of Va. - appointed Adjt. of 56th 5/3/62; forced to resign 10/31/62 due to chronic inflammation of bladder and urethra; in ordnance dept. Danville 9/63; G.C. Wharton requested 9/25/63 Otey be appointed to his staff of 3rd Brigade, East Tennessee; b. 12/20/1837 Lynchburg to John Mathews and Lucy W. Norvell Otey; attended Hanover Academy; matriculated VMI 7/17/1855 age 17; graduated *7/4/1859* 10th in class of 29- held highest military rank Cadet 1st Capt. 1858/1859 - one of 5 brothers who attended VMI; 3 days after graduation appointed VMI assistant professor of French and

English and assistant instructor of infantry tactics with rank of Lt; 12/1859 assigned to accompany contingent of VMI cadets to help preserve order in Charles Town at execution of John Brown; 1860 taught at Alabama Military Academy - appointed temporary commandant - resigned when felt unfairly replaced; after war opened insurance office in Lynchburg with his brother Major Peter J. Otey; m. Sarah Elizabeth Dandridge Wyatt 4/25/1866 Lynchburg – 5 children; d. 4/21/1890 Lynchburg.

OVERBY, L. W.: enl. 12/1/61 in Mecklenburg, Field and Staff - Quarter Master Sgt.; special orders to proceed to Richmond 12/4/62; furloughed 2/27/63-3/9/63; received clothes 10/14/64 and 12/30/64; surrendered with one horse and baggage by Lee at Appomattox; b. Lunenburg; member of Va. Legislature 1885-1889,

OVERSTREET, WILLIAM R.; enl. 7/18/61 Co. I in Charlotte; present 7/18/61-10/31/61; KIA Hatcher's Run.

PAINTER, SILAS A.: enl.. 7/9/61 Co. C in Louisa; present 7/9/61-10/31/61; d. 6/20/1878 from inflammation caused by wooden leg and liver trouble; widow applied for pension 4/21/1900 - m. 1858 Louisa - $25 approved.

PALMER, JOHN T.: enl. 7/18/61 Co. I in Charlotte, 2nd Lt./1st Lt; present 7/18/61-10/31/61; appointed Capt 11/19/61; POW near Bowling Green, Ky. 1/20/62; letter from Col. William D. Stuart 5/3/62 concerning Palmer's AWOL - not reelected to his command - dropped 5/5/62.

PALMER, WILLIAM PRICE: original member of Richmond Howitzers; in John Brown's raid; Lt. and Capt of 1st Co.; Surgeon to 54th Va.; had to collect dead bodies after Battle of 1st Manassas; appointed Field and Staff Surgeon 56th Va. 5/19/62; vacated position 6/19/62 because of falling health; transferred from 56th to Camp Lee; b. 8/14/1821 to Charles Price and Mary Jane Randolph Palmer in Richmond; attended Berkeley's Academy, Hanover Co. 4 years and then grammar school in New York; UVA 1840; became doctor at father's insistence - received M.D. from University of Pennsylvania and trained in Baltimore hosp.; practiced medicine Richmond and on Richmond-Danville Railroad until father's death; never married; loved literature and history – member of Virginia Historical Society and its executive committee; 1891-1896 V.P. of VHS - wrote many articles on Va. History; Va. Legislature selected him to select, arrange, and edit state manuscripts extending from 1652-.1781 - *Calendar of State Papers* 5 volumes - 5th volume completed by Sherwin McRae due to Palmer's failing health; elected Richmond sheriff 11/8/1870; d. *3/4/1896* Richmond.

PALMORE, JOHN THOMAS: enl. 7/12/61 Co. G in Charlotte; present 7/26/61-10/31/61; WIA Gaines's Mill - minie ball through left thigh cut artery - furloughed 7/4/62-8/4/62; POW Gettysburg; confined Ft. McHenry,

Ft. Delaware, and Pt. Lookout 10/26/63 - look oath and joined U. S. Service at Pt. Lookout 2/11/64; pension application 5/14/1888 age 60 living Chesterfield - $15 approved.

PAMPLIN, WILLIAM JAMES: enl. 9/3/63 Co. K in Lunenburg; present 11/63-1263 and 4/1/64; admitted Richmond hosp. 6/2/64; furloughed 6/11/64 - returned to duty by 8/31/64; admitted Farmville hosp. 8/15/64 with wd, of right foot involving loss of the 4th toe followed by planta abscess - wd. received 6/2/64: remark on hosp. slip - "he ought to be transferred to heaven" - furloughed 30 days 8/16/64; readmitted 8/16/64 - returned to duty 9/16/64; b. Lunenburg; admitted Lee Camp Soldiers' Home 1/13/1900 age 71 due to old age and indigence; lived in Mecklenburg before entering Soldiers' Home; d. 4/23/1907 age 78 - bur. East 27, Hollywood Cem.

PARHAM, GEORGE L.: enl. 7/20/61 Co. B in Mecklenburg; d. 8/23/61 Camp Lee; death claim filed by mother Nancy Parham 12/61 - owed $37.10.

PARRISH, JAMES M.: enl. 7/26/61 co. F in Louisa; sick furlough with measles 7/27/61-8/31/61; present 9/61-10/61; reported as missing since battle of Ft. Donelson on rolls of 9/63-12/63 and 5/64-6/64.

PARRISH, WILLIAM D.: enl. 2/9/63 Co. E in Brunswick; present 9/63-12/63; admitted Chimborazo 8/4/64 with remittent fever - returned to duty 10/23/64; POW Burkeville 4/6/65 - took oath and released from Pt. Lookout 6/16/65; light complexion, dark brown hair, blue eyes, 5'7 3/4"; b. about 1829 to Goodwyn and Mary Martha Williams Parrish in Brunswick; overseer before war; m. Matilda A. Day 5/27/1857; after war laborer and farmer; applied for pension 5/21/1900 age 75 living Edgerton, Brunswick Co. - partially disabled due to age and chronic diarrhea - $15 approved; made statement 8/19/1902 - suffered from exposure Pt. Lookout; rerated 4/24/1906 - totally blind - $30 approved.

PARROTT, CHARLES B.: enl. 8/22/62 Co. H in Richmond; 7/63-12/63 detached service war dept. in N.C.; 3/63-1/64 extra duty as teamster; present 4/1/64 and 5/64-8/64; admitted Richmond hosp. 1/19/65 - furloughed 15 days 1/20/65; admitted U.S. Hosp. 3/31/65 with gunshot wd. of left side - d. no date given.

PARSONS, CORNEIJUS W.: enl. 7/10/61 Co. E in Brunswick; present 7/10/61-8/31/61; POW Gettysburg - confined FL McHenry and Ft. Delaware; d. 11/2/63 of chronic diarrhea; bur. Finn's Point, N.J. Nat. Cem.; b. about 1835; 1860 working as overseer for Dr. John A. Field.

PARSONS, NATHANIEL: enl. 7/26/61 Co. F in Louisa; present 7/27/61-8/31/161; in Richmond hosp. with measles.

PATE, J. S.: Co. F; POW in Richmond hosp. 4/3/65 - on roll of Richmond hosp. 5/28/65.

PATTERSON, REUBEN A.: Field and Staff, Asst Surgeon/Surgeon;

contract physician paid $80 per month; assigned to Lynchburg Gen. Hosp. #2 10/28/62; relieved of duty 11/18/62; assigned Asst. Surgeon 56th Va. – n.d.g.; resident of Henrico Co.; took amnesty oath 7/17/65 age 39 in Richmond; also farmer.
PATTERSON, S. J.: Co. D; discharged 8/31/61 by S.O. 249 A.G.O. 61, Par. 6.
PATTESON, CAMM: enl. *7/8/61* Co. D in Buckingham, Capt.; present 7/8/61-10/31/61; appointed Capt. 7/10/61 - paid $130 per month; dropped as Capt. 5/5/62; b. Amherst Co. 2/21/1840 son of David Patteson; graduate of undergraduate and law schools UVA; lawyer; Democratic Presidential elector from Va. 1884; represented Buckingham in Va. General Assembly after war; member UVA Board of Visitors; still living 6/1902.
PATTESON, (PATTERSON) CHARLES L: enl. 7/23/61 Co. D in Buckingham; present 7/8/61-10/31/61; d. 5/64 in Richmond of disease contracted in army; widow Mildred A. Patteson applied for pension 10/8/1888; rn. in Buckingham 12/1857 - $30 approved.
PATTESON, CORNEULIS W.: enl. 7/8/61 Co. D in Buckingham; present 7/8/61-10/31/61; POW Ft Donelson - sent from Camp Morton to Vicksburg for exchange; sick furlough 10/21/62; received clothes at Scottsville hosp. 6/26/63; present 9/63-12/63, 4/1/64, and 5/64-8/64; admitted Chimborazo 10/20/64 with lumbago - furloughed 11/30/64; POW Burkeville 4/6/65; took oath and released from Pt. Lookout 6/16/65; fair complexion, auburn hair, blue eyes, 5'11 5/8"; resident of Buckingham; farmer. applied for pension *4/21/1903* age 63 living Centenary, Buckingham Co.; had measles during service; disabled due to Bright's disease and indigestion for 20 years - exposure and "rough" diet during war - $15 approved; d. 3/25/1911 of consumption Buckingham; wife applied for pension 5/17/1924 - m. 2/1/1877 - $20 approved.
PATTESON, DAVID R.: enl. 7/8/61 Co. D in Buckingham; Sgt.; present 7/8/61-8/31/61; d. 9/10/61 typhoid fever - death claim filed 10/28/61 - owed $26.63.
PATTESON, THOMAS ANTHONY: enr. as conscript 2/28/64 - assigned Co. D 3/64; present 4/1/64 and 5/64-6/64; admitted Chimborazo with wd. 8/25/64; paroled Charlottesville 5/16/65; d. 4/26/1900 from acute dysentery; widow Antonia M. Patteson applied for pension 9/25/1924 - m. Buckingham 12/18/1878 - S20 approved.
PATTILO, JOHN H.: enl. 7/8/61 Co. A in Mecklenburg; Pvt./2nd Sgt.; present sick with measles 7/8/61-10/31/61; present 9/63-12/63 and 5/64-8/64; POW Farmville 4/6/65 - took oath and released from Pt. Lookout 6/16/65; resident Mecklenburg; light complexion and hair, blue eyes, 5'7 1/2".
PATILLO, SAMUEL G.: enl. 7/8/61 Co. A in Mecklenburg; Pvt./Sgt.;

present sick with measles 7/8/61-8/31/61; present 9/61-10/61; d. 3/15/62 age 20 in Gate City Hosp., Atlanta - bur. Oakland Cem. Atlanta, Row 6, No. 5 - claim of deceased soldier filed by father I. P. Pattillo 7/15/62 - owed $98.56; b. Mecklenburg; farmer; dark complexion and hair, blue eyes, 5'10".

PATTON, WILLIAM: enl. 7/10/62 Co. E in Richmond; deserted 7/11/62.

PEACE, EDWIN M.: enl. 8/6/61 Co. K in Mechanicsville; Cpl.; present 8/6/61-10/31/61; POW Ft. Donelson - sent from Camp Morton to Vicksburg for exchange; sick furlough 10/24/62-11/24/62; admitted Chimborazo 8/11/63 with scorbutus – deserted hosp. 8/23/63 - returned 8/26/63; made Cpl. 10/15/63; present 9/63-12/63, 4/1/64 and 5/64-8/64; POW High Bridge 4/6/65 - took oath and released from Pt. Lookout 6/16/65; native of Hanover; light complexion, black hair, light blue eyes, 5'5"; applied for pension 5/12/1900 age 73 living Old Church, Hanover Co. - partially disabled due to weakness of body - $15 approved - made statement 6/5/1902 - totally disabled to do manual tabor.

PEACE, WILLIAM H.: enl.. 8/6/61 Co. K in Mechanicsville; present 8/6/61-10/31/61; POW Ft. Donelson; d. Camp Morton Prison hosp. 5/21/62 of typhoid fever - bur. Green Lawn Cem. - reinterred Crown Hill Cem; death claim filed by widow Mildred Peace 10/24/62 - owed $128,76 b. Hanover.

PEELE, HENRY T.: enl. 5/2/62 Co B in Richmond; deserted 5/6/63.

PENNIER, ROBERT G.: no Co. given; surrendered by Lee at Appomattox.

PENNINGTON, FRANKLIN: enl. 7/9/61 Co. C in Louisa - entered service 10/18/61 as substitute for $550; mother wrote 12/61 asking for his discharge because of death of his wife who left 3 infant children - she was widow and unable to raise thern - also said that Frank was in poor health and had terrible vision - Capt. Timoleon Smith answered that Frank was very healthy and had fine vision - was examined by surgeon when entered service; on 9/63-12/63 rolls reported as AWOL since 1/62; lawyer; father was hosp, surgeon in War of 1812.

PERKINS, HENRY J. W.: enl. 7/26/61 Co. F in Louisa, Sgt./2nd CpL; present on all rolls; POW Sharpsburg – confined Ft. McHenry; paroled and sent to Ft. Monroe for exchange 10/13/62; received clothes 12/3/63, 10/19/64 and 12/28/64.

PERKINS, JAMES GIDEON: enl. 7/10/61 Co. E in Brunswick; sick furlough 7/10/61-8/31/61; POW Ft. Donelson - d. 8/6/62 at Camp Morton of bilious fever - bur. Green Lawn Cem. - reinterred Crown Hill Cem.; death claim filed by widow 6/3/63 - owed $173.20; b. 1824 Brunswick to Gideon and Elizabeth Jessee Perkins; m. Amanda V. Johnson 1852 - 2 girls.

PERKINS, JOHN BENJAMIN: pwl; enl. 1861 Co. E; POW Ft Donelson;

d. Camp Morton before 8/62 - bur. Green Lawn Cem. - reinterred Crown Hill Cem; b. 1822 – brother of James G. Perkins, Co. E.

PERKINS, THEODORA MARION: pwl; enl. *2/12/62* Co. F at Camp Lee; left service on detail at Appomattox and paroled in Hanover, b. Hanover; farmer; applied for pension 2/25/1915 age 75 living Beaver Dam, Hanover Co. - $500 real estate - $25 personal property - partially disabled due to old age, rheumatism, and bad leg where accidentally shot after war - $43.20 approved; d, 5/15/1919 of heart failure; widow Elizabeth Anne Perkins applied for pension 7/17/1919 - m. 12/24/1857 Hanover; $60 approved.

PERRY, WILLIAM: enl. 7/26/61 Co. F in Louisa; sick furlough with measles 7/27/61-8/31/61; 9/61-10/61 AWOL; on roll 9/63-10/63 listed as deserted 10/8/61.

PETTUS, THOMAS F.: Co. I; received clothes 10/29/64; asked to be detailed as farmer 11/12/64 – assistant surgeon said unfit for duties of soldier due to obesity and enlarged liver, given extra duty accounting for animals; letter from his wife 2/12/65 asking to forgive him for not making weekly reports because his orders were sent to wrong place - asked that he be able to remain accounting for arimals at Drakes Branch; took oath Charlotte 5/15/65

PEYTON, LAWSON: pwl; Co. I - from Charlotte; KIA Boonsboro.

PILKINTON, JOHN T.: enr. as conscript 1/14/64 in Essex Co. – assigned to Co. K 1/15/64; present 4/1/64 and 5/64-8/64; POW Sutherland Station 4/2/65 - admitted Petersburg hosp. with gunshot wd. of left thigh - d. 7/24/65 Richmond hosp..

PLACE, ROLAND: enl. 10/23/63 Co. K in Richmond, Pvt./Sgt.; present 9/63-12/63 and 4/1/64: admitted Chimborazo 6/27/64 with liver congestion - returned to duty 8/27/64; admitted Chimborazo 12/3/64 with hepatitis - returned to duty 1/16/65: POW Hatcher's Run 3/31/65 - took oath and released from Pt. Lookout 6/16/65; resident of Richmond; light complexion, dark hair, hazel eyes; 5'7 ¼".

PLEASANTS. CHRISTOPHER S.: enl. 5/3/62 Co. B in Richmond; POW and WIA Gettysburg; sent to Gettysburg hosp. with compound fracture of right leg - confined Ft. Delaware and Pt. Lookout 10/26/63 - paroled from Pt. Lookout 2/18/65; admitted Richmond hosp. 2/27/65 – furloughed 30 days; paroled Charlottesville 5/19/65; Page Co. pension list.

POINDEXTER, CHARLES T. (G.): enl. 7/9/61 Co. C in Louisa; present 7/9/61-8/31/61.

POINDEXTER, EDWARD W.: enl. 7/9/61 Co. C in Louisa, Pvt./1st Lt.; present on all rolls; elected 1st Lt. 1/18/64; paroled Columbia 5/15/65.

POINDEXTER, WILLIAM THOMAS: enl. 9/26/61 Co. C in Louisa, Pvt./Sgt.; present 9/61-10/61; AWOL Court Martial 2/23/63; found guilty of specification and charge – forfeited 2 months pay and had to cut wood and bring water for Co. and Regt. Until 4/1/63; POW Gettysburg - sent DeCamp General Hosp. with gunshot wd. of right middle finger - hand amputated – exchanged 9/16/63; present 5/64-8/64; admitted Richmond hosp. 2/14/65 - furloughed 30 days 2/15/65.

POLLARD, JOHN W.: pwl; entered service as member Co. B 1st Batt. of Va. Reg. Reserves and then Co. I, 56th Va. Inf. - ran away from home 1/64 age 15 to join army; had measles during war, b. Charlotte; applied for pension 4/1/1901 age 54 living Abell, Charlotte Co. - partially disabled with bladder trouble and poor eyesight due to measles; reapplied 7/1912 age 65 – almost blind; income $100 annually as mechanic - may not have been approved; member H. A. Carrington Camp - given Cross of Honor ; admitted Lee Camp Soldiers' Home *7/5/1922* age 75 for old age.

POOL, A.G.: Co. A; received clothes 12/28/64; surrendered by Lee at Appomattox.

POWELL, GILBERT W.: enl. 5/3/62 Co. B in Richmond; admitted Charlottesville hosp. 7/15/63 with debilitas - furloughed 40 days 10/3/63; readmitted 11/12/63 with ascites - returned to duty 4/20/64; 5/64-6/64 AWOL; readmitted hosp. 8/23/64 with ascites; discharged from service 8/29/64.

POWELL, JAMES WILLIAM: pwl; enl. 1862 Co. B; b. Brunswick 11/29/1846 to Robert Simmons and Martha A. Powell; never married; d. 5/29/1928 age 81 - bur. Powell Family Cem, Highway 644 near Ebony.

POWELL, LEONARD A.: enl. 7/8/61 Co. D in Buckingham; present 7/8/61-10/31/61; reenlisted 5/3/62 admitted Richmond hosp. with jaundice 2/16/63 -transferred 4/12/63; probably KIA Gettysburg - death not reported to Company which dropped his name from rolls 7/63-8/63; death claim filed 7/25/64 by widow Mary S. Powell - left one child.

POWELL, RICHARD: pwl; enl. 1864 Co. F: from Goochland.

POWELL, T. (TOM) N.: pwl; Co. D; wrote letter 10/11/62 to Secretary of War (10/15/1862) asking for discharge because would not be 18 until May and not fit for service; applied for pension 5/31/1900 age 55 living Nelson - disabled by heart palpitation during war - $15 approved; "dead" written across application.

POWELL, WILLIAM H.: enl. 2/22/64 Co. E at Chaffin's Farm; present 4/1/64; admitted Richmond hosp. 5/31/64 - furloughed 30 days 7/16/64; POW Farmville 4/6/65 - took oath and released 6/15/65; resident Greenville Co.; dark complexion. brown hair, blue eyes, 5' 51/2".

POWELL, WILLIAM L.: enl. 7/15/61 Co. H in Albemarle; present 7/29/61-10/31/61; d. 5/30/62 in Emory and Henry Hosp. of disease; death claim filed 1/51/63 - owed $113.

POWERS, JOHN F.: pwl; Co. I; b. 9/20/1828 Charlotte; d. 7/21/1903 Charlotte.

POWERS, JOHN W.: enl. 6/22/61 Co. B in Mecklenburg; present 9/61-10/61; d. 4/27/1862 in Mecklenburg - death claim filed 9/19/62 - owed $140.26.

PRATT, G. T.: pwl; enl. 4/61 Co. B; WIA Gettysburg; from Washington Co.

PRICE, WILLIAM H.: enl. 7/18/61 Co. I in Charlotte, 2nd Lt.; present 7/18/61-10/31/61; appointed 2nd Lt. 11/19/61 - dropped 5/5/62; on forage detail 5/63-6/63; furloughed 10 days 11/64; admitted Richmond hosp. 3/17/65 with Catarrh - returned to duty 3/29/65; POW Hatcher's Run 3/31/65 - confined Johnson's Island 4/9/65 - took oath and released 6/17/65 age 40; resident Aspinwall; fair complexion, dark hair, grey eyes, 6'; 1896 reported as died since war.

PRITCHETT, PETER: enl.. 7/15/61 Co. H in Albemarle; present 9/61-10/61 - refused to report until he saw he was to be arrested - mustered in 9/20/61; 7/63-12/63 and 5/64-6/64 under arrest for desertion 10/25/63; admitted Richmond hosp. 12/15/63 with pneumonia - sent to Castle Thunder 1/9/64; 7/64-8/64 present - 6 months salary deducted by order of court martial; paroled Charlottesville 5/19/65.

PROFFIT, HARVEY: Co. C; admitted Chimborazo 6/23/62 with diarrhea; discharged 10/3/62 because a minor.

PRYOR, R.: pwl; Co A; bur. Oakwood Cem.

PRYOR, SAMUEL E.: enl. 7/17/61 Co. I in Charlotte; transferred *8/1/61* age 27 Co B; 3rd Regt. Va.. Vols.; transferred 8/8/61 Co. D, 3rd Regt. Va. Vols.; appointed Quartermaster Sgt.; discharged 10/5/61 for disability, b. Dinwiddie; farmer.

PUGGH, (PUGH) JOSEPH A.: enl. 6/1/61 Co. D in Buckingham; reenlisted 8/11/62; admitted Chimborazzo 2/20/63 with continual fever. present 9/63-12/63; furloughed 15 days 12/14/63 with pneumonia; present 4/1/64 and 5/64-6/64; admitted Chimborazo 7/20/64 with chronic diarrhea - furloughed 40 days 7/23/64; received clothes 10/13/64 and 10/19/64.

PUGH, DAVID S. (C.): pwl; enl. 1861 Co. I in Richmond; surrendered by Lee at Appomattox; farmer; applied for pension 8/4/1900 age 58 living Rough Creek, Charlotte Co. - $15 approved; rerated 3/1/1909 age 69 - disabled due to heart disease and lung trouble - $36 approved.

PUGH, JOHN O.: pwl; Co. I Charlotte Co.; WIA Hatcher's Run.

PUGH, PRESLEY ALLEN: enl. 7/18/61 age 31 Co. I in Charlotte; Pvt.; present 9/61-10/61; furloughed 8/28/62-9/18/62; present 7/63-12/63 and 5/64-8/64; POW last battle of War 4/6/65 Sayler's Creek; with Lee and his army until 3 days before Appomattox surrender; took oath and released from Pt. Lookout 6/16/65; resident Charlotte and Prince Edward Co.; light complexion, brown hair, blue eyes. 5'6 3/4"; b. 2/13/1830; m. "Miss Betsey" Sarah Elizabeth Driscoll (Driskill) of Charlotte Co.12/2/1854; 3 children; farmed near Prospect, Va. after War; She lived to age 85; Called "GramPugh" by family, Pvt. Pugh lived to age 95. Both are bur. in Oakwood Cem. Richmond in the Armour family plot.

In childhood, Great-Grandaughter Iris Keir Armour Baughman attended Civil War reunions in Richmond with him. She later served as Chamber of Commerce Executive Director during 14 vital developmental years of Ft Walton Beach and Destin, Florida

Here is Pvt. Presley Allen Pugh's brief personal description of his four years in Co. I, 56th Virginia Infantry Regiment:

"Enlisted in what at that time was the Charlotte Greys on or about the first of May 1861 & with other Virginia Companies was formed into the 56th Virginia Regiment & did duty in & around Richmond until sometime in November of that year when the Regiment was sent to Pound Gap on the line between Virginia & Kentucky & after a short time was ordered to Fort Donelson in Tennessee & attached to Floyd's Brigade & fought in the battles around that place until it was surrendered to Grant.

The 56th with a portion of Floyd's Brigade escaped up the Cumberland River to Nashville to find that city surrendered also. But the march was continued to Murphreesboro where I was detailed to take charge of the wounded who were sent to Atlanta & there helped to establish the first Confederate hospital in Georgia.

I left Atlanta in March & rejoined the 56th near Seven Pines shortly before the Seven Pines fight & the Regiment was there attached to what was then known as Pickett's Division which with other Virginia Brigades formed Pickett's Division.

It is generally known what Pickett's Division fought through during the four years of the War. I think there was no general battle fought by General Pickett & Lee in which that Division did not take a part & but one, If I remember rightly, in which the 56th was not engaged that being the Battle of the Wilderness or Chancellorsville & at the time that battle was fought the Brigade was near Suffolk, Virginia on its march from North Carolina to Richmond, Virginia.

I was with the Regiment until April 6th, 3 days before the surrender at Appomattox having been captured at Sayler's Creek & taken to Point Lookout & remained there until the 20th of June in the year 1865."

Pvt. Pugh's daughter, Ella Thomas Pugh Anderson was Manager of the Millinery department at Miller & Rhodes in Richmond. His Granddaughter Ida May Anderson Armour (Cole) was Head Dietician of the Cafeteria at Thomas Jefferson HS in Richmond until retirement. Great-Grandson Alexander Presley Armour was President and Chairman of Richmond's Davenport & Co. stock brokerage firm until his death at the age of 93. Great-Granddaughter Jean Armour Moore was Secretary to the Dean of Randolph-Macon College. Great-Granddaughter Ellen Elizabeth Armour Cox was an executive of Richmond's State ABC Board office. Great-Granddaughter Francis May Armour Bryant and her husband became highly successful owners of large motel and restaurant businesses after his retirement as a Roanoke Dr Pepper VP. Pvt. Pugh's Great-Great Grandchjildren have followed similar patterns as University Professor, Architect, prominent business and land owners, elected official, and civic involvement as well as re-publishing this history of his Regiment's Civil War years.

PUGH, WILLIAM J.: enr. as conscript 4/21/64 at Camp Lee - assigned to Co. I 4/28/64; present 5/64-8/64; received clothes 10/13/64, 11/14/64 and

12/2//64.

PULLER, GOLDER W.: Co. K; POW Southside Railroad 4/3/65 - took oath and released from Pt. Lookout 6/16/65; resident Hanover; dark complexion, black hair, dark hazel eyes, 5'10"; d. 3/17/1874 of liver disease in Hanover; widow Margaret E. Puller applied for pension 6/19/1905 - m. 11/27/1842 King William Co. - $25 approved.

PURCELL, J.: pwl; Co. G; d. in service.

PURCELL, JOHN PEMBERTON: enl. 7/12/61 Co. G in Charlotte, Pvt./2nd Lt.; present 7/26/61-10/31/61; records appear to show that attempted unsuccessfully to get discharge 10/8/62 age 22; furloughed 2/27/63-3/29/63 and 11/1/63-12/31/63; present 4/1/64 and 5/64-8/64; POW Sayler's Creek 4/6/65 - confined Johnson's Island - took oath and released 6/19/65 age 24; b. Charlotte; resident of Dupree's Old Store; dark complexion and hair, hazel eyes, 5'10"; member H. A. Carrington Camp 5/15/1922; applied for pension 1/6/1926 age 86 living Drakes Branch, Charlotte Co. - said fought at Fort Donelson, Gaines's Mill, 2nd Manassas, and others - doctor said senile - $140 approved.

PURCELL, THOMAS H.: enl. 8/20/64 Co. G in Richmond; present 7/64-8/64; received clothes 9/27/64, 10/13/64, and 12/28/64; native Washington, D.C.; Georgetown University alumnus, class of 1865.

PURDY, JAMES, JR,: enl. 1862 Co. E; sick 1863; conscripted 1864 in Lawrenceville and assigned to Co. E; present 4/1/64 and 5/64-8/64; WIA Five Forks 4/1/65; paroled Burkeville 4/14/65-4/17/65; b. Portadown, Armagh County, Ireland 11/15/1827 to James and Sarah Henry Purdy; m. Elizabeth Wells of Ireland 5/7/1847 and left for U.S 2 weeks later - settled near White Plains in Brunswick - 7 children; became naturalized citizen 1859; farmer; lifelong member of Methodist church - member of Orange Society in Ireland founded to protect Protestant interests - did not believe in slavery - member Camp No. 70 UCV of Brunswick and of Brunswick Lodge A. F. and A. M.; 1915 celebrated 68th wedding anniversary - article in "Brunswick Times Gazette" 5/17/1915; oldest citizen of Brunswick at his death 8/31/1917 almost 90 - bur. Oakwood Cem., Lawrenceville; survived by wife (married 70 years) 4 sons, and daughter.

PURDY, WILLIAM S.: enl. 2/17/63 Co. B in Richmond; WIA and POW Gettysburg – admitted DeCamp Hosp. with gunshot wd. of face and foot - exchanged 9/16/63; retired by Medical Examining Board 8/15/64 as totally disqualified - assigned Invalid Corps; m. Charles W. Thomas's sister Tinker 1882 - Thomas referred to him in letter as "Irish scoundrel."

PURYEAR, ROBERT: enl. 7/8/61 Co. A in Mecklenburg; AWL 7/8/61-8/31/61; present 9/61-10/61; admitted Richmond hosp. 9/25/62; discharged 10/5/62 age 45 and 5 months - over 45; b. Mecklenburg; farmer; fair complexion, dark hair, grey eyes. 5'.

PURYEAR, RUFFIN: enl. 7/8/61 Co. A in Mecklenburg; present sick with measles 7/8/61-8/31/61; present 9/61-10/61; admitted Richmond hosp. 7/3/62 - d. 9/25/62 with diptheria.
QUARLES, FREDERICK J.: Co. F; Lt.; paroled Louisa 5/15/65.
QUARLES, JOHN M.: enl. 7/9/61 Co. C in Louisa; sick furlough 7/9/61-8/31/61; present 9/61-10/61; discharged 11/12/61 age 21 due to epileptic fits; b. Louisa; farmer; light complexion and hair, grey eyes, 5'7".
QUESENBERRY, V: Field and Staff - Assistant Surgeon; 11/63-12/63 absent sick; admitted Gordonsville hosp. 11/30/64.
QUIM, JAMES: enl. 8/1/62 Co. H in Richmond; 7/63-12/63 listed as deserter.
RAGLAND, CHARLES: pwl; Co. D.
RAGLAND, ROBERT: enl. 7/23/61 Co. D in Buckingham; present 7/8/61-10/31/61; discharged 6/4/62 age 34 due to disease of muscle of left leg so distorted that could not be used; b. Buckingham; carpenter, dark complexion, black eyes and hair, 5'8".
RAGSDALE. IRWIN (IRVING) S.: enr. as conscript 3/14/64 in Brunswick - assigned Co. E 3/21/64; present 4/1/64 & 5/64-8/64; admitted Chimborazo 10/2/64 with intermittent fever - returned to duty 10/30/64; received clothes 9/27/64, 10/27/64, 11/14/64, 11/26/64, and 12/28/64; transferred to Capt. Cornelius T. Allen's Artillery Co.; b. 1833 to Herbert and Elizabeth Abernethy Ragsdale; storekeeper; bonded to marry Marietta E. Scoggin 4/10/1854 - 4 children; after her death m. Adeline R. Bennett 1/17/1866; 1870 census, 1 child; member Bethel Methodist Church; 10/1870 moved to Kentucky.
RAINEY, JOHN T.: enl. 7/1/61 Co. B in Mecklenburg; present 9/61-10/61.
RAINEY, JOSEPH H.: enl. 6/26/61 Co. B in Mecklenburg; present 9/61-10/61; WIA Frazier's Farm 6/30/62; believed KIA Gettysburg, but no Federal records.
RAINEY, MADISON L.: enl. 6/22/61 Co. B in Mecklenburg; present 9/61-10/61.
RAINEY, ROBERT W.: enl. 9/12/61 Co. B in Richmond, Pvt./Cpl. – substitute for W. G. Jackson; present 9/61-10/61; sick furlough 9/3/62-3/31/63; present 9/63-12/63 and 4/1/64; transferred to Goochland Heavy Artillery as Pvt. 5/29/64 in exchange for Sam J. Rock; present 7/64-8/64, 11/64-12/64, and 1/65-2/65.
RAINEY, WILLIAM H.: enl. 6/24/61 Co. B in Mecklenburg, Pvt./Sgt.; present 9/61-10/61; WIA Gaines's Mill; admitted Petersburg hosp. 5/6/63 with catarrh - returned to duty 7/12/63; readmitted 7/13/63 with intermittent fever - remarks said "paroled prisoner" - returned to duty 8/17/63; present 9/63-10/63; 15 day furlough 11/63-12/63; present 4/1/64 and 5/64-8/64; POW Burkeville 4/6/65 - took oath and released from Pt. Lookout 6/17/65; resident of Mecklenburg; light complexion, brown hair, grey eyes, 5'9 5/8".

RAMEY, THOMAS G.: enl.10/9/61 Co. A in Mecklenburg - substitute for John P. Hayes; present 9/61-10/61; discharged 9/9/62 age 37 because over 35; b. Mecklenburg: farmer; dark complexion and hair, grey eyes, 5'11".
RAMSEY, SAMUEL W.: enl. 7/18/61 Co. I in Charlotte; present 7/18/61-10/31/61; deserted 12/20/62; present in arrest 11/63-12/63; court martial 2/10/64; absent in arrest 5/64-8/64; released from confinement 12/1/64; admitted Chimborazo 12/17/64 - furloughed 30 days 1/31/65; MWIA and POW Hatcher's Run 3/31/65 - admitted Campbell Hosp., Washington, D.C. 4/7/65 *age* 32 gunshot wd. of right thigh and left leg - d. 5/6/65; wife - Mrs. M. J. Ramsey.
RASH, C. N: pwl; Co. H or Co. F; applied for pension 5/16/1900 age 56 living Meridian, Dinwiddie Co. partial disability caused by partial paralysis of rt. side.
RASH, JAMES S. (A.): enl. 7/18/61 Co. I in Charlotte; absent on furlough beyond time 7/18/61-8/31/61; present 9/61-10/61; WIA Gaines's Mill; admitted Richmond hosp and on 9/62-10/62 hosp. roll; furloughed 10/31/63-12/31/63; present 5/64-8/64.
REA, ANDREW A: enl. 7/15/61 Co. H in Albemarle; present 7/29/61-10/31/61; admitted Richmond hosp. 6/22/62 - transferred Danville 7/3/62; admitted Charlottesville hosp. with wd. 4/9/63; returned to duty 9/22/63; present 10/63-12/63 and 4/1/64; admitted Richmond hosp. with wd. 5/2/64 - furloughed 90 days; admitted Charlottesville hosp. 8/11/64 with chronic diarrhea - admitted Chimborazo 12/9/64 with chronic diarrhea – d. 12/26/64 of chronic diarrhea - left $20.50 in effects - bur. Oakwood Cem.
REA, JEFFERSON: pwl; Co. H; d. in service.
REA, RYLAND B.: enl. 7/15/61 Co. H in Albemarle, discharged 8/20/61 - unfit for duty.
REA, WILLIAM: pwl; Co. H.
REA, ZEPHENIAH: enl. 7/15/61 Co. H in Albemarle; present 7/29/61-10/31/61; admitted Chimborazo 6/28/62 with gunshot wd. of head - transferred to Albemarle 7/7/62; discharged 3/28/63 age 45 because over 45; b. Albemarle; farmer; dark complexion, eyes, and hair, 5'8".
READ, MELANCHTHON C.: pwl; entered service 2/64 age 44 Co. I; fought at Gaines's Mill; b. 1829; had pension; d. 1919 - bur. Woodlawn Cem., Tampa, Fla.
READ, THOMAS NELSON: enl. 7/18/61 Co. I in Charlotte, Sgt.; absent sick in Richmond 7/18/61-8/31/61; present 9/61-10/61; discharged 1/15/62; joined 14th Va. Cav.; d. after war according to SHSP 1896.
REAMEY, JAMES H.: pwl; Co. A; (may be Ramey, Thomas G.)
REDD, (REID) RICHARD LEE: enl. 7/12/61 Co. G in Charlotte, Pvt./Comsy Sgt.; present 7/26/61-10/31/61, 9/63-12/63 and 5/64-8/64; absent detached service 4/1/64; surrendered by Lee at Appomattox with

one horse and baggage.
REDMOND, WILLIAM H.: enl. 10/18/63 Co. G in Charlotte; present 4/1/64; absent sick 5/64-6/64; admitted Richmond hosp. 6/4/64 with debility – returned to duty 6/25/64; admitted Chimborazo 7/16/64 with typhoid fever - d. 7/21/64.
REDMOND, WYATT T.: enl. 10/15/63 Co. G in Charlotte; present 9/63-12/63.
REEVLY, G. W. (REWELY, G. R.): Co. G; Sgt.; surrendered by Lee at Appomattox.
REVELEY, DAVID ROBERTSON: pwl; Co. G; Sgt.; VMI 1865 - attended 8 months; resident of Nebraska, Va.; d. 1900.
REYNOLDS, WILLLAM M.: enl. 7/9/61 Co. C in Louisa; AWOL 9/61-10/61.
RHODES, FRANKLIN: enl. 7/15/61 Co. H in Albemarle; present 7/29/61-10/31/61; present 7/63-12/63; admitted Charlottesville hosp. 8/3/63 with chronic diarrhea - returned to duty 8/10/63; present 4/1/64; absent sick 5/64-8/64; admitted Chimborazo 8/27/64 with diarrhea - furloughed 50 days 8/31/64; admitted Charlottesville hosp. 10/23/64 with chronic diarrhea - furloughed 10/25/64.
RHODES, HEZEKIAH (T.): enl. 7/15/61 Co. H in Albemarle; present 7/29/61-8/31/61; sick furlough 9/61-10/61; admitted Charlottesville hosp. 12/16/61 with erysipelas – returned to duty 12/18/61; WIA Gaines's Mill; admitted Chimborazo 6/29/62 with gunshot wd, of neck - transferred Charlottesville hosp. 7/3/62; deserted and arrested 10/31/63 by 1st Lt. F. M. McMullan, Co. D, 4th Va. Heavy Artillery; furloughed 1/1/64-6/8/64; admitted Chimborazo 6/4/64 - furloughed 40 days 6/9/64; WIA Cold Harbor - admitted Charlottesville hosp. 7/14/64 with gunshot wd. of left hand - furloughed 7/14/14 - furlough extended 8/9/64 - readmitted 9/5/64 - transferred to Lynchburg hosp, 4/11/65; b. Orange Co. 2/2/1829 farmer, applied for pension 5/25/1910 age 75 living Eastham, Albemarle Co. (lived there 56 years) - $50 income - $640 real estate -disability due to useless left hand as result of wd. Cold Harbor - $36 approved; d. 8/3/1921 in Eastham of old age - bur. Riverview Cem., Charlottesville; widow Catherine Rhodes applied for pension 10/6/1923 - m. 4/8/1876 Albemarle - owned 1/3 of 1000 acres, 2 pigs, and few chickens - $76 approved.
RHODES, W.: Co. H; present 4/1/64.
RICE, WILLIAM H.: enl. 7/15/61 Co. H in Albemarle; discharged 8/20/61 because unfit for service.
RICHARD, JOHN L.: enl. 7/15/61 Co. H in Albemarle – excused by governor before mustered in - entry cancelled.
RICHARDS, DR. JOHN R.: entered service in 7th N,C. Infantry; appointed 2nd Lt. 7/29/61 in Co. H - appointed assistant surgeon 5/3/62.
RICHARDS, ROBERT: Co. D; 1st Lt; 9/61-10/61 roll showed promoted

to Commissary of Regt.

RICHARDSON, JOHN: enl. 7/26/61 Co. F in Louisa; Capt.; present 7/27/61-10/3/61; entered service as Capt. and elected Capt .5/3/62; present 9/63-12/63; furloughed 20 days 1/9/64 - had only one other furlough of indulgence in 2 years; furloughed 30 days 10/17/64 with chronic diarrhea and internal fever, admitted Richmond hosp. 11/21/64 - transferred Gordonsville; POW Sayler's Creek 4/6/65 - confined Old Capitol Prison and Johnson's Island - took oath and released 6/19/65 age 32; b.. 5/30/1833 Louisa; resident of Jackson, Louisa Co.; teacher and surveyor after war – excellent mathematician; dark complexion and hair, brown eyes; 6'6"; d. 6/16/1892 of heart and kidney infection near Orchid, Louisa Co.; widow Elizabeth McC. Richardson applied for pension 8/9/1902; m. 1861 Louisa - owned 2 shares of stock worth $100 each - $25 approved.

RICHARDSON, ROBERT P. (T.): enl. 8/19/61 age 17 Co. K in Richmond - substitute for Edmond Alexander – permission given by father Lt. William H. Richardson; present 9/61-10/61; POW Ft. Donelson - d. Camp Morton Prison Hosp. 3/31/62 of pneumonia; bur. Green Lawn Cem. - reinterred Crown Hill Cem.; death claim filed by father 11/24/62 - owed $80.

RICHARDSON, WILLIAM: enl. 7/26/61 Co. F in Louisa; present 7/27/61-10/31/61; admitted Charlottesville hosp. 8/26/62 with debility – sent Lynchburg hosp. 8/27/62; furloughed 2/1/63-2/16/63; present 9/63-12/63 and 4/1/64; on 5/64-6/64 roll reported as killed in battle since mustered for pay.

RICHARDSON, WILLIAM T.: enl. 8/6/161 Co. K in Mechanicsville; present 8/6/61-8/31/61; AWOL 9/61-10/61; absent detached service 7/63-12/63 and 4/1/64; 7/64-8/644 roll reported as AWOL - came in since last muster - dated 8/31/64; admitted Chimborazo 9/15/64 with intermittent fever - returned to duty 10/1/64; captured with wagon train near end of war but escaped; POW and paroled Richmond 4/24/65;
b. Hanover; laborer; applied for pension 4/25/1903 age 65 living Old Church, Hanover Co. - bad varicose veins and rheumatism-- described by his comrades as uneducated man, but faithful and true to Confederate army - $30 approved.

RIDDEL, RICHARD JONSON: enl. 7/26/61 Co. F in Louisa; present 7/27/61-10/31/61; on detached duty after 11/62 to tan leather for Confederacy in Louisa; b. Goochland; tanner; applied for pension 5/28/1922 age 84 living Louisa – no income or property - totally disabled by age - $130 approved.

RIDEOUT, DAVID T.: enl. 6/22/61 Co. B in Mecklenburg; present 9/61-10/61; in hosp. Russellville, Ky. 2/4/62; POW Ft. Donelson - sent from Camp Morton to Vicksburg for exchange – admitted Richmond hosp.

10/12/62; furloughed 30 days 10/24/62; furloughed 5/1/63-8/31/63; sick furlough 8/28/63-9/28/63; present 9/63-12/63, 4/1/64 and 5/64-8/64; WIA and POW Sayler's Creek 4/6/65 – in Union hosp. with gunshot wd. of right thigh - paroled Burkeville 4/14/65-4/17/65; applied for pension 5/17/1897 age 59 living Black's Ridge, Mecklenburg Co. – application disallowed – approved when amended 8/16/1897; member Armistead Camp UCV 1898.

RIGGINS, WILLIAM H.: enl. 7/8/61 Co. A in Mecklenburg; present 9/61-12/61; waggoner - 1862; detached for duty on Pickett's Supply Train in Chesterfield as waggoner 9/63-12/63, 5/64-8/64, and 9/64-12/64.

RIGNOR, J. H.: pwl; Co. G.

RIORDAN, LAFAYETTE W.: enl. 7/26/61 Co. F in Louisa; present 7/27/61-10/31/61; discharged 10/2/62 age 36 because served one year and over 35; farmer; light complexion, blue eyes, 5'6".

RIPLEY, JAMES M.: enl. 7/23/61 Co. D in Buckingham; present 7/8/61-10/31/61; MWIA Frazier's Farm - gunshot wd. of head - admitted Chimborazo 7/2/62 unconscious - d. 7/4/62 – death claim filed 2/24/63 by father - owed $45.46.

RIVES, EDWARD: pwl; Field and Staff; Surgeon.

ROACH, JAMES R.: enl. 10/1/61 Co. G at Camp of Instruction - substitute for Charles Bumley; present 9/61-10/61; discharged 11/24/61 age 27 - no reason given - had been listed as physically qualified for service 10/2/61; teacher; light hair and complexion. 5'8".

ROBERTS, A. S.: pwl; enl. 8/64 Co. A; from Orange Co.

ROBERTS, ELBERT H.: enl. 7/12/61 Co. G in Charlotte; present 7/26/61-10/31/61; d. 3/15/62 age 26 - death claim filed by father Joseph H. Roberts – owed $65; b. Charlotte; farmer; light hair and complexion, dark eyes, 5'11".

ROBERTS, GEORGE JOSEPH WILLIAM: enl. 7/l2/61 Co. G in Charlotte; present 7/26/61-10/31/631; WIA Ft. Donelson - discharged 5/13/62 age 21 due to gunshot wd. of right elbow joint resulting in anchylosis; farmer, light complexion and hair, blue eyes, 5'11"; b. 1840 Charlotte; applied for pension 6/7/1897 age 56 - arm paralyzed from wd. received Ft Donelson - $15 approved – paid $24 1909; d. 1912 Charlotte.

ROBERTS, GEORGE T.: pwl; Co. G - from Charlotte; d. 2/11/1896 of paralysis in Charlotte; widow Maria Roberts applied for pension 4/19/1900 - m. 11/17/1858 Mecklenburg - $25 approved.

ROBERTS, JAMES H.: enl. 10/3/61 Co. C; present 9/61-10/61; POW Ft. Donelson; AWOL 9/63-12/63.

ROBERTS, ROBERT: enl. 7/15/61 Co. H in Albemarle; excused by governor before mustered in - entry cancelled.

ROBERTSON, ARCHIBALD T.: Co. D; POW Hatcher's Run 4/2/65 - took oath and released from Pt. Lookout 6/17/65; resident of

Buckingham; fair complexion, grey hair and eyes, 5'10 3/4".
ROBERTSON, (ROBINSON) BENJAMIN F.: enl. 7/9/61 Co. C in Louisa; present 7/9/61-8/31/61; d. 10/19/61. (may be Benjamin Franklin Robertson ,Co. I)
ROBERTSON, BENJAMIN FRANKLIN: pwl; Co. I; b.. Campbell Co. 1846; bur. Evington Methodist Church, Rt. 24, Campbell Co.
ROBERTSON, EDWARD G.; enl. 7/12/61 Co. G in Mecklenburg; present 7/26/61-10/31/61 transferred to Capt. W. H. Jones's Va. Cav. 11/22/61.
ROBERTSON, ELISHA ZACHARIAH: enl. 7/8/61 Co. D in Buckingham; present 7/8/61-10/31/61; reenlisted 5/3/62; furloughed 1/12/63-2/1/63: present 9/63-12/63, 4/1/64, and 5/64-8/64; POW Burkeville 4/6/65 - took oath and released from Pt. Lookout 6/17/65; resident of Buckingham; dark complexion, brown hair, hazel eyes, 5'7 1/2"; applied for pension 5/21/1900 age 70 living in Oslin Mill, Buckingham Co.; struck by minie ball in right shoulder during war - $15 approved; made statement 8/11/1902 - owned property worth $55.
ROBERTSON, (ROBINSON) JOHN H. W.: enl. Co. A, 5th Batt. Va. Inf. - disbanded 5/62; enl. 2/9/63 Co. E in Brunswick; admitted Chimborazo 6/17/63 - furloughed 40 days 7/8/63; 9/63-10/63 sick In hosp.; 4/1/64 present; admitted Chimborazo 5/26/64 with chronic inflammation of stomach - furloughed 60 days 5/28/64; 5/64-8/64 absent sick; admitted Chimborazo 2/25/65 with dyspepsia - returned to duty 3/29/65; surrendered by Lee at Appomattox; b. 1833 to Bennett and Pamela S. Wilson Robinson; m. Ida V. Glidewell 8/26/1869 - 3 children; killed in Brunswick 12/14/1873.
ROBERTSON, REPS O.: Co. G; resident of Mecklenburg; received clothes 10/19/64; took amnesty oath in Richmond 5/10/65; b. 3/9/1831; d. 7/27/1903 - bur. Woodland Cem., Part 2, Mecklenburg - CSA marker.
ROBERTSON, WILLIAM J.: enl. 7/8/61 Co. D in Buckingham, Pvt./Cpl.; present 7/8/61-10/31/61; reenlisted 5/3/62; admitted Farmville hosp. 8/15/62 - deserted hosp. 11/6/62; POW Gettysburg - confined Ft Delaware and Pt. Lookout 10/26/63 - paroled and exchanged 2/18/65; paroled Farmville 4/11/65-4/21/65.
ROBEY, T. P.: Co. unknown; paroled Burkeville 4/14/65-4/17/65
ROBINS, REV. WILLIAM F.: Chaplain 56th Va. Inf.; present 1/28/65 in trenches near Howlett's House; present 1/30/65 in trenches near Bermuda Hundred; also on roll dated 1/30/65 as missionary in Barringer's Cav. Brigade in Belfield, Va.
ROBINSON, CALVIN (WILLIAM) A.: enl. 7/9/61 Co. C in Louisa; present 7/9/61-10/31/61; admitted Chimborazo 11/23/62 with debility - returned to duty 2/10/63; MWIA and POW Gettysburg - d. 7/4/63 of gunshot wd. in head in U.S. XII Corps Hosp. at George Bushman's house - bur. there as Calvin Robinson.

ROCK, SAMUEL J.: enl. 1/9/63 Goochland Light Art. in Fluvanna; absent sick 1/63-2/63; admitted Episcopal Church Hosp., Williamsburg with chronic diarrhea 6/17/63; returned to duty 6/30/63; present 9/63-10/63 - 1 month's pay deducted by sentence of Court Martial; admitted Chimborazo hosp. 12/10/63 with stricture - deserted hosp. 12/18/63; present 1/64-2/64; roll of 3/64-4/64 showed transferred to Co. B, 56th Va. in exchange for Robert W. Rainey; admitted Richmond hosp. 6/11/64 with acute dysentery; deserted hosp. 6/16/64; 5/64-8/64 listed as AWOL; paroled in Richmond 4/28/65.

ROSS, BEVERLY (BEVIL) GRANVILLE: enr. as conscript in Lawrenceville 3/14/64 - assigned to Co. E 3/21/64; present 4/1/64; 5/64-8/64 listed as AWOL since 6/16/64; paroled Burkeville 4/14/65-4/17/65; b. 9/3/1829 to Peter Wyche ("man of large wealth") and Elizabeth B. Green Ross; attended Randolph Macon College 1 or 2 years; farmer; m. Virginia Ann Goodrich 5/29/1852 - 2 children; after her death m. Violetta Clarke 8/1/1870 - 3 children; d. about 1910 - bur. on his farm east of Lawrenceville.

ROTHWELL, JAMES (JOSEPH) WARREN: enl. 5/3/62 Co. D; d. 8/6/63 of typhoid fever in Gordonsville - bur. Rothwell Family Cem., Crozet; b. 12/3/1830 near Crozet; death claim filed by widow Lucinda C. Rothwell - owed $145.10 - 4 children; widow applied for pension 6/4/1888 living Albemarle - m. 2/20/1855 near Wellington, Albemarle Co. - $30 approved.

RUDISILL, JACOB (JAKE) R.: enl. 7/1/61 Co. D in Buckingham. 2nd Lt./1st Lt.; elected 2nd Lt. 5/3/62 - resigned 12/25/62; elected 1st Lt. 7/6/64; WIA and POW Gettysburg - captured at stone wall - confined Ft. Delaware and Johnson's Island 7/18/63 - exchanged from Pt. Lookout 3/14/65; b. Nelson Co. 1836; applied for pension 2/4/1903 age 67 living Avon. Nelson Co.- farmer since 1896 - partially disabled due to age and hernia - $15 approved; d. by 9/1909.

RUSH, H. H.: Co. G; surrendered by Lee at Appomattox.

RUSSELL, WILLIAM: enl. 7/8/61 Co. A in Mecklenburg, 2nd Lt.; AWL 8/24/61-9/2/61; present 9/61-10/61; appointed 2nd Lt. 7/30/61 - dropped 5/5/62; had long spell of fever in Nashville, TN - could not endure infantry service; enr. as conscript 1/24/64 - assigned Goochland Art.; present 1/64-2/64 and bounty due; present 3/64-8/64; absent 12/15/64 - detailed for 10 days by Lt. Col. Pemberton to purchase hosp. supplies; spent most time in army in heavy artillery at Ft. Chaffin - in army at surrender; b. 3/11/1839 in Mecklenburg to Richard and Miranda Jeffries Russell; attended Hampden-Sydney 8 months before matriculated at VMI 1857 - attended VMI 18 months; farmer on large estate on Staunton River before and after war; m. Kate S. Hardy 5/ 1/1861 - 2 daughters and 3 sons; elder in Bluestone Presbyterian Church; member Armistead Camp, UCV 1896; d. 8/30/1914 age 76 in Jeffress, Mecklenburg Co. of

paralysis - bur. Bluestone Presbyterian Church graveyard, Mecklenburg.
RUTHERFORD, THOMAS J.: Co. F; received clothes 12/28/64; POW Hatcher's Run 3/31/65 - took oath and released from Pt. Lookout 6/17/65; resident of Goochland; dark complexion and hair; hazel eyes, 5'9 1/4".

Chapter 17

Roster, 56th Virginia Regiment, S thru Y

SADDLER, CHARLES: enl. 7/12/63 Co. G in Charlotte; present 9/26/61-8/31/61; discharged 9/4/61 age 18 due to physical disability; b. Halifax; dark complexion, hair, and eyes, 5'4 1/2"; farmer.

SADLER, CHARLES A.: enl. 7/10/61 Co. E in Brunswick, drummer, 7/16/61-8/31/61 sick furlough with measles; admitted Charlottesville hosp. 8/26/62 with debility; discharged 10/8/62 because over 35 and did not reenlist; dark complexion and hair; blue eyes, 5'10"; b. about 1823 to Henry and Elizabeth R. Sadler in Brunswick; overseer, plasterer and stone mason; m. Agnes C. Pritchett 1841 - 3 children; Agnes d. 1847; m. Rebecca L. Dugger 1848 - d. 1850's; after war moved to Halifax, N.C. – m. Nannie C. ? – 6 children; Methodist; son Willis, Co. F, 12th Va. KIA 5/12/64,

SADLER. JOHN F.: enl. 2/9/63 Co. E in Brunswick; present 9/63-12/63, 4/64-8/64; admitted Chimborazo 6/2/64 with gunshot wd. of hand - transferred Danville hosp, - furloughed 6/10/64; admitted Chimborazo 9/29/64 with concussion - returned to duty 10/17/64; still on duty as late as 2/65 - letter from Bevil G. Ross to his wife mentioned being on picket duty with John; b. about 1825 in Brunswick - brother of Charles A. Sadler; overseer before war; bonded to marry 12/18/1848 - 6 children; d. 8/2/1887 in Sturgeon District, Brunswick - bur. family cem., Hwy. 611.

SADLER, SAMUEL CARLETON (COLEMAN): enl. 7/10/61 Co. E in Brunswick; sick furlough 7/10/61-8/31/61; admitted Richmond hosp. 10/20/62 with nephritis - transferred to Petersburg hosp. 11/25/62; admitted Richmond hosp. 12/17/62; present 9/63-12/63; AWOL 4/1/64; absent sick 5/64-8/64; admitted Chimborazo 6/11/64 with chronic diarrhea - furloughed 60 days 7/26/64; b. 2/26/1833 in Brunswick - brother of Charles A. and John F. Sadler; planter before war; brick mason after war; m. Martha Frances Anderson (brother William D. Anderson KIA Gettysburg) 10/24/1852 in Northhampton, N. C. - 11 children; d. 8/'15/1890 of peritonitis in Brunswick - bur. family cem., Hwy. 611; widow applied for pension 9/20/1902 - $25 approved.

SANDERS, (SAUNDERS) THOMAS L.: enl. 2/9/63 Co. E in Brunswick; present 9/63-12/63, 4/1/64, and 5/64-8/64; admitted Richmond hosp. 9/12/63 - returned to duty 9/13/63; on register of rebel deserters who took oath at H.Q. Bermuda Hundred, Army of the James 2/8/65 – sent to City Point Va., Washington, D.C., and then Baltimore, Maryland.

SANDRIDGE, GEORGE W.: enl. 5/3/62 Co. H in Richmond, Cpl.; admitted Charlottesville hosp. 10/12/62 with debility - returned to duty 10/24/62; Co. reported as absent and supposed to be POW Gettysburg 7/12/63; believed KIA Gettysburg, but no Federal records concerning him.
SANDRIDGE, WILLIAM: (probably George W.) enl. 7/15/61 Co. H in Albemarle; present 7/29/61-10/31/61; d. 1863.
SARGENT, G. A.: pwl; Co. D.
SAUNDERS, ANDERSON H.: Co. E; Cpl.; resident of Louisa; paroled Louisa Court House 5/22/65; also shown as Co. E, 1st Va. Eng.
SAUNDERS, BEVERLY B.: enl. Co. A, 5th Va. Inf. Batt - disbanded 1862 and men over 35 discharged; enl. Co. E in 1863 or 64; received clothes 12/28/64; surrendered by Lee at Appomattox; b. 1822 to Turner and Lucy Vaughn Saunders; farmer, m. Mary Moore 1/8/1863 - no children; estate inventoried 1888 in Meherrin, District, Brunswick.
SAUNDERS, J. H.: enl. 5/6/62 Co. K in Richmond; AWOL 7/63-8/63. dropped from roll by order of Gen. Garnett.
SAUNDERS, JOHN T.: (probably TURNER): enl. 7/10/61 Co. E in Brunswick; present 7/10/61-8/31/61; POW Ft. Donelson - sent from Camp Morton to Vicksburg for exchange; POW and WIA Gettysburg - confined Ft. McHenry, Ft. Delaware, Pt. Lookout 10/27/63 - transferred to Hammond Gen. Hosp. 1/64 - d.1/3/64 of chronic diarrhea - bur. Pt. Lookout; b. about 1843 - probably Beverly B. Saunders's brother.
SAUNDERS, MATHEW W.: pwl; Co. F; applied for pension 9/16/1889 age 57 living Brooking's, Goochland Co. - shot in left shoulder at Hatcher's Run 4/1/65 - left arm stiff as result and could not raise or lower anything with it - pension denied at first - Col. B. O. James, Goochland representative in Virginia House of Delegates wrote letter 2/4/1892 saying Saunders should have pension because arm might as well have been lost - $15 approved.
SCOGGIN, FENTON T.: enl. 7/10/61 Co. E in Brunswick; sick in Richmond with measles 7/10/61-8/31/61; discharged 9/2/61 due to illness; d. 9/22/61 age 21 in Brunswick; death claim filed by father Manson Scoggin 1/30/1862 - owed $45.53; son of Manson and Jane Moore Scoggin.
SCOTT, THOMAS WATKINS.: enl. 7/12/61 Co. G in Charlotte; present 7/26/61; discharged 9/9/62 age 17 because under 18; b. Charlotte; tanner, light complexion and hair; b. 4/11/1844 son of Rev. William C. and Martha Martin Scott; m. Ruth Josephine Watkins 11/16/1865; joined Charlotte Defenders at 18 - nicknamed "captain"; wded. in service and carried scar through life; carne to Drake's Branch, Charlotte Co. about 1872 as merchant and built first warehouse; U.S. Marshal under Grover Cleveland; member Presbyterian Church; Commander H. A. Carrington Camp. UCV from its organization until his death - voted Commander

Emeritus for life after became invalid; attended reunion in Newport News 10/1911; badly injured in 1914 and invalid until death 7/10/1924 - bur. in Drake's Branch Presbyterian Church grave yard.

SCRUGGS, WILLIAM G.: enl. 7/8/61 Co. D in Buckingham; present 7/8/61-8/31/61; sick furlough 9/61-10/61; POW Ft Donelson - sent from Camp Morton to Vicksburg for exchange; admitted Richmond hosp. 10/19/62 - deserted hosp. 12/3/62; present 9/63-12/63 and 4/22/6]\4; AWOL 5/63-8/63; paroled Farmville 4/11/654-4/21/65.

SERGEANT, WILLIAM B.. enl. 7/8/61 Co. D. in Buckingham, Sgt; present 7/8/61-10/31/61; d. from exposure on retreat from Ft. Donelson; claim of deceased soldier filed 10/6/62.

SEYMOUR, OCTAVIOUS LITTLETON: pwl; Co. B, 56th Va. until 1864 in Co. D 44th Va. Inf. Batt; b. 3/12/1846 to John Hardaway and Theophane Rebecca Rose Seymour in Brunswick; farmer; 11/11/1876 "Brunswick Times Gazette" said of him, "has a splendid crop of tobacco. He is one of our most enterprising farmers and always raises good crops." m. Annie (Nannie) Susan McAden 11/16/1892 - 5 children; member Bethany Methodist Church – lay minister when no minister available; a founder and trustee of Broadnax Methodist Church – 1905; trustee of school board 1905-1910; d. 1912 of heart trouble - bur. Butterworth Family Cem. - body later moved to Oakwood Cem., South Hill.

SHACKLEFORD, R. F.: enl. 5/3/62 Co. H in Richmond; on rolls 7/63-12/63 listed as taken prisoner in Maryland and said to have taken the oath.

SHARP, C. A: pwl; enl. 1864 Co. A.

SHARP, JOSIAH F.: enl. 7/18/61 Co. I in Richmond; discharged 8/5/61 age 26 due to hernia; b. Prince Edward Co.; wheelwright, sallow complexion, sandy hair, grey eyes; 5'10".

SHELTON, R. L.: pwl; Co. B - entered army in Charlotte Reserves at Staunton River Bridge 1663 - transferred to Co. B, 56th Va.; POW 4/6/65 - paroled 6/65; b. Charlotte; farmer and barn builder; applied for pension 5/5/1900 age 52;. resident of Randolph, Charlotte Co. - had liver disease so could not work in summer - $15 approved; rerated 2/1/1909 age 66 - disabled due to cirrhosis of liver, dyspepsia, and age - $36 approved.

SHEPHERD, PETER: enl. 7/9/601 Co. C in Louisa; present 7/9/61-10/31/61; d. Lynchburg hosp. of erysipelas 6/7/62 - bur. Lynchburg Cem. Row 3, Grave 4 - claim of deceased soldier filed 3/4/63.

SHIFLETT, ADAM L.: enl. 7/29/61 Co. H in Albemarle; refused to report to his company until arrested - mustered in 10/1/61; on rolls of 7/63-12/63 and 5/64-8/64 listed as deserter.

SHIFLETT, ALBERT: enl. 7/15/61 Co. H in Albemarle; absent when company mustered and refused to report until arrested 9/14/61; rolls of 9/63-12/63 and 4/1/64 listed as deserter; Note : Telegraph No. 3309 received at Richmond 11/26/61 from Louisa Court House to Sec. of

War said 7 Shifletts belonging to Co. H and ordered to southwest Va. were discovered in Louisa 11/25/61 – 3 were captured, admitted they were deserters, and were in jail - others have escaped - signed "John Hunter."

SHIFLETT, DURRETT DAVIS: enl. 7/15/61 Co. H in Albemarle; present 7/29/61-10/31/61; rolls of 7/63-12/63 listed as deserter; b. 10/1837 Orange Co.

SHIFFLETT, GUSTIN: enl. 7/15/61 Co. H in Albemarle; present 7/29/61-10/31/61; on rolls of 7/63-1263, 4/1/64, and 5/64-8/64 listed as deserter.

SHIFLETT, JOHN: enl. 5/3/62 Co. H in Richmond; on rolls of 7/63-12/63, 4/1/64, and 5/64-8/64 listed as deserter.

SHIFLETT, LINEUS: enl. 7/5/61 Co. H in Albemarle; absent when mustered in and still absent 9/2/61 - entry cancelled.

SHIFLETT, MARSHAL: enl. 7/15/61 Co. H in Albemarle; absent when mustered in - refused to report until arrested 9/14/61; admitted Richmond hosp. 10/18/62 - returned to duty 10/22/62; on rolls of 7/63-12/63 and 7/64-8/64 listed *as* deserter - believed to have been shot by mistake.

SHIFFLETT, OVERTON: enl. 7/15/61 Co. H in Albemarle; present 6/29/61-8/31/61; on rolls of 7/63-12/63 listed as deserter.

SHIFLETT, SMITH: enl. 7/15/61 Co. H in Albemarle; present 7/29/61-8/31/61; on rolls of 7/63-12/63 listed as deserter.

SHIFLETT, WESLEY: enl 7/15/61 Co. H in Albemarle; present 7/29/61-10/31/61; d. 3/6/62 Gate City Hosp., Atlanta - bur. Oakland Cem., Atlanta, Row 5, Grave 1; claim of deceased soldier filed *11/22/62*

SHISLER, JOHN R.: enl. 7/9/61 Co. C in Louisa; present 7/9/61-8/3161; absent 9/61-10/61; discharged 10/8/61.

SHOEMAKER, JACOB: enr. as conscript 2/22/64; assigned 2/24/64 to Co. H at Chaffin's Farm; 4/1/64 in arrest; confined in E. D. M. prison and volunteered to defend Richmond in 1864 - pardoned by Jefferson Davis 8/3/64; admitted Richmond hosp. 5/11/64 with diarrhea; transferred to Castle Thunder 5/21/64; admitted Chimborazo 6/24/64; d. 7/25/64 of disease.

SHOEMAKER, NOAH: enr. as conscript 2/22/64 at Chaffin's Farm - assigned to Co. H 2/24/64; 4/1/64 in arrest; received clothes 5/14/64 at Castle Thunder, on list of those released and pardoned 8/3/64 from E. D. M. Prison to defend Richmond from Sheridan's Raid; absent sick 7/64-8/64; admitted Richmond hosp. 7/17/64 with continual fever - d. 7/27/64 - probably bur. Oakwood Cem..

SHORT, JOHN T.: enl. 7/10/61 Co. E in Brunswick; discharged 7/20/61 age 18 due to rheumatism that made hands almost completely useless; dark complexion, black hair and eyes, 5'11"; b. 1842 to William and Martha B. Harris Short in Brunswick - brother of Richard H. and William B. Short - sister Juliette m. Needham S. Cheely and sister Martha M. m. William A. Blick; overseer; never married; 1870 census he and widowed

sister living together and farming; 1880 census farm laborer.
SHORT, RICHARD HENRY: enl. 8/24/61 Co. E in Brunswick; present 7/10/61-8/31/61; MWIA Ft. Donelson - d. 2/18/62 - bur. at Ft. Donelson; b. 2/26/1837 Brunswick - brother of John T. and William B. Short.
SHORT, RICHARD OSCAR: enl. 7/1/61 Co. E in Brunswick; d. 3/8/63 in Petersburg hosp. of typhoid fever - bur. Blandford Cem., Petersburg; b. about 1834 Brunswick to Anderson W. and Amanda E. O. Harrison Short; m. Harriet Ann Duane 9/7/1854 - 5 children.
SHORT, WILLIAM BURCH ("SAMBO"): exempted from service 3/15/62 due to stomach disease; enr. as conscript 2/9/63 Co. E in Brunswlck; described as tallest man in Co. E; POW Gettysburg - confined Ft. McHenry and Ft. Delaware - transferred to Chester, Penn. Hosp. 8/10/63 - d. 9/6/63 of scorbutus - bur. Grave 184, Chester Cem. - reinterred Philadelphia Nat. Cem., C.S.A. Section; b. 1832 Brunswick - brother of John T. and Richard H. Short; descendant of signer of Declaration of Independence; m. Barbara (Babie) Short 12/10/1861 - daughter of Capt. Armistead Short - no children.
SIMMONS, SAMUEL S.: enl. 6/22/61 Co. B in Mecklenburg; present 9/61-10/61; POW Ft. Donelson - sent from Camp Morton to Vicksburg for exchange; furloughed 3/28/63-4/11/63; admitted Charlottesville hosp. 8/23/63 - returned to duty 9/14/63; present 9/63-12/63 - pay withheld 2 months because overdrawn at hosp.; present 4/1/64 and 5/64-8/64; POW Burkeville 4/6/65 - took oath and released from Pt. Lookout 6/20/65; b. 3/28/1840; resident of Mecklenburg; farmer and carpenter; dark complexion, black hair, blue eyes, 5'10 ¼"; member Armistead Camp No. 26, UCV; applied for pension 5/20/1904 age 65 living Stony Cross, Mecklenburg Co. - had small pox and typhoid fever during war - $15 approved; d. 4/6/1915 of heart disease Mecklenburg - bur. family cem., Rt. 678, Mecklenburg; widow Virginia Simmons applied for pension 5/18/1915 – m. .2/18/1868 Mecklenburg; $30 approved.
SIMMONS, WILLIAM: enl 7/22/61 Co. B in Mecklenburg; present 9/61-10/61; WIA Gaines's Mill - admitted Richmond hosp. 6/28/62 - returned to duty 10/1/62; admitted Chimborazo 5/8/63 with rheumatism - transferred Blacks and Whites hosp.; present 9/63-12/63; detailed to Chaffin's Farm hosp. as cook 2/8/64; admitted Chimborazo 6/19/64 with wd. of rt. hip - furloughed 30 days 6/19/64; present 7/64-8/64; deserted to Union and took oath 1/29/65 - sent to Bermuda Hundred, Baltimore, and Pittsburg, Penn. 2/4/65.
SIMPSON, F.: enl. 4/25/? Co. K in Richmond; AWOL 7/63-8/63 - dropped from rolls by Gen. Garnett's order.
SIMS, JAMES B.: enl. 7/25/61 Co. F in Louisa; present 9/63-12/63; d. 12/5/63.
SIMS, MERRIWETTIER B.: enl. 7/9/61 Co. C in Louisa; present 7/9/61-

8/31/61; on 9/63-10/63 roll as deserted 3/62 at Abingdon; present 5/64-8/64; deserted to Union and took oath 2/3/65 - sent to Portsmouth, Washington, D.C., and Philadelphia.
SINGLETON, WILLIAM L.: enl. 4/20/64 Co. B in Richmond; present 5/64-8/64; received clothes 10/13/64, 10/14/64, and 10/19/64.
SLATE, GILES B.: enl. 7/10/61 Co. E in Brunswick; present 7/10/61-8/31/61; POW Ft. Donelson - d. 3/6/62 or 5/4/62 in Camp Morton Prison Hosp. of typhoid fever - bur. Green Lawn Cem. - reinterred Crown Hill Cem.; death claim filed by his daughter and only surviving heir Emily Jane Slate 7/31/63 -owed $92.46; b. about 1837 to William and Julia Slate; m. Virginia A. Lewis 3/17/1858; 1860 census - laborer.
SLATE, THOMAS F.: enl. 7/10/61 Co. E in Brunswick; present 7/10/61-8/31/61; d. 9/21/62 in Culpeper of typhoid fever - death claim filed 3/12/63 by mother Julia Slate – owed $205; personal letter to Julia Slate dated 9/24/62 informing her of her son's death from typhoid fever near Plain's - papers show he had been in hosp. and discharged as fit for duty - when Gen. Jackson's command came through about a month before Thomas's death, he, "sick and weary" turned to nearby house, and the family took him in and nursed him; b. about 1837 - probably brother of Gilles B. and William Pryor Slate; 1860 census, laborer for farmer in Brunswick.
SLATE, WILLIAM PRYOR:: enl. 7/10/61 Co. E in Brunswick; present 7/10/61-8/31/61; discharged 6/4/62, but reenl; POW Farmville 4/6/65 - took oath and released from Pt. Lookout 6/20/65; florid complexion, light brown hair, grey eyes, 6'1"; b. about 1830 Brunswick - brother of Giles and Thomas F. Slate; m. Martha R. Lilley 1854; m. Louisa Lewis 2/10/64; 7 children; shoemaker and farmer; moved to Nottoway Co.; d. Nottoway 12/23/1894; widow applied for pension 1900.
SLAUGHTER, PHILIP PEYTON: entered service 4/61 as volunteer with Montpelier Guards; Lt.; went to Harper's Ferry 5/61; commissioned Capt. and Major by Gov. Lecher and ordered to defenses of Gloucester Point - before left for his post promoted Lt. Col. 56th Va.; served with Floyd in W.Va.; morning reports of 1/12/62, 1/13/62, and 1/17/62 showed him commanding regiment in Bowling Green, Kentucky; elected Lt. Col. of 56th 5/3/62; WIA Gaines'e Mill - field glasses driven into his groin when shot in hip by shrapnel shell; 8/1/63 in Richmond on detached service with the Commission for the Exchange of Prisoners - learned Col. Stuart had died and wrote he would return to the field immediately if his absence interferred with promotion - health was rapidly improving; appointed Col. of 56th 8/5/63; applied for retirement 5/20/64 due to wd. received Gaines's Mill - on register of Invalid Corps and assigned to Gen. Kemper 5/17/64; on staff duty of War Dept. in Richmond until Richmond evacuated; paroled 3/65 Scottsville; b. Madison Mills, Orange Co. 8/10/1834 to Dr. Thomas Towles

and Jane Madison Chapman Slaughter; matriculated VMI 9/1/1853. graduated 8th in class of 23 7/4/1857 - 1st Captain of Cadet Corps 185.-1857; Associate Professor of Latin and Assistant Instructor of Tactics 1857-1858 VMI; private tutor for family of William Fort in Baton Rouge, La.; m. Emma Thompson 1/10/1871 Orange Court House - one daughter Elizabeth Pendleton; railroad agent of Va. Midland Railroad in Orange 1866-1891; applied for pension 12/23/1889 age 55 in Orange Co.; right leg useless without crutch and in constant pain - leg shortened - totally disabled for manual labor; admitted Lee Camp Soldiers' Home 5/26/1892 age 58 for general debility, d. 4/21/1893 - bur. Orange., Va.

SMITH, ACHILLES J.: enl. 7/8/61 Co. A in Mecklenburg; admitted Charlottesville hosp. 8/26/62 with debility; admitted Richmond hosp. 12/11/62 - furloughed 30 days 2/19/63; absent sick 9/63-12/63 and 5/64-8/64; on pay register for discharged soldiers 5/15/64 age 35;
 b. Mecklenburg; farmer, dark complexion and hair, gray eyes, 5'10".

SMITH, ALBERT A.: enl. 7/9/61 Co. C in Louisa; sick furlough 7/9/61-8/31/61; present 9/61-10/61.

SMITH, DR. AUDUBON CUSTIS: enl. 7/63 Co. C in Louisa; WIA and POW Gettysburg – given water and carried off field to field hosp. by Union soldier Albert N. Hamilton - sent to West's Buildings Hosp. - paroled and exchanged 9/23/63; admitted Chimborazo 9/24/63 with gun shot wd of both shoulders, 10/7/63 furloughed 40 days; dentist; member Methodist Church; attended 50th Gettysburg reunion; 7/12/1913; d. 6/7/1915 age 72 "Mt. View" Gordonsville of paralysis - survived by wife and 2 daughters - bur. Maplewood Cem. Gordonsville; widow Mrs. Isaac Garrison (remarried 1920) applied for pension 3/12/1937 living Orange Co. - m. Smith 2/26/1891 Cove College - $100 approved.

SMITH, BENJAMIN J.: enl. 6/29/61 Co. B in Mecklenburg, Pvt./Sgt.; present 9/61-10/61; admitted Richmond hosp. 9/27/62 with chronic diarrhea; admitted Richmond hosp. 2/17/83 with gunshot wd. of shoulder and hepatitis - transferred to Danville hosp. 3/12/63 age 30 - returned to duty 5/18/63; present 4/1/64 and 5/64-6/64; letter from his wife to Jefferson Davis asking that he let Ben come home and work so they could give to the needy - said that Ben was only physically with the company since he could not use gun because of shoulder wd. - at home he could raise beef and pork and would give 400 pounds of each to the government and would sell any left to soldiers' families at government price, n. d.; detached for agricultural purposes until able for field service by Sec. of War 8/10/64; living 1905; member Armistead Camp No. 26, UCV.

SMITH, C. P.: Co. C; POW Petersburg hosp. 4/3/65 - transferred Gen. Hosp, 4/25/65.

SMITH, EDWARD.: enl. 6/23/62 Co. A in Richmond - substitute; listed as deserter on rolls 9/63-12/63.

SMITH, EDWARD A.: enl. 7/8/61 Co. A in Mecklenburg, Pvt./Cpl.; d. 3/4/62 - death claim filed by widow Elizabeth F. Smith 12/24/62; owed $78.73.

SMITH, E. T. (H.): enl. 7/18/61 Co. I in Charlotte; present 7/18/61-10/31/61; at Ft. Donelson; d.4/5/62 age 27 in Atlanta, Ga.- claim filed by wife Ann Smith - owed $67.36; resident of Charlotte; farmer; dark complexion and hair, black eyes, 5'8".

SMITH, GEORGE W.: enl. 7/9/61 Co. C in Louisa, Cpl./Sgt.; admitted Chimborazo 11/21/61 - returned to duty *12/17/62;* present 9/63-12/63 and 5/64-8/64; admitted Richmond hosp. *4/4/64* - furloughed 30 days 4/5/64; admitted Richmond hosp. 12/27/64 - furloughed 48 hours 12/28/64; paroled Beaverdam 5/7/65; watchmaker & musician; d. age 90 Bells Cross Roads, Louisa Co.

SMITH, JAMES: enl. 7/15/681 Co. H in Albemarle; present 7/29/61-10/31/61; POW sent from New York to Aiken's Landing for exchange 10/6/62; admitted Richmond hosp. 10/11/62 - sent to Camp Lee 10/17/62; Manuscript 1528 entitled "deserter" - dated 10/25/62 on rolls 7/63-12/63, 4/1/64, and 5/64-8/64 listed as AWOL or deserter.

SMITH, JAMES A. J.: enl. 6/22/61 Co. B in Mecklenburg, Sgt.; discharged 9/9/62 age 36, over 35 & served 1 year; b. Mecklenburg; farmer; dark complexion, black hair, hazel eyes; 5'8".

SMTH, JAMES C.: enl. 7/9/61 Co. C in Louisa; sick furlough 7/9/61-8/31/61; present 9/61-10/61; AWOL 9/63-12/63.

SMITH,JAMES H.: pwl; Co. C.; Sgt.

SMITH, JAMES L.: enl. 7/18/61 Co. I in Charlotte; sick furlough beyond time 7/18/61-8/31/61; present 9/61-10/61; wded.. 2nd Manassas; discharged 3/7/63 age 28 due to anchylosis of elbow joint from gunshot wd. in left arm; b. Charlotte; farmer; fair complexion, dark hair, grey eyes, 5'8".

SMITH, JOEL: pwl; Co. I.

SMITH, JOHN: Co. D; paroled 5/15/65 Louisa.

SMITH, JOHN A.: enl. 7/8/61 Co. A in Mecklenburg; 7/8/61-8/3/61 on guard duty; present 9/61-10/61; admitted Danville hosp. 7/30/62 with debilitas - returned to duty 8/20/62.

SMITH, JOHN M.: enl. 7/18/61 Co. I in Charlotte; 7/18/61-8/31/61 sick furlough beyond time; present 9/61-10/61; b. Campbell Co:, farmer; dark eyes and hair, fair complexion, 5'8"; d. 3/28/62 in Chattanooga, TN - death claim filed by widow Mary E. Smith 9/5/62 - owed $79.26.

SMITH, JOHN O.: enl. 7/9/61 Co. C in Louisa, Cpl.; present 9/61-12/61; admitted Richmond hosp. 7/29/62 - transferred to Danville; present 5/64-8/64; received clothes 9/27/64, 10/13/64, 12/28/64; paroled Louisa 5/15/65; miner and farmer; applied for pension 4/17/1907 age 80 living Louisa - totally disabled due to age and hernia - $36 approved; attended 1898 reunion in Philadelphia; d. 9/25/1912 in Mineral of paralysis - $25 funeral expenses paid 11/13/1916 under Pension Act 1902; widow Mattie A. Smith applied for pension 5/10/1924 - m. 7/21/1881 Louisa - $80 approved.

SMITH, JOHN P.: enl. 6/64 Co. C. at Cold Harbor; admitted Richmond hosp. 1/19/65; furloughed 15 days 1/20/65; returned to duty 2/6/65; WIA and POW Hatcher's Run 4/1/65 age 20 - admitted Petersburg hosp. 4/1/65 with fracture of left arm by conoidal ball -arm amputated at shoulder joint - transferred Pt of Rocks hosp. 5/8/65 - then confined Ft. Monroe and Newport News - took oath and released 6/16/65; resident of Augusta Co.; fair complexion, dark hair, blue eyes, 5'8".

SMITH, JOSEPH HENRY: enl. 7/9/61 Co. C in Louisa, Sgt./2nd Lt; present 7/9/61-10/31/61; elected 2nd Lt. 5/3/62; KIA Gettysburg; b. 3/30/1842.

SMITH, LARKIN: pwl; Field and Staff - Quartermaster.

SMITH, LEONIDAS CLAIBOURNE: enl. 7/9/61 Co. C in Louisa, Sgt; present 9/63-12/63 and 5/64-8/64; furloughed 2/6/63-2/26/63; paid for reconnoitering service 11/1/63-12/31/63 and 6/30/64-12/31/64; also in 24th Va. Cav.; b, 12/17/1843 Louisa; joined Caroline Co. vets group 1903; d. 4/19/1924 Caroline Co.

SMITH, MILES B.: enl. 7/9/61 Co. C in Louisa, Pvt./Sgt; present 7/9/61-10/31/61; WIA Gettysburg - admitted Richmond hosp. 7/12/63 with gunshot wd. - returned to duty 9/7/63; admitted Richmond hosp, 4/1/64 – 9/22/64 with chronic diarrhea; readmitted hosp. 10/6/64 with tonsillitis - returned to duty 11/31/64; paroled Ashland 5/2/65; harness maker and miner, applied for pension 4/21/1900 age 66 living Cuckoo, Louisa Co.- disability due to hernia – S15 approved; made statement 5/12/1902 - $100 property - tumor on leg and fistula on arm; rerated 6/4/1910 age 75 living Mineral, Louisa Co. - annual income $100 as miner - $70 personal property - $24 approved.

SMITH, ROBERT J.: enl. 7/8/61 Co. A in Mecklenburg; guard duty 7/8/61-8/31/61; present 9/61-10/61; applied for pension 4/24/1900 age 81 living Chase City, Mecklenburg Co. - totally disabled due to age and weakness - $30 approved; made pension statement 5/6/1902 age 83.

SMITH, ROBERT S.: enl. 7/9/61 Co. C. in Louisa, Pvt./2nd Lt. present on all rolls; WIA Gaines's Mill; elected 2nd Lt. 5/21/64; absent on 15 day furlough from trenches near Clay's House 11/25/64; POW Hatcher's Run 3/31/65 - sent to Johnson's Island 4/9/65 from Old Capitol Prison - took oath and released 6/17/65 age 25; b. Louisa; farmer; dark complexion and hair. blue eyes, 5'11"; applied for pension 3/21/1908 age 69 living near Oakland, Louisa Co. - rheumatism from exposure during war and kidney trouble - $36 approved.

SMITH, SAMUEL J.: enl. 7/9/61 Co. C in Louisa; present 7/9/61-10/31/61; discharged 5/13/62 age 22 due to heart disease; b. Louisa; farmer; fair complexion, brown hair, light hazel eyes, 6'1".

SMITH, THOMAS B. (S.): enl. 7/18/61 Co. I in Charlotte, Sgt./Pvt.; present 7/18/61-1031/61; sick in Atlanta 1862; WIA and POW Gettysburg - sent Gettysburg hosp. and Hammond Gen. Hosp. with gunshot wd. in ankle - paroled and exchanged from Pt. Lookout 4/27/64; admitted Chimborazo 5/1/64 with deblilitas - furloughed 30 days 5/8/64; shown as Pvt. on rolls beginning 7/63-8/63.

SMITH, TIMOLEON: organized Capt. Timoleon Smith's Va. Volunteers 6/3/61; enl. 7/9/61 Co. C in Louisa; Capt./Lt. Col.; appointed Capt. 7/9/61 and elected Capt. 53/62; WIA Gaines's Mill and Frazier's Farm; commissioned Major 7/31/63; paroled Louisa *5/22/65;* during war sent to Pennsylvania on secret mission, got information, and returned safely; b. Louisa; d. Louisa 4/30/1905 with hernia - bur. Smith Farm, Rt. 33, Louisa Co.; widow Bettie V. Terrell Smith applied for pension 4/8/1914; m. 1867 Orange Co.

SMITH, WLLIAM G.: enl. 7/18/61 Co. I in Charlotte; present 7/18/61-10/31/61*;* discharged 9/8/62 age 39 because over 35; carpenter; dark complexion and hair, blue eyes; pension application 5/5/1900 age 77 living Abell, Charlotte Co. - totally disabled because hands paralyzed - $30 approved - made statement 5/12/1902 age 80.

SMITH, WILLIAM J. O.: enl. 7/9/61 Co. C in Louisa. (may be John O. Smith)

SMITH, WILLIAM LEE: enl. 6/15/61 Co. I in Charlotte; 7/18/61-8/31/61; sick furlough beyond time; present 9/61-10/61; sick in Atlanta after Ft. Donelson; reenlisted 5/62; WIA and POW 6/28/62 Frazier's Farm - on roll of POWS on board Steamer *Coatzacoalos* - confined Ft. Columbus and Ft Delaware 7/9/62 age 27- exchanged Aiken's Landing 8/5/62; KIA Gettysburg - death claim filed by widow Sarah K. Smith 2/25/65- owed $74.64 - 3 children; b. Campbell Co.; light complexion and eyes, dark hair; 5'8".

SMITHEE, JOSEPH J.: enl. 8/6/61 Co. K in Mechanicsville; furloughed 8/6/61-8/31/61; present 9/61-10/61; AWOL since 10/24/61; POW Ft. Donelson - sent from Camp Morton to Vicksburg for exchange; furloughed 10/21/62-11/24/62*;* POW Gettysburg - confined Ft. Delaware and Pt. Lookout 10/26/63 - took oath and released 2/18/65.

SMITHSON, EDWARD S.: Co. A; served 1 year; from Charlotte; admitted Richmond hosp. 3/25/65; captured Richmond hosp. 4/3/65 - confined Jackson Hosp., Libby Prison, and Newport News - d. of chronic diarrhea 6/13/65 U.S. Prison hosp. and Newport News; bur. grave 109 Greenlawn Cem., Newport News; widow Isabella C. Smithson applied for pension – m. 10/18/1848 Charlotte; $30 approved.

SMITHSON, PERCY: enr. as conscript 4/23/64 in Mecklenburg - assigned to Co. A. 4/25/64; admitted Chimborazo with fever 6/12/64 - returned to

duty 6/20/64; KIA in skirmish 8/25/64.
SMYTH, ROBERT G.: pwl; Co. unknown; d. Henrico Co. 11/30/1910. (may be Robert S. Smith)
SNEAD, CHARLES: pwl; Co. G.
SNEAD, GEORGE H.: enr. as conscript 3/7/64 - assigned to Co. G 3/16/64; present 4/1/64; transferred to Lunenburg Artillery 4/19/64.
SNEAD, JOSEPH (JAMES): pwl; Co, G.
SNEAD, PARKES E. (PARKIE): enl. 4/4/64 Co. H at Chaffin's Farm age 19; present 4/1/64 and 5/64-8/64; WIA Hatcher's Run - admitted Farmville hosp. 4/8/65 with gunshot wd. of left hand, second finger - finger amputated; paroled Farmville 4/11/65-4/21/65; b. Albemarle; applied for pension 2/28/1898 age 56 living Stuarts Draft, Augusta Co. - partial disability due to loss of finger -pension disallowed - no loss of limb; lived in Waynesboro prior to entering Lee Camp Soldiers' Home 6/24/1908 age 63 due to rheumatism - discharged at own request 8/22/1920 - readmitted 11/11/1920 - discharged at own request 8/8/1922; readmitted 10/10/1925; discharged at own request 2/26/1929.
SNEAL, JOHN Q.: Co. G.; paroled 4/26/65 Headquarters 1st Division, 6th Army Corps.
SNEED, JOHN: enl. 7/8/61 Co. A in Mecklenburg - rejected as too young - name cancelled.
SNELSON, WILLIAM G.: enl. 7/26/61 Co. F in Louisa; measles 7/27/61-8/31/61; present 9/61-10/61; d. Abingdon 4/10/62 of fever - death claim filed 7/24/62 - owed $73.66.
SNYDER, DANIEL W.: enl. 7/26/61 Co. F in Louisa - substitute for J. W. Mallory; present 9/61-10/61; signed name receiving quartermasters property 4/9/62 and 4/14/62 in Abingdon.
SPAIN, SAMUEL: Co. I; POW Farmville 4/6/65 - took oath and released 6/20/65; resident of Charlotte; fair complexion, grey hair, blue eyes; 5'11".
SPAIN, THOMAS C.: Co. I; Pvt./Cpl.; POW Burkeville 4/6/65 - took oath and released from Pt. Lookout 6/20/65; resident of Charlotte; fair complexion, brown hair, blue eyes, 5'10".
SPAULDING, SAMUEL C. (EDWARD): Co. G; POW Burkeville 4/6/65 - took oath and released 6/20/65; resident of Charlotte; dark complexion, dark brown hair, blue eyes, 5'9"; b. 9/6/1830 or 9/20/1832; d. 4/16/1900 - bur. Wyllesburg Baptist Church, Rt. 15, Charlotte Co.
SPENCER, H. L.: enl. 4/20/64 Co. K at Chaffin's Farm; admitted Richmond hosp. 6/1/64 with gunshot wd. of right wrist - furloughed 60 days 6/20/64; admitted Richmond hosp. 2/24/65 with pnuemonia - returned to duty 3/6/65; readmitted 3/19/65 with pneumonia - transferred to Farmville hosp.; paroled Farmville 4/11/65-4/19/65.
SPENCER, J. J.: enr. as conscript 2/20/64 - assigned to 56th 2/22/64 - no

Co. given; (may be John A. Spencer).
SPENCER, JAMES W.: enl. 7/8/61 Co. D in Buckingham, Pvt./Cpl;. present 7/8/61-10/31/61; KIA Gettysburg.
SPENCER, JOHN A.: enr. as conscript 2/16/64 Camp Lee - assigned Co. G. Chaffin's Farm 2/23/64; on register of Medical Director's office, Richmond - recommended to hospital for treatment of skin problem left leg of 8 years duration.
SPENCER, W. G.: pwl; Co. I.
SPENCER, WILLIAM J.: enl. 7/8/61 Co. D in Buckingharn; present 9/61-10/61; reenlisted 5/3/62 Fulton Hill - paid $50 bounty; admitted Farmville hosp. 8/5/62 - deserted hosp. 11/6/62; on detached duty for most of 1863 and 1864 as teamster for Pickett's Supply Train, Chesterfield Co.; paroled Charlottesville 5/19/65.
SPICER, DAVID J: enl. 7/26/61 Co. F in Louisa; present 7/27/61-10/31/61; on all rolls shown as missing since Ft. Donelson; d. 3/1/62; . death claim filed by father Rice H. Spicer - due $123.33.
SPICER, JAMES H.: enr. 2/16/64 as conscript at Camp Lee - assigned Co. C. 2//23/64; paroled Ashland 5/2/65; resident of Louisa; farmer;
SPICER, WILLIAM H.: Co. F; received clothing 12/28/64 in Louisa; paroled 5/8/65 Columbia; member Hill Camp, CV - No. 6.
SPROUSE, DYER M.: enl. 7/15/61 Co. H in Albemarle; present 9/61-10/61; d. 7/15/62 of chronic diarrhea contracted in service - d. at home in Albemarle on sick leave; widow Dicey Ann Sprouse applied for pension 5/7/1888. m. 7/17/1854 Albemarle -$30 approved.
ST. JOHN, ALEXANDER A.: enl. 9/3/62 Co. I Charlotte; MWIA and POW Gettysburg - d. 7/26/63 of shoulder wd. in U. S. 1st Division, I Corps Hosp., Gettysburg.
ST. JOHN, MATT T.: enl. 10/1/64 Co. I at Camp Lee; admitted Chimborazo 11/20/64 with chronic diarrhea; 1/31/65 ordered to report to Surgeon McCaw at Chimborazo for detail - unfit for field service; retired 2/6/65 due to chronic diarrhea.
ST. JOHN, ROBERT C.: Co. I; POW High Bridge 4/6/65 - took oath and released from Pt. Lookout 6/20/65; resident of Charlotte; fair complexion, brown hair, hazel eyes, 5'71/4".
STAINBACK, GEORGE WASHINGTON: enl. 7/10/61 Co. E in Brunswick; present 7/10/61-8/31/61; admitted Richmond hosp. 10/15/62 - returned to duty 10/22/62; received clothes in Richmond hosp. 7/21/63; present 9/63-12/63, 4/1/64, and 5/64-6/64; KIA 9/29/64 Chaffin's Farm; son of Robert Alexander, Sr. and Lucy Bass Stainback.
STAINBACK, JOHN MASON: enl. 7/10/61 Co. E in Brunswick, Cpl: present 7/10/61-8/31/61; discharged 12/1/62; b. about 1846 to John G. and Indianna J. C. Mason Stainback in Brunswick; 1870 census described as invalid; d. 8/6/1875 of typhoid fever.

STAINBACK, JOHN MOORE: pwl; enl. Co. E; b. 1840 to Peter and Ann Eliza Moore Stainback; studied medicine after war,
rn. Izora Gouldman 1869 - 4 children; 1880 living in Baltimore, Md. on Lexington St. with wife's family.

STAINBACK, ROBERT ALEXANDER: enl. 7/10/61 Co. E in Brunswick; Pvt./2nd Lt./Capt.; present 7/10/610-8/31/61, 9/63-12/63, 5/64-8/64; POW Ft. Donelson; sent from Camp Morton to Vicksburg for exchange; admitted Charlottesville hosp. 6/15/63; returned to duty 6/19/63; elected Lt. 12/31/63; became Capt. Co. E after Capt. Fraser POW Gettysburg; signed roll as commanding Co. 1/24/64; POW Sayler's Creek 4/6/65 age 22 – confined Johnson's Island 4/17/65 - released and took oath 6/20/65; florid complexion, dark hair, hazel eyes. 5'5"; b. about 1843 in Brunswick - brother of John Moore Stainback; attended Randolph Macon; moved to Clarke Co., Miss. after war, m. Belle West - several children; still living In 1880.

STAINBACK, ROBERT ALEXANDER, JR.: enl. 7/10/61 Co. E in Brunswick; present 7/10/61-8/31/61; POW Ft. Donelson - confined Camp Morton - d. 4/25/62 age 24 of typhoid fever at Indianapolis - bur. Green Lawn Cem. - reinterred Crown Hill - death claim filed by father Robert A. Stainback, Sr. 3/12/63; b. 2/29/1837 Brunswick - brother of George Washington Stainback.

STANLEY, GEORGE M.: enl. 2/17/63 Co. B in Richmond; present on all rolls; admitted Richmond hosp. 10/15/62 with rheumatism - returned to duty 10/22/62; admitted Richmond hosp. 5/16/63 with debility- furloughed 50 days 6/20/63; readmitted 7/14/63 and 9/8/63 with intermittent fever; POW Burkeville 4/6/65 - took oath and released from Pt. Lookout 6/19/65; resident of Brunswick; dark complexion, dark brown hair, blue eyes, 5'31/2".

STARKE, HORACE C.: enl. 3/15/62 Co. B in Richmond; admitted Chimborazo 7/4/62 with typhoid fever - furloughed 60 days 8/25/62; d. 9/1/62 of typhoid fever - death claim filed by mother Matilda Starke - due $105.89.

STARKE, JOHN: enl. 10/26/61 Co. C.

STEEL, ADISON PETER: enl. 7/18/61 Co. I in Charlotte; WIA Ft. Donelson; present on all rolls; Court Martial 2/23/63 AWOL - guilty of specification and charge - forfeited 2 months pay and had to cut wood and bring water for Co. and Regt. until 4/1/63; WIA and POW Gettysburg - confined Ft. Delaware and Pt. Lookout - exchanged 2/18/65; on list of those not present with command, but surrendered by Lee at Appomattox.

STEEL, JOHN D.: enl. 7/12/61 Co. G in Charlotte; present 7/26/61-8/31/61; discharged 9/27/61 age 38 due to heart disease; farmer; dark complexion, eyes, and hair.

STEEL, (STELL) R. R.: pwl; Co. I; WIA Ft. Donelson and Gettysburg.

STEGAR, C. E.: pwl; Co. D. (may be Charles E. Steger)
STEGER, (STEGAR) CHARLES E. (R.): enl. 7/8/61 Co. D in Buckingham; Pvt./Cpl.; present 7/8/61-10/31/61; WIA Gaines's Mill; reenlisted 5/3/62; POW Gettysburg - paroled from Ft. Delaware 8/1/63; admitted Scottsville hosp. 8/30/63; present 9/63-12/63, 4/1/64, and 5/64-8/64; b. Buckingham; farmer; applied for pension 4/21/1908 age 68 living Tucker, Buckingham Co. - had pneumonia and fever during war - left service at Amelia Court House just before surrender - totally disabled due to infirmities of age - $36 approved - signed pension application of Thomas Patteson's widow 1924.
STEGER, JOHN W.: enl 7/18/61 Co. D in Buckingham; present 7/8/61-8/31/61; 10 day sick furlough on roll 9/61-10/61; WIA Gaines's Mill - right leg amputated at thigh 6/27/62 - in association for relief of maimed soldiers; b. Buckingham; discharged 8/13/62 age 24 due to loss of leg; dark complexion and hair, blue eyes; farmer; applied for artificial leg 9/27/64; applied for pension 4/9/1888 age 49 – resident Beesville, Buckingham Co. - $30 approved; living 1909 - paid pension of $85.
STERNBRIDGE, SILAS W.: enl. 7/8/61 Co. A in Mecklenburg; 7/8/61-8/31/61 sick with measles; present 9/61-10/61.
STINSON, DAVID W.: enl. 7/8/61 Co. D in Buckingham, Pvt./Lt.; present 7/8/61-10/31/61; admitted Richmond hosp. 7/23/62; furloughed 8/25/62; reenlisted 8/11/62; admitted Scottsville hosp. 3/6/63 with typhoid fever - there until 9/63; present 9/63-12/63, 4/1/64 and 5/64-8/64; appointed 1st Sgt. 5/20/64; paroled Farmville 4/11/65-4/21/65; applied for pension 6/15/1904 age 62 living in Dianna Mills, Buckingham Co. - could do no manual labor because left leg disabled by explosion of shell while in army; b. Buckingham; farmer - school trustee beginning 1902; $36 annual salary; served in army 3 years 9 months - left service 4/7/65 between Burkeville and Farmville - $15 approved; d. 5/11/1914 of heart disease; widow Mary Lee Stinson applied for pension 12/1/1934 - m. 11/14/1901.
STINSON, WILLIAM A.: enl. 7/8/61 Co. D in Buckingham; Sgt.; present 7/8/61-8/31/61; d. 9/25/61 of typhoid fever - death claim filed by mother Jane R. Stinson; owed $69.77.
STITH, LITTLETON EZRA: enl. 3/1/62 in Coleman's Art.; discharged 12/28/62 with kidney disease; enr. as conscript Co. E 2/9/63 in Brunswick; admitted Farmville hosp. 3/27/63 with urinary calculus; furloughed 15 days 5/9/63; deserted hosp. 6/5/63; absent sick 9/63-10/63; AWOL 11/63-12/63; discharged 4/20/63 age 36 due to kidney disease; farmer before war, light complexion, dark hair, hazel eyes, 5'8"; b. 1829 son of Obadiah and Mary Hunnicutt Stith in Brunswick; m. Mary Jane Hawthorne 7/9/1856 in Lunenburg -11 children - she d. *8/26/1875; m.* Sallie L Hawthorne (Mary's sister) 4/25/1877 - 3 children; appointed county surveyor 1875; died 5/22/1886 age 57 of consumption.

STRONG, NATHANIEL H.: enl. 7/26/61 Co. F in Louisa; 7/27/61-8/31/61 in hosp. with measles; present 9/61-10/61, 9/63-12/63, and 4/1/64; sick 5/64-6/64; present 7/64-8/64; admitted Chimborazo 8/27/64 with diarrhea; furloughed 40 days 9/13/64 to Louisa; paroled Ashland 4/25/65; applied for pension 4/28/1900 age 61 living Frederick Hall, Louisa Co. - partially disabled - $15 approved - made statement 6/9/1902 - $30 real and personal property.

STUART (STEWARD) MICHAEL: enl. 9/14/61 Co. H; substitute for James C. Gentry; POW Ft Donelson – confined Camp Morton - d. 3/20/62 of pneumonia - bur. Greenlawn Cem.; reinterred Crown Hill Cem.

STUART, WILLIAM DABNEY: Colonel, 56th Virginia Regiment.; 5/61 appointed 1st Lt in Provisional Army of Va; in a few weeks was promoted to Lt. Col. in Col. Thomas P. August's 15th Va. Regiment - command fell largely on Stuart because August was in poor health; Stuart gallantly commanded Regt. on Va. Peninsula when Butler was repulsed at Big Bethel; Virginia Gov. Letcher was uncertain how to select a Commander for the new 56th Virginia Regiment being formed from Companies and fractions of Companies already in service - so Gov. Letcher allowed Company officers to select; near unanimously they elected Lt. Col. Stuart as Commander of the 56th Virginia Regt. from 9/17/61 until his death; he was elected full Colonel 5/3/1862; Stuart distinguished self at the Battle of Sharpsburg; Gen. "Stonewall" Jackson wanted to promote him to Brigadier Gen., but Stuart's health was bad from 1st Maryland Campaign, so he went home to Staunton and did not get promotion; Col. Stuart was MWIA in Pickett's Charge at Gettysburg age 32; he was sent home to Staunton where he died; b. Staunton 9/30/1830 to Thomas Jefferson and Martha M. Dabney Stuart; grandfather Archibald Stuart fled to America from Ireland in the 1700's; one of Archibald's great grand-sons was father of Confederate Gen. J.E.B. "Jeb" Stuart; Col. Stuart's father was member of Va. Legislature from Augusta Co.; Stuart was educated at Staunton Academy-"distinguished for gentlemanly deportment and attention to his scholastic duties"; matriculated VMI 7/6/1847 age 17; at the time his father was worth nothing and had a nervous disease of head - mother supported family; 7/4/1850 was graduated 3rd in class of 17 from VMI; Stuart was 6' tall and had large muscular frame; was appointed Assistant Professor of Math and Instructor of Tactics VMI 1850-1853 where he developed friendship with Stonewall Jackson; 1853 became headmaster of large classical school Washington, D.C.; in Georgetown met Frances Harris from Loudoun Co, married her in the 1850' s - 2 daughters and son; 1855 became Headmaster of classical school in Richmond where he stayed until war; Stuart died 7/29/1833 in Staunton Hosp. which was temporarily operating in the Methodist School for Girls; on the day of his burial a letter was received asking Stuart if he was able to accept a promotion to Brigadier General; He was bur. in Thornrose Cem., Staunton.

SUMMERSON, JAMES E.: enl. 8/22/62 Co. H in Richmond; POW Gettysburg –confined Ft. Delaware and Pt. Lookout - admitted Smallpox Hosp. Pt. Lookout 11/17/63 - exchanged 5/3/64; present 5/64-8/64; received clothes 9/27/64, 10/13/64, and 12/3/64.

SWIFT, LUTHER RICE: enl. 7/26/61 Co. F in Louisa; present 7/27/61-10/31/61; detailed as Assistant to Commissary 10/1/61.

SYDNOR, STEPHEN C.: enl. 8/6/61 Co. K in Mechanicsville; discharged 8/20/61 age 32 for debility and disease of spinal cord; b. Hanover; farmer, dark complexion and hair, grey eyes, 5'9".

TALLEY, GEORGE F.: enl. 7/26/61 Co. F in Louisa; present on all rolls; WIA slightly 6/1/64-6/4/64; paroled Louisa 12/3/65.

TALLEY, HANSWOOD: enl. 8/6/61 Co. K in Mechanicsville - never mustered in - rejected by surgeon.

TALLEY, ROBERT B.: enl. 7/26/61 Co. F in Louisa; Pvt./Cpl.; sick furlough 7/27/61-8/31/61; present on all other rolls; admitted Chimborazo 6/11/64 wtth chronic diarrhea - returned to duty 7/1/64; POW near Howlett's House 8/25/64 - confined Ft. Monroe and Pt Lookout - admitted hosp. 11/4/64 with typhoid fever - d. 11/17/64 - bur. Conf. Cem. Pt. Lookout.

TALLEY, VERGIL F.: pwl; Co. F - from Louisa.

TALLEY, WILLIAM EDWIN:: enl. 8/6/61 Co. K in Mechanicsville; Cpl./2nd Lt.; present 8/6/61-10/31/61; carried Edmond Longan Co K home sick; elected 2nd Lt. 5/3/62 - resigned 10/10/62 as only 7 men in company - became Sgt. Co. F, 25th Va. Battery; 11/19/62 wrote asking for job in war department in Richmond because wanted to be near aging father and mother who lost elder sons in trying to reclaim Maryland.

TALLEY, WILLIAM H.: enl. 7/26/61 Co. F in Louisa, Cpl./Lt; 7/29/61-8/31/61 absent with measles; promoted 5th Sgt. 10/21/61; present on all other rolls; elected 2nd Lt. 5/3/62; admitted Chimborazo 7/28/62 - transferred to private quarters; appointed 1st Lt 2/1/63; on 11/63-12/63 roll shown as commanding company; admitted Richmond hosp. 8/10/64 with remittent fever and diarrhea; furloughed 30 drays 8/18/64 to Louisa.

TALLEY, WILLIAM J.: enl. 6/22/61 Co B in Mecklenburg; present 9/61-10/61; d. 3/25/62 in Murfreesboro;. death claim filed by father Levi Talley 5/21/62 - owed $77.80.

TANNER, JOHN E.: enl. 6/22/61 Co. B in Mecklenburg; present 9/61-10/61; d. 3/9/62 in Atlanta; Ga.; death claim filed by father Evens Tanner 5/21/62 - owed $80.90.

TAPPS, CHARLES: enl. 7/15/61 Co. H in Albemarle; present 7/29/61-

10/31/61; admitted Chimborazo 7/4/62 with rheumatism - returned to duty 8/16/62.

TAPSCOTT, GEORGE A.: pwl; Co. D - entered service age 15 spring 1864 at Chaffin's Farm; left service after Cold Harbor - broken in health; b. Buckingham; surveyor and notary public; applied for pension 10/16/1923 age 74 living Albernerle - $100 income as notary - $500 personal property - total disability due to heart disease and rheumatism - $140 approved.

TAPSCOTT, GEORGE N.: enl. 6/1/61 Co. D. in Buckingham; 9/63-10/63 AWOL; present 11/64-12/63 and 4/1/64; 5/64-8/64 absent wded. - admitted Chimborazo 6/3/64 with flesh wd. of right hip - furloughed 40 days 6/29/64..

TAPSCOTT, VINCENT A.: enl. 7/8/61 Co. D in Buckingham, Cpl./2nd Lt.; present 7/8/61-10/31/61; reenlisted 8/11/62; present 9/63 - 10/63; absent on detail 11/63-12/63; present 4/1/64 and 5/64-8/64; promoted 2nd Lt. 5/20/64; 7/64-8/64 signed roll as commanding company; 9/6/64 wrote letter requesting election of 2nd Lt. in his company because Capt. John P. Jones and Jacob Rudisill captured at Gettysburg and he was the only officer left; paroled Richmond 5/17/65; 1911 living Imperial Hotel - Red Bluff, Calif.

TARRY, (TERRY) THOMAS L.: enl. 7/12/61 Co. G in Charlotte; discharged 8/10/61 age 21 due to palpitations of heart after exercise and family history of lung disease; Capt. Thomas D. Jeffress wrote that he saw no reason why he should be discharged because had been healthy and strong during 6 weeks of drilling; b. Mecklenburg; farmer, light complexion, dark hair, black eyes. 5'8 ¾".

TATE, BICKERTON: pwl; Co. F (probably James H. B. Tate)

TATE, CALVIN O.: enl. 7/26/61 Co. F in Louisa; 7/27/61-8/31/61 home with measles; present 9/61-1061; admitted Chimborazo 6/23/62 with dysentery - transferred Danville - deserted hosp. 7/9/62; WIA Gettysburg; present 9/63-12/63; 4/1/64 listed as deserter; 5/64-8/64 present; pardoned by Jefferson Davis and released from E. D. M. Prison 8/3/64; b. Louisa; farmer; applied for pension 8/20/1910 age 83 living Louisa - said in hosp. when Lee surrendered - totally disabled - no income or property - $36 approved.

TATE, FLEMING D.: enl. 7/26/61 Co. F in Louisa; in hosp. with measles; 7/27/61-8/31/61; WIA Gaines's Mill; present on all rolls; admitted Chimborazo 5/15/63 with debility - returned to duty 6/5/63; received clothes 10/13/64 and 10/19/64; paroled Ashland 4/25/65; applied for pension 5/9/1892 age 55 living Bumpass, Louisa Co.- minie ball passed between 1st and 2nd ribs and upper lobe of left lung - equal to loss of limb - disallowed - reapplied 5/11/1896 - $15 approved.

TATE, FRANK: pwl; Co. F; widow Anna Wood Tate applied for pension

7/26/1954 living Crozet, Albemarle Co. - m. 4/26/1910 - received $19 per month from dept. of welfare - $480 approved; Mrs. Tate had to construct her own pension application because there were no originals left in 1954 - she was born in 1878.

TATE, GEORGE F.: enl. 7/26/61 Co. F in Louisa; present 7/27/61-10/31/61; d. 3/19/62 in Chattanooga, TN - death claim filed by father William A. Tate 2/27/64 - owed $68.98

TATE, HENRY: enr. as conscript in Hanover 3/11/64 - assigned to Co. K 3/14/64; AWOL 4/1/64 and 5/64-6/64; absent in arrest 7/64-8/64 - forfeited 7 month's pay by order of court martial; admitted Chimborazo 11/22/64 with acute diarrhea and hernia - transferred to private quarters 12/15/64 - returned to duty 12/22/65; d. Hanover of consumption - n. d.; widow Caroline W. Tate applied for pension 11/23/1910; m. 5/14/64 Hanover - $25 income - $456 real estate -$25 approved - said husband had been on pension roll of Hanover.

TATE, JACK: enl. 7/26/61 Co. F in Louisa; 7/27/61-8/31/61 in hosp. with measles; present 9/61-10/61; d. 2/17/62 in Nashville - death claim filed by father Reuben Tate 7/3/62 - owed $56.36.

TATE, JAMES H. B. (HENRY) (BICKERTON: enl. 7/26/61 Co. F in Louisa; present 7/27/61-10/31/61; deserted 6/1/63; listed as absent on rolls 9/63-12/63 and 4/1/64 - escaped from prison; on rolls 5/64-8/64 listed as deserted 5/15/63 and underwent sentence of Court Martial; received clothes at Castle Thunder 5/14/64 and 11/12/64 - released from confinement 12/1/64 by *S.O. 285/22;* captured by Union at Ft. Pocahontas 11/28/64 - listed as rebel deserter - took oath of allegiance at Bermuda Hundred - sent Washington, D.C. and New York 12/7/64.

TATE, JAMES L.: enl. 7/26/61 Co. F in Louisa; 7/27/61-8/31/61 in hosp. with measles; present 9/61-10/61; admitted Williamsburg hosp. 4/26/63 with diarrhea - transferred Farmville hosp. with abscessed foot - furloughed 30 days 5/13/63 - returned to duty 6/5/63; admitted Chimborazo hosp. 8/6/63 with chronic rheumatism - furloughed 60 days 9/8/63.

TATE, JOHN S.: enl. 7/26/61 Co. F in Louisa; present 7/27/61-10/31/61; admitted Chimborazo 6/4/62 with diarrhea - returned to duty 6/25/62; admitted Williamsburg hosp. 4/26/63 - returned to duty 5/8/63; admitted Chimborazo 8/5/63; furloughed 1/1/64-2/29/64; admitted Chimborazo 6/17/64 with wd. received 6/16/64 age 35 - transferred to Louisa 8/5/64; farmer, paroled Richmond 4/27/65.

TATE, NATHAN G.: enl. 7/26/61 Co. F in Louisa; 7/27/61-8/31/61 in Richmond hosp. with measles; present 9/61-10/61; WIA Gaines's Mill; present 5/64-6/64; POW near Howlett's House 8/25/64 –confined Bermuda Hundred, Ft. Monroe, and Pt. Lookout 8/27/64; d. 3/4/65 of gangrene at Pt. Lookout; bur. POW graveyard Pt. Lookout.

TATE, REUBEN (JR. or SR.): pwl; Co, F (may be Richard Tate)

TATE, REUBEN N. (JR. or SR.): enl. 7/26/61 Co. F in Louisa; 7/26/61-8/31/6 in Richmond hosp. with measles; present 9/61-10/61; deserted 1/1/63, 5/15/63 or 6/1/63 - escaped from prison according to roll 4/1/64; 7/64-8/64 roll said undergoing sentence of court martial; deserted to Union 3/22/65 - sent to Washington, D.C.

TATE, RICHARD: enl. 7/25/61 Co. F in Louisa; present 4/1/64; deserted 5/20/64; paroled Columbia 5/8/65.

TATE, WOODY: pwl; Co. F.

TAYLOR, CHARLES S.: pwl; Co. F; POW Elmira, New York; d. 3/4/65 bur. Woodlawn Nat. Cem., Elmira.

TAYLOR, DAVID M.: enl. 5/3/62 Co. H in Richmond, on detached duty 5/22/63 – 6/8/63; furloughed 7/1/63-8/31/63; present 9/63-12/63, 4/1/64, and 5/64-8/64.

TAYLOR, GEORGE W.: enl. 5/3/62 Co. B in Richmond; Court Martial 2/23/63 AWOL. - guilty of specification and charge. forfeited 6 months pay; WIA Gettysburg - POW Greencastle, Pa. 7/5/63 - sent from Chester, Pa. hosp. to Hammond Gen. Hosp., Pt. Lookout 10/4/63 - exchanged at City Point 3/3/64; admitted Chimborazo 6/10/64 with wd. of right thigh and syphilis - furloughed 7/64-8/64 – readmitted hosp. 8/15/64 - returned to duty as guard 9/16/64; shown on roll of Invalid Corps, Co. A, 1st Batt. 10/25/64; Medical Board said unfit for field duty 3/3/65; b. Albemarle; resident of Richmond 1919; admitted to Lee Camp Soldiers' Home *8/12/1919* age 74 due to infirmities of age; d. 10/20/1919 - bur. by H. M. Reinhard, Richmond.

TAYLOR, HENRY CLAY: exempted from service 3/15/62 due to dyspepsia; enl. 2/8/63 Co. E in Lawrenceville, age 23; discharged 6/6/63 as unfit for field duty - wrote and asked for job in quarter-master or commissary dept. because wanted to serve country; enr. as conscript 3/14/64 - assigned Co. B 3/21/64; present 4/1/64 and 5/64-8/64; in hosp. 8/21/64; fair complexion, brown hair, grey eyes; 5'11"; surrendered by Lee at Appomattox; b. 1840 to George Washington and Eveline G. Hawkins Taylor; teacher before war; m. Lavinia Augusta Nash Walker 12/14/1870 - 3 children; lived in home called "Aspen Grove," Mecklenburg; ran store and post office in Blackridge section of Mecklenburg; member Armistead Camp, UCV 1898; d. 3/21/1923 - bur. Olive Branch Baptist Church near Blackridge.

TAYLOR, ISAAC A.: enl. 6/22/61 Co. B in Mecklenburg, Pvt./Cpl.; present 9/61-10/61; POW Ft. Donelson - sent to Camp Morton - d. 3/10/62 of typhoid fever - bur. Green Lawn Cem.; death claim filed 9/25/63 by father Isaac Taylor.

TAYLOR, JAMES: enl 7/15/61 Co. H in Albemarle; present 7/29/61-10/31/61; d. 2/22/62; death claim 4/18/62; owed $66.06.

TAYLOR, ROBERT A.: Co. B; POW Farmville 4/6/65 - sent to Pt.

Lookout - d. 6/3/65 of chronic diarrhea; bur. Confederate. Cem., Pt. Lookout - No. 2013.

TAYLOR, ROBERT J.: enl. 6/22/61 Co. B in Mecklenburg; 9/61-10/61 furloughed; POW Ft. Donelson - sent from Camp Morton to Vicksburg for exchange; POW Gettysburg - Co. roll indicated KIA Gettysburg, but no Federal records concerning him; b. 1837; 1860 census, overseer.

TAYLOR, DR. THOMAS JAMES: organized Ebenezer Greys; enl. 7/10/61 Co. E in Brunswick, Capt./Pvt.; appointed Capt. 7/15/61 - dropped 5/5/62; promoted to Surgeon of 56th Va.; enl. 3/28/64 Co. E in Richmond; listed as Pvt. on 4/1/64 roll; AWOL 5/64-6/64; 7/64-8/64 roll showed discharged by Gen. Lee's orders near Howlett's House 8/13/64; b. 1/6/1837 to Capt. John J. and Sarah Ann Walker Taylor, attended UVA Medical School late 1850s; farmer and doctor; never married; one of Brunswick's outstanding citizens; elected to County Board of Supervisors and Chairman of County Board of Health; awarded Cross of Honor at Lawrenceville reunion of CV 6/1911; d. 1/6/1918 - bur. St. Mark's Episcopal Church Cem., Cochran.

TAYLOR, WILLIAM PLEASANT: enl. 7/10/61 Co. H, 9th Va. Cav.; discharged on surgeon's certificate 8/23/61; enl. Co. B, 56th Va., n.d.g.; POW Farmville 4/6/65 - took oath and released from Pt. Lookout 6/30/65; resident of Brunswick; light complexion, brown hair, blue eyes, 5'7".

TAYLOR, WILLIS L: enr. as conscript 2/16/64 - assigned to Co. C 2/23/64; absent sick 7/64-8/64; admitted Chimborazo 9/16/64 with chronic diarrhea - furloughed 60 days to Charlotte 10/2/64; admitted Chimborazo 3/19/65 with intermittent fever - transferred to Danville hosp. 4/3/65.

TEMPLE, THOMAS PRICE: enl. *8/6/61* Co. K in Mechanicsville, 1st Lt; present 8/6/61-8/21/61; resigned 9/2/61 - appointed Asst. Surgeon 9/5/61.

TERRELL, JOHN E.: enl. *7/25/61* Co. F in Louisa; present 9/63-12/63; transferred to Alexandria Battalion Artillery.

TERRELL, RICHMOND Q. (T.): enl. 7/26/61 Co. F in Louisa, Pvt./Sgt; present 7/61-10/61; WIA Gettysburg; absent wded. on rolls 9/63-10/63 and 4/64-6/64; present 7/64-8/64; admitted Chimborazo 12/9/64 with wd. of rt. side; POW Farmville 4/6/65 - released from Pt. Lookout 6/21/65; resident of Louisa; fair complexion, brown hair, blue eyes, 5'10"; d. 3/28/1909.

THACKER, GRANVILLE: enl. 8/6/61 Co. K in Mechanicsville; discharged age 36 due to pneumonia 8/21/61; b. Hanover Co.; farmer; dark hair and complexion, blue eyes, 5'6".

THACKER, PHILIP: enl. 8/6/61 Co. K in Mechanicsville; discharged 8/31/61 age 28 with hernia; b. Hanover Co.; overseer. dark eyes, brown hair, 5'10".

THOMAS, BENJAMIN J.: enl. 6/22/61 Co. B in Mecklenburg; d. 9/24/1861/.

THOMAS, CHARLES W.: enl. 6/22/61 Co. B in Mecklenburg; present

9/61-10/61; POW Ft. Donelson - sent from Camp Morton to Vicksburg for exchange; absent sick 9/63-12/63 and 4/1/64; present 5/64-8/64; admitted Chimborazo 9/13/63 with chronic diarrhea - furloughed 35 days 9/19/63; POW Farmville 4/6/65; d. of pneumonia at Pt. Lookout 4/26/65 – bur. grave 1572 Confederate Cem., Pt. Lookout; farmer Mecklenburg before war; m. Mary Rebecca Pearson 11/10/1852 Warren Co., N. C. - 3 children.

THOMAS, D. RICE: enl. 7/18/61 Co. I in Charlotte; present 7/61-10/61; KIA Ft. Donelson - 1st man in Co. I killed,

THOMAS, HENRY ROBINSON: pwl; Co B; entered service in Coleman's Arty. 1861; left when Lee surrendered; b. about 1841 to John J. and Martha L. Thomas in Mecklenburg; 1880 living Brunswick in home of John S. Thomas and working as merchant; m. Leona L Seymour 10/181865; applied for pension 8/27/1902 in Brunswick age 81 living Elam, N.C.- rheumatism; $15 approved.

THOMAS, ROBERT N.: enl. 7/27/61 Co. F in Louisa, 1st Lt./Capt. Co. G; absent on sick furlough with measles 7/27/61-8/31/61; present on all other rolls; escaped with Floyd from Ft. Donelson; on register of Richmond hosp. - returned to duty 8/12/62; appointed Capt. Co. G 1/15/63; furloughed 15 days 12/23/64; WIA Hatcher's Run - POW Fairground Post Hosp. Petersburg 4/3/65 - admitted with wd. of rt. shoulder - paroled 5/28/65; b. 1834 Louisa; attended Chamber's Commercial College in Baltimore; resident of Chesterfield Co.; member Richmond police force over 30 years - Sgt. of Police Court 1895 - retired 1905; d. 8/10/1907 Richmond - survived by wife and daughter.

THOMAS, ROBERT W.: enr. as conscript 6/8/64 and assigned to Co. B 6/11/64; absent sick in hosp. 5/64-6/64; admitted Chimborazo 7/25/64 - furloughed 60 days 8/6/64; d. 9/16/1864.

THOMAS, WILLIAM E.: enl. 7/15/61 Co. H in Albemarle: 7/29/61-9/3/61 sick In hosp.; present 10/61; admitted Charlottesville hosp. 11/24/62 with debility - returned to duty 3/2/63 - special duty to Capt. Dejarnett, Enrolling Officer, 8th Congress District; present 7/63-12/63 and 4/1/64; WIA Frazier's Farm - admitted Chimborazo 8/17/64 age 21 - upper third of arm amputated - furloughed 60 days 7/24/64; admitted Charlottesville hosp. 9/23/64 with wd. of humerus shaft - furloughed 9/23/64.

THOMAS, WILLIAMSON C.: enl.. 6/10/61 Co. E in Brunswick, present 7/10/61-8/31/61; MWIA Gaines's Mill - admitted Richmond hosp. 6/29/62 with wd. - d. 7/12/64; death claim filed 12/11/63 by widow Indiana V. Thomas - m. 1852 - 3 children; b. Brunswick about 1831 to Robertson C. and Sally Rainey Thomas.

THOMASON, ANDREW J.: enl. 7/10/61 Co. B in Mecklenburg; present 9/61-10/61; KIA Gaines's Mill - mother applied for $50.00 bounty.

THOMASON, WILLIAM R. E.: enl. 8/15/63 Co. K in Thicksford; conscripted 1/9/64 and assigned to 56th Va. Inf. 1/15/64; present 4/64-

6/64; transferred to Co. B 6/26/64 in exchange for Allen W. Bingham; POW Amelia Co. 4/6/65 - took oath and released from Pt. Lookout 6/20/65; resident of Greenville Co.; fair complexion, light brown hair, grey eyes, 5'6 ¾".

THOMPSON, CHARLES, JR.: enl. 7/26/61 Co, F in Louisa; Pvt./Sgt. Major; present on all rolls; promoted to Sgt Major on roll of Field and Staff for 11/63-12/63; admitted Chimborazo 8/10/64 with internal fever - returned to duty 8/15/64; 12/30/64 made Asst. Adjutant; POW Burkeville 4/7/65 - took oath and released from Pt. Lookout 6/21/65; resident of Louisa; light complexion, brown hair, grey eyes, 5'7 ½"; living 3/1911.

THOMPSON, JAMES E.: enl. 6/22/61 Co. B in Mecklenburg, Sgt.; present 9/61-10/61; appointed Sgt. 9/1/61; WIA Frazier's Farm; discharged 9/13/62 age 36 because over 35; b. Lunenburg Co.; farmer; florid complexion, blue eyes, black hair, 5'10"; indebted to CSA for $12.25 on account of clothing given in duplicate at camp near Hagerstown, Md.

THORP, CHARLES A.: pwl; Co. A; applied for pension 5/5/1900 age 74 living Hugh, Charlotte Co. - disabled due to rheumatism caused by hardship of war - $15 approved - pension statement 10/11/1902 age 77.

THROCKMORTON, (THOCKMORTON) CHARLES R.: enl. 7/18/61 Co. A in Mecklenburg; present 7/8/61-10/61.

THROCKMORTON, JOHN W.: enl. 7/8/61 Co. A in Mecklenburg; present 7/8/61-8/31/61; absent on sick furlough 10/9/61 - 10/19/61.

THROGMARTIN, (THROGMORTON) T. E.: enr. as conscript 1/1/64 in Henrico - assigned to Co. K 1/15/64; present 4/1/64; AWOL 5/64-8/64.

THURSTON, G. H.: enr. as conscript 5/3/61 Co. H in Richmond; discharged 5/12/62 age 32 with hernia; b. Goochland Co.; farmer; sallow complexion, blue eyes, light hair, 5'7".

TIBBS, PLEASANT J.: Co. C; POW High Bridge 4/6/65 - took oath and released from PL Lookout 6/21/65; resident of Henrico; dark complexion, black hair, hazel eyes, 5'11".

TIMBERLAKE, ALPHEUS R.: enl. 8/6/61 Co. K in Mechanicsville, Sgt./1st. Lt.; present 8/6/61-10/61; promoted to 2nd Lt. 8/13/61; elected 1st Lt. 9/6/61; resigned 10/28/61.

TIMBERLAKE, CHARLES: enl. 7/9/61 Co. C in Louisa; AWOL 9/6-10/61.

TIMBERLAKE, PHLIP: enl. 10/18/61 Co. C; present 9/61-10/61.

TIMBERLAKE, S. W.: Co. K; Sgt; transferred 9/61 from Howitzer Battalion at Yorktown where had been Pvt.

TINDALL, LOUIS C.: enl. 7/8/61 Co. D in Buckingham; present 7/8/61-8/31/61; sick furlough 9/61-10/61; paroled at Warrenton, Va. 9/29/62; paid $50 bounty 12/3/62; present 9/63-12/63; absent sick furlough 4/22/64; KIA Cold Harbor.

TOOMBS, RICHARD: enl. 7/12/61 Co. G in Mecklenburg; present 7/26/61 -10/61; waggoner 2/18/62 - 3/31/62; discharged 10/10/62 age 36 because over 35; dark complexion, hair and eyes, 5'9"; b. Charlotte Co.; farmer, applied for pension 5/5/1900 age 72 living Red Oak, Charlotte Co. - disabled due to rheumatism and general debility -$15 approved.

TOONE, JOHN R.: enl. 7/8/61 Co. A in Mecklenburg; present 7/20/61-8/19/61; AWL 8/20/61-9/2/61; present 9/61-10/61; d. 4/62 Chattanooga, TN; m. Margaret R, Toone.

TOWNSEND, GEORGE: enl. 7/20/61 Co. A in Mecklenburg; rejected because too young.

TRAINER, BURNET: enl. 7/9/63 Co. C in Louisa; absent on detached service in Richmond on all rolls - building gun boats on James River.

TRAINHAM, ANDREW J: enl. 7/26/61 Co. F in Louisa; absent 7/27/61-8/31/61 in Richmond Hosp. with measles; present 9/61-10/61; discharged age 36 6/4/62 due to atrophy of muscles; dark complexion, black hair and eyes, 5'9"; paroled Ashland – 4/30/65; b. Louisa; farmer, applied for pension 5/15/1900 age 64 living Hewlett, Hanover Co. - bad health caused by exposure during war - partial disability due to rheumatism and asthma - $15 approved; made pension statement 4/24/1903.

TRAINHAM, CHRISTOPHER C. (B.): enl. 7/26/61 Co. F in Louisa. Cpl./Hosp. Steward; appointed Cpl./Hosp. Steward 11/25/62; present on all rolls; furloughed 3/1/63-3/10/63.

TRAINHAM, DAVID C.: enl. 7/9/61 Co. C in Louisa; present 7/9/61-10/61; WIA and POW Gettysburg; in Gen. Hosp. Gettysburg and transferred West's Buildings Hosp. with gunshot wd. of right lung - exchanged 8/23/63; absent wded. 9/63-12/63; absent on detached service as woodchopper 1864 in Abingdon; admitted Chimborazo for 30 days beginning 8/25/64.

TRAVIS, WILLIAM J.: Co. F; paroled Louisa 5/15/65.

TRENT, BOOKER F.: enl. 7/18/61 Co. I in Charlotte; absent sick on furlough beyond time 7/18/61-8/31/61 - put in guardhouse because thought trying to desert, but soon released; present 9/61-10/61; d. 4/3/62 age 20 in Gate City Hosp., Atlanta, Ga. of typhoid fever - bur. Oakland Cem., Atlanta, Row 4, No. 17; death claim filed 9/5/62 by father Marshall Trent - owed $81.10; b. Charlotte; farmer; blue eyes, dark hair, florid complexion, 5'8".

TREVILLIAN, JAMES: pwl; Co. D.

TRICE, ADDISON L.: enl. 5/2/61 Co. D, 13th Va. Inf. in Loudoun Co. - discharged 6/9/61, epilepsy; enl. 7/9/61 Co. C in Louisa; Cpl; present 7/9/61-10/31/61; MWIA Ft. Donelson - severely wded. and ordered to hosp., but refused to go - led charge on enemy's works using his musket as crutch - fell dead on works, pierced by dozen bullets - d. 2/15/62 age 25 - death claim filed by mother Adella H. Trice 11/13/63 - owed $63.50; b. 1833? Louisa; farmer, light complexion, blue eyes, light hair, 5'8".

TRICE, ALFRED W.: Co. C; received clothes 10/19/64 and 12/28/64;

paroled Louisa 5/15/65; applied for pension 4/28/1900 age 70 living Louisa - lost 1 eye - $15 approved; made statement 7/14/1902 age 72 - $291 personal property.

TROTTER, ISHAM EDWARD: enl. 7/10/61 Co. E Brunswick; Pvt./Sgt.; present 7/10/61-8/31/61; POW Ft. Donelson - sent from Camp Morton to Vicksburg for exchange; admitted Richmond hosp. 11/25/62 - returned to duty 12/8/62; POW Gettysburg - confined Ft McHenry, Ft. Delaware, and Pt. Lookout 10/27/63 - paroled and exchanged 5/3/64; present 5/64-8/64; POW Burkeville 4/6/65 - took oath and released from Pt. Lookout 6/30/65; fair complexion, light hair, hazel eyes, 6'; b. Brunswick 1/30/1838 to Col. Isham and Agnes Thweatt Manson Trotter -father Col. of Brunswick Militia many years; farmer; never married; attended Lawrenceville Reunion CV 1908; entered Lee Camp Soldiers' Home 7/9/1922 age 84 due to infirmities of age - d. 11/18/1923 - remains taken by family; bur. Oakwood Cem., Lawrenceville.

TRUMAN, THOMAS J.: enl. 8/6/61 Co. K in Mechanicsville – transferred to Capt Binford's Co. as deserted from him 8/20/61; present 9/61-10/61; POW Ft. Donelson - sent from Camp Morton to Vicksburg for exchange; admitted Richmond hosp. 9/12/63 - returned to duty 9/13/63; extra duty as laborer at Chaffin's Farm building ice house 1/1/64-1/5/64; MWIA Cold Harbor - admitted Chimborazo 6/2/64 with gunshot wd. penetrating thorax - d. 6/20/64 - death claim filed by widow Rebecca Jane Truman 10/29/64 - owed $75; b. Henrico.

TRUMAN, WILLIAM: enl. 8/6/61 Co. K in Mechanicsville; present 8/6/61-10/31/61; POW Ft. Donelson - sent from Camp Morton to Vicksburg for exchange,

TUCKER, BENTLEY HUNTLEY: enl. 8/6/61 Co. K Mechanicsville; Sgt.; present 8/6/61-10/31/61; sick furlough 2 weeks 10/14/61; admitted Williamsburg hosp. 4/30/63 with rheumatism - transferred Farmville hosp. 5/8/63; WIA and POW Gettysburg - right arm amputated at shoulder joint in West's Buildings Hosp. 7/25/63 - stump healed - paroled for exchange 9/27/63; POW at his home 3/1/64 - paroled from Pt. Lookout for exchange 4/27/64; admitted Chimborazo 5/1/64 - furloughed 60 days 5/12/64 - another record reported deserted 6/23/64; retired to Invalid Corps 8/5/64; admitted Chimborazo 3/16/65; m. Richmond 7/3/1873 Sarah Jane Butkins; applied for pension 4/18/1888 age 55 living Old Church, Hanover Co. - lost right arm Gettysburg - $30 approved; d.10/17/1913 of Bright's disease In Old Church; widow applied for pension 2/24/1923 - owned widow's portion of 75 acres and $100 personal property - $76 approved.

TUCKER, HENRY T.: enl. 8/6/61 Co. K in Mechanicsville, Cpl./Pvt; present 8/6/61-10/31/61; POW Ft. Donelson - sent from Camp Morton to Vicksburg for exchange; reenlisted 1862; sick furlough 11/21/62-12/21/62; admitted Petersburg hosp. 6/4/63 with fever - furloughed 30 days 6/11/63;

present 7/63-12/63, 4/1/64 and 5/64-8/64; admitted Chimborazo hosp. 11/20/64 due to wd. and debilitas - returned to duty 12/6/64; paroled Richmond 4/27/65,

TUCKER, JAMES E.: enl. 8/6/61 Co. K in Mechanicsville; AWOL from 8/31/61; present 9/61-10/61; POW Nashville. TN 4/25/62 - paroled and exchanged 10/15/62; sick furlough 3/5/63-3/25/63; present 7/63-12/63, 4/1/64, and 5/64-8/64; paroled Richmond 4/24/65.

TUCKER, JAMES T.: enl. 6/29/64 Co. K at Howlett's House; present 5/64-8/64; POW Southside Railroad 4/2/65 - took oath and released from Pt. Lookout 6/21/65; b. Hanover, fair complexion, brown hair, blue eyes; 5'7".

TUCKER, JOHN D.: enl. 8/26/64 Co. K in Richmond; absent sick 7/64-8/64; admitted Chimborazo 11/11/64 - returned to duty 11/18/64; b. Hanover; admitted Lee Camp Soldiers' Home 2/24/1897 age 53 for paralysis; d. 7/15/1910 age 66 - bur. East 123, Hollywood Cem.

TUCKER, JOHN T.: enl. 8/6/61 Co. K in Mechanicsville; AWOL from 8/31/61; present 9/61-10/61; WIA Gaines's Mill - admitted Richmond hosp. with gunshot wd. - furloughed 30 days to home in Hanover; Manuscript 1444 listed as deserted 11/19/62; present 9/63-12/63, 4/1/64, and 5/64-8/64; d. of consumption in Hanover, n.d.; widow Elizabeth Tucker applied for pension 5/29/1902 - m. 3/9/ n.d.g. Pole Green, Hanover Co. - no Income or property - $25 approved.

TUCKER, JOSEPH: enl. 8/6/61 Co. K in Mechanicsville - never mustered in - did not appear.

TUCKER, LEWIS W.: enl. 8/15/61 Co. G in Charlotte; present 9/61-10/61; discharged 9/9/62; POW Burkeville 4/6/65 - took oath and released from Pt. Lookout 6/20/65; b. Halifax; resident of Mecklenburg; dark complexion, dark eyes, black hair, 5'11".

TUCKER, S. D.: Co. unknown; POW paroled 4/27/65.

TURNER, GEORGE W.: enl. 2/20/64 Co. H at Chaffin's Farm; present 4/1/64 and 5/64-8/64; received clothes 9/27/64.

TURNER, JAMES W.: enl. 7/9/61 Co. C in Louisa; Cpl./Pvt.; sick furlough 7/9/61-8/31/61; present 9/61-10/61; AWOL 9/63-12/63;

TURNER, ROBERT: enl. 7/25/61 Co. F in Louisa (other rolls Co. A); present 4/1/64; roll 5/64-6/64 listed as deserted 5/20/64; roll 7/64-8/84 showed absent - in division guard house.

TURNER, STEPHEN W.: enl. 6/22/61 Co. B in Mecklenburg, 2nd Lt.; present 9/61-10/61; appointed 2nd Lt. 7/15/61; in command of Co. in Russellville, Ky. 2/4/62; POW Ft. Donelson - confined Camp Chase and Johnson's Island 4/10/62 - sent to Vicksburg for exchange 9/1/62 - exchanged 11/8/62; dropped as 2nd Lt. 5/5/62; went to Texas after his exchange with members of the 7th Texas who had been POWS with him - joined Chambers' Batt. and 13th Texas Inf.; b. Warren Co. N.C. to Charles Granderson and Sara Rainey Turner; lived in Marengo,

Mecklenburg Co. from age 5 until war started; entered Emory and Henry College at age 15 - taught school in Mecklenburg; settled in Smith Co., TX after war; m. Dora Ann Shuford Long 2/10/1874 in Tyler, TX - 7 boys and 2 girls; founded Commercial Dept. at Polytechnic College, Fort Worth, Texas 1895 and taught there; also taught Latin and Greek at Weatherford College, Weatherford, TX; tax assessor for Smith Co., TX - 2 term; minister in Methodist Church 50 years; got pension from TX; d. 5/22/1916 Cisco, TX - bur. Gatesville, TX.

TURNER, VINES: enl. 7/10/61 Co. E in Brunswick, Cpl./Pvt.; present 7/10/61-8/31/61; admitted Richmond hosp. 11/22/62 - returned to duty 12/62; absent wded. and unfit for duty 9/63-12/63, 4/1/64, and 5/64-8/64; got pension in Faulkner Co., Ark.; d. 3/15/1902

TUTOR, SAMUEL A.: enl. 6/22/61 Co. B in Mecklenburg, Pvt./Sgt; present 9/61-10/61; WIA Gaines's Mill - furloughed from Richmond hosp. with gunshot wd.; admitted Charlottesville 11/6/62 with pneumonia - transferred to Farmville hosp. 11/12/62 - returned to duty 1/7/63; admitted Chimborazo 7/13/63 with debility - returned to duty 7/30/63; present 9/63-12/63 with exception of 15 day furlough; present 4/1/64; admitted Chimborazo 6/4/64 with acute dysentery; age 23 - furloughed 30 days 7/23/64; received clothes 10/13/64 and 10/19/64; resident of Mecklenburg; farmer, fair complexion, dark hair, hazel eyes; 5'6"; living Mecklenburg 4/1911.

TYLER, JOHN W.: enl. 7/15/61 Co. H in Albemarle; present 7/29/61-10/31/61; WIA Frazier's Farm; with unit at Gettysburg; native Haymarket; Georgetown University alumnus class of 1835,

VAUGHAN, ASA JORDAN: pwl; Co. H; from Dinwiddie.

VAUGHAN, JAMES M.: enl. 7/8/61 Co, A in Mecklenburg; AWL 7/8/61-8/31/61; present on all other rolls; furloughed 5/8/62-6/18/62; admitted Danville hosp. 9/24/62 with debilitas - returned to duty 10/7/62: teamster on rolls 9/10/63-11/14/63 and 3/1/64-6/30/64; admitted Chimborazo 11/10/64 with typhoid fever - returned to duty 11/29/64; surrendered by Lee at Appomattox.

VAUGHAN, JOHN L.: enl. 6/22/61 Co. B in Mecklenburg; present 9/61-10/61; MWIA and POW Gettysburg - left arm amputated in field hospital - d. Camp Letterman, U.S. Gen. Hosp., Gettysburg 7/29/63; bur. Sect, 1, Grave 5 of hosp.'s cem. - disinterred to Richmond 6/13/1872 Box 32 - reinterred Hollywood Cem.

VAUGHAN, MARTIN: enl. 7/8/61 Co. A in Mecklenburg; present 7/8/61-10/31/61; furloughed 5/8/62-5/11/62 and 3/1/63-3/28/63; present 9/63-12/63 and 5/64-6/64; admitted Chimborazo 7/15/64 - d. 7/24/64 of typhoid fever - probably bur. Oakwood Cem.; pension application filed by widow Mary A. Vaughan of Mecklenburg - m. 5/13/1849 Mecklenburg - $30 approved.

VAUGHAN, WILLIAM ASHTON: enl. 8/6/62 Co. A. 5th Va. Inf. Batt. - disbanded 1862; men transferred to Co. H, 53rd Va. Inf.; discharged 3/9/63 - got Richard S. Lewis as substitute; later enl. Co, E; POW Hatcher's Run 3/31/65 - took oath and released from Pt. Lookout 6/21/65; light complexion, red hair, blue eyes, 5'9"; b. 4/10/1844 to William Henry and Mary W. Griffin Vaughan; farmer and Road Superintendent for Totaro District, Brunswick; m. Susan Sills Griffin 2/16/1870; 10 children; d. 1909.
VAUGHAN, WILLIAM J.: enl. 6/22/61 Co. B in Mecklenburg; present 9/61-10/61; d. Richmond hosp. 8/20/62 of disease - left effects of $2.50.
VAWTER, (VAUGHTER) MERRITT G.: enl. 7/18/61 Co. I in Charlotte; present 7/18/61-10/31/61; d. Emory and Henry College Hosp. 4/28/62 of disease - left effects of $5.
VAWTER, WILLIM T.: enl. 7/9/61 Co. C in Louisa; d. at home in Louisa 8/5/61 from disease contracted in army - death claim filed 3/28/63 - owed $36.84; widow Mary Jane Vawter applied for pension 4/12/1888 - m. 10/15/1852; $30 approved.
VIA, EDWARD: enl. 8/6/61 Co. K in Mechanicsville, Pvt./Sgt.; furloughed 10/4/62-11/4/62; WIA Gettysburg - admitted Chimborazo 7/17/63 with gunshot wd. - furloughed 30 days 9/12/63; foot scout 10/29/63-12/15/63; furloughed 1/1/64-2/29/64; present 5/64-8/64; POW in Petersburg hosp. 4/3/65 with gunshot wd. of head - paroled Farmville 4/11/65-4/21/65 - admitted Pt. of Rocks Hosp. 5/1/65; drew pension under 1888 act in 1911; d. Hanover; widow Martha Ann Via applied for pension 6/24/1912; m. Hanover 12/12/1865 - owned cow and a few chickens - $25 approved.
VIA, HARRISON: enl. 8/6/61 Co. K in Mechanicsville, Pvt./2nd Lt; present 8/6/61-10/31/61 and 7/63-12/63; absent sick 5/64-8/64; elected 2nd Lt. 6/18/64; absent wded. 7/64-8/64.; admitted Chimborazo 6/3/64 with wd.- furloughed 8/31/64 -also furloughed 60 days 9/2/64 to Hanover - still in hosp. 1/28/65; admitted Farmville hosp. 4/10/65 - POW and paroled in U.S. Hosp. Farmville 4/11/65-4/21/65 age 22; b. Hanover; merchant; fair complexion, light hair, blue eyes.
VIA, MANOAH G.: enl. 7/15/61 Co. H in Albemarle; present 7/29/61-10/31/61 and 7/63-10/63; admitted Richmond hosp. 7/17/63 - probably WIA Gettysburg - furloughed 20 days; AWL 11/63-12/63; admitted Charlottesville hosp. 1/12/64 with chronic diarrhea - furloughed 60 days 8/26/64; d. 9/25/84 Albemarle - death claim filed 2/9/65.
VIA, WALLER T.: enl. 7/15/61 Co. H in Albemarle; present 7/29/61-10/31/61; POW Camp Douglas, Illinois on roll dated 8/1/62; AWOL on roll 7/63-12/63 as of 10/25/63
VIA, WILLIAM H.: enr. as conscript 2/13/64; assigned Co. H at Chaffin's Farm 2/23/64; present 5/64-6/64; absent sick 7/64-8/64;admitted Richmond hosp. 8/3/64 - furloughed 30 days 8/11/63; admitted Charlottesville hosp. 9/9/64 with chronic diarrhea - returned to duty 11/20/64; certificate of

disability granted by Medical Examining Board 3/25/65- sent to hosp. to report to officer; admitted Richmond hosp. 4/7/65 - POW in Richmond hosp. 4/3/65 - sent from hosp. to Libby Prison 4/14/65 and then City Point; b. Albemarle; laborer, applied for pension 3/27/1909 age 66 living Doylesville, Albemarle Co. - totally disabled due to blindness and age - wded. in thigh in lines below Richmond - $36 approved; state paid family $25 toward funeral expenses 1919.
VORCHAN, FERDINAND: enl. 5/3/62 Co. H in Richmond; on rolls of 7/63-12/63 listed as deserter.
VORSBERG, AUGUST: pwl; , Lt., Quartermaster and Engineer.
VOWELL, J. H.: pwl; Co, G.
WADDELL, ANDREW J.: enl. 1/22/64 Co. G at Chaffin's Farm; present 4/1/64; absent sick 5/64-6/64; present 7/64-8/64; POW Farmville 4/6/65 - took oath and released from Pt. Lookout 6/22/65; b. Amherst Co.; resident of Henrico; florid complexion, light brown hair, grey eyes.,5'4 1/2"; admitted Lee Camp Soldiers' Home 11/15/1915 age 75 due to age; d. 8/29/n.d.g.; Allens Creek while on furlough.
WADDELL, SAMUEL H.: Co. K; POW Farmville 4/6/65 - took oath and released from Pt. Lookout 6/22/65; resident of Charlotte; dark complexion, dark brown hair, blue eyes, 5'10 1/4".
WADE, B. W.: Co. unknown, Sgt; paroled Richmond 4/26/65.
WAGGONER, JAMES R.: Chaplain - sought appointment as Chaplain in army - officers of 56th Va. requested Waggoner be appointed to their Regiment; Methodist minister from Louisa; appointed 6/1/62; resigned 7/10/63 to accept appointment in Soldier Trust Society of Methodist Church Southern Conference.
WAGNER, (WAGONER) WILLIAM HENRY: enl. 7/10/61 Co. E in Brunswick; present 7/10/61; discharged 11/1/61 age 28 due to diseased lungs; reenlisted; surrendered at Lynchburg 4/65; light complexion and hair, grey eyes, 5'7"; b. about 1829 to William and Mary Wagoner in Brunswick; m. Elizabeth Virginia Stainback 11/5/1856 (sister of George W. and Robert A. Stainback, Jr.) - 4 children; farmer and carpenter; applied for pension 7/12/1902 age 73 living Brunswick and working in store; said left service when detailed at Lynchburg - $30 approved; d. 1/25/1915 – bur. Sturgeonville.
WAGSTAFF, CHRISTOPHER R.: enl. 7/10/61 Co. A in Mecklenburg: on guard duty 7/8/61-8/31/61; present 9/61-10/61; discharged 9/8/62 age 38 because served one year and over 35; farmer, dark complexion, hair, and eyes, 5'10".
WAGSTAFF, WILLIAM: pwl; Co. A.
WALDROP, JOHN F.: enl. 7/26/61 Co. F in Louisa, Cpl.; absent sick with measles 7/27/61-10/31/61; discharged 3/8/62 due to poor health; clerk-accountant; applied to Treasury Dept. for clerk's job in CSA 3/21/63.

WALDROP, JOHN THOMAS.: enl. *7/26/61* Co. F in Louisa; present 7/27/61-10/31/61; listed as missing since Ft. Donelson on all other rolls; b. 8/2/1843; William David Waldrop's brother.
WALDROP, WILLIAM DAVID: enl. 7/26/61 Co. F in Louisa; present 7/27/61-10/31/61; sick furlough 7/13/6-8/13/63; present 9/63-12/63; present 4/1/64; absent sick 5/64-8/64; admitted Chimborazo 10/27/64 with chronic diarrhea - furloughed 60 days 11/1/64; paroled 5/17/65; b. 7/18/1841; John Thomas Waldrop's brother; d. 7/16/1866 of pneumonia - bur. Waldrop Family Cem., Rt. 632 -1/2 mile from Waldrop's Chapel.
WALDROP, W. F.: pwl; Co. I.
WALDROP, WILLIAM F. (D.): enl. 7/26/61 Co. F in Louisa; present 7/27/61-10/31/61; MWIA Ft. Donelson - d. 3/11/62 Clarksville, TN - death claim filed by father Francis Waldrop 5/30/62 - owed $65.17.
WALKER, ALFRED W.: enl. 6/29/61 Co. B in Mecklenburg; present 9/61-10/61.
WALKER, DAVID R: enl. 6/22/61 Co. B in Mecklenburg; present 9/61-10/61; discharged 9/9/62 age 48 because over 35; resident of Mecklenburg; farmer, dark complexion, blue eyes, grey hair.
WALKER, J. S. (C.): pwl; Co. I.
WALKER, JAMES: pwl; Co. D.
WALKER, JOHN JEFFERSON: enl. 7/8/61 Co. D in Buckingham, Pvt./Sgt.; present 7/8/61-10/31/61; enl. 10/1/62 Co. E 21st Va. Inf. at Bunker Hill; Sgt./1st Lt.; present 11/62-12/62 and 1/63-4/63; elected 1st Lt. 2/23/63; discharged 3/21/63; d. of wds. 5/5/63; native of Florida.
WALKER, JOHN OLIVER: enl. 6/22/61 Co. B in Mecklenburg; Cpl./Pvt; present on all rolls; in hosp. Bowling Green, Ky. 2/4/62; POW Ft. Donelson - sent from Camp Morton to Vicksburg for exchange; admitted Chimborazo 11/8/62 with fever - returned to duty 9/18/63; POW Burkeville; took oath and released from Pt. Lookout 6/5/65; dark hair and complexion, grey eyes, 5'11 3/4"; resident of Mecklenburg; applied for pension 4/30/1900 age 70 living Mecklenburg near Brunswick line - disabled by age - $15 approved - pension statement 6/14/1902 age 73; d. 2/26/1906.
WALKER, JOSHUA E.: enl. 6/22/61 Co. B Mecklenburg; 1st Lt.; present 9/61-10/61; elected 1st Lt. 7/15/61 - dropped 5/5/62.
WALLER, JOHN J.: enl. 6/22/61 Co. B in Mecklenburg; present 9/61-10/61; POW Ft. Donelson and missing at exchange; d. Vicksburg - claim filed 12/17/63.
WALLER, JOHN W.: enl. 7/10/61 Co. B in Mecklenburg; furloughed 9/61-10/61.
WALTON, ERASMUS: enl. 7/15/61 Co. H in Albemarle - absent when Co. mustered in and still absent 9/2/61- entry cancelled.
WALTON, GEORGE E. M.: enl. 7/9/61 Co. C in Louisa; AWOL 9/61-10/61.

WALTON, NEWELL J.: enl. 7/15/61 Co. H in Albemarle; sick furlough 7/29/61-8/31/61; present 9/61-10/61; d. Emory and Henry hosp. 6/8/62 of disease - claim filed by widow Amanda E. Walton 7/11/63 - 3 children - owed $35.93.
WALTON, THO: pwl; Co. G,
WALTON, WILLIAM G.: enl. 7/22/61 Co. F in Louisa, 2nd Lt.; sick in city with measles 7/27/61-8/31/61; appointed 2nd Lt. 7/27/61 - declined 5/3/42.
WALTON, WILLIAM JACKSON: enl. 7/26/61 Co, F in Louisa; Sgt./2nd Lt; sick in city with measles 7/27/61-8/31/61; present 9/61-10/61; elected 2nd Lt. 5/3/62 - declined.
WARD, JOHN: enl. 7/15/61 Co. H, Albemarle; present 7/29/61-10/31/61.
WARD, SAMUEL: enl. 7/15/61 Co. H in Albemarle; Cpl.; discharged 8/20/61 age 35 due to hernia: b. Albemarle; farmer; fair complexion, dark hair, hazel eyes, 5'9"; reenlisted 5/3/62 Camp Fulton - discharged 5/9/62.
WARREN, FELIX: enl. 8/6/61 Co. K in Mechanicsville; present 8/6/61-8/31/61; absent sick 9/61-10/61; discharged 12/31/61 with disability; d. Richmond during war.
WASH, ROBERT D.: enl. 7/26/61 Co. F in Louisa; Sgt.; present 7/27/61-10/31/61; Richmond hosp. list showed returned to duty 8/12/62; WIA Gettysburg - absent wded. and unfit for duty 9/63-10/63; admitted Chimborazo 7/20/64 with dysentery - returned to duty 8/25/64; paroled Richmond 5/3/65.
WATKINS, JAMES A.: enl. 7/26/61 Co. F in Louisa; present 7/27/61-10/31/61; disabled at Manassas 8/31/62; absent 9/63-12/63, 4/1/64, and 5/64-6/64; on detached duty at Pickett's Headquarters and Quartermaster Dept. of Pickett's Division 7/64-8/64; surrendered by Lee at Appomattox; b. and raised Louisa Co.; applied for pension 5/23/1900 age 57 living Pine Top, Orange Co. -disabled due to gunshot wd. through left ankle joint at 2nd Manassas - $15 approved; 1905 teaching school in Orange and making $1 per day - got no pension because had $500 worth of property.
WATKINS, JOHN C.: enr. as conscript 2/27/64 in Charlotte -assigned same day to Co. G; absent on detached service baling hay 3/64-5/64.
WATKINS, WILLIAM LEIGH: pwl; Co. I; applied for pension 4/141900 age 66 living Smithville, Charlotte Co. - left side paralyzed - $15 approved; made pension statement 8/5/1902 age 68.
WATSON, JOSEPH E.: enl. 7/8/61 Co. A in Mecklenburg, Cpl.; present 7/8/61-8/31/61; discharged 8/30/61 - got substitute William H. Williams.
WATSON, JOSEPH W.: enr. as conscript 5/3/62 - discharged 5/27/62 age 25 due to disability; enr. as conscript 3/8/64 at Camp Lee - assigned Co. G 3/16/64; present 4/1/64 and 5/64-8/64 – claimed to be a Nazarene and opposed to fighting - refused to receive pay for fighting; deserted to enemy 1/6/65 - took oath of rebel deserter at Bermuda Hundred - supposedly sent to Henderson, Ky.; b. Albemarle; painter, fair complexion, dark hair, blue

eyes, 5'6".

WEBB, BENJAMIN F.: enl. 9/15/63 Co. G in Franklin Co.; present 9/63-12/63; laborer building ice house at Chaffin's Farm 1/64; deserted to enemy 1/6/65 - took oath of rebel deserter at Bermuda Hundred - supposed to be sent to N.Y. City - later record indicated transferred to Henderson, Ky.

WELCHER, (WILSHIRE) ROBERT A.: Co. F; paroled Ashland 5/1/65; miller; (may be Robert A. Wilshire).

WELLS, I. T.: pwl; joined Armistead Camp, UCV 1898.

WHARTON, RICHARD GOODE: Field and Staff; Adj./1st Lt.; drilled troops at Camp Lee and Richmond College 4/23/61-10/61 with no compensation; Pvt. in 1st Co. Richmond Howitzers 8 months; Col. William Dabney Stuart wrote Comm. of VMI if Wharton could return to VMI and finish his courses since his age kept him from employment in army, and business in Va. was stagnated˜, Stuart wrote Conf. Sec. of War 1/5/62 supporting Wharton for Cadetship in Conf. Army to 1/5/62; widowed mother wrote Conf. Sec. of War 1/30/62 to call attention to fact that Wharton had applied for Cadetship in Army – and needed job to pay back money he borrowed to go to VMI; Stuart wrote to Brig. Gen. Corse from camp near Culpeper Court House 11/9/62 and 11/12/62 saying that Lt. Otey had resigned as Adi. - Lt. E. B. Goode was assigned to take his place, but Goode was taken sick after fall of Donelson and did not report - said 56th was poorly officered and If War Dept. had assigned Goode to other duty, Stuart wanted Wharton to be Adj.; appointed Adj. 56th Va. 11/26/62; admitted Richmond hosp. 7/24/63 with scorbutis, scabies, and wd. - Transferred to private quarters 11/2/63; WIA 8/25/64 near Howlett's House; 11/5/64 found unfit for field service for 5 months because of gunshot wd. of lung with indications of phthisis; S.O. 270/22 11/12/64 ordered to report to Brig. Gen. W. M. Gardner, commanding post Richmond for temporary assignment to light duty as inspector of Guards at Libby Prison and Castle Thunder; 12/7/64 Wharton wrote and asked If he could keep horse of his predecessor - in 5/63 he exchanged his private horse with Capt. Carter, Adj. 56th Va., for a horse branded CS and equal in value to his - his old horse was used as draught horse, attached to baggage wagon and captured by enemy when army was returning from Gettysburg - Carter died soon after horses were exchanged so Wharton did not get certificate - granted permission to keep horse; 1/28/65 listed as on sick furlough due to wds. received in trenches near Howlett's House; paroled at Richmond 4/22/65; b. 2/3/1842 Hanover Co. to Dr. Robert Henry and Lucy Hylton Dabney Wharton; entered VMI 1858 - declared graduated 12/12/61, 7 months prior to normal graduation because drilled troops in Richmond at start of war; taught school several years after war; entered Medical College of Virginia - graduated c. 1871; m. Elizabeth Allen Courts

1873 - daughter of Daniel W. Courts, treasurer of North Carolina; one son and two daughters; practiced medicine Ruffin, NC, - became blind and lived with son; still living 2/4/1921.
WHITE, CHARLES WILLIS: pwl; enl. Co. C 21st Va. in Christiansville - transferred to 56th, Co. unknown; AWOL 11/61-12/61; discharged 6/9/62 by providing substitute; d. Drakes Branch, n.d.g. from softening of brain; widow Susan M. White applied for pension 6/6/1900; m. Mecklenburg - n.d.g. - $25 approved.
WHITE, HUGH L.: enl. 7/8/61 Co. A in Mecklenburg, Sgt; on guard duty 7/5/61-10/31/61; d. Nashville, TN hosp. 3/5/62 - death claim filed by mother Jane White 8/21/62 - owed $95.83.
WHITE, JAMES E.: enl. 8/6/61 Co. K in Mechanicsville - never mustered in and did not appear.
WHITE, WILLIAM: enl. 8/6/61 Co. K in Mechanicsville; present 8/6/61-10/31/61 - last 2 days AWOL.; POW Ft. Donelson - sick at Camp Morton - sent to Vicksburg for exchange; POW Gettysburg - d. 10/30/63 of chronic diarrhea at Ft. Delaware - bur. Finn's Point, N.J.
WHITEHEAD, JOHN M.: enl. 7/12/61 Co. G in Charlotte, 2nd Lt; appointed 2nd Lt. 7/26/61 - dropped 5/5/62; enr. as conscript 2/16/64 - assigned to 56th 2/25/64; d. 3/22/64 Richmond of pneumonia.
WHITLOCK, ANDREW J.: enl. 7/9/61 Co. C in Louisa; discharged 7/26/61 age 30, hernia; b. Louisa; farmer, light complexion, blue eyes, 6'2 1/2".
WHITLOCK, JESSE ANDERSON: enl. 4/1/64; Co. C at Chaffin's Farm; present 5/64-8/64; admitted Chimborazo 1/23/65 with scrofula - returned to duty 1/30/65; paroled Ashland 5/2/65; b. Louisa; farmer; applied for pension 3/14/1910 age 69 living Mineral, Louisa Co. - disability due to age and wd. in right side received 1865 - no income - $24 approved; rerated 3/18/1918 - $75 approved; bur. Rt. 654, Mineral, land owned by Walton Lumber Co.
WHITLOCK, JOHN H.: enl. 7/9/61 Co. C in Louisa; sick furlough 7/9/61-8/31/61; present 9/61-10/61 and 9/63-12/63; furloughed 1/1/64-2/29/64; admitted Richmond hosp. 4/2/64 - furloughed 30 days 4/3/64 - returned to duty 5/5/64; present 5/64-8/64; received clothes 10/13/64, 12/2/64, and 12/28/64; paroled Ashland 5/2/65; farmer.
WHITLOCK, SAM A.: pwl; Co. C - from Louisa.
WHITLOCK, WILLIAM J. (H.): enl. 7/9/61 Co. C in Louisa; sick furlough 7/9/61-8/31/61; present 9/61-10/61; d. 8//20/62 in Louisa of typhoid fever.
WHITLOCK, WILLIAM JOSEPH: pwl; Co. D; b. 1849; d. 1921.
WHITTEMORE, (WHITMORE) HENRY E.: enl. 6/22/61 Co. B in Mecklenburg; Pvt./Sgt.; admitted Richmond hosp. 1/30/63; transferred Blacks and Whites Hosp. 4/3/63 with rheumatism - note from Inspector of 102 to McCaw asked if Whittemore and John O. Walker are still in Chimborazo and if so what was their condition; present 9/63-12/63, 4/1/64,

and 5/64-8/64; POW Burkeville 4/6/65 - took oath and released from Pt. Lookout 6/22/65; florid complexion, brown hair, dark hazel eyes, 5'11 1/2": b. Mecklenburg; farmer; applied for pension 5/6/1903 age 73 living Mecklenburg - disability due to exposure during war - $15 approved; rerated 1/24/1906 age 76 - old age, liver disease, varicose veins - $30 approved; member Longstreet Camp UCV,

WICKER, WASHINGTON: enl. 8/6/61 Co. K in Mechanicsville; present 8/6/61-10/31/61; Manuscript 1444 concerning desertion 11/19/62; admitted Chimborazo 2/16/63 - returned to duty 4/21/63; readmitted 6/7/63 with dysentery - returned to duty 8/25/63; present 7/63-12/63, 4/1/64 and 5/64-8/64 - had to forfeit one month's pay by sentence of Court Martial; paroled at Richmond 4/20/65.

WIDDIFIELD, MARTIN V.: enl. 5/3/62 Co. B in Richmond; POW Gettysburg - confined Ft. Delaware and Pt. Lookout 10/27/63 - exchanged 2/18/65.

WIGLESWORTH, JOSEPH W.: enl. 10/26/63 Co. K in Richmond; paid $50 bounty; present 9/63-12/63, 4/1/64, and 5/64-8/64; received clothes 9/27/64, 10/13/64, 10/19/64, 12/30/64; paroled Ashland 4/25/65.

WILKERSON, WILLIAM: pwl; Co. A.

WILKES, BENJAMIN CALVIN (H.): enl. 7/18/61 Co. I in Charlotte; present 7/18/61-10/31/61; admitted Chimborazo 8/1/62 with fever – transferred Lynchburg 8/6/62; POW Gettysburg – confined Ft. McHenry and Ft. Delaware 7/10/63 - exchanged from Pt. Lookout 12/25/63; detailed to hosp. guard duty in Lynchburg 2/24/65 age 29; name on list of those surrendered by Lee at Appomattox, but not present with command for parole.

WILKES, BURWELL BASSETT, JR.: pwl; Co. E; assigned guard duty Lynchburg where was examined monthly by Post Medical Examining Board; discharged before surrender; surrendered in Lynchburg few days after 4/9/65; b. 1/30/1836 to Burwell and Lucy Gray Feild (Dr. Richard Feild's daughter); attended UVA before war - highly recommended by Latin and Greek professors; farmer and teacher; never married; elder in Concord Presbyterian Church, Brunswick; d. 4/21/1895 of consumption - bur. Wilkes' Family Cem. on plantation "Charlie's Hope", Brunswick.

WILKINS, THOMAS F.: enr. as conscript 1/1/64 at Gloucester - assigned to Co. K 1/15/64; absent sick 4/1/64 and 5/64-6/64; POW near Howlett's House 8/25/64 - confined Bermuda Hundred, Ft. Monroe, and Pt. Lookout 8/27/64 - paroled and transferred to Aiken's Landing 9/18/64; admitted Chimborazo 9/23/64 with fever - furloughed 40 days 9/26/64 to Gloucester.

WILKINSON, ALEXANDER (ALLEN): enl. 8/10/64 Co. A in Mecklenburg; present 7/9/64-8/31/64; admitted Chimborazo 3/30/65 with debility; captured in Richmond hosp. 4/3/65 - sent to Jackson Hosp., Libby Prison, and Newport News 4/23/65; resident of Mecklenburg; fair complexion, red hair, grey eyes, 5'7".

WILKINSON, WILLIAM M.: Co. C; captured Rollsburg, Va. 12/13/62 age 25 - confined Athenum Prison, Wheeling, Va. - transferred Camp Chase; resident of Bridgeport, Harrison Co.; bar keeper; fair complexion, light hair, blue eyes; 6'.

WILLIAMS, A. B.: pwl; 1st Lt./Ensign; (probably Alexander Lafayette Price) he and his personal baggage surrendered by Lee at Appomattox.

WILLIAMS, ALEXANDER LAFAYETTE PRICE: enl. 7/18/61 Co. I in Charlotte, Pvt./Lt./Ensign; sick furlough 7/18/61-8/31/61 - absent beyond time; special leave granted 8/20/61; present 9/61-10/61; at Ft. Donelson; WIA and POW Gettysburg - gallant color bearer captured inside enemy's line with flag of 56th Va. Inf. - gunshot wd. in thigh - admitted Chester Hosp. - paroled and exchanged 9/23/63; appointed Ensign 6/15/64; admitted Chimborazo 8/27/64 with dysentery - furloughed 30 days 9/13/64 to Mecklenburg - furlough extended 30 days; surrendered by Lee at Appomattox; b. 5/14/1838 Halifax Co. to Isaac James and Mary Morton Crews Williams (uncle was Hiram George Crews); joined Missionary Baptist Church 1850 and Ellis Creek Church in Halifax 1858; lived in Lunenburg when enl.; farmer, parents owned 10 slaves and 150 acres of land at outbreak of war, but he owned none; lived In Charlotte after war until 1870 when moved to Ky.; living Greenbrier, TN 1921.

WILLIAMS, ANDREW JACKSON: enl. 7/10/61 Co. E in Brunswick; present 7/10/61-8/31/61: signed power of attorney at Camp Lee 11/4/61; enl. 1863 Co. F 25th Batt. Local Defense Troops; b. about 1828 to Thomas R. and Elizabeth M. Harrison Williams.

WILLIAMS, B. T.; pwl; Co. B.

WILLIAMS, BENJAMIN HARRISON: enl. 2/9/63 Co. E in Brunswick; present 9/63-10/63; AWOL 11/63-12/63; present 4/164; MWIA and POW Cold Harbor - d. Armory Square USA Gen. Hosp., Washington, D.C. 6/15/64 age 40 of gunshot wd. rt. thigh and/or breast; resident Brunswick; widow Margaret Williams; b. about 1826 Brunswick - brother of Andrew J. and Charles W. Williams.

WILLIAMS, CHARLES B.: enl. 7/18/61 Co. I in Charlotte, Pvt./Cpl.; present 7/18/61-8/31/61; sick in Richmond hosp 9/61-10/61.; admitted Richmond hosp. 9/7/62 – transferred Farmville hosp. 9/29/62 with debility - returned to duty 12/6/62; furloughed 6/30/63-10/31/63; present 7/63-12/63 and 5/64-8/64; d. after war, but before 1896.

WILLIAMS, CHARLES W. (H.): enl. Co. E 1883; MWIA Gettysburg; d. 7/8/63 Gettysburg hosp. of gunshot wd. leg; body reinterred Hollywood Cem; b. about 1833 Brunswick - brother of Andrew J. and Benjamin H. Williams; m. Martha A. Rideout 1/15/1863.

WILLIAMS, CLEMENT W.: enl. 7/18/61 Co. I in Charlotte; admitted Danville hosp. with debilitas 9/17/62; in Richmond hosp. 12/6/62;

admitted Chimborazo 2/18/63 with flesh wd. left side of head and debility - transferred to Farmville hosp. 3/16/63 - furloughed to Charlotte 40 days 3/26/63 - returned to duty 5/26/63 - varicose veins of scrotum - to be furnished with suspensory bandage and returned to Regt.; deserted near Gettysburg 7/3/63, probably while on march to field, and captured 2 days later - took oath of allegiance to U.S. 7/7/63.

WILLIAMS, DAVID P.: enl. 6/25/61 Co. B in Mecklenburg; present 9/61-10/61; POW Ft. Donelson - sent from Camp Morton to Vicksburg for exchange; WIA and POW Gettysburg - sent Gettysburg hosp. and DeCamp Hosp. with gunshot wd. in hip; paroled 9/16/63; retired to Invalid Corps 4/27/64; admitted Richmond hosp. 3/7/65 - returned to duty 3/11/65; surrendered by Lee at Appomattox - name on list of those who took amnesty oath administered to paroled POWS remaining in Richmond 5/13/65; applied for pension 4/18/1892 age 58 living Marengo, Mecklenburg Co. - disallowed; reapplied 2/17/1896 age 62 - $15 approved.

WILLIAMS, EDWARD: Co. C; received clothes 10/19/64 and 12/28/64; admitted Chimborazo 3/9/65; paroled Gordonsville 6/23/65.

WILLIAMS, EMBREN EMBREY or EMBRA) E.: enl. 6/13/61 Co. E in Brunswick, Pvt./Sgt; POW Ft. Donelson - sent from Camp Morton to Vicksburg for exchange 9/11/62; declared exchanged Aiken's Landing 11/10/62; WIA and POW Gettysburg - in Gettysburg hosp. with wd. of left arm - paroled 8/23/63 at Baltimore, Md. - delivered City Point 8/24/63 - admitted Petersburg hosp. 8/24/63 – furloughed 8/28/63; rolls of 4/1/64 and 7/64-8/64 showed him as clerk in office of Comdt. of Conscripts for Va.; certificate of disability for retiring invalid soldier 3/3/65 age 26 - arm amputated; light complexion, dark hair, grey eyes, 5'8"; b. Brunswick 10/29/1835 to John L and Mary C. Jones Williams; brother Leonidas Fenton Williams KIA Gettysburg; farmer; m. Mary Elizabeth Boswell 12/27/1864 Lunenburg, 2 children; son Thomas F. represented Lunenburg in Va. House of Delegates; d. 5/11/1920 - bur. Woodland Cem., Chase City, Mecklenburg Co.

WILLIAMS, GREEN W.: enl. 610/61 Co. E in Brunswick; discharged with disability 8/19/61 age 36; exempted from service 3/15/62 because of foot injury; reenl. 2/9/63 Co. E; admitted Farmville Hosp. 3/9/63 with lumbago; WIA and POW Gettysburg; admitted Gettysburg hosp. 7/5/63 with gunshot wd. of right thigh - paroled from Pt. Lookout 3/16/64 - admitted Chimborazo 3/20/64 – furloughed 30 days; dark complexion, eyes, and hair, 5'10"; b. about 1826 in Brunswick - brother of Embry Williams; 1849 m. Rebecca Birdsong, daughter of Nathaniel Birdsong, Co. E; after her death, m. Lucretia C. Clayton 1852 - 1 child; after her death m. Frances A. E. Drummond in Brunswick 1/71857 - 4 children; farmer.

WILLIAMS, HENDERSON S.: enl. 7/8/61 Co. A in Mecklenburg; sick with measles 7/8/61-8/30/61; d. 9/25/61 in Richmond - death claim filed by father Thomas L. Williams.

WILLIAMS, J. S.: Co. unknown; paroled at Richmond 4/26/65.

WILLIAMS, JAMES A.: enl. 7/10/61 Co. E in Brunswick; present 7/10/61-8/31/61; POW Ft. Donelson 2/16/62 - sent from Camp Morton to Vicksburg for exchange; furloughed 10/24/62-11/24/62; MWIA and POW Gettysburg - d. US II Corps Hosp. 7/19/63 from gunshot wd. that fractured hip - bur. Row 1, Yard D of hosp. cem. in Jacob Schwartz's cornfield on Rock Creek; moved to Richmond 6/13/62 with 110 others in 10 boxes labeled "S" - reinterred Hollywood Cem.

WILLIAMS, JAMES H.: exempted from service because overseer for widowed mother 3/20/62; exemption ceased later, so enl. 2/9/63 Co. E in Brunswick; POW Gettysburg – confined Ft. Delaware; sick in hosp. 9/63-10/63; AWOL 11/63-12/63, 4/1/64, and 5/64-6/64; absent sick 7/64-8/64; paroled Burkeville between 4/14/65-4/17/65; b. about 1839 to Edmund and Jane K. Delbridge Williams; m. Mary E. Nanny 2/64 in Brunswick - 1 daughter; James and daughter probably d. in 1868.

WILLIAMS, JAMES L: enl. 3/14/64 Co. B in Richmond; present 4/1/64; admitted Chimborazo 8/25/64 with gunshot wd. of left hand - furloughed 60 days 9/24/64 to Brunswick; admitted Chimborazo 3/7/65 with pneumonia; applied for pension 5/21/1900 age 62 living Brunswick - partially disabled due to age, shortness of breath, and rheumatism - $15 approved - "dead" written across front of application.

WILLIAMS, JERRY: pwl; Co. E (may be James A. or James H. Williams).

WILLIAMS, JOHN DANIEL: enl. 7/8/61 Co. D in Buckingham; present 7/8/61-10/31/61; reenlisted 5/3/62 at Fulton Hill - paid $50 bounty; WIA and POW Sharpsburg 9/14/62 – minie ball wd. left hand and arm – confined Ft. McHenry and Ft. Monroe 10/17/62 - exchanged at Aiken's Landing 10/19/62; - admitted Scottsville hosp. 10/20/62 - furloughed 50 days 10/30/62 - still on hosp. roll 8/63 – admitted Chimborazo 9/21/683 - deserted hosp. 10/14/63; b. 1836; farmer; applied for pension 8/29/1889 age 52 living Arrington, Nelson Co.; $15 approved; made statement 5/4/1911 age 74 living Lynchburg; d. 1920 in Lynchburg.

WILLIAMS, NATHANIEL HARVEY: enr. as conscript 3/14/64 Camp Lee - assigned to Co. B 3/22/64; 4/1/64 present; admitted Chimborazo 6/4/64 with severe gunshot wd. of hand - furloughed 60 days 6/11/64.

WILLIAMS, PETER T.: pwl; Co. D; applied for pension 5/14/1900 age 74 living Forkland, Nottoway Co. - disabled by age - $30 approved.

WILLIAMS, RICHARD JONES: enl. 7/10/61 Co. E in Brunswick; present 7/10/61-8/31/61; furloughed 1/1/62-2/1/62 and 5/12/64-5/30/64; present 9/63-12/63, 4/1/64, and 5/64-6/64; absent on furlough 7/64-8/64; POW Farmville 4/6/65 - took oath and released from Pt. Lookout 6/22/65; dark complexion, brown hair, grey eyes, 5'10 1/2"; b. about 1833 to John and

Sarah W. Williams; 1850 living in home of William H. Mitchell in Brunswick; m. Virginia Ann Blanks 8/27/1856 - 9 children; farmer; applied for pension 5/10/1900 age 71 living Nottoway, suffering from diseases; d. 1916 - bur. Pleasant Grove Church Cem.

WILLIAMS, STERLING J.: enl. 7/10/61 Co. E in Brunswick; absent sick with measles 7/1/61-8/31/61; present 9/63-10/63; on rolls 11/63-12/63 and 1/64-8/64 listed as on detached service as shoemaker in C.S. Clothing Depot Richmond; KIA picket line Howlett's Farm 8/25/64 - estate inventoried in Brunswick 1866; pension application filed by widow 4/2/1888; m. Martha E Moore 11/28/1849 Brunswick; 1860 census – farmer; 3 daughters.

WILLIAMS, THOMAS, J.: *enl.* 7/10/61 Co. E in Brunswick; present 7/10/61-8/31/61; admitted Chimborazo 7/1/62 with gunshot wd. of hand; furloughed 7/2/62-8/3/62 and 1/15/63-2/5/63; MWIA and POW Gettysburg - confined Ft. McHenry & Ft. Delaware where d. n.d.g.; b. about 1845 Brunswick to Nathaniel Hicks and Susan P. Wray Williams; m. Martha J, Hanks 2/23/1863; farmer.

WILLIAMS, THOMAS B.: enl. 7/8/61 Co. I in Charlotte; present 7/18/61-10/31/61; discharged 6/4/62 due to broken down condition; d. 6/7/62 *age* 27 Charlotte of disease; b. Charlotte; farmer, dark complexion, light hair, blue eyes. 5'5".

WILLIAMS, WILLIAM H. H.: enl. 8/31/61 Co. A in Mecklenburg - substitute for Joseph E. Watson; discharged 9/24/62 age 46 because over 35; b. Lunenburg; farmer; dark complexion and hair, grey eyes, 5'10".

WILLIAMS, WILLIAM JESSE: enl. 2/9/63 Co. E Brunswick; WIA and POW Gettysburg - d. Ft Delaware 8/26/63 of rubeola – bur. Finns Point, N. J.; b. about 1831 - brother of James H. Williams.

WILLIAMS, WILLIAM W.: enl. 7/18/61 Co. I in Charlotte; Pvt./Capt.; present 7/18/61-10/31/61; appointed 1st Lt 11/19/61; elected Capt. 5/3/62 - resigned 8/4/62 due to laryngitis of long standing; d. after war but before 1896.

WILLIAMSON, FRANK: Co. A - substitute - deserted 9/63-10/63.

WILLIAMSON, THOMAS: Co. K, 1st Lt; elected 1st Lt 5/3/62 - resigned 3/20/63.

WILLS, N. H.: Co. C; paroled Columbia 5/65.

WILMOTH, (WILMOUTH) JAMES WILLIAM: enl. 7/10/61 Co. E in Brunswick; listed *as* being absent sick with jaundice; d. 1862 yellow jaundice - death claim filed 9/15/62; b. Brunswick about 1829; 1860 census - living Lunenburg with wife Mary Jane Turner - 3 children - working as overseer.

WILMOTH (WILMOUTH) RICHARD H.: enl. 2/9/63 Co. E; present 9/63-12/63 and 4/1/64; WIA Cold Harbor in right forearm - absent wded. 5/64-8/64 and unfit for service; discharged 2/65 age 24; paroled 5/26/65 in

Richmond; light complexion, black hair, hazel eyes; 5'4"; son of Jesse and Martha Wilmouth of Mecklenburg; m. Rebecca A.Westmoreland 1/3/63 in Brunswick - 4 children; farmer; d. 1/29/1873 from wd. received in war; widow Rebecca A. W. Westmoreland (remarried) applied for pension 9/27/1900 living Brunswick - $25 approved,

WILSHIRE, ROBERT A.: enl. 7/26/61 Co. F in Louisa; present 7/27/61-10/31/61; deserted 9/13/63; on 7/64-8/64 roll listed as absent - in division guard house. (may be Robert A. Welcher.)

WINFREY, GEORGE HILL.: enr. as conscript 2/23/64 at Camp Lee - assigned Co. D 3/7/64; present 4/1/64; WIA Cold Harbor - admitted Chimborazo 6/1/64 with wd. of right shoulder, listed as absent wded. 5/64-8/64; examined by Farmville Hosp. Board 10/14/64 and ordered to return to Command; admitted Chimborazo 3/15/65; paroled at Farmville 4/27/65; b.1835 or 38 Buckingham; m. Judith Catharine Robertson; applied for pension 5/12/1900 age 65 living in Well Water, Buckingham Co. - right leg amputated because of T.B. - $30 approved; made statement 3/26/1903 – owned property worth $330.25; d. 1918; grandson was George Herman Layne Winfrey, secretary, treasurer, and business manager of Medical Society of Virginia.

WINGFIELD, ALBERT BURTON: enl. 6/1/61 Co. D in Buckingham; listed as deserted on roll of 9/61-10/61; reenlisted 5/3/62; Court Martial for desertion 1/13/63; found guilty of AWOL - forfeited pay and allowances for 12 months and when not on march had to be on detail cutting wood until 4/1/63; admitted Chimborazo 2/22/63 with chronic diarrhea - transferred Lynchburg 3/18/63; admitted Williamsburg hosp. 5/8/63 – transferred Petersburg; absent sick 9/63-12/63, 4/1/64, and 5/64-6/64; listed 4/64 and 7/64-8/64 as on detached duty driving wagon; furloughed 5/1/64-8/8/64; admitted Chimborazo 8/16/64 with chronic diarrhea - returned to duty 8/30/64; came home from army sick with chronic diarrhea and never able to do anything again; said to be "a funny fellow, the life of the camp"; b. 4/15/1834; miller, applied for pension 5/12/1911 age 77 living Schuyler, Nelson Co. - blind, hernia and chronic diarrhea -served until surrender - $24 approved; d. 12/25/1916 in Schuyler of chronic colitis - bur. Rock Springs United Methodist Church, Rt. 620, Nelson Co,; widow Alice Wingfield applied for pension 11/16/1923 – m. 1874 Salem - $76 approved.

WINGFIELD, NIMROD T.: enl. 5/3/62 Co. B in Richmond; admitted Charlottesville hosp. 5/28/62 with rubeola; returned to duty 7/21/62; POW Boonsboro - sent from Ft. Delaware to Aiken's Landing for exchange 10/2/62 - declared exchanged 11/10/62; admitted Charlottesville hosp. 3/2/63 with debilitas; WIA and POW Gettysburg – confined Ft. Delaware - paroled 7/30/63 and sent from Pt. Lookout for exchange 8/63 - admitted Farmville hosp. 8/29/63 with wds. and chronic diarrhea; deserted hosp. 9/4/63.

WINN. JAMES W.: enl. 7/8/61 Co. A in Mecklenburg; present sick with measles 7/8/61-8/31/61; present 9/61-10/61; reenlisted 5/3/62; d. 2/24/63 of disease in Clarksville, TN - death claim filed by father Britton Winn 11/15/64 - owed $244.48

WINSTON, RICHARD W.: Pvt.; conscripted 1864 in Co. F; received clothes 12/28/64; POW Hatcher's Run 3/31/65 - took oath and released from Pt. Lookout 6/22/65; resident of Goochland; b.12/11/1837; black hair, dark complexion, hazel eyes, 5'7".

WOOD, AMMON HANCOCK: pwl; Co. H.

WOOD, CALEB: pwl.; Co. D; from Nelson Co.

WOOD, CHRISTOPHER C.: enl. 8/22/62 in Co. H; POW Gettysburg - admitted Chester, Pa, Hosp. - paroled and exchanged 9/23/63; WIA skirmish line Cold Harbor - admitted Chimborazo 6/2/64 with gunshot wd. of right arm - transferred to Charlottesville hosp. 6/9/64 - furloughed 7/29/64 for 60 days; declared totally disabled 12/30/64 age 20 due to wds.; b. Albemarle 12/11/1843; farmer; applied for pension 3/26/1888 age 44 living Nelson Co. - right arm and hand useless due to wds. - $15 approved.

WOOD, JESSE H.: enl. 5/3/62 Co. D; d. Richmond hosp. 7/25/62 of typhoid fever.

WOOD, JOHN M.: enl. 7/15/61 Co. H in Albemarle; present 7/29/61-10/31/61; WIA Gaines's Mill; admitted Charlottesville hosp. 6/26/63 with ulcers - furloughed 7/15/63-8/15/63; listed as deserted 9/3/63; absent sick on roll 7/63-12/63; admitted hosp.1/64 - returned to duty 4/4/4 - AWL 4/1/64; present 5/64-8/64; received clothes 10/19/64 and 12/30/64; d. suddenly with hemorrhage of lungs - n.d. - widow Julia A. E. Wood applied for pension 3/11/1904 living Albemarle; m. 1856 - said he was on pension list when he died; $25 approved.

WOOD, JOHN T.: enl. 7/15/61 Co. H in Albemarle; listed as refusing to report on roll 7/29/61-10/31/61.

WOOD, JOSIAH H.: Co. H; paroled Charlottesville 5/20/65.

WOOD, RICHARD I. (T.): Co. A; paroled 5/12/65 Headqtrs. 6th Army Corps; d. 7/15/1877 in Mecklenburg when struck by lightning; widow Elizabeth Wood applied for pension 5/1/1900; rn. 2/16/1852 in Boydton - $25 approved.

WOOD, ROBERT W. Co. H; KIA Gaines's Mill.

WOOD, WILLIAM: pwl; Co. D.

WOOD, WILLIAM H.: enl. 5/3/62; Co. K; admitted Charlottesville hosp. 11/24/62 - returned to duty 12/2/62; POW Gettysburg - confined Ft. Delaware - exchanged 7/30/63 - admitted Charlottesville hosp. 8/18/63 with debility - returned to duty 11/11/63; present 9/64-12/64; AWL 4/1/64; on roll of 5/64-6/64 dated 8/31/64 listed as absent since last mustered; paroled 6/21/65; resident of Hanover; dark complexion and hair, grey eyes; took

oath 6/21/65. (may be William Henry Wood)
WOOD, WILLIAM HENRY: enl. 8/6/61 Co. K in Mechanicsville; Pvt./Cpl.; present 8/6/61-10/31/61; POW Ft. Donelson - sent from Camp Morton to Vicksburg for exchange; furloughed 10/24/62-11/24/62; POW Gettysburg – confined Ft. McHenry and Ft. Delaware - took oath and released 6/21/65; sallow complexion, dark hair, grey eyes, 5'6"; alive in 1905.
WOOD, WILLIAM RICE: enl. 7/15/61 Co. H in Albemarle; Sgt.; present 7/29/61-8/31/61; sick furlough 9/61-10/61; furloughed 11/6/61-4/19/62; reenlisted 5/1/62 - paid $50 bounty; on detached service 8/5/62-12/20/62; POW Gettysburg – confined Ft. Delaware and Pt. Lookout - took oath and received for exchange at Venus Point, Savannah River 11/15/64; POW Harper's Farm 4/6/65 - released 6/22/65; fair complexion, black hair, hazel eyes, 5'7 3/4"; b. 9/2/1834; resident Albemarle; bur. Mt. Moriah Cem., Albemarle.
WOODDY, GEORGE W.: enl. 2/23/64 Co. K at Chaffin's Farm; present 4/1/64; AWOL 5/64-6/64; absent in arrest 7/64-8/64; received clothes 10/19/64.
WOODDY, JOHN H.: enl. 2/23/64 Co. K at Chaffin's Farm; KIA Hanover Junction 5/25/64; death claim filed 3/6/65; b. Hanover.
WOODY, PLEASANT J.: enl. 8/6/61 Co. K in Mechanicsville, Pvt./Cpl.; present 8/6/61-10/31/61; POW Ft. Donelson - sent from Camp Morton to Vicksburg for exchange; furloughed 11/11/62-12/11/62 and 1/1/64-2/29/64; POW Burkeville 4/6/65 - took oath and released from Pt. Lookout 6/22/65; resident of Hanover; light complexion, light brown hair, hazel eyes, 5'81/2"; lived Richmond prior to admittance to Lee Camp Soldiers' Home 1/16/1914 age 78 due to age - discharged at own request 3/31/1915 - readmitted 12/26/1916 - discharged at own request 5/28/1917.
WRAY, WILLIAM ANDERSON: enl. 2/9/63 Co. E in Brunswick; POW Gettysburg - confined Ft. McHenry and Ft. Delaware; took oath and released 6/20/65; sallow complexion, dark hair and eyes, 6'3"; b. about 1830 to Anderson and Nancy Gibbs Wray in Brunswick; farmer; m. Virginia B. Wright 4/29/1857 Brunswick - 6 children; d. 1908 – will probated 9/12/1908.
WRIGHT, ALBERT J.: enl. 6/22/61 Co. B in Mecklenburg; MCV hosp. roll 8/5/61-8/14/61; POW Ft. Donelson; d. Camp Morton of typhoid pneumonia 3/17/62 - bur. Green Lawn Cem. - reinterred Crown Hill Cem.; death claim filed by father 5/21/62 - owed $73.76.
WRIGHT, C. T.: Co. G; received clothes 12/64; surrendered by Lee at Appomattox.
WRIGHT, COLEMAN F.: enl. 2/17/83 Co. B in Richmond; detailed 9/5/63 hosp. guard – recorded on duty 9/63-12/63; present 4/1/64; recommended for furlough 5/28/64 due to phthisis pulmonalis- d. 6/27/64.
WRIGHT, GEORGE H.: enl. 8/6/61 Co. K in Mechanicsville; present

8/6/61-10/31/61; in hosp. 3/62-8/62; present 7/12/63, 4/1/64, and 5/64-8/64; furloughed 1/1/64-2/29/64; admitted Chimborazo 8/25/64 with wd. - right ring and middle fingers amputated - furloughed 40 days 9/1/64 - readmitted 10/16/64 - deserted hosp. 10/30/64; residence Hanover.

WRIGHT, JACKSON: enl. 7/8/61 Co. A in Mecklenburg; present 7/8/61-8/31/61; detached service at Armory in Richmond 10/16/61 per S.O. 306/1.

WRIGHT, JAMES L.: enl. 6/22/61 Co. B in Mecklenburg; present 9/61-10/61; POW Ft. Donelson - sent from Camp Morton to Vicksburg for exchange; WIA and POW Gettysburg - admitted West's Buildings Hosp. 7/3/63 with gunshot wd. of head - paroled 8/24/63; admitted Williamsburg Hosp. 3/5/64 with wd. - returned to duty 3/7/64; retired to Invalid Corps 5/2/64; POW Farmville 4/6/65 - took oath and released from Pt. Lookout 6/22/65; fair complexion, dark brown hair, hazel eyes, 5'7 1/4"; resident Mecklenburg; applied for pension 1/15/1903 age 72 living Meridian, Dinwiddie Co.; disabled due to wd. at Gettysburg and rheumatism - property worth $400 - $30 approved.

WRIGHT, JOHN W.: enl. 7/10/61 Co. B in Mecklenburg; present 9/61-10/61; POW Ft. Donelson - sent from Camp Morton to Vicksburg for exchange; furloughed 2/6/63-2/19/63; WIA and POW Gettysburg - shot through hip so could hardly move body and sent to West's Buildings Hosp. - paroled 8/23/63; retired to Invalid Corps 5/2/64; farmer; applied for pension 7/20/1896 age 54 living North View, Mecklenburg Co. - $15 approved; member Armistead Camp No. 26, UCV; d. 12/19/1926 of heart trouble Mecklenburg; widow Rebecca C. Wright applied for pension 5/10/1927; m. 11/24/1886 Mecklenburg - $90 approved.

WRIGHT, JOHN W.: enl. 8/6/61 Co. K in Mechanicsville; discharged age 22 due to partial paralysis of right hand caused by spider bite 8/16/61; b. Hanover; dark complexion and hair, blue eyes, 5'10".

WRIGHT, JOSEPH: enr. as conscript 10/1/63 and assigned Co. A; present 9/63-12/63; sick furlough 2/4/64; AWOL 5/64-8/64; received clothes 12/64.

WRIGHT, P. C.: pwl; enl. 1884 on Howlett Line in Co. B; discharged in 1865; served 6 months; b. Mecklenburg; farmer; applied for pension 5/8/1903 age 76 living La Crosse, Mecklenburg Co. - partial disability due to age, rheumatism, weakness, and nervousness - $15 approved.

WYANT, JAMES C.: enl. 7/29/61 Co. H; Capt.; elected Capt. 5/3/62; admitted Chimborazo 6/24/62 with pneumonia; MWIA Gettysburg by gunshot wd. of face - d. 7/31/63 of erysipelas in Chester Hosp., Gettysburg - bur. Grave 90 Chester Hosp. Cem.; left $3, pocket book, papers, and Testament - reinterred Nat. Cem. Philadelphia; death claim filed by widow Samantha A. Wyant - owed $442; widow filed pension application 6/4/1888 - m. 12/15/62 near White Hall, Albemarle Co. - $30 approved.

WYNN, J. C.: Co. K; Cpl.; POW Gettysburg - in College Hosp. and then taken to Baltimore.

YANCEY, (YANCY) ABSALOM: enl. 8/15/62 Co. A in Mecklenburg; WIA and POW Gettysburg - admitted DeCamp Hosp. with gunshot wd. of forearm and back - paroled and exchanged 8/24/63; AWOL on roll 11/63-12/63; present 7/64-8/64; POW near Howlett's House 8/25/64 - confined Ft. Monroe and Pt. Lookout – exchanged 3/15/65.

YANCY, (YANCEY) JOHN R.: enl. 7/8/61 Co. A in Mecklenburg; present 7/61-10/31/61; discharged 9/9/62 age 36 because over 35 and did not reenlist; dark complexion, hair and eyes, 6'; b. 4/27/1826 in Mecklenburg; farmer - owned 500 acre farm 5 miles n. of Clarksville; m. Virginia Jones White -7 children; member Methodist Episcopal Church; applied for pension 11/17/1906 age 80 living Skipwith, Mecklenburg Co.; totally disabled - suffered from exposure during war - $30 approved; member Armistead Camp, UCV; d. 3/12/1907 - bur. family cem., Rt. 697, Mecklenburg Co.

YANCY, (YANCEY) J. R.: pwl; enl. 7/61 Co. A; served 4 years. (could be John R. Yancy).

YANCY, (YANCEY) JOHN WILLIAM: enl. 7/8/61 Co. D in Buckingham, Pvt./Lt.; present 7/8/61-10/31/61; present 9/63-12/63, 4/1/64, and 5/64-8/64; on detached duty 7/64-8/64; received clothes 10/19/64, 11/14/64, 12/2/64, and 12/28/64; farmer; applied for pension 9/6/1902 age 62 living in Lawfords, Buckingham Co. - neuralgia and rheumatism from exposure during 2nd year of war -marched through 6 states and in 7 battles during war - home on sick furlough last 2 or 3 months - $15 approved; d. 1904 of heart disease; widow Mary J. Yancey applied for pension 4/29/1908 – m, 1867 Buckingham - she owned 90 acres of land - rented it for $25 annually - $25 approved.

YATES, JAMES WILLIAM: enl. 7/12/61 Co. G in Mecklenburg; present on all rolls; furloughed 10/8/62-11/8/62 and 3/28/63-4/18/63; d. Halifax Co. in 1891 from "La Grippe"; widow Susan A. Yates applied for pension - m. Charlotte 1660's - $25 approved.

YOUNG, JOSEPH E.: enl. 7/26/61 Co. F in Louisa; present 7/27/61-10/31/61; d. 6/1/62 in Louisa of rheumatism - death claim filed by widow Margaret Young 7/30/63.

YOUNG, THOMAS JACKSON: enl. 7/9/61 Co. C in Louisa; sick furlough 7/9/61-8/31/61; WIA 2nd Manassas - minie ball in calf of left leg; present 9/63-12/63 and 5/64-8/64; paroled Ashland 5/2/65; farmer before war; b. about 1843; miner after war; m. Mary Catherine Holliday of Spotsylvania; filed pension application 4/14/1890 age 49 living in Mineral, Louisa Co. - pension disallowed; reapplied 9/12/1892 - paralysis of left leg below wd. bad circulation in foot - totally disabled - $15 approved; d. 4/1900 Mineral - bur. Baptist Church of Mineral Cem.

YOUNG, WILLIAM H., JR.: enl. 7/9/61 Co. C in Louisa, Cpl./Pvt.; present 7/9/61-10/31/61; Court Martial 2/23/63 - found guilty of specification and charge of AWOL - reduced to ranks and forfeited 2 months pay; POW Gettysburg - confined Fort Delaware and Pt. Lookout - paroled and released 5/2/65; tanner.

Chapter 18

Photographs and Maps, 56th Virginia Regiment

Pvt. Robert B. Agee, Co. D.

Left, General Richard B. Garnett, Brigade Commander, KIA Gettysburg. Right, Pvt. Robert B. Agee, Co. D

View from the Howlett Line 1864.
Drawing by Private Thomas A. Patteson, Co. D.

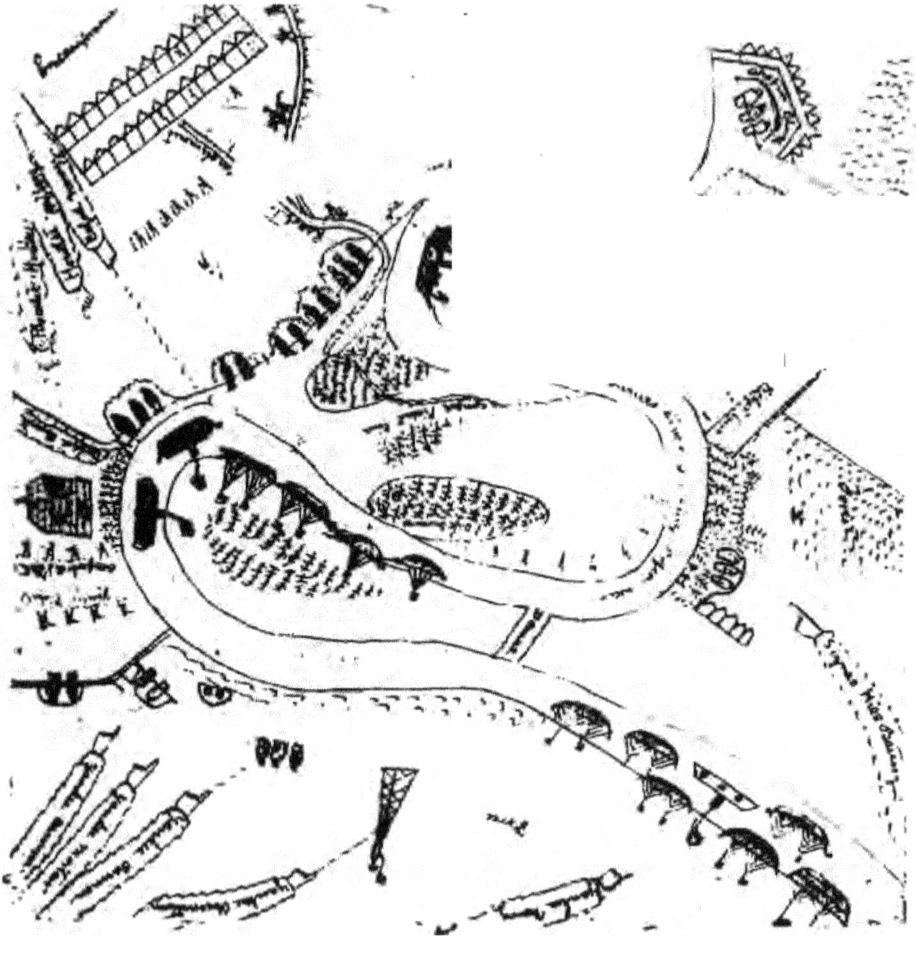

Battle flag, 56th Virginia - Army of Northern Virginia pattern.

Left, Capt. Robert P. Dickinson, Co. C., Right, Pvt. Charles W. Thomas, Co. B, died in prison.

Left, Sgt.Maj. Thomas Thweatt Jones, Co. E, POW Ft. Donelson., Right, Lt. Stephen W. Turner, Co. B, captured Ft. Donelson.

Right, silver ID disk worn by Private Pvt. John W. Barret, Co. F.
Right, Daniel W. Snyder, Quartermaster, Co. F.

Left, ivory field glasses made by Ringard Opticien of Paris. inscribed "Col. P. P. Slaughter, 1864, 56th Reg. Va. Infty, A.N. Va."
Right, Pvt. Robert J. Newman, Co. F.

Left, Pvt. David Gardner, Co. H. disabled by wound at Gaines's Mill. Right, Col. Philip P. Slaughter.

Left, Pvt. Jesse A. Whitlock, Co. C, Right, Pvt. William J. Harlow, Co. C, WIA

Left, Pvt. Marcellus Holt, believed to be M. C. Holt, Co. I., Right, Pvt. Samuel J. Harlow, Co. H, WIA Gaines's Mill.

Left, Private Henry Tate, Co. K, Right, Capt. Henry C. Michie, Co. H, WIA 2nd Manassas and Gettysburg.

Left, Pvt. John L. Holt, Co. I, KIA Gettysburg. Right, Pvt. Burrell N. M. Holt, Co. I, WIA Frazier's Farm and Gettysburg

Left, Pvt. William N. Boswell, Co. A. 11 year old drummer boy holding sword that Jefferson Davis presented to him. Right, Dr. William P. Palmer, Regimental Surgeon.

Top Left, Pvt. Freeman W. Jones, Co. E, WIA Howlett Line. Top right, Lt. George W. Finley, Co. K, captured at Gettysburg, one of the "Six Hundred".

Bottom left, Pvt. John R. Agee, Co. D. Bottom right, Pvt. James H. Norris, Co. H.

Top left, Capt.Thomas D. Jeffress, Co. G, WIA Gaines's Mill. Top right, Capt. Dabney C. Harrison, Co. K, KIA Fort Donelson. Bottom left, Pvt. James Purdy, Co. E, WIA Five Forks. Bottom right, Pvt. James W. Jeffress, Co. G. KIA Fort Donelson.

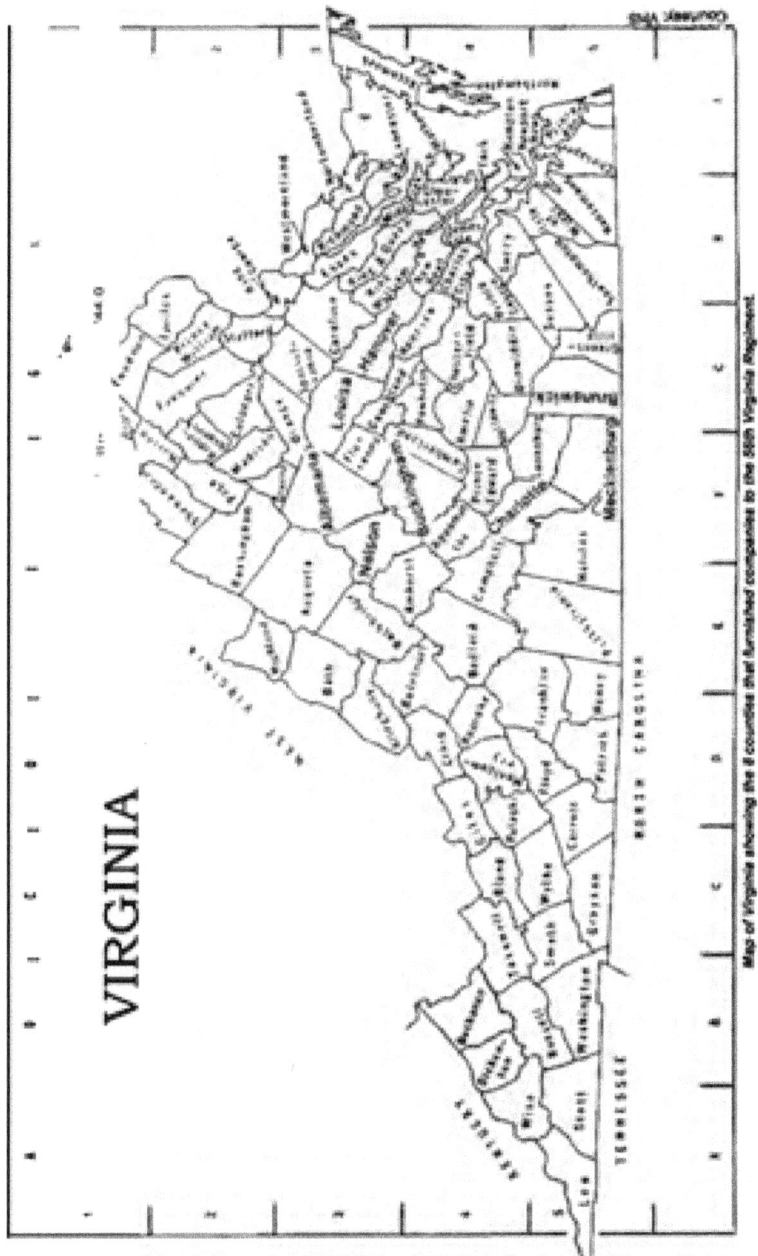

Map illustrating Virginia Counties in which were the homes of soldiers in the 56th Virginia Infantry Regiment.

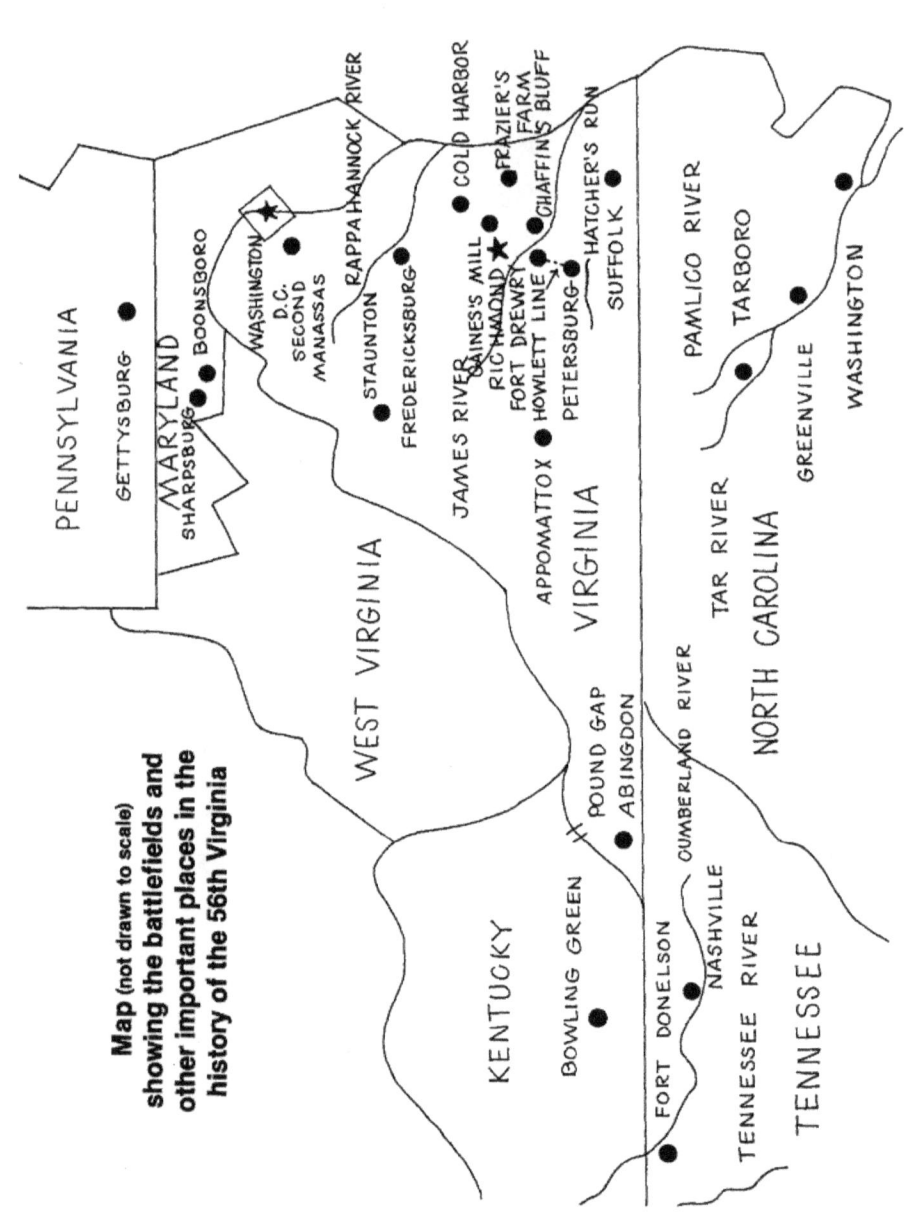

Map (not drawn to scale) showing the battlefields and other important places in the history of the 56th Virginia

BIBLIOGRAPHY

Manuscripts

Alleman, Glenn L., "A Biographical Study of William Dabney Stuart, Colonel C. S. A. and his 56th Virginia Volunteers." Abstract of a thesis. Brigham Young University 1960.
Brydge, Jean H., "Lonely Path to Glory." 1977.
Calkins, Christopher M., Notes on Howlett Line.
Crews, Hiram., Portions of his diary received from Richard L. Smith.
Groves, Lieutenant Richard H. (Ret.), " 1st Lt. John Thomas Chaffin: Company "G", 56th Virginia Volunteer Infantry Regt.."
Gunn, Ray W., Files on Virginia Confederate Soldiers.
Harlow, Gerald W., Burial files.
Howard, Harold E., File on 56th Virginia infantry.
Hutchinson, Scott W., Cemetery records.
Krick, Robert K., File on 56th Virginia.
Mann, B. David., VMI file.
McFall, F. Lawrence., Cemetery records.
Kelley, Fannie, Petition for damages to her Cold Harbor property - filed December 5, 1877. Copy in possession of John H. Armstrong, Ill.
R. E. Lee Camp of Confederate Veterans, Soldiers' Home Burial Ledger. Hollywood Cemetery, Richmond, Virginia.
Short, William B., Letters in possession of Mrs. Caleb Short.
Stein, Carl F., List of Confederate soldiers buried Oakland Cemetery, Atlanta, Georgia.
Stonesifer, Roy P., Jr., "The Forts Henry-Heiman and Fort Donelson Campaigns: A Study of Confederate Command." Diss. Pennsylvania State University, 1965.
Stribling, Reverend Charles, "Of Whom the World Was Not Worthy." Centennial speech of Concord Presbyterian Church, Brunswick County. Papers of Mrs. Mary Meade Dameron Woodson.
Thomas, Charles W., His letters. Copies owned by Richard L Baird.
Turner, Grady T., "Fifty-Sixth Regiment Virginia Volunteers in the

Civil War." 1931.
United Daughters of the Confederacy, application forms. Virginia Division, UDC. Richmond, Virginia.
University of Virginia Archives
John Warwick Daniel Papers
Jane Chapman Slaughter Papers
Virginia Historical Society
Armistead Camp, No. 28, UCV Minute Book
Carrington Papers
Grisby Papers
Krick, Robert K., Compiled Inmates of Lee Camp Confederate Soldiers' Home, 1986.
Short Papers
Virginia Military Institute
Virginia Military Institute, Alumni Records
William Dabney Stuart Papers
Virginia State Archives
Complied Roster of Regiments, Vol. 6
Confederate Prisoners of War, Johnson's Island 1862-1864 Accession No. 25829
Joseph Bidgood Papers, Unit Record Department, Adjutant General's Office,
Confederate Military Records, Box 60
Reverend George Williamson Finley Papers
S. Bassett French Papers
Pension Applications, Acts of 1888, 1900, and 1902
Williams, Alexander Lafayette Price, His Confederate Questionnaire. **Tennessee State Library,** Roll No. 8.

Public Documents

National Archives, War Department Collection of Confederate Records.
Complied Service Records, Confederate General and Staff Officers and Non-regimental Enlisted Men. M 331.
Compiled Service Records, Volunteer Soldiers Who Served in

Organizations from the State of Virginia. M 324, Rolls 972-978.
General Orders, Confederate Adjutant and inspector General's Office. M 1782.
Letters and Telegrams, Sent by the Confederate Adjutant and Inspector General, 1861-1865. M 627.
Letters Received, Confederate Adjutant and Inspector General M 474.
Unfiled Papers and Slips, Belonging to Confederate Complied Service Records. M 347.
Unit Locations, M 861
National Archives, Record of the Bureau of the Census
Seventh Census of the United States, 1860
Tenth Census of the United States, 1880
Twelfth Census of the United States, 1900
Thirteenth Census of the United States, 1910

Newspapers

Ezekiel, Herbert T., "Abbyville's Captain Frank Nelson Pickett's Man," The News Progress, (Clarksville) December 30, 1987.
Finley, George W., "Bloody Angle," Buffalo Evening News, May 28, 1894. In Gettysburg Newspaper Clippings, IV, 43.
Pritchett, Dr. W. M., "Our Civil War Soldiers from Brunswick County," The Brunswick Times Gazette, weekly article for 10 years.
Richmond Enquirer, June 14, 1864, Vol. LXII No. 6.
Richmond Times Dispatch. May 28, 1904, August 10, 1907, April 14, 1915, June 9, 1915.

Periodicals

Confederate Veteran, 1893-1932.
Cooling, B. Franklin, "Virginians and West Virginians at Fort Donelson," West Virginia History, 28:101-120. January, 1967.
---------, **ed.,** "A Virginian at Fort Donelson: Excerpts from the Prison
Journal of John Henry Guy, Tennessee Historical Quarterly, 176-

190. Spring, 1968.
Halsey, Ashley, "Ancestral Gray Cloud Over Patton," American History illustrated, 19:42-48. March, 1984.
"Mulberry Hill Families." The Southsider - Local History and Genealogy of Southslde, Virginia. 4:86-89. Fall, 1985.
Southern Historical Society Papers, 52 vols. Richmond, 1876-1959.
Sylvia, Steve, "Lt. Robert S. Ellis, Jr.: KIA Pickett's Charge," North South
Trader's Civil War, Special Gettysburg Edition 25: No. 4. May-June, 1988.
"Two Gettysburg Encounters," The Literary Digest, 47: 75. July 12, 1913.
Wright, Porter C., "The Confederate Monument at Louisa, Virginia," Louisa County Historical Society Magazine. 9:3. Summer, 1977.
"Oakland Academy," Louisa County Historical Society Magazine. 2: No. 2, 19-22, December, 1970.

Published Sources

Ailsworth, Thomas S., et al., eds. Charlotte County: Rich indeed. Charlotte County, Virginia: Charlotte County Board of Supervisors, 1979.
Barbier, Joseph, Scraps from the Prison Table at Camp Chase and Johnson's Island. Doylestown, Pennsylvania: W. W. H. Davis, 1868.
Bearss, Ed and Christopher M. Calkins, The Battle of Five Forks. Lynchburg, Virginia: H. E. Howard, Inc. 1985.
Beitzell, Edwin W. Point Lookout Prison Camp for Confederates. Abell, Maryland: privately printed, 1972.
Bracey, Susan L., Life by the Roaring Roanoke. Mecklenburg County, Virginia: Mecklenburg Bicentennial Commission, 1977.
Brook, Robert A., Hardesty's Historical and Geographical Encyclopedia Illustrated. Special Virginia Edition. New York: H. H. Hardesty and Company, 1884.
Brown, Brigadier General George H., ed. Records of Service of

Michigan Volunteers in the Civil War. Michigan: Michigan Legislature.

Bruce, Philip A., History of Virginia. 6 volumes. Chicago: The American Historical Society, 1924.

---------- **Virginia,** 5 volumes. Chicago, 1929.

Burrell, Charles Edward. A History of Prince Edward County Virginia. Richmond, Virginia: Williams Printing Company, 1922.

Busey, John W. and David G. Martin., Regimental Strengths at Gettysburg. Baltimore: Gateway Press, 1982.

Chappelear, George Warren., Families of Virginia: Volume III - Barret. Harrisonburg, Virginia: Cavalier Press, 1934.

Couper, William., The V.M.I. New Market Cadets: Biographical Sketches. Charlottesville, Virginia: The Michie Company, 1933.

Cooling, Benjamin Franklin. Forts Henry and Donelson - the Key to the Confederate Heartland. Knoxville: University of Tennessee Press, 1987.

Davis, James A., 51st Virginia infantry. Lynchburg, Virginia: H. E. Howard, inc., 1983.

DeVere, Schele Maximilian, ed. Students of the University of Virginia: A Semi-Centennial Catalogue with Brief Biographical Sketches. Baltimore: Charles Harvey and Company, 1878.

Dictionary of Select and Popular Quotations Which are in Daily Use: Taken from the Latin, French, Spanish, and Italian Languages. Philadelphia: J. B. Lippincott and Company, 1859.

Dinwiddie County: the County of the Apamatica. Richmond: Writers' Program of Work Projects Administration in the State of Virginia, 1942.

Divine, John E., 8th Virginia Infantry. Lynchburg: H. E. Howard, Inc., 1984. .

----------- **35th Battalion Virginia Cavalry.** Lynchburg: H. E. Howard, Inc.,1985.

Dombusch, Charles E., Military Bibliography of the Civil War. 3 vols. New York: New York Public Library, 1972.

Evans, General Clement A., ed. Confederate Military History. Vol. III. Atlanta: Confederate Publishing Company, 1899.

Freeman, Douglas Southall, Lee's Lieutenants: A Study in

Command. 3 vols. New York: Charles Scribner's Sons, 1942-44.
Georg, Kathleen R. and John W. Busey, Nothing But Glory - Pickett's Division at Gettysburg. Hightstown, New Jersey: Longstreet House, 1987.
Harris, Malcolm H., M. D., History of Louisa County, Virginia. Richmond, Virginia: Dietz Press, 1936.
Harrison, Walter, Pickett's Men: A Fragment of War History. New York: D. Van Nostrand, 1870.
Hoge, William James. "Sketch of Dabney Carr Harrison," University Memorial Biographical Sketches. Ed. Reverend John Lipscomb Johnson. Baltimore: Turnbull Brothers, 1871.
Hogg, Ann M., ed. with Dennis A. Tosh. Virginia Cemeteries: A Guide to Resources. Charlottesville: UVA Press, 1986.
Hollywood Memorial Association. Register of the Confederate Dead Interred in Hollywood Cemetery, Richmond, Virginia. Richmond: Gary, Clemitt, and Jones, 1869.
Hotchkiss, Major Jed, Confederate Military History – Virginia - Vol. III. Dayton, Ohio: Morningside Bookshop, 1975.
Howe, Thomas J., The Petersburg Campaign - Wasted Valor, June 15-18 1864. Lynchburg: H. E. Howard, Inc., 1988.
Hummel, Ray O., Jr. List of Places Included In 19th Century Virginia Directories. Virginia State Library Publication, 1960.
Hunton, Eppa, Autobiography of Eppa Hunton. Richmond: William Byrd Press, 1933.
Ingmire, Frances Terry and Carolyn Ericson. Confederate Prisoners of War: Soldiers and Sailors Who Died in Federal Prisons and Military Hospitals in the North. St. Louis, Missouri: Ericson Books, 1984.
Johnson, Robert U. and C. C. Buels, eds. Battles and Leaders of the Civil War. 4 vols. New York: Thomas Yoseloff, Inc., 1956.
Jones, Freeman W. "A Daring Expedition" and "Experience at Pt. Lookout," War Talks of Confederate Veterans. Ed. George S. Bernard. Fenn and Owen Publishers, 1892.
Jordan, Ervin L., Jr. and Herbert A. Thomas, Jr. 19th Virginia Infantry. Lynchburg: H. E. Howard, inc., 1988.
Krick, Robert K., The Gettysburg Death Roster - The Confederate

Dead at Gettysburg. Dayton, Ohio: Morningside Bookshop Press, 1981.
---------- **Inmates of Lee Camp Confederate Soldier's Home**. 1986.
---------- **Lee's Colonels,** A Biographical Register of the Field Officers of the Army of Northern Virginia. Dayton, Ohio: Morningside Bookshop Press, 1979.
30th Virginia infantry. Lynchburg: H. E. Howard, inc.
Lea, Reba F., Nelson County Civil War Soldiers. Virginia Book Company, 1979.
Lilley, David A., ed. Confederate Veteran ... Obituary Index. Dayton, Ohio, 1978.
Louisa County Centennial Committee, Louisa County and the War Between the States. Charlottesville: Wayside Press, 1964.
Maloney, Eugene A., A History of Buckingham County. Waynesboro, Virginia: Charles F. McClung, inc., 1976.
Markham, Jerald H., Compiled Veterans of Lee Camp Soldier's Home Buried In Hollywood 1894-1946. Lynchburg: J. H. Markham, 1986.
Moore, Evelyn Lee, Behind the Old Brick Wall: A Cemetery Story. Richmond, Virginia: Lynchburg Committee of the National Society of the Colonial Dames of America, 1968.
Moore, Munsey Adam, Cemetery and Tombstone Records of Mecklenburg County, Virginia. 2 Vols. Chase City, Virginia: Moore Publications, 1982.
Mumper, James A., Compiled I Wrote You Word: The Poignant Letters of Private Holt - John Lee Holt 1829-1863. Privately printed, c. 1980.
Murray, J. Ogden, The Immortal Six Hundred, A Story of Cruelty to Confederate Prisoners of War. Roanoke, Virginia: Stone Printing and Manufacturing Co., 1911.
Neagles, James C., Confederate Research Sources: A Guide to Archive Collections. Salt Lake City: Ancestry Publishing, 1986.
Neale, Gay, Brunswick County, Virginia 1720-1975. Richmond: Whittet and Shepperson, 1975.
Nine, William G. and Ronald G. Wilson, The Appomattox Paroles

April 9-15, 1865. Lynchburg: H. E. Howard, 1989.
Medical and Surgical History of the War of the Rebellion. 6 Vols. Washington, D.C.: Government Printing Office, 1870-1888.
Richey, Homer, ed. Memorial History of John Bowie Strange Camp, UCV. Charlottesville: Michie Company, 1920.
Riggs, David F. 7th Virginia Infantry. Lynchburg: H. E. Howard, Inc., 1982.
----------. **13th Virginia Infantry.** Lynchburg: H. E. Howard, Inc., 1988.
Robertson, James I., Jr., ed. An Index Guide to the Southern Historical Society Papers 1876-1959. 2 Vols. New Jersey: Kraus international Publications, 1980.
---------- **18th Virginia Infantry,** Lynchburg: H. E. Howard, inc., 1984.
Scott, J. L. , 36th Virginia infantry. Lynchburg: H. E. Howard, inc., 1987.
Sellers, John R., ed. Civil War Manuscripts: A Guide to Collections In the Manuscript Division, Library of Congress. Washington, D.C.: Library of Congress, 1986.
Sommers, Richard J., Richmond Redeemed: The Siege at Petersburg. New York: Doubleday and Company, 1981.
Stewart, George R., Pickett's Charge: A Micro-history of the Final Attack at Gettysburg, July 3, 1863. Cambridge, Massachusetts: Riverside Press, 1959.
Sussex County - A Tale of Three Centuries, Compiled by workers of Writers' Program of Work Projects Administration in State of Virginia: Richmond: Whittet and Shepperson, 1942.
Swank, Walbrook Davis, The War and Louisa County 1861-65. Charlottesville: Privately printed, 1986.
Confederate Letters and Diaries 1861-1865., Charlottesville: Privately printed, 1988.
Tyler, Lyon G., ed. Men of Mark in Virginia. Vol. II. Washington, D. C.: Men of Mark Publishing Company, 1907.
United States War Department., The War of the Rebellion: A Compilation of the Official Records of the Union and Confederate Armies. 128 vols. Washington, D.C.: Government Printing Office,

1880-1901.
Virginia Pensioners 1908-1909. Compiled by Auditor of Public Accounts. Richmond, 1909.
Walker, Charles D., Memorial Virginia Military Institute, Biographical Sketches of the Graduates and Eleves of the Virginia Military Institute Who Fell During the War Between the States. Philadelphia: J. B. Lippincott and Co., 1875.
Wallace, Lee A., Jr. A Guide to Virginia Military Organizations 1861-1865. Lynchburg: H. E. Howard, Inc., 1986.
Weisiger, Benjamin B., III. Buckingham County, Virginia - 1850 U. S. Census. 1984.
Wise, Jennings C., The Military History of the Virginia Military Institute From 1839-1865. Lynchburg: J. P. Bell, 1915.
Wood, William N., Lt., Reminiscences of Big "I ", Company "A ", Nineteenth Virginia Regiment. McCowat - Mercer Press, 1956.
Woodward, Major E. M., History of the 198th Pennsylvania Volunteers. New Jersey: MacCrellish and Quigley, 1884.

www.ingramcontent.com/pod-product-compliance
Lightning Source LLC
Chambersburg PA
CBHW031307150426
43191CB00005B/117